Sm02000278
11/02
£21·99
uYA
(Sug)

Power Games

Critical and radical perspectives have been central to the emergence of the sociology of sport as a discipline in its own right. This ground-breaking new book is the first to offer a comprehensive theory and method for a critical sociology of sport. It argues that class, political economy, hegemony and other concepts central to the radical tradition are essential for framing, understanding and changing social and political relations within sport and between sport and society.

The book draws upon the disciplines of politics, sociology, history and philosophy to provide a critical analysis of power relations throughout the world of sport, while offering important new case studies from such diverse sporting contexts as the Olympics, world football, boxing, cricket, tennis and windsurfing. In the process, it addresses key topics such as:

- nations and nationalism
- globalisation
- race
- gender
- political economy

Power Games can be used as a complete introduction to the study of sport and society and will be essential reading for any serious student of sport. At the same time, it is a provocative book that by argument and example challenges those who research and write about sport to make their work relevant to social and political reform.

John Sugden is Professor of the Sociology of Sport at the University of Brighton's Chelsea School. His work on the political sociology of sport in divided societies and on the politics of world football governance has been widely acclaimed.

Alan Tomlinson is Professor of Sport and Leisure Studies at the Chelsea School. He is well known for his historical and sociological work on leisure and consumption, particularly relating to sport and spectacle, and for his pioneering work on the history and culture of FIFA, world football's governing body.

Power Games

A critical sociology of sport

Edited by John Sugden and Alan Tomlinson

London and New York

First published 2002 by Routledge
11 New Fetter Lane, London EC4P 4EE

Simultaneously published in the USA and Canada
by Routledge
29 West 35th Street, New York, NY 10001

Routledge is an imprint of the Taylor & Francis Group

© 2002 John Sugden and Alan Tomlinson

Typeset in Garamond by T & F Books Ltd

Printed and bound in Great Britain by Antony Rowe Ltd,
Chippenham, Wiltshire

British Library Cataloguing in Publication Data
A catalogue record for this book is available from the British Library

Library of Congress Cataloging in Publication Data
A catalog record for this book has been requested

ISBN 0–415–25100–1 (hbk)
ISBN 0–415–25101–X (pbk)

Contents

vi *Contents*

Contributors

Alan Bairner was educated at the universities of Edinburgh and Hull and is currently Professor in Sports Studies at the University of Ulster. He is co-author of *Sport, Sectarianism and Society in a Divided Ireland* (1993), joint editor of *Sport in Divided Societies* (1999) and author of *Sport, Nationalism and Globalization: European and North American Perspectives* (2001). He has published widely on the relationship between sport and national identity in Ireland, Scotland and Sweden and has also written on the theme of sport and masculinity. He is a member of the editorial boards of the Sociology of Sport Journal and Football Studies.

Ben Carrington studied at the universities of Loughborough and Leeds Metropolitan and currently teaches sociology and cultural studies at the Chelsea School, University of Brighton. He has researched and published widely in the areas of race, masculinity and popular culture. Ben is co-editor, with Ian McDonald, of *'Race', Sport and British Society*, also published by Routledge.

Leon Culbertson studied at the University of Brighton, where he completed his undergraduate studies and conducted doctoral research on the potential contribution of the work of Jean-Paul Sartre to critical theorisations of sport. He is interested in contemporary French philosophy, Marxism, phenomenology and the application of critical theory to the study of popular culture. He is currently lecturer in sports studies at Edge Hill College of Higher Education, where he teaches courses in the socio-cultural analysis of sport, cultural studies and critical theory.

John Hargreaves graduated from, and obtained his doctorate at the London School of Economics. His teaching and research posts include the Simon Marks Research Fellow in Economic and Social Studies at the University of Manchester and Emeritus Reader in Sociology at the University of London Goldsmiths' College. Currently, John is Professor of Sociology at the University of Brighton. He has written extensively on sport, politics, power and culture, and his book, *Sport, Power and Culture* is an internationally acclaimed text. His latest book, *Freedom For Catalonia?*, is an analysis of Catalan nationalism based on fieldwork carried out in Spain on the Barcelona Olympic Games.

Marc Keech is a Senior Lecturer in Sport and Leisure studies in the Chelsea School at the University of Brighton. He completed his undergraduate degree and PhD at Staffordshire University and also holds a PGCE in Further and Higher Education. Having worked in Further Education he joined the university in 1999. His research interests are in the politics and history of domestic and international sports policies. Recently, he has written a number of articles on the history and politics of sport in South Africa and is currently engaged in a series of commissioned research projects examining the utility of sport development policies in England.

Gill Lines earned her undergraduate and doctoral degrees at the University of Brighton's Chelsea School where she now works as a Senior Lecturer and Course Leader in Sport and Leisure Studies. Her main research interests and publications focus on the connections between gender and media representations, with a particular emphasis on youth and youth culture.

Ian McDonald studied at the Universities of Liverpool and Leicester. He lectures on sociology, politics and sports policy in the Chelsea School at the University of Brighton. Ian has researched and published widely in the areas of sport politics, social policy, nationalism, ethnicity, and race relations. He is co-editor, with Ben Carrington, of *Race, Sport and British Society*, also published by Routledge.

Graham McFee is Professor of Philosophy at the University of Brighton. He studied at the University of Keele and University College, London. His major interests are in the philosophy of Wittgenstein and in philosophical aesthetics, especially the aesthetics of dance. He has published widely in many areas of philosophy, his principal publications including *Understanding Dance* (Routledge 1992), *The Concept of Dance Education* (Routledge 1994) and *Free Will* (Acumen 2000). He is Vice President of the British Society of Aesthetics.

Jon Magee studied at University of Ulster, Loughborough University and the University of Brighton's Chelsea School, attaining a PhD at the latter institution. He worked at Edge Hill College of Higher Education before moving to the University of Wales Institute, Cardiff (UWIC) as a Senior Lecturer. He is Discipline Director for Sports Sociology and is broadening the focus of his doctorate to form a series of papers on sports labour migration, of which the chapter in this book is the second. Jonathan also holds an UEFA 'A' Soccer Coaching Licence and is Head Coach to UWIC Inter Cardiff of the Welsh League. As a soccer player, Jonathan represented Northern Ireland at every level up to under-21, played for Northern Irish, Irish and Great Britain Students, competed in three World Student Games and won medals in Northern Irish and English non-league competitions.

Udo Merkel holds degrees in the Social Sciences and Sport Sciences from the University of Cologne and the German Sport University. His MA in the Sociology of Sport is from the University of Leicester, whilst he completed his PhD at the University of Oldenburg, supervised by Professor Bero Rigauer. Before joining the University of Brighton in 1994, he was in charge of a Research Centre for Comparative European Sport and Leisure Studies at the German Sport University in Cologne. His research and academic interests are in the Politics and Sociology of Sport and Leisure, comparative European Studies and Football Cultures. He has published widely in these areas and is currently preparing a monograph entitled *Sport in Divided Germany*.

John Sugden studied at the universities of Essex and Liverpool in the UK, and the University of Connecticut in the USA. He worked for fourteen years at the University of Ulster before moving to the University of Brighton in 1996 where he is currently Professor in the Sociology of Sport and Deputy Head of Chelsea School. He has published widely in the political sociology of sport and has been acclaimed for his ethnographic and investigative research and reportage. His books on sport in Ireland (with Alan Bairner) and international boxing have won national and international awards and his investigative work on FiFa, with Alan Tomlinson, is recognised to be ground-breaking.

Alan Tomlinson studied humanities and sociology for his BA at the University of Kent, and sociological studies for his master's and doctorate degrees at the University of Sussex. He also studied for his professional postgraduate qualification (University of London) in English and Social Studies. He has worked at the Chelsea School, University of Brighton since 1975, where he is currently Head of the Chelsea School Research Centre. He is Chair of the University of Brighton's Research Degrees Committee and Professor of Sport and Leisure Studies. He has edited, co-authored and authored more than 20 volumes on consumption, sport and leisure, and has worked on international sports cultures and politics since the early 1980s. His current interests are in the comparative and historical analysis of sports spectacle, and its relation to forms of consumption. He is editor of the *International Review for the Sociology of Sport* (2000–2003).

Belinda Wheaton rejoined the University of Brighton's Chelsea School, from where she earned her doctorate, as a postdoctoral Senior Research Fellow in 2002. Previously, Belinda was with the Centre for Sport and Cultural Research (CSCS) at the University of Surrey Roehampton, where she taught on undergraduate and postgraduate courses in the sociology of sport and leisure. Her main research and publications have focused around the sociological significance of alternative sport, particularly the performance of gendered identities, and new forms of sport consumption. Her current research interests focus around the politics of popular culture. She has also been a contributor to various specialist sport magazines, and is editing a book for Routledge on 'Lifestyle Sports'.

Preface

The study of and research into the sociology of sport is a relatively new enterprise in Argentina. Led by Pablo Alabarces, a study group emerged in the 1990s dedicated to developing the subject there. In order to stimulate further interest the Argentinians invited a small number of scholars from the UK to talk to them about their work and this book has its origins in a presentation that the co-editors were invited to make to a group of academics at the University of Buenos Aires in 1997. In the invite we were asked to speak about the nature of the research and scholarship emanating from the University of Brighton's Chelsea School Research Centre, which they (not us) claimed as distinctive. This caused us to ask ourselves what, if anything, was different about the work that we, and other colleagues at the University of Brighton, were engaging in.

The answer, first framed in Buenos Aires, is developed in the pages of this book and spelled out particularly in the opening chapter. In short, if our work does distinguish us, it is not because there is a theoretical orthodoxy slavishly followed by our group, but because we have a number of shared concerns that we seek to understand and comment about, and a style of research through which we pursue these interests. Central among these concerns are questions of power. What is it? Who has it and who does not? And what are the consequences of it being wielded, resisted, and reformulated in different sport and leisure settings? We seek to make sense of power relations through an informed critical gaze, and a commitment to qualitative empirical research and its interpretation through a range of theoretical arguments. We are also committed to reconnecting the academic analysis of sport and leisure to a wider policy agenda and the processes of social change and political reform.

Our distinctiveness also has a lot to do with recruiting a critical mass of well-trained, highly motivated, and hard working social scientists who not only share ideas and collaborate on research, but who also review and critique each other's work. Indeed those who read this book from cover to cover will note that, while there is much sharing of concepts and themes, there is an equal amount of mutual critique of work current and past, some of which is self-reflective and self-critical.

While the emphasis differs in each chapter, all contributors engage with questions of theory, method and critique. In some cases, particularly in the early chapters, issues of general theory predominate, or the contribution of a single theorist is re-evaluated and/or applied to a particular empirical setting or context. Some contributions re-evaluate the contributor's own work. In other later chapters an individual method is featured in the context of lived experience of sport and leisure and/or detailed studies of particular practices. In summary, the book is not intended to be a serial unfolding of some grand design with a beginning, middle and end, but a coherent collection of independent examples of the Brighton approach to doing the sociology of sport. Throughout, all chapters are characterised by an appropriate balance of theory, method, empirical evidence and critical analysis. The book is organised in three parts: Part I comprises a single overview chapter dealing with overarching theoretical and methodological issues and debates; the contributions in Part II emphasise general theoretical re-evaluations and interventions; Part III prioritises national case studies and ethnographic studies and sport practices.

We would like to dedicate this book to the University of Brighton for its ongoing support of the Chelsea School Research Centre and for its particular willingness to invest in the recruitment of high quality academics and researchers in the sport and leisure cultures research area. Professor Stuart Laing, (Pro-Vice Chancellor) Academic Affairs, deserves special thanks for his faith in and backing for our endeavours. Finally we would like to thank Professor Peter Donnelly of the University of Toronto and Dr Jim McKay of the University of Queensland for their full and frank critical responses to versions of the chapters presented at the annual meeting of the North American Society for the Sociology of Sport (NASSS) in Colorado Springs in November 2000.

Not all of the contributors work at the University of Brighton, but those that do not are either former doctoral research students of the Chelsea research group or have long-standing collaborative links with key members of the Brighton group and share the ethos outlined above. Both of the editors and most of the contributors work at the Chelsea School. Alan Bairner is at the University of Ulster, Jordanstown, Leon Culbertson at Edge Hill College, and Jon Magee at University of Wales Institute Cardiff.

John Sugden and Alan Tomlinson
Brighton and Eastbourne, September 2001

Part I
Theory and method

1 Theory and method for a critical sociology of sport[1]

John Sugden and Alan Tomlinson

The title of this book *Power Games* has a double meaning. On the one hand, it refers in a general sense to the game of power, that is the manifold schemes, strategies and techniques through which individuals and groups struggle with and against one another for position and dominance, and against subservience. On the other hand, it points towards how such power games are played out in the institutional setting of sport which, in late modernity, has become a very highly valued global commodity, and an important vehicle for the acquisition of wealth and status and the exercise of power. In this book we offer a collection of essays which, incorporating both of these meanings, in different but overlapping ways, illuminates how the dynamic, interactive and embodied nature of power in sport can be researched, interpreted and theorised. In this opening chapter we outline a way of thinking about and researching power that is fundamental to our own work and much that follows.

The centrality of power in sociological analysis hardly comes as a surprise to those grounded in the classical debates of modern Western social science. What has always been at issue is the source of power, and the nature of the context within which power relations are lived out: the mode of production for Marx; new forms of the division of labour for Durkheim; particular forms of authority for Weber, and the individual drive or will to acquire and use power for theorists such as Habermas, Freud and Nietzsche.

More recently, Giddens (1984) has developed structuration theory, an attempted departure from the dichotomous agency–structure debates, which tries to synthesise elements of these classical positions and rework them in an integrated and interpretative sociology centred around power relations. For Giddens, power is the central dynamic of all human societies, at all levels of institutional life, interpersonal relations and everyday practice. It is not merely a matter of having power or not having power, it is that power relations are inherent in and integral to all social life. As Giddens (1984: 15) puts it, 'The use of power characterises not specific types of conduct but all action'. It is the omnipresent transformative capacity of power discovered in all facets of social interaction that is important. Rather than seeing power relations as a zero sum game in which the power of some can only be accumulated and exercised at the expense of others losing all their power, Giddens draws our attention to what he calls the 'dialectic of control'.

This notion involves two key elements. The first centres on the idea that all human beings possess some power in the form of their ability to transform, to some extent, the circumstances in which they find themselves. It is this ability to respond to the social environment and to manipulate it in some way that is a basic human characteristic. The second element follows from this and points to the fact that although it is usually one person or a group that dominates in a power relationship, 'the subordinate party always has some power ... which enables them (in varying degrees) to counter or offset the power of the dominant party' (Layder 1995: 16). This is a concept that we found very useful, for instance, in helping us to unravel the Byzantine power networks within the governing body of world football FIFA (Sugden and Tomlinson 1998: 44).

This is not such a radical formulation, though some of its implications may have radical consequences for the scope and direction of contemporary theory and method. Indeed, philosophy, particularly in the writings of Bertrand Russell, has already provided a powerful rationale for this position. Writing in the context of Nazi and Stalinist totalitarianism, Russell (1940: 10) claimed that orthodox Marxist economists 'were mistaken in supposing that economic self-interest could be taken as the fundamental motive in the social sciences'. For Russell, 'love of power' must be seen as the critical determinant of social affairs. Only then, he argues, can history be rightly interpreted. His study is therefore an attempt:

> to prove that the fundamental concept in social science is Power, in the same sense that Energy is the fundamental concept in physics. Like energy, power has many forms, such as wealth, armaments, civil authority, influence on opinion. No one of these can be regarded as subordinate to any other, and there is no one form from which the others are derived. The attempt to treat one form of power, say wealth, in isolation can be only partly successful, just as the study of only one form of energy will be defective at certain points, unless other forms are taken into account.
>
> (Russell 1940: 10)

Russell defines power as the 'production of intended effects ... it is easy to say, roughly, that A has more power than B, if A achieves many intended effects and B only a few' (*ibid.*: 35). Clearly this does not mean that B is powerless, but simply that B is less powerful than A. For Russell, power over human beings involves the influencing of individuals by (a) direct physical power, typically exercised by organisations such as the army and the police; (b) inducements on the basis of rewards and punishments, typically used by employer or economic organisations; and (c) the influencing of opinion, or propaganda, including the cultivation of 'desired habits in others', such as military drill, by organisations such as schools, churches and political parties. Russell, taking a leaf out of Weber's book, also distinguishes between traditional, naked and revolutionary power, and explores different forms of the power of individuals: the business executive, the politician and the wire-puller behind the scenes.

Russell's argument for the recognition of power as the core concept of the social sciences – to understand the power relation, the 'impulse to power', as the central drive of social life – is matched by an historical and cross-cultural sensitivity to the nuanced and multiple manifestations of power relations in different places and at different times. It is a reminder that, no how matter how seductive and eloquent such arguments might be, theorisations of power should not be, Marcuse-style, one-dimensional (Marcuse 1972). Social scientists should recognise and seek to understand and explain when, why and how power transforms from one of its dimensions, or balance of dimensions, to another.

Too often, treatments of power have lacked Russell's detail and subtlety. By locating power in only one source or another, or confusing the consequences of power (for instance domination) with power per se, such analyses are over-simplified and incomplete. Some key works on the sociology of sport have tended to fall into this trap. Take George Sage's *Power and Ideology in American Sport* (Sage 1990). Sport is presented throughout this book as 'one of various cultural settings in which the hegemonic structure of power and privilege in capitalist society is continually fortified' (*ibid.*: 209). Once this all-pervasive power structure is established, alternatives to the present sports system – counter hegemonic initiatives – can then be considered. For Sage these are important but somewhat marginal gestures of resistance to programmes or policies cast by and for dominant social groups. He then catalogues selected forms of political resistance, placing a particular emphasis on gender and race which he sees as having 'given rise to opposition and transformation' (*ibid.*: 211–14).

It is not Sage's careful and sound critical analysis that is at fault here. In his adaptation of Hargreaves's (1986) model to the USA, Sage's depiction of the ideological nature of sport is convincing and his recognition of sources of resistance appropriate enough. But the picture that is painted is of a monolithic and systemic power structure in sports against which some resistance might be possible, and even some marginal transformation, but in terms of significant change we are still left waiting for the revolution. It is an all or nothing model of resistance, which separates the process of resistance from the embodied power dynamic itself. The Sage version could be formulated syllogistically: you/they are powerful, I/we resist, things change. For all its sociological subtlety, and its acknowledgement of the importance of hegemony theory, recognising the reflexive and interactive nature of power relations, Sage's model is too top-down and is not an adequate portrayal of the dynamics of power within sports cultures and practices.

Sage oversimplifies Hargreaves's position who, in *Sport, Power and Culture*, offers a concise, flexible and accessible definition of power when he says:

> When we use the term power, we are referring ... to a relationship
> between agents, the outcome of which is determined by agents' access to
> relevant resources and their use of appropriate strategies in specific
> conditions of struggle with other agents.
>
> (Hargreaves 1986: 3)

Critical here is the recognition that power is a relationship, a dynamic, and
that the relationship involves human agents struggling over resources and
outcomes. There are various forms in which power relations are manifest,
and Hargreaves outlines four such forms by which the compliance of subordinate groups may be obtained: physical force or its threatened use;
economic sanctions; the assertion of authority or prestige; and persuasion. In
translation, this breakdown is similar to Michael Mann's fourfold classification of the sources of power that, in shorthand, he refers to as the IEMP –
ideological, economic, military and political. These are not totally separate
and monolithic dimensions, but 'overlapping networks of social interaction'
(Mann 1986: 2) Like Mann, Hargreaves is at pains to emphasise that the
exercise of power is always by agents, however much power has become
invested in and circulated throughout the social body. Thus it is people,
either individually or collectively, and not systems, that wield, challenge,
seek or reaffirm power. They act, of course, within the context of institutional structures, but those structures are themselves contingent upon
ongoing and embodied power relations.

Rather than working with the couplet Power/Resistance, it is surely
important to see resistance as a form of power itself, as a response to say,
domination, or in Russell's terms, to a particular form of power, say naked or
traditional power. For if actors have some capacity to affect outcomes, they
are exercising some degree of power. Lukes (1974) has problematised
simplistic formulations on the exercise of power and urged that a deeper
study of power must recognise how, in complex and subtle ways the inac-
tivity of leaders and sheer weight of institutions is a form of power. Doing
nothing can have great impact on events as surely as can doing something.
More generally he stresses the relational dimensions of power:

> Power is the capacity to produce, or contribute to, outcomes – to make a
> difference to the world. In social life, we may say, power is the capacity
> to do this through social relationships: it is the capacity to produce, or
> contribute to, outcomes by significantly affecting another or others.
>
> (Lukes 1993: 504)

By such a definition, resistance to domination – as in the refusal to
comply – must itself be seen as a form of power. Indeed in a note on historical method, Nietzsche specified resistance as a central process. In *The
Genealogy of Morals* (1956: 210), he talked of how 'the whole history of a

thing', such as a custom, constitutes a 'chain of reinterpretations and rear-rangements'. Such a history:

> is a sequence of more or less profound, more or less independent processes of appropriation, including the resistances used in each instance, the attempted transformations for purposes of defence or reaction, as well as the results of successful counterattacks. While forms are fluid, their 'meaning' is even more so.
>
> (Nietzsche 1956: 210)

Echoes of Nietzsche inform Foucault's writings on power and resistance, particularly his section on method in *The History of Sexuality* where Foucault disputes that any 'over-all unity of domination' is 'given at the outset' (1981: 92). He argues that power must be understood as 'the multiplicity of force relations immanent in the sphere in which they operate and which constitute their own organisation' (*ibid.*), and furthermore, involving struggles and confrontation that affect the power relations by transforming, strengthening, or reversing them. These force relations might also form a chain or a system, or be isolated from one another, and they take effect as strategies. According to Foucault, power is not an institution, and not a structure; yet neither is it a certain strength we are endowed with; it is the name one attributes to a complex strategic situation of struggle in a particular society. With, not apart from, these very power relations, resides the potential for resistance, not a sporadic, dramatic, revolutionary intervention, but something more internal to the power dynamic itself. 'Where there is power there is resistance, and yet, or rather consequently, this resistance is never in a position of exteriority in relation to power' (*ibid.*: 95).

Foucault goes on to emphasise the relational character of power relations, arguing that:

> Their existence depends on a multiplicity of points of resistance: these play the role of adversary, target, support, or handle power relations. These points of resistance are present everywhere in the power network ... There is a plurality of resistances, each of them a special case: resistances that are possible, necessary, improbable; others that are spontaneous, savage, solitary, concerted, rampant, or violent: still others that are quick to compromise, interested, or sacrificial; by definition, they can only exist in the field of power relations.
>
> (Foucault 1981: 95–6)

Foucault's abstract account at least implies that nobody is excluded from the power game and that individuals can operate in a myriad of ways at points of resistance while playing it. In processes of appropriation and resistance, it is human agents who, in Lukes's (1974) terms, make a difference to the world.

Thus, the question of agency has to be located within any adequate conceptualisation of power. Giddens recognises this when he says:

> Action depends upon the capacity of the individual to 'make a difference' to a pre-existing state of affairs or course of events. An agent ceases to be such if he or she loses the capacity to 'make a difference', that is, to exercise some sort of power.
>
> (Giddens 1984: 14)

Sport is one cultural form in which these agency/power dynamics can be studied. In de Certeau's terms, it is a prominent practice of everyday life. His project is to develop a multifaceted analysis of culture that he views as the product of the tension inherent in the political dynamics of power relations at every level of society (1988: xvii). Fiske (1989: 32–42) draws upon de Certeau's theory in his argument for the recognition of everyday life as a significant sphere in which 'the people' undermine the 'strategies of the powerful, make poaching raids upon their texts or structures, and play constant tricks upon the system' (*ibid.*: 32).

Fiske uses this approach to illustrate the progressive, rather than radical, nature of popular culture, and highlights the interpretative and creative capacity of human agents to employ such tactics. Although such an approach can be criticised for an over-celebration of the everyday and the popular, it is nevertheless a reminder that there is no everyday practice without interpretation. It also points to the fact that the interpretative act itself is a form of human agency, an act of appropriation and a potential form of resistance.

Within popular culture, there is what Stuart Hall (1981: 228) calls 'the double stake ... the double movement of containment and resistance, which is always inevitably inside it'. The study of particular sport cultures can demonstrate this, showing how power relations themselves involve an ebb and flow of influences, illustrative of the reflexive and generative capacity of human actors to confirm, adapt, negotiate, and at times remake their institutions and cultures. Indeed, the history of sport hitherto is not that of a 'hidden hand' modelling sport behind our backs, neither is it only the story of a powerful elite, of great men and a few great women shaping sport in their own image and likeness. It is rather an ongoing narrative of struggle that blends individual and collective action or agency with political, economic and cultural flows and forces. It is to understand this narrative that is the key task for a critical sociology of sport.

In substantive work on sport and popular culture, as a way of considering the main social and political components engaged in power relations, Hargreaves's (1996) understanding of hegemony has a hugely inclusive potential, and the Gramscian concept is invoked in a number of the contributions to this book. The inclusivity promised involves a transcendence of any traditional anchorage of the concept in social class. However, this is a transcendence that is rarely realised. As Carrington (2000) has argued, instead of hegemony being opened up as a concept within which the other important constituencies of oppression and resistance in the post-colonial epoch – most notably race and gender – could be accommodated, not much more than lip service has been paid to social categories outside of class. The idea that come the revolution, and with it the resolution of class struggle, all other forms of repression will simply wither away, was always fanciful, even when communism was a vibrant political force. In the post-communist era it is completely bankrupt. With a residual Marxist orthodoxy fettering the inclusive potential of hegemony, other theoretical positions broadly within a postmodern and postcolonial framework have gained ground, not in addition to, but in opposition to, hegemony. We believe that such turf wars are both unproductive and unnecessary, and that it would be folly to abandon a notion of hegemony that illuminates the nature of the contest and struggle over resources, the conditions whereby consent is secured by the dominant, and the persisting significance of the economic in the constitution of the relations of political economy.

Nevertheless, thus far we have ducked a problem, the solution to which has evaded most, if not all, abstract theorists of power: the question of primacy or determinacy. Which if any of the dimensions of power is the most powerful? Returning to Mann's classification, for instance, is it the ideological, the economic, the military, or the political? For Mann there can be no simple answer, because he recognises that his IEMP model is ideal-typical and that society as lived out is a much more fluid enterprise. Societies, as he puts it, 'are much messier than our theories of them' (Mann 1986: 4) and 'whether we can single out economic power as ultimately decisive in determining the shape of societies … is an empirical question' (*ibid.*: 30), not a theoretical imperative.

It is insufficient for social scientists to merely identify a power relation. They must also learn to understand what that power relation means to those engaged within it. In other words, as Layder (1995) argues from a method-ological perspective, and Flyvberg (1998) illustrates through concrete fieldwork, an understanding of power relations, and especially of the question of determinacy, cannot be gained in the abstract, but necessitates sustained empirical research. Thus, having clarified some of the key theoretical underpinnings of our concept of power and established its centrality to the critical sociology of sport, we next turn to the vexed question of how to research power in the field.

We have established that power relations are social relations. However, these relations are seldom conducted on the surface of public life. The often-heard characterisation of the mysteries surrounding family politics, 'no one knows what goes on behind closed doors', could be used to charac-terise power relations in general. Things that look like public displays of power relations – the candidates' debate, for instance – are usually precisely that, caricatured, choreographed and simplified *displays* of power that belie the complex struggles taking place in the icebergs under the surface bulk. How to get at and make sense of the deep, insider information below the surface of everyday life is not usually taught in graduate school research methods courses or available in manuals of research practice. After many years of collaboration we have developed a style of qualitative research and scholarship which, while not particularly special in terms of its single dimensions, as a totality has been seen by some to be relatively distinctive. This has led to some commentators (not us) labelling our approach as 'the Brighton method' – referencing the fact that we, and all of the authors included in this volume, either work for the University of Brighton, or have been research students there, or have strong and regular collaborative links with colleagues at that institution. For instance, Giulianotti (1999: 184) has referred to the distinctive contribution of 'Brighton-based researchers' in studying football cultures in a critically comparative way. This has caused us retrospectively to consider what exactly our approach to research and scholarship is and to ask what, if anything, is distinctive about that approach?

An understanding of our style of social research requires the consideration of six overlapping elements: historiography; comparative methods; critical sociology; ethnography; investigative research; and gonzo. In practice, these are simultaneous interrelated elements of a research process, orchestrated and conducted from the centre by the researcher. For the purpose of this chapter, however, we have summarised our understanding of the significance of each separately.

Unlike many historians, we believe that the painstakingly detailed, usually archive-based, 'factual' reporting of history can and should be connected and concerned with a sociology of the present. To paraphrase Marx (1979: 103), people make history, but how they make history is to some extent determined by what tools and raw materials they can get access to and the range of imagined possibilities that existing economic, political and cultural circumstances suggest. Society is not reinvented on a daily basis. Social change (evolution and revolution) is but the cutting edge of institutional processes that are deeply rooted and time-honoured. In order to make full sense of what happens today we must come to understand why it happened, at least in part, in terms of yesterday's events.

Thus, it is vital to give research into contemporary phenomena a dynamic historical dimension – to identify and connect the key institutional developments and critical moments of individual and collective action that underpin the area of social interaction under scrutiny, help to frame its contemporary form and suggest its legacy. Social history is not coterminous with social theory, but it is a valuable resource in its development. Any interpretation and theory of the present that does not account for history is bound to be seriously weakened.

The fundamental purpose behind a methodology that embraces the comparative is to learn more about ourselves by understanding more about 'the other' – both horizontally across space and vertically through history. This is more than an abstract academic principle, it is also the premise of a contemporary global citizenship that undermines the formation of ethnocentrism and stereotyping – the basis of so much conflict in the modern world. In a developing corpus of work we have sought to generate studies, which, when taken together, constitute a broader comparative project. These might be a single case study, informed by comparative thinking, such as our analysis of sport in Cuba (Sugden, Tomlinson and McCartan 1990). Collections of cases – for instance, our edited volume on world football cultures – *Hosts and Champions* (Sugden and Tomlinson 1994) – offer the reader a choice from a range of individual cases that stand alone, but also have an accumulative impact in terms of a more comprehensive understanding of football cultures and politics world-wide. Likewise *Boxing and Society* (Sugden 1996), in perhaps a more concentrated example, offers deeply-grounded, free standing commentaries on the social location of boxing (in the USA, Northern Ireland and Cuba) that, when read together constitute a comparative international analysis. In *Sport in Divided Societies* (Bairner and Sugden 1998) case studies are placed alongside each other to examine sport's potential to act as a cohering or conflictual influence upon the wider society. The study of single cases should always be informed, however implicitly, by a wider understanding of how a particular society stands in relation to others, in terms, for example, of contemporary trends towards globalisation. Well developed case studies providing detailed and deeply situated comparative data are essential if abstract theorisations are to be avoided.

In its most simple sense, to be critical is to be sceptical – that is, never take things at face value. For instance, seek out official statistics, but expecting them to be unreliable, in some cases even fraudulent; go in search of evidence that contradicts official wisdom. In other words, question authority. It is a main task of the sociologist to get under the skin of daily life and to understand what passes as 'routine' in the context of broader issues of power, control and resistance to domination. In our invocation of this concept we follow the example of the great USA sociologist C. Wright Mills in his exhortation (1959) to understand, in integrated fashion, biography and history, self and structure, private life and public issues. Mills was also masterful in his eclectic use of the most appropriate concepts and theories when applying his critical gaze. He railed against the use of grand theory and of measurement-led research ('abstracted empiricism'). Likewise Giddens, although himself an exclusively library-based theorist, has preached against an over-dependency on quantitative methods and recommends more interpretative and ethnographic approaches. Indeed, when asked for empirical examples of structuration theory, he regularly cited (Giddens 1989: 430) the widely influential ethnography of working-class male youth by Willis (1977). Our own work encapsulates both an informed eclecticism, as Mills put it, and a research mission that is located at the point of agency and structure – that is, where and how humans live out their lives in particular times and places and what contribution this makes to the social construction of reality.

Interpretations and theorisations benefit greatly from research that is grounded in the lived experiences of those engaged in the area of cultural production under scrutiny, including a sensitivity to life histories (for a convincing example of the latter, see Coakley and Donnelly 1999). By ethnography we refer to a comprehensive package of qualitative research techniques (observation, participant observation, oral histories, interviewing, still photography, video recording, and so forth) in the application of which the researcher first gains empathetic access to a particular social milieu, then, second, develops an authentic gaze enabling previously invisible power relations to be seen, and, finally, is able to reproduce its more salient features for the edification of a wider readership.

There are different levels of ethnography, ranging from classic, long-term, depth-immersion studies, such as those employed by the Chicago School, through to more fleeting forms of 'ethnographic visiting'. It takes time to learn to see the invisible and we favour approaches towards the classic end of this continuum. In the sociology of sport, the work of Alan Klein on baseball in the Dominican Republic (1991) and bodybuilding on the US West Coast (1993) is exemplary, as are aspects of Wacquant's (1995) and Sugden's (1996) work on boxing. However, even if classic Chicago-style ethnography is not the main research tool, gaining a sense of space, place, character and culture – which can only be achieved through spending some time in the living research environment – sharpens a researcher's critical gaze, helps the formulation of questions and enhances interpretation and theorisation. The latter is not ethnography per se (although too often shallow reportage is claimed as such), but can be used to enhance other forms of research and theory.

Furthermore, our experience tells us that passive forms of ethnography – that is fieldwork in which the researcher's role is dictated and constrained by the flow of events presented to him or her as 'natural' – rarely allows for the full impressionist canvas to be filled. Recognising the unpredictable complexities of the researcher's place and role in relation to the topics and human subjects of research, we believe that an investigative imperative is faithful to the spirit of a critical social science. Investigative sociological research is an important dimension of the critical gaze. It is not a new category (although, it has for some years lain dormant within the social scientist's methodological repertoire). Classic subcultural studies by Robert Park and his contemporaries in the Chicago School in the 1920s and 1930s were, in part, dependent upon the methods of investigative and muckraking journalism. This made an important contribution to the democratic process in the early twentieth-century US, in particular in the legendary figure of Lincoln Steffens (Kaplan 1975). In the 1960s and 1970s, Jack Douglas at the University of California retrieved this tradition, arguing that any valid critique of what is really going on must go beyond passive observation and embrace the investigative. His investigative mission combines a quest for truth with the recognition that observation is essential: 'Direct observation of things in their natural state (uncontrolled) is the primary basis of all truth ... this bedrock facticity of concrete experience and observation pervades our everyday lives' (Douglas 1976: 12).

To get at the truth, direct observation, for Douglas, necessarily goes beyond gazing at the surface. His research strategy is based upon the assumption that everyday social life has a tendency to be duplicitous: that individuals and groups construct and present images of who they are and what they do that can mask underpinning social realities:

> The investigative paradigm is based upon the assumption that profound conflicts of interest, values, feelings and actions pervade social life. It is taken for granted that many of the people one deals with, perhaps all people to some extent, have good reason to hide from others what they are doing and even lie to them. Instead of trusting people and expecting trust in return, one suspects others and expects others to suspect him. Conflict is the reality of life; suspicion is the guiding principle.
>
> (Douglas 1976: 55)

Douglas's view of the nature of social life is framed by his experience of researching relatively microscopic, albeit 'deviant', subcultures. However, his basic principles can be taken to apply to all walks of life. He does not believe that all people are fraudulent all of the time, but he does maintain that even the most trivial areas of social interaction can be distorted through combinations of misinformation, evasions, outright lies and stage management or 'front'. He argues that social research must account for this and advocates mixed methodologies that are simultaneously 'cooperative and investigative' (Douglas 1976: 56) – that is, methodologies that take note of self-generated and freely given legends, but that also subject such 'official histories' to scrutiny from a multitude of vantage points.

In this regard we have been able to learn much from the likes of Vyv Simson and Andrew Jennings, whose work on the politics and economics of international sport, particularly as in the context of the International Olympic Movement, has been seminal (Simson and Jennings 1992). They have shown that organisations like the International Olympic Committee (IOC), the International Amateur Athletic Federation (IAAF) and the Fédération Internationale de Football Associations (FIFA) are part of the apex of a multi-billion dollar global sports political economy. As such, these bodies have much to show off, but even more to hide. Jennings has been particularly critical of 'tame' fellow journalists and academics whose work has failed to penetrate far beneath the surface and rhetoric of international sport. In 1994 he challenged the academic community to go beyond secondary sources, institutionally generated accounts and outright propaganda (Jennings 1994). For Jennings there can be no substitute for first-hand, investigative fieldwork (see Jennings 1996) based on principles similar to those outlined by Douglas. In a more conventionally academic vein, and from an anthropological pedigree, MacAloon has challenged critical sociologists and cultural analysts to use 'face-to-face observation and extended "listening-in"' (1992: 117) in order to discover what the world is really like.

A note of caution, however, on the investigative journalistic mode. To make a living, the investigative journalist is too often over-dependent upon sensationalist headlines and juicy stories. Thus, co-operative methods (and findings) tend to be jettisoned in favour of an approach that is totally investigative and negative. 'Ignore the good, hound the bad and the ugly.' For us, what separate the investigative journalist from the investigative social scientist are: the pursuit of objective understanding; the generation of theory; and the value of interpretation and explanation rather than mere exposé. Yes, by all means disclose – reveal the bad and the ugly – but also, when it can be justified, balance this with accounts and interpretations of the good.

The final element of our methodological approach is drawn from the world of gonzo journalism pioneered by Hunter S. Thompson. Appropriately, while Thompson has written on many topics, including features on the absurdities of the American political landscape, some of his most significant works have centred on sport and leisure pursuits. Best selling books such as *Hell's Angels* (1967), *The Great Shark Hunt* (1980), *Fear and Loathing in Las Vegas* (1972) are built around his idiosyncratic reportage of bikers, fishermen and off-terrain car racers. Likewise he has published essays loosely based upon marathon running, horse racing, 'iron man' contests and boxing matches. There are two elements of the gonzo approach to journalism: the method and the stream of consciousness personalised reportage.

Thompson consistently displays the capacity to get close to the centre of the action without ever being totally incorporated within it. As Tomlinson has observed of Thompson, 'by entering sports settings on his own terms he was able to emphasise the nature of sports values by looking at them through the eyes of the marginal individual' (Tomlinson 1984: 30). Thompson believes that the reporter has to be a part of the scene that is being reported upon, *at the same time* being semi-detached from that experience. This makes the reporter more conspicuous than the anonymous 'fink', as Goffmann (1989) put it, and the Thompson style runs the risk of having too much effect upon the setting. But in his hands, observation has a dual quality whereby the researcher watches his own impact on the scenes that he is studying, using the reactions to his performance as a means of getting under the skin of social life:

> *gonzo* journalism is a style of 'reporting' based on William Faulkner's idea that the best fiction is far more *true* than any kind of journalism ...

True *gonzo* reporting needs the talents of a master journalist, the eye of an artist/photographer and the heavy balls of an actor. Because the writer *must* be a participant in the scene, while he's writing it – or at least taping it.

(Thompson 1980: 114–15)

For Thompson, investigative reportage is necessarily about risk-taking. People with something to hide do not routinely invite social commentators and confirmed sceptics into their inner sanctums. Albeit quite often narcotically or booze enhanced, Thompson reveals a capacity to ignore conventional gate-keeping processes. With his *Rolling Stone* press card in one hand and a bottle of Wild Turkey in the other, Thompson drifts in and out of the scenes he is studying, seemingly oblivious to the barriers which would leave most of us standing outside in the cold. In this regard, Thompson is widely regarded as the *enfant terrible* of 'new journalism': somebody who never gets invited to the party, but who inevitably turns up.

While perhaps not on the same scale as Thompson's risk-taking, individually (Sugden 1996: 2001) and as a team (Sugden and Tomlinson 1998) we have taken, and continue to take, many gambles in the service of our investigative fieldwork. In many ways the fieldwork strategy of our FIFA projects (1998, 1999), researching the structures, values and ideologies of the governing body of world football, emerged from a series of, more or less, successful gambles. Based upon the knowledge that powerful FIFA personnel always gather at international events such as the national championship of a confederation, a junior global tournament, or the World Cup Finals themselves, we target such events as sites for our fieldwork. If you want to watch the power brokers playing their games, invited or not, you have to turn up and invent strategies to get inside. It is not absolutely necessary to get into the spectacles themselves (although this can help), but it is essential to gain access to the five-star hotel lobbies, press receptions and embassy parties where the big brokers can be watched, photographed, overheard, targeted for on-the-hoof interviews and follow-up appointments.

Another of Thompson's qualities which we draw upon is the way he connects his personalised, microscopic reportage with the wider social and political landscape – in sociological terms, his ability to interpenetrate agency and structure. *Hell's Angels* (1967), for instance, is not just about the interpersonal dynamics of a motor cycle gang, it is also a vivid interpretation of social change in the United States in the post-war generation. Likewise, *Fear and Loathing in Las Vegas* (1972) is more than a narrative of a booze and drug-crazed sojourn in Nevada, it is also, as the sub-title tells us, *A Savage Journey into the Heart of the American Dream* (1972).

Albeit, with neither Thompson's eloquence nor excess, some of our own work attempts both to record the detail of everyday experience while, at the same time, animate such detail with reference to the wider social and political forces which frame it. *Boxing and Society* (Sugden 1996), for instance, explores the work-a-day lives of boxers in an American ghetto, in the back streets of Belfast and in the tumble-down of Old Havana, in each case animating the boxers' stories with the overarching dynamics of 1980s' urban poverty in America, the machinations of sectarian strife in Northern Ireland and the contradictions of life in Castro's Cuba. *FIFA and the Contest for World Football* (Sugden and Tomlinson 1998) is an institutional and interpersonal history of the governance of world football, but it is also informed and informing of a global history of twentieth-century social, economic and political development. At the local and regional level, Tomlinson's (1992) study of knur-and-spell is situated within a broader analysis of embryonic consumer culture in working-class communities.

A second issue that has hitherto been ducked is that of realism versus relativism, and we conclude this chapter with a discussion of the epistemological position within which the framework outlined herein is embedded. We agree with Gouldner that one meaning of sociological objectivity is the ability of the sociologist to

> take the standpoint of someone outside of those most immediately engaged in a specific conflict, or outside of the group being investigated … It is only when we have a standpoint somewhat different from the participants' that it becomes possible to do justice to their standpoints.
>
> (Gouldner 1973: 56–7)

Whereas some important critiques (such as variants of feminism) privilege a standpoint epistemology 'which holds that women's subjugation puts them in a privileged position to produce true knowledge' (Wacquant 1993: 497), we believe that to adopt such a position takes away the interpretative role of the sociologist. It makes of sociological work a series of generated accounts in which, say, experiential narratives are not necessarily related to the wider picture. It is a version of realist epistemology, in which social-science-based knowledge aspiring to be objective can be distinguished from ideological accounts, rather than this sort of standpoint position, which is absolutely essential for any empirical work that aims to avoid the pitfalls of cultural relativism. Steven Ward has argued that realist epistemology has become unfashionable in much of contemporary sociology:

> This attack [on realist epistemology] has been instigated, at least in part, by a loose confederation of deconstructionists, feminist theorists, science studies practitioners and cultural studies theorists. These theorists, who are often grouped under the convenient label of postmodernists, question the possibility of ever grounding scientific knowledge in any firm absolutes … They reject the notion that scientific truth can ever transcend the local semantic practices, power dynamics, social hierarchies or cultural forms which shape it. Truth, therefore, is not a result of the unearthing and reporting of the already

there, but always and forever a product of rhetoric, power and per
sion.

(Ward 1997: 7

Ward refers to the relativist position in the theory of method as 'standpoint
epistemology' whereby, 'all knowledge is localised perspective and all interpretations are mediated by and can be reduced to the linguistic or social
characteristics of the groups which produce them' (1997: 774). He goes on
to reveal the ontological weaknesses in the standpoint position, and
concludes his attack on postmodernist and culturally relativistic thinking by
staking out a middle ground between standpoint epistemology and scientific realism. He calls for an 'associational epistemology': a theory of method
based on the moral commitment of a community of scholars to objectively,
rigorously and systematically seek out universal truths (*ibid.*: 83–5).

We believe, however, that Ward's case is overstated and oversimplified.
By grouping together under the heading of 'standpoint epistemology' a wide
and diverse body of scholarship, particularly in feminist and postcolonial
theory, he fails to notice that it is not so much the standpoint of the
researcher that is important, but what she or he says about this in relation to
the observations and interpretations made and theories constructed. As
Wheaton and Carrington demonstrate in this volume, it is possible to
research and theorise about power relations in ways that are honest about the
perspective that frames the gaze of the researcher, while, at the same time,
through self-reflection and dialogue with existing theory and research,
contribute to the accumulation of 'associational' sociological knowledge.

By singling out a narrowly defined positive-realism as the only standpoint from which to embark on research, Ward could also leave himself open
to the charge of academic elitism. We are strongly committed to the view
that sociologists should talk to one another in a shared language that is also
accessible to a wider audience. The development of this code of communication is a democratic project. In other words, it cannot be white, middle
class, Western and male-dominated, but must be inclusive across all social
categories (race, class, gender, region and so forth). However, neither can it
be a melting pot or battlefield of ideologies and local perspectives. On the
contrary the code of communication becomes the metalanguage, a kind of
exchange rate system, through which interpretations of and debates about
distinctive spheres of social life are conducted on common ground. Without
such a language relativism prevails and the 'disenchantment of the world'
cannot be achieved.

We are not against the empowerment of the marginalised and oppressed
through the authentic reporting of local perspectives. However, if local
voices are to make a contribution to this shared understanding, we firmly
believe that such perspectives must themselves be re-evaluated through the
metalanguage of social science. Our investigative work has never prejudged
the meaning or significance of data, evidence and respective experiential or

interpretative accounts. In Cuba, for instance, we were as sceptical of the official accounts of the apologists of the state sports system (Sugden, Tomlinson and McCartan 1990) as we were of the claims and boasts of the hustlers on the streets of Old Havana (Sugden and Tomlinson 1995). The task is always to relate different accounts to each other, and to construct the bigger picture. Willis (1977) never left the voices of his kids to speak merely for themselves. His ethnography of the kids is mediated by his interpretative conceptualising intervention, and then – separately – densely theorised in the metalanguage of social science, and so avoids falling into any reductionist relativism or romantic celebration of the voices of the less powerful. There will always be problems with any relativist position that privileges the assumed authenticity of any single voice. In our own work we have always sought to avoid such imbalance. Some of the premises of the investigative approach have sustained the sort of scepticism necessary for the defence of an associational realism upon which the metalanguage of the critical social science community must be based.

We believe that in our own work we manifest a strong moral commitment to the objective, rigorous and systematic quest for truth. But ours is not the philosophical or absolute truth that Ward seems to be talking about, rather it is a sociological truth. Following Clegg (2000), we argue that whereas the former asks what is truth (a question that Foucault believed unanswerable), sociological truth is 'what passes for truth' (*ibid.*: 141), in other words what people believe to be true in the context of the social worlds within which they abide. Given this formulation, and given that there are multiple vantage points, there are multiple truths. In the context of particular networks of power, it is the task of the researcher to identify, gain access to and share as many of these vantage points as possible. On this basis it is possible to construct an overall interpretation that may not be true to any single vantage point, but which, by taking account of them all, including that of the researcher, is the most honest representation of a given milieu's shared truth about itself at a given point in history.

To clarify this, think of the difference between a photograph and an impressionist painter's canvas. The photograph captures a moment of reality (or truth) that is immediately transient and dependent on prevailing and instantly passing conditions of light, shade, expression, and so forth. And remember, just like respondents in interviews, the camera can lie. The impressionist painting, on the other hand, is constructed over time and incorporates the various dimensions of the artist's gaze and what is known about the places and people that are painted. It also leaves room for interpretation by those who view the work in the gallery. Thus, what is produced is not reality per se, but an informed *impression* of that reality. The artist then offers the painting for public appraisal, acclaim or ridicule, implicitly challenging other artists to depict the chosen scene differently. In this way we regard ourselves as rigorous social scientists and as *social impressionists*.

The essays included in this volume, either directly or indirectly, at different levels of sport's institutional framework, address the power dynamics inherent in contemporary sport. They are timely reminders of the centrality of the conceptualisation of power for a critical sociology of sport, and of the need for a detailed empirical study of the sources of power within sports cultures, and the responses generated within those cultures to particular forms of power. They offer no single perspective on the analysis of power, but all recognise that different conditions of, and response to, particular forms of power must be identified and revealed as relational, and that sociological and cultural analyses must be sensitive to the varying forms of resistance that can be expressed within these power relations. They are, in other words, *impressions* of power games.

Notes

1   This chapter is in part a reworking of Sugden and Tomlinson (1999) and Tomlinson (1998), and also owes much to discussions with colleagues in seminars and reading groups held in Sport and Leisure Cultures, Chelsea School Research Centre, University of Brighton.

References

Bairner, A. and Sugden, J. (eds) (1998) *Sport in Divided Societies*, Aachen: Meyer & Meyer.

Carrington, B. (2000) 'A theoretical critique of power, politics and resistance within neo-Gramscian sport sociology', paper presented at the North American Society for the Sociology of Sport annual conference, *Sport and Social Justice*, Colorado Springs, USA, November.

Clegg, S. (2000) 'Theories of power', *Theory, Culture and Society* 17(6): 139–47.

Coakley, J. and Donnelly, P. (eds) (1999) *Inside Sports*, London: Routledge.

De Certeau, M. (1988) *The Practice of Everyday Life*, trans. S. Rendall, Berkeley: University of California Press.

Douglas, J. (1976) *Investigative Social Research: Individual and Team Field Research*, Beverly Hills: Sage.

Fiske, J. (1989) *Understanding Popular Culture*, London: Routledge & Kegan Paul.

Flyvberg, B. (1998) *Rationality and Power: Democracy in Practice*, Chicago: Chicago University Press.

Foucault, M. (1981) *The History of Sexuality: An Introduction*, trans. R. Hurley, Harmondsworth: Penguin/Pelican.

Giddens, A. (1984) *The Constitution of Society: Outline of the Theory of Structuration*, Cambridge: Polity Press.

—— (1989) *Sociology*, Cambridge: Polity Press.

Giulianotti, R. (1999) *Football: A Sociology of the Global Game*, Cambridge: Polity Press.

Goffmann, E. (1989) 'On fieldwork', *Journal of Contemporary Ethnography* 18(2): 123–32.

Gouldner, A.W. (1973) *For Sociology: Renewal and Critique in Sociology Today*, London: Allen Lane.

Hall, S. (1981) 'Notes on deconstructing "the popular"', in R. Samuel (ed.) *People's History and Socialist Theory*, London: Routledge & Kegan Paul.

Hargreaves, J. (1986) *Sport, Power and Culture: A Social and Historical Analysis of Popular Sports in Britain*, Cambridge: Polity Press.

Jennings, A. (1994) 'Investigative journalism and sport', unpublished address to the North American Society for the Sociology of Sport, Savannah, Georgia, USA, November.

—— (1996) *The New Lords of the Rings: Olympic Corruption and How To Buy Gold Medals*, London: Simon and Schuster.

Kaplan, J. (1975) *Lincoln Steffens: A Biography*, London: Jonathan Cape.

Klein, A.M. (1991) *Sugarball: The American Game, the Dominican Dream*, New Haven and London: Yale University Press.

—— (1993) *Little Big Men: Bodybuilding Subculture and Gender Construction*, Albany: State University of New York Press.

Layder, D. (1995) *New Strategies in Social Research*, London: Blackwell.

Lukes, S. (1974) *Power: A Radical View*, London: Macmillan.

MacAloon, J. (1992) 'The ethnographic imperative in comparative Olympic research', *Sociology of Sport Journal* 9(2): 104–30.

Mann, M. (1986) *The Sources of Social Power. Vol. 1: A History of Power from the Beginning to A.D. 1760*, Cambridge: Cambridge University Press.

Marcuse, H. (1972) *One Dimensional Man*, London: Abacus.

Marx, K. (1979) 'The eighteenth brumaire of Louis Bonaparte' (1852), in K. Marx and F. Engels, *Collected Works, Vol. II, Marx and Engels 1851–1853*. London: Lawrence & Wishart.

Mills, C.W. (1959) *The Sociological Imagination*, Harmondsworth: Penguin.

Nietzsche, F. (1956) *The Birth of Tragedy* and *The Genealogy of Morals*, trans. F. Golffing, New York: Doubleday.

Russell, B. (1940) *Power: A New Social Analysis*, London: Basic Books/Allen & Unwin.

Sage, G. (1990) *Power and Ideology in American Sport: A Critical Perspective*, Champaign, IL.: Human Kinetics Books.

Simson, V. and Jennings, A. (1992) *The Lords of the Rings: Power, Money and Drugs in the Modern Olympics*, London: Simon & Schuster.

Sugden, J. (1996) *Boxing and Society: An International Analysis*, Manchester: Manchester University Press.

—— (2001) 'We are Leeds!', in M. Perryman (ed.) *Hooligan Wars: Causes and Effects of Football Violence*, Edinburgh: Mainstream.

Sugden, J. and Tomlinson, A. (eds) (1994) *Hosts and Champions: Soccer Cultures, National Identities and the USA World Cup*, Aldershot: Avebury/Ashgate.

—— (1995) 'Hustling in Havana: ethnographic notes on everyday life and mutual exploitation between locals and tourists in a socialist economy under siege', in G. McFee, W. Murphy and G. Whannel (eds) *Leisure Cultures: Values, Genders, Lifestyles* (LSA Publication No. 54), Brighton: Leisure Studies Association.

—— (1998) *FIFA and the Contest for World Football: Who Rules the Peoples' Game?* Cambridge: Polity Press.

—— (1999) 'Digging the dirt and staying clean: retrieving the investigative tradition for a critical sociology of sport', *International Review for the Sociology of Sport* 34(4): 385–97.

Sugden, J. Tomlinson, A. and McCartan, E. (1990) 'The making and remaking of white lightning in Cuba: politics, sport and physical education thirty years after the revolution', *Arena Review* 14(1): 101–9.

Thompson, H.S. (1967) *Hell's Angels: A Strange and Terrible Saga of the Outlaw Motor Cycle Gangs*, Harmondsworth: Penguin.

—— (1972) *Fear and Loathing in Las Vegas: A Savage Journey to the Heart of the American Dream,* London: Paladin.

—— (1980) *The Great Shark Hunt: Strange Tales from a Strange Time*, London: Picador.

Tomlinson, A. (1984) 'The sociological imagination, the new journalism and sport', in N. Theberge and P. Donnelly (eds) *Sport and the sociological imagination*, Fort Worth: Texas Christian University Press [also in *The Game's Up: Essays in the Cultural Analysis of Sport, Leisure and Popular Culture*, Aldershot UK: Ashgate/Arena, 1999].

—— (1992) 'Shifting patterns of working class leisure: the case of knur and spell', *Sociology of Sport Journal* 9(2): 192–206.

(1998) 'Domination, negotiation and resistance in sports cultures', *Journal of Sport and Social Issues* 22(3): 235–40.

Wacquant, L.J.D. (1993) 'Positivism', in W. Outhwaite and T. Bottomore (eds) *The Blackwell Dictionary of Twentieth Century Social Thought*, Oxford: Blackwell.

—— (1995) 'Pugs at work: bodily capital and bodily labour among professional boxers', *Body and Society* 1(1): 65–93.

Ward, S. (1997) 'Being objective about objectivity: the ironies of standpoint epistemological critiques of science', *Sociology* 31(4): 773–91.

Willis, P. (1977) *Learning to Labour: How Working Class Kids Get Working Class Jobs*, Farnborough: Saxon House.

Wolfe, T. (1968) *The Electric Kool Aid Acid Test*, New York: Bantam.

Part II

Theory: interventions and re-evaluations

2 Globalisation theory, global sport, and nations and nationalism

John Hargreaves

Introduction

In the last decade a growing number of sociologists of sport, as well as other social scientists writing on sport, have used concepts and theories of globalisation to help them understand the significance of the increasing tendency of sport to operate on a world scale (Harvey and Houle 1994; Houlihan 1994; Maguire 1999; Miller *et al.* 2001). There are many problems in doing so and it would be inappropriate to attempt to deal with all the issues comprehensively here – whether globalisation is a myth, as the 'sceptics' claim, or a new age or world order which is qualitatively different from previous eras; whether it develops in linear fashion towards some predictable end, or is a discontinuous process having unforeseen outcomes; whether it is a homogenising force or generates global heterogeneity and diversity; whether a global culture exists already, or if not to what extent it is a possibility; whether it is more appropriate to conceptualise the global order in terms of Western domination and cultural imperialism, or the expansion of capitalism; whether globalisation is better characterised as an extension of modernisation processes or as a postmodern phenomenon; and whether it can be explained in terms of a single prime cause, or only in multi-causal terms. I take a sceptical position on some of these issues in focusing on the main problem I wish to discuss, namely, the effects of globalisation on national identities and nationalism and the role that globalised sport plays therein. A major drawback in this enterprise, despite the large literature embracing a variety of approaches, is that as yet we have no unified, coherent theory of globalisation. Also, the fact that the term has become an article of faith for many politicians, interest group spokesmen and for broad swathes of the intelligentsia, including a lot of academics, clearly, has not helped.

In the first part of this chapter, I very briefly sketch the main types of approach among globalisation theorists and make some critical points about them. In the second part of the chapter, I take some selected examples of work on globalisation and sport, focusing on how globalised sport may or may not impinge on national identity, national interests and nationalism.

Globalisation theory

Globalisation theorists can be divided, firstly, into the more extreme or radical adherents of the thesis, the 'hyperglobalisers', and, secondly, the apparently more moderate 'transformationists' who are more careful to qualify their claims, somewhat more tentative and, on the whole, rather more perceptive (Held *et al.* 1999).[1]

In the ranks of the hyperglobalisers we find individuals from across the political spectrum, from Marxists to neo-liberals, although obviously their opinions differ on whether globalisation is benevolent or exploitative and on the overall impact it is having. At the risk of oversimplifying, hyperglobalisers see globalisation as inevitable. There is no hiding place left for insulated economies, autarkic polities and diverse traditional cultures. A single world embracing all levels has emerged, with its own structure, organisation, culture and dynamics, integrating regions, states, nations and localities, into a single increasingly undifferentiated economic, political and cultural space. The process is unidirectional and inexorable, and it is moving towards a predictable end – the emergence of a global society, whether peacefully, or by other means. Many processes are involved, but the prime mover or cause is the expansion of the market, or, for those on the left, advanced consumer-oriented capitalism. Probably the most important single feature of hyperglobaliser doctrine is the decline and fall of the 'nation-state'. Its powers diminished, its sovereignty and autonomy undermined and eroded by global forces, it is seen as an anachronistic political unit whose powers are passing inevitably to emergent political structures at regional and global levels. Attempts to resist and defend the nation-state, motivated by national identity and nationalist sentiment, tend to be castigated as irrational, as based on nostalgia and as potentially dangerous delusions. National identities are giving way to global, cosmopolitan identities.

I will not spend time assessing the hyperglobalisers separately since it is more fruitful to assess the rather more rigorous version of the globalisation thesis advanced by the transformationists, which, in fact, does much to correct the former's tendency to exaggerate the impact of globalisation and to over-simplify the complex processes involved. This is not to say that they do not share certain common features, one of which is a tendency to couch key propositions in such a way as to make testing them difficult, if not impossible, and to be highly selective in the evidence they adduce in support of their generalisations.

The transformationists

The leading light among the transformationists is Anthony Giddens, although the most thorough account to date is by Held and his associates, on whom I will concentrate for that reason, unless otherwise stated. For transformationists, while contemporary globalisation constitutes a unique order, a new era, globalisation as such is not new and various attempts have been made to periodise its development. Held *et al.* put forward a four-phase model: pre-modern (up to circa 1500); early modern (1500–circa 1850); modern (1850–1945); contemporary (1945 to the present). Robertson (1990) has a five-stage model which overlaps with Held *et al.*'s; and Giddens simply gives two stages: from the end of the nineteenth century to the Second World War, and from the Second World War onwards to the present with, like Robertson, an emphasis on the special significance of the later years of the period. The process is not unilinear and the end is not predictable; rather, global development is discontinuous and its direction open. Nevertheless, Giddens does assert that globalisation is irreversible, and Robertson that its development is 'inexorable' (Giddens 2000). Held *et al.*, on the other hand, entertain doubts as to whether the contemporary pattern of neo-liberal globalisation is as secure as it seems. Transformationists agree that no single force drives globalisation, such as the market, or advanced capitalism: instead a number of major factors steer global development. So, in principle, explanation has to be in multi-causal terms.

Giddens's earlier statements adumbrate the emergence of a global capitalist economy, the system of nation-states, the world military order, the international division of labour and new communications technology as prime factors in the development of globalisation (Giddens 1990). More lately he has emphasised the last factor, referring to the power of the 'electronic economy' and instantaneous electronic communications across the globe as the prime mover (Giddens 1999). Robertson lists capitalism, Western imperialism and global communications with, like Giddens, an emphasis on the efficacy of the last factor.

Held *et al.* borrow elements of the conceptual framework developed by Mann (Mann 1986). Transnational networks of economic, political, military and cultural power intersect and interact with each other, no single network having ultimate primacy, although any one of them can be dominant at any given time depending upon the nature of the particular conjuncture of forces. The different networks of power, however, are not necessarily synchronised for they have their own dynamics. So globalisation is not a single process and the different processes involved may work in opposing ways. Nor does it automatically reproduce itself. Held *et al.* usefully point out that we need to take account of dimensions of globalisation other than its extensiveness, on which most of the commentators tend to concentrate. Analysis must also be in terms of the intensity and velocity of global flows and interactions, and in terms of their 'impact propensity'. In substantive terms, what is unique about contemporary globalisation for transformationists, then, is the unprecedented conjunction of forces, institutions, organisations and infrastructures that have led to a flood of goods, services, people, images and symbols across the globe, a development that, for Giddens, is revolutionary.

First, the contemporary pattern of globalisation is said to be characterised by the emergence of a new political world order replacing that based on the outcome of the Second World War and its aftermath (the bipolar balance of power in the Cold War era and the existence of the UN, and decolonisation and the formation of new states in the Third World). The break-up of the Soviet bloc and the ensuing second wave of new states has created a near universal world of 'nation-states' overlaid by multilateral regional and global systems of regulation and governance. This global pattern is no longer reliant on the expansionary logic of coercive institutions of empire, or on a single hegemonic power, the USA having eschewed that role. New infrastructures and means of global surveillance and governance have transformed the terms on which the structure of global relations is reproduced and contested.

Second, the global economic network set up in the aftermath of the Second World War (the International Monetary Fund, World Bank, etc.), together with the wave of neo-liberal deregulation in the core Western economies since the seventies, has led to an explosion of world trade, investment and financial flows (Giddens cites the fact that more than a trillion dollars is traded each day on global markets). This economic interaction is overseen by tighter mechanisms, an intensification of multilateral economic surveillance and regional supervision and a deepening of regulatory activity.

Third, the global cultural network, established by developing older technology further (dedicated cables, radio, TV, film, publishing) and the appearance of new technologies (satellites, computers) has transformed cultural and social interactions, and the majority of such interactions are now through popular cultural media and artefacts, not between elites as in previous eras. The key institutions in this connection are the emergent multinational media corporations. There have also been major shifts in migration patterns – from the Third World and Eastern Europe to the West, from Asia to the Gulf States, from Latin America to North America – and of asylum seekers from areas of instability in the non-West to the West.

All these changes have stimulated the most significant historical attempts to regulate and institutionalise global flows and networks, with international treaties, laws, organisations, political networks and alliances. The result is a unique pattern of interconnections extending into every domain: the international trading system encompasses almost every state; cultural products and technologies circulate in every continent; and no state is disconnected completely from the global telecommunications network.

Contrary to the hyperglobalisers, transformationists deny that globalisation necessarily weakens the 'nation-state' and induces its decline; rather, for them, the nation-state is challenged and pressurised by global forces into adapting and undergoing reconstruction. Indeed Giddens explicitly states that it is still the most important political actor (Giddens 1999). While he stresses the uncertainty and anxiety that the unpredictablity of globalisation produces, Held *et al.*, in contrast, insist that a globalised world is not a world out of control. On the contrary, what is distinctive about contemporary globalisation is the magnitude and institutionalisation of its political regulation, but which, at the same time, is also highly contested, since the infrastructures and institutions of global politics generate new arenas and mechanisms through which conflicts are played out – the EU, WTO, alternative G7 summits, NGOs, etc. Hence, contrary to the hyperglobalisers, the scope for political action is expanded, not narrowed. However, this does not mean that globalisation is under the control of national governments and that the power of the nation-state is unaltered, for the states in advanced capitalist society have been transformed. One of the key aspects of globalisation for transformationists is the steadily advancing de-territorialisation of politics that is occurring through the reconfiguring of the state system, with the emergence of new institutions and means of regulation at the supranational level. Thus a new conception of sovereignty is in operation. Non-interference in the affairs of sovereign states is no longer accepted as the basis of international relations. Human rights, for example, now take precedence over state sovereignty.

The critique of globalisation theory

Although the transformationist account of globalisation is certainly an advance on the hyperglobalisers' approach in some important respects, it is by no means entirely satisfactory. The conception of contemporary globalisation as a unique conjuncture and the claims made about its impact are still rather unconvincing in certain respects. It is debatable whether periodisation schemes that rewrite world history as the development of globalisation add much to our understanding of the past. Indeed, historical sociologists, Giddens among them, have found it possible to write on the development of Western capitalism, state formation, the interstate system, international relations and cultural change without referring at all to globalisation (Giddens 1985).

In terms of understanding the present, the argument that politics is being de-territorialised as political processes are taken over by institutions of global governance – the EU, WTO, G7, etc. – to which all governments are equally subject as interstate relations are reconfigured, in some ways is far from convincing. Clearly, there is some sort of an infrastructure of supranational governance and regulatory institutions – such as the regime of human rights law – but one cannot assume, as Held *et al.* do, that it actually works in practice. When they claim that: 'The idea of a political community of fate – of a self-determining collectivity – can no longer be meaningfully located within the boundaries of a single nation-state' (Held *et al.* 1999: 447), one wants to ask was this ever the case anyway? Historical sociologists' work on state formation and the interstate system shows that, actually, it never was in practice (Mann 1986). What is missing here is a systematic analysis of the actual impact of the contemporary supranational infrastructure; only then is it possible to ascertain with any accuracy the extent to which it is effective. If we take, for example, the UN implementation of human rights law over say, Kosovo and Ruanda, we see at once that actual outcomes are determined not by the 'international community', but by the decision of the US and its Nato allies to intervene or not, and that in significant ways intervention, whether by Nato or the UN, can be quite ineffective in terms of its ostensible aim to protect human rights. The efficacy of a good proportion of so-called global institutions of governance, particularly the UN, is doubtful, to say the least. Their existence is often no more than an expression of pious hope or a cover for special interests, and there is little evidence that they are becoming more effective.

We can infer from these examples, and from others such as American action in the Gulf War, that it is by no means clear that the US has eschewed the pursuit of world hegemony. Held *et al.* argue that global economic expansion after the 1973 oil crisis and economic deregulation took place when US power was in relative decline. But this neglects the fact that the American economy recovered in the 1990s to regain its place as the most powerful economic engine of all and, of course, its global political and military power was confirmed by its victory in the Cold War.

As for the contemporary pattern of economic expansion, Held *et al.* admit that much of this is between the triad of Western Europe, North America and Japan/East Asia. They are surely right in contending that it increasingly enmeshes many other areas of the world, but they fail to provide convincing evidence in terms of their own recommended framework – that is to say, in terms of the extensiveness, intensity, velocity and impact of global economic expansion. Instead, their analysis is focused on six of the advanced capitalist states (the US, Britain, France, Germany, Sweden and Japan) rather than a systematic examination of global economic relations as such, a procedure that hardly constitutes an adequate test of their propositions about globalisation. Although they admit that their narrow focus leaves a misleading impression of rising intensity of globalisation, they nevertheless proceed to concentrate on the growing intensity of 'global flows' (!) in trading markets with respect to Western economies and OECD countries. In so doing they are forced to concede that levels of direct foreign investment for some countries are actually less now than they were at the height of the nineteenth century. The key point here is that Held *et al.*'s notion of the 'impact propensity' of globalisation processes fudges the issue: what is needed instead is a systematic examination of the actual impact of globalisation in empirical terms that takes its evidence from across the whole globe (Hirst and Thompson 1996).

The treatment of the nation, national identity and nationalism

The problems which globalisation theorists have with the nation, national identity and nationalism stem from their uncritical use of that misleading, ubiquitous, category, the 'nation-state'. The fact is that a significant proportion of so-called 'nation-states' are nothing of the kind: many are, on the contrary, multinational and multi-ethnic entities (O'Connor 1994). Also, of course, a good proportion of nations do not possess their own state. When state and nation are thus conflated the danger is that the latter's significance is downgraded and misinterpreted. Indeed, most of the material in texts on globalisation purportedly dealing with the so-called 'nation-state' actually deals more with the state component than the nation component. It is not that theorists like Giddens and Held are unaware of the distinction between nation and state. It is that in the literature on globalisation modernist theories of the nation and nationalism predominate, i.e. nations and nationalism are treated as essentially modern phenomena dating back no more than 200 years or so, from the late eighteenth and early nineteenth centuries in Europe. As such, they are treated overwhelmingly as ideological entities: as 'imagined communities' (Anderson 1983), as the cement of societies fragmented by the trauma of modernisation and rapid change (Gellner 1983), as 'psychological' phenomena (Giddens 1985), or as 'invented traditions' (Hobsbawm and Ranger 1983; Hobsbawm 1990); and whether diffused from above or emanating from below, useful to elites in the struggle over state power and the construction of modern cohesive societies. The trouble with this is that it is at best only half the story. Nationalism, like liberalism and socialism, may be a modern creation, but as theorists of nationalism, like Smith, Hastings, Armstrong and many others point out, if the perennial aspect of nations and nationalism, i.e. their deep historic, ethnic origins, is neglected, we will never understand the significance of the nation and the power of nationalism, the capacity of nations to endure through the most profound changes and terrible traumas, and the current revival of nations and nationalism in the modern world (Armstrong 1982; Hastings 1997; Smith 1998). Nations are one of the main types of historical community, founded by ethnies or peoples out of their historic experiences and having their own values, myths, memories, traditions, institutions, customs, organisations and deep attachment to territory. As such, nations, and the deep sense of belonging they generate, cannot be merely imagined, invented or conjured out of nothing, or imposed on people willy nilly.

While globalisation theorists like Giddens and Held *et al.* readily recognise that globalisation may reinforce or stimulate national identity and encourage the emergence of nationalist movements, this is largely a token recognition, for their main object of analysis is, in fact, the state system rather than nations and nationalism. The resulting lacunae means that they have difficulty in explaining the origins, the survival and the strengthening of the nation and nationalism in the contemporary period.[2]

Crucially, it means that their analysis of the expansion of the political and cultural network of globalisation is seriously deficient. Global expansion is supposed to generate supra-national, more cosmopolitan loyalties and identities as part of the emergence of a global culture. But this idea fails to recognise that the entrenchment of national identities, and nationalist sentiment places strong limits on the development of global identity and global culture. As Smith argues, if the outlines of a global culture are discernible, there are, nevertheless, strict limits to the construction of a global culture *sui generis*, and these lie in the existing plurality of cultures, each embedded in a specific history and attached to a specific location. This applies especially to the existence of national cultures with their own memories, traditions, identities, values, myths, customs and sense of destiny, each of them tied to a specific time and place (Smith 1995). To one or other extent they insulate their members from direct exposure to global influences and enable them to interpret 'global culture' according to their own values, and to reformulate and use it according to their own interests. Unless the content of global culture can be harmonised with a given national culture, establish a continuity with it, and be compatible with the prevailing sense of collective identity and destiny, it has little or no chance of surviving and flourishing, for global culture draws its content from, among other sources, such already constructed national cultures. The more there is a tendency towards the emergence of a global culture, the more the plurality of national cultures tends to be accentuated (*ibid.*).

Global sport, national identity and nationalism

The recent accelerated expansion of capitalism on a global scale is characterised by greater commercialisation and commodification of both the private and public spheres, involving an enhanced role and power of multinational companies (MNCs). The development of sport as a global phenomenon has become a more or less integral part of the global expansion of the economic network, as business interests led by the MNCs move into, associate themselves with and increasingly impinge on major sports in search of profits and image enhancement. In the vanguard of the ensuing commodification of sport on a world scale are the media MNCs, in particular the television networks, whose capacity to market sport to the world and influence the course of its development has been greatly facilitated by recent advances in communications technologies (Miller *et al.* 2001: ch. 3). Political elites in the constituent states of the new world order have, for some considerable time, tended to intervene in and to promote sport as an important instrument for the creation of a sense of national identity and as a way of enhancing their state-nation's prestige and influence internationally. Those who manage and control sport within national borders, and the elites in charge of the international non-governmental organisations (INGOs) that control international sport, now well understand the material benefits that may accrue from commercialisation and governmental support, and accordingly they accommodate to commercial and government pressures, forming mutually beneficial alliances with commercial and political interests (Hargreaves 2000: ch. 3). Globalised sport is, by and large, driven by the West, and since America in so many ways leads the West, it should come as no surprise to learn that globalised sport is highly Americanised.

Major sectors of elite competitive sport are, then, in one way or another globalised or advancing rapidly along that path (Maguire 1999; Miller *et al.* 2001), but it is important to understand that the extensiveness, intensity, velocity and impact of globalisation in the sphere of sport varies considerably. For example, association football under the control of FIFA (the International Federation of Football Associations) and the Olympic Games under the aegis of the IOC (International Olympic Committee) are unrivalled in terms of each of these aspects of globalisation (Sugden and Tomlinson 1998; Hargreaves 2000). On the other hand, sports like cricket, baseball, basketball, rugby union and ice hockey may be globalised in terms of the intensity, velocity and impact of the processes involved, but globalisation of such sports is not so extensive in comparison. They have a grip on certain areas of the world rather than a universal popular presence. Less popular sports that are also subject to globalisation processes, like golf, tennis and motor racing, tend to have less impact propensity. The extensiveness of a recently globalised sport, American football, is clearly limited, and so its impact outside the US and Canada is relatively weak, yet it is intensely involved in processes of globalisation (Maguire 1999). Also, the extensiveness, intensity, velocity and impact of the processes involved across the whole of globalised sport may fluctuate considerably.

Thus the globalisation of sport is uneven and exhibits great variation, an indication that it is not an inevitable product of a single cause or uniform process, but that rather it is the product of interaction between interdependent economic, political and cultural forces. We will see that this point has a particular bearing on the issue upon which we wish to focus – the relationship between globalised sport, the nation, national identity and nationalism.

Although there is a general awareness of the global expansion of sport and of the continuing political significance of the nation and nationalism, the amount of sociologically informed work on the relationship between them is still quite limited and its quality uneven; and the work rarely focuses specifically on nationalism, as such, as the prime object of attention. We need to know the extent to which globalised sport helps to activate the growth of national identity and nationalism, the types of national identity it may help to foster, i.e. reactionary or anti the status quo, state nationalism or nationalism against the state, and the extent to which it can help counteract globalisation processes and foreign domination. By the same token we need to know the conditions in which national identity may be rendered problematic by globalised sport, and whether the manifestations of national identity that we see in it represent one of the last gasps of the nation-state and nationalism in the modern world.

It is reasonably clear that that the transformation of nation-based sport into globalised sport may help to stimulate national sentiment and provide a rallying point around which it can be reinforced and reconstructed, as Miller *et al.* point out in a wide-ranging account of sport and globalisation, drawing on globalisation theory, Marxism and postmodernism. The

Australian authorities, among others, for example, have attempted to use soccer for that purpose (Miller *et al.* 2001). However, echoing one of the main tenets of globalisation theory, the main thrust of this analysis is that globalised sport, driven by free market forces and the activities of the MNCs, is de-territorialised, making it more problematic for people to identify with it as an expression of their nation. What has happened to Canadian ice hockey and English Premier football league are taken as cases in point. In the latter case, an increasing number of star foreign players have been imported – not only from nearby Europe, but also from the countries of the former Soviet bloc, Latin America and Africa, and even from the US and Australia. Foreign managers have taken over some of best known, successful teams, like Arsenal and Chelsea, and even the England team itself now has a Swede as manager. Second and third generation black British players have risen to the top echelons of English football including representing England. The last restrictions on the free movement of players across frontiers have been lifted and the market in soccer labour deregulated as a result of the European Court of Justice decision (the Bosman judgement) and EU legislation banning the quota system (Miller *et al.* 2001).

ˎ It has been argued that, in the English case, globalisation provides the conditions for the emergence of a regressive form of national identity, i.e. a defensive, nostalgic and dangerously racist form of national identity, which is expressed in the way football matches are reported in the tabloid press and in the way fans behave: a fragile male 'little Englander' identity is said to wrestle with 'fluid, pluralisitic and less male-defined global identities' (Maguire 1999: see pp. 189–206). This is attributed to a general sense of 'English dislocation', uncertainty and anxiety about national identity among the English population due to the decline of the British nation-state in the context of contemporary globalisation, i.e. loss of empire and of 'world hegemony', external pressure deriving from Britain's membership of the EU, internal pressure from Irish, Scottish and Welsh nationalism, and the increasingly multi-ethnic composition of the population. ˎ

There is not much doubt that globalised football is intimately tied up with national sentiment (Sugden and Tomlinson 1998). Its global expansion has been closely associated with the increasing assertiveness of newly emerging states and nationalist movements in the second and third worlds. Driven by a simultaneous expansion of the global economic network in which major multinational companies ally themselves with the FIFA oligarchy, football's trajectory is increasingly subject to the interests of transnational capital as well as certain national interests.

On the other hand, globalised football has to a significant extent worked to the advantage of non-Western countries and peoples. It has enabled some of them – on the African continent, for example – to acquire valuable material help as well as access to the world stage; it has stimulated nationalist sentiment and resistance to perceived domination and oppression (Sugden and Tomlinson 1998). In these respects it could be said to have done something significant to help alter the balance of power between the West and the rest. Sugden and Tomlinson argue that the expanded power over the game of the multinational commercial interests in the consumer goods and cultural and media industries are the real winners, together with the FIFA oligarchy. In the final analysis, they conclude that this control amounts to a form of Western hegemony and cultural imperialism over countries like Sudan, Nigeria, Malaysia, Singapore and South Africa: 'for the post-colonial third world affiliation to FIFA and participation in international football represented a tacit acceptance of the deep structure left behind by the colonists' (Sugden and Tomlinson 1998: 228).

Similar conclusions have been drawn about the impact of US dominated baseball in the Dominican Republic and Mexico (Klein 1991, 1997). Such countries are said to be simultaneously developed and underdeveloped in accordance with US interests, and baseball is held to be part of the cultural armoury of US hegemony, all the more effective for its immense popularity in Latin American countries in and around the Caribbean region: 'The dream of baseball shines radiantly for the individual, but it blinds society' (Klein 1991: 59). It absorbs the energies and hopes of youth better invested in other things. Indeed, the American major franchises are said to function exactly like multinational companies, siphoning off the best Latino players through lucrative offers and thus impoverishing and retarding the local game. Latino players imported into the US are said to experience racial/ethnic stereotyping. Agreements between US major league and Mexican and Dominican local clubs, ostensibly aimed at assisting the latter by providing management and training expertise, are seen as subordinating them to the interests of the American partner and as spreading American norms and values. US star players, imported to play for local teams at higher salaries and better conditions than their Latino local team mates, are reported to be arrogant and ethnocentric.

Just as US political and economic domination breeds a degree of resentment and nationalist hostility against the US, so Mexican and Dominican baseball's dependency on US baseball is seen as doing the same. In the Dominican case, Klein goes so far as to claim baseball is the main vehicle for resistance to American cultural domination. Latino players resent the privileges and ethnocentric behaviour of 'gringo' imports to their teams and what they perceive as American franchises' insensitivity to Latino culture, when Latinos play for US teams. Mexican and Dominican baseball management takes an anti-American stance in the press on occasions in disputes with American baseball interests. Dominican press coverage of the game, in particular, seethes with anti-American nationalism: Dominican players in American major league games are treated as national heroes, the Dominican professional league is all-important, the game in the premier baseball nation, America, is ignored, and America is blamed for the decline of the Dominican professional and amateur leagues. The sense of national pride that is taken in the success of Latino players in the US and in the performance of national teams contrasts starkly with the widespread lack of success of people in these countries at improving their lot, and the consequent self-loathing and the sense of inferiority to Americans.

The consensus among commentators on sport and globalisation, then, seems to be that, while globalised sport may stimulate national identity and nationalism in given cases, in the final analysis it is, nevertheless, overwhelmingly a manifestation of the power and universal triumph of advanced consumer capitalism that negates national identity and reduces nationalism to a spent force. Such accounts have their merits, not least the wealth of information on globalised sport they have gathered, but they also possess serious weaknesses. An over-reliance on globalisation theory and its Marxist alternatives and an uncritical use of modernist theories of nationalism lead to an underestimation of the power of the nation and nationalism to resist and counteract the effects of globalisation. The result is that insufficient attention is paid to endogenous cultural factors, with a resultant failure to explain variations in the capacity of different state-nations and peoples to resist and counteract globalising processes.

Commentators like Miller *et al.*, Maguire and Klein mistakenly rely on Anderson's idea of the nation as merely an 'imagined community' and on Hobsbawm's notion that national institutions, values and beliefs are merely 'invented traditions' (Anderson 1983; Hobsbawm and Ranger 1983).[3] All three seem to be totally unaware of the importance of ethno-nationalist elements, which has been pointed out by the perennialist critics of modernist theories of nationalism, such as Anthony Smith (Smith 1995, 1998). Thus, as characterised by Maguire, English national identity constitutes nothing more than a 'phantasy shield', a 'dream' – 'wilful nostalgia' for a great lost past. The main problem with this characterisation stems precisely from his narrowly modernist approach. It results in a picture of contemporary English identity as nothing more than a rather nasty delusion, and so the complexity of a form of national identity, whose origins go much further back in the history of Britain than modernists can imagine, is grossly underestimated (Hastings 1997). To reduce a deeply rooted, autonomous, historical phenomenon with its values, customs and traditions, memories, institutions, attachment to territory and symbols to a mere phantasy or delusion is to caricature English national identity.[4] Of course there are outbursts of xenophobic sentiment in England which manifest themselves in sport, as there are in almost all countries, but they have nothing like the importance that Maguire suggests (Hargreaves 2000, ch. 1: 6–7). The danger here is that the received wisdom of the liberal-left intelligentsia, with its domain assumptions that further European integration is a foregone conclusion and that opposition in Britain to further losses of sovereignty is simply irrational, take over and blind us to the real difficulties in understanding English national identity and the role sport plays in it. In addition, the existence of 'global identities' is taken for granted here which, as we have seen, is itself a delusion.

One wonders whether press comment on sport and on the reported comments of sports stars, sports managers and other sports officials, and of politicians – a lot of which amounts to little more than anecdote – is an accurate barometer of the state of national identity. Too often it is assumed that expressions of national identity articulated by the sports press coincide with those expressed elsewhere, whereas, for all we know, they may be untypical. For example, the contents of the sports pages have relatively little interest for women and are unlikely therefore to reflect this large section of the population's opinion. Little or no direct evidence on the fans' or on the wider audience's national sentiments is presented. It is simply assumed, rather than demonstrated empirically, that there is a commensurate ideological effect on sports fans and the wider audience for sport.

Miller *et al.* and Klein employ different versions of dependency theory to explain asymmetrical power relations between the West and the rest and how they manifest themselves in globalised sport. The fly in the ointment in Miller *et al.*'s case is that they also want to draw on postmodernism and Foucaultian notions such as 'governmentality'. Now, the latter kinds of discourse dismiss the whole enterprise of theory construction and claims to scientific knowledge about the world as mythological 'grand narratives'. For Foucault and his ilk, knowledge and truth claims are social constructions: they are the material of social power. So there is a contradiction here between the economic determinism and scientific pretensions of dependency theory and the ostensible indeterminacy of postmodernism and of Foucault's post-structuralist variant of it. Logically, of course, Miller *et al.* cannot have it both ways, but they do persist in trying to do so. Consequently, at one moment capitalist power is overwhelming, the next it is negated and globalised sport is the rallying point for resistance and challenge to the monster's power. Miller *et al.*'s disdain for any notion of a value-free, objective analysis and their commitment to an anti-capitalist and anti-Western political ideology means that no serious attempt is made to test their propositions in a rigorous manner, and every attempt is made to select and interpret evidence so that it fits their preconceptions.

The problem with dependency theory itself, of course, is that it cannot explain how some post-colonial countries manage to escape dependency to a significant extent (most of the Asian tiger economies, for example), while others remain very much dependent (virtually all of Africa, for example); that is, it cannot explain dependency and variations in dependency at all because it treats politics and culture as mere epiphenomena, rather than as they should be treated – as autonomous sources of power. Klein exemplifies the problem when he attempts to combine dependency theory with the Gramscian notion of hegemony. It was to deal with the deficiencies of economic determinism in the Marxist tradition that Gramsci formulated his notion of hegemony. Klein wants to argue that there is a significant cultural resistance centred on baseball in the Dominican Republic to US hegemony, but his attempt to employ two incompatible universes of discourse, one determinist, the other granting agency to subordinate groups, vitiates his argument. Gramsci's notion is not of a populace being 'blinded', but of subordinate groups, conscious of their interests, being won over, persuaded, negotiated with and led by dominant groups – a notion that grants to politics and culture an autonomy unrecognised in dependency theory (Hargreaves 1986).

In fact, Mexico's and the Dominican Republic's dependency on the US is due, in part at least, to endogenous factors. Their political systems have been, and still are to a great extent, notoriously corrupt and undemocratic, political unity has been lacking, and elites have been incapable of and/or unwilling to develop their economies, and certain features of their cultures militate against escaping dependency. Little wonder that poverty is rife and that these countries are vulnerable to foreign domination.

Klein's material itself actually reveals that a good deal of the troubles of Mexican and Dominican baseball can be directly attributed to Latino culture. The fact that Dominican and Mexican professional players are paid less than American imported players is the responsibility of the Mexican and Dominican team owners, not of Americans, who do not even own Dominican and Mexican league teams. On the other hand, Latino players in American leagues are paid handsomely, on a par with North American players. It is Dominican team owners who are responsible for keeping down salaries by opposing 'free agency' for players, whereas in American professional baseball opposition to it has been overcome. It is significant that in Klein's study of the bi-national team, the Tecos of Laredo and Nuevo Laredo, Mexican fans and team members expressed their strongest feelings against the team management, rather than against American influence, and that in the Dominican Republic fans vent their anger against Dominican players contracted to American major league, rather than American baseball as such, because of their refusal to support the Dominican game. The reason that Dominican professional and amateur leagues are in decline is not just because of the pull of America, it is because they are badly and corruptly run. Also, Latino players so often encounter problems of adjustment to life in the US and experience failure, not just because of racism and cultural stereotyping, but because they often lack the requisite cultural resources to function in the more competitive, hard-working US baseball environment – for example, a sufficient level of education and linguistic capability, and appropriate attitudes to work and social discipline. Such deficiencies can often be traced to the rampant, exaggerated form of egotism at the core of Latino male culture, the cult of 'personalismo' and machismo. That is to say there are weaknesses in Latino culture which limit the development of effective resistance to US cultural domination and which Klein has difficulty making sense of within his dependency theory framework and his oversimplified notion of hegemony.

In any case, Latino players are not so dependent on the US game as might appear. The recent entry of Japan into the market for Latino players is likely to reduce the power of the American leagues over Latin baseball, since they can play Japanese baseball off against US baseball interests.

The essential point is that we need to distinguish the specific characteristics of a country's structure and culture if we are to understand its relationship with the West and the impact of globalised sport on national identity. It is easy to fall into the trap, as Sugden and Tomlinson and other commentators do, of assuming that very different types of society are equally subordinate to the West. While it may be true that African countries like the Sudan and Nigeria are in a subordinate and dependent position vis-à-vis the West, this is unlikely to be true of other countries like Malaysia and Singapore, that are hardly Third World countries any more. These can fall back on strongly developed economic, as well as cultural and political, resources to counterbalance Western power and influence. Similarly, the fact that the newly independent states of eastern and south-eastern Europe, following the collapse of the Soviet Union, the Soviet bloc and Yugoslavia, with their fierce national pride, as evidenced by Serbia's resistance to Nato, have been drawn into a closer association with the West through their thorough integration into globalised football, would not seem to have the inevitable effect of enhancing Western domination. Whether or not this happens depends on the capacity of states and nations to exert their autonomy. Sugden and Tomlinson eventually concede this point, but unfortunately it does not inform their analysis.

The different way that some sports have been received in contrasting cultures shows that given the appropriate political and cultural resources, foreign domination can be successfully resisted. Take the cases of Japan and Cuba, two sharply contrasting cultures, where baseball was enthusiastically taken up and became the national game. In both cases this game is now popularly understood in these countries as theirs, and it has come to express, not American cultural domination, but specific aspects of Japanese and Cuban culture (Whiting 1989; Jamail 2000). Many observers have noted the capacity of the Japanese to live within their own culture and Western culture simultaneously; Horne and Jary suggest that among Japanese youth attracted to the game there may be a subtle modification of national identity which takes the form of a synthesis of Japanese and Western identities (Horne and Jary 1994). Others have argued that the Japanese have learned to switch between the two cultures rather than synthesise them (Morishima 1982; Reischauer 1995). Whether syncretism or switching is involved, undeniably the Japanese have a remarkably strong sense of national identity and well-developed cultural resources to cushion them against the impact of globalised culture. If Klein is right in thinking that the importation of baseball to the Dominican Republic and Mexico is part of a pattern of American domination over those countries, in contrast to Japan and Cuba where it seems not to have served this purpose, perhaps the explanation for the different outcome lies in part, at least, in the relatively weaker cultural resources of Mexico and the Dominican Republic.

Huntington has documented the different ways in which non-Western civilisations have proved to be capable of resisting Western influence and domination, which he accounts for in terms of the ineradicable cultural differences between them and the West. There are variations in the type and strength of challenge they present to the West. East Asian (Sinic and Japanese) and Islamic challenges are the strongest and most successful; Orthodox (Russia and her Balkan co-religionists) and Hindu resistance and difference is entrenched; Latin American resistance is growing; and African civilisation, while seemingly incapable of mounting a challenge to the West, maintains its vast cultural distance (Huntington 1997). The first lesson here is surely that a strong sense of cultural identity and, especially, of national identity, and a confidence among a population about its national culture, impose severe limits on the capacity of globalised sport to serve as a vehicle of globally organised economic, political and cultural domination. And the second lesson is that social power cannot be adequately analysed in terms of a zero-sum game conception of power relations – that is, a conception in which power is a fixed sum and gains by one party to a power relationship are necessarily gained at the expense of the other(s).

These lessons are amply confirmed by the Barcelona Olympic Games and the manner in which they functioned as an arena for the interplay of Catalan and Spanish identities and interests (Hargreaves 2000). The fact that the Games intensively enmeshed Spain, and in particular Catalonia, in an extensive global network of economic and cultural power, instantly activated the national and local political fields. The Olympics stimulated both Spanish and Catalan nationalist sensibilities, in so far as it provided opportunities for the Spanish state to intervene in, and exert control over, Catalan affairs (questions of public investment in improvements to Barcelona's infrastructure, Espanolisation of the Games, control over the degree to which the Games were Catalanised, etc.), thereby threatening Catalan autonomy. On the other hand, Catalan nationalist activity around the Games challenged Spanish sovereignty. A spiralling struggle developed over the degree of control each would exercise over the Games and, in particular, over the extent to which the Games would represent the Spanish and Catalan nations and express their different identities.

However, contrary to what might be thought, in fuelling Catalan nationalism globalised sport did not in any sense weaken the Spanish state. On the contrary, the latter gained considerably from the great success of the Games – in national prestige and in terms of the positive effect the Games had in certain ways on national integration. The gains for Catalonia were even greater and, on the whole, were not made at the expense of the Spanish state – that is, globalised sport did not entail a zero-sum game in this case. The way this conflict turned out enabled all the main agents involved to make perceived gains. Catalonia gained immensely in economic, cultural and political terms – from the flow of national and global capital into the region; the extent to which it was able to flood the Games with its cultural and political symbols; the way it projected itself to the world as an important, attractive nation – and in the process Catalan nationalism was strengthened in its own constituency vis-à-vis the political opposition.

Among the main reasons why globalised sport did not contribute to weakening the Spanish state or help to subordinate Catalonia to the hegemony of this or that transnational force, was the strength and flexibility of the democratic, pluralist Spanish state, and the character of Catalan nationalism, which is founded on the long existence of Catalonia as a historic nation from mediaeval times, with a well-developed civil society, strong cultural institutions, a firm, although not rigid, sense of national identity, and a confidence among the Catalan population in their own culture. There is no doubt that global capital and the IOC oligarchy profited from these games and exerted a significant influence over them, and that Americanisation was well to the fore. These forces co-existed with, rather than dominated, the national and the local, which were shielded from the full impact of global forces.

Conclusion

Globalisation is not a myth, but neither is it as significant as is often made out. In so far as it exists it is best understood as a continuation or extension of modernisation processes. A good proportion of the issues on which the concept of globalisation is intended to throw light can be adequately understood in terms of already available theory and concepts, as Mann's notion of power operating through transnational networks demonstrates. Where globalisation theory falls down quite badly is in its failure to comprehend the real significance of the nation, national identity and nationalism.

The expansion of sport on a global scale is one of the most striking examples of the propensity for power networks to expand exponentially and in promiscuous fashion; that is, through sport, economic, cultural and political power networks intersect and interact with each other to produce outcomes which are often unintended and unforeseeable. The resulting tie-up between sport, national identity and nationalism is a pertinent instance which is being paid increasing attention by sociologists.

Although the need to avoid determinism and reductionism is widely acknowledged in the literature on sport and globalisation, and there is a lot of attention paid to multi-causal explanation and the capacity of subjects to resist the imposition of power, there is still a tendency to succumb to the temptation to give explanations in terms of the ultimate primacy of some factor or other. There is also a tendency to exaggerate the capacity of the powerful to dominate, and to underestimate the capacity of the less powerful to counteract them, and to take advantage of, and benefit from, global sport. This stems from the propensity to treat power relations exclusively as a zero-sum game.

One of the major constraints on the further development of a global power system, and the emergence of a homogenised global culture and global identity, is the existence of nations, national identities and nationalism. Strong, diverse national cultures in which people have confidence are priceless assets. It is time that nations, national identity and nationalism came to be seen as potentially major bulwarks against domination by the globally powerful, and not simply as bogey men responsible for so much of the world's ills.

Notes

1   In practice it is not so easy to pigeonhole proponents of globalisation. Some, like Robertson, could possibly fit into either category or could be said to straddle the division (Robertson 1990).
2   Giddens, for example, puts Catalan nationalism down to the weakening of the Spanish state in the context of globalisation (Giddens 1999), whereas the weakening of the host state and the emergence and consolidation of Catalan nationalism occurred well before the contemporary era.
3   Wieber provides one of the few incisive critiques of Anderson's influential notion of nations as 'imagined communities' (Wieber 2000). See also Smith's comments (1998: ch. 6) on both Anderson and Hobsbawm in this connection.
4   If the culture of any other nation or ethnic group were to be so denigrated, there is little doubt that politically correct eyebrows would be raised.

References

Anderson, B. (1983) *Imagined Communities*, London: Verso.
Armstrong, J. A. (1982) *Nations before nationalism*, Chapel Hill: University of North Carolina Press.
Gellner, E. (1983) *Nations and Nationalism*, Oxford: Blackwell.
Giddens, A. (1985) *The Nation-State and Violence*, Cambridge: Polity Press.
—— (1990) *The Consequences of Modernity*, Cambridge: Polity Press.
—— (1999) *Reith Lectures*, BBC Radio 4, weekly 7 April–5 May.
—— (2000) address to the Association for the Study of Ethnicity and Nationalism Annual Conference, London School of Economics.
Hargreaves, J.E. (1986) *Sport, Power and Culture: A Social and Historical Analysis of Popular Sports in Britain*, Cambridge: Polity Press.
—— (1998) 'Reply to Keating, ethno-nationalist movements in Europe: a debate', *Nations and Nationalism* 4(4): 569–74.
—— (2000) *Freedom for Catalonia? Catalan Nationalism, Spanish Identity and the Barcelona Olympic Games*, Cambridge: Cambridge University Press.
Harvey, J. and Houle, F. (1994) 'Sport, world economy, global culture, and new social movements', *Sociology of Sport Journal* 11(4): 337–55.
Hastings, A. (1997) *The Construction of Nationhood*, Cambridge: Cambridge University Press.
Held, D., McGrew, A., Goldplatt J. and Perraton, J. (1999) *Global transformations*, Cambridge: Polity Press.
Hirst, P. and Thompson, G. (1996), *Globalisation in Question*, Cambridge: Polity Press.
Hobsbawm, E. (1990) *Nations and Nationalism since 1780*, Cambridge: Cambridge University Press.

Hobsbawm, E. and Ranger T. (1983) *The Invention of Tradition*, Cambridge: Cambridge University Press.

Horne, J. and Jary, D. (1994) 'Japan and the World Cup: Asia's first World Cup Final hosts?', in J. Sugden and A. Tomlinson (eds) *Hosts and Champions: Soccer Cultures, National Identities and the USA World Cup*, Aldershot: Arena.

Houlihan, B. (1994) *Sport and International Politics*, Hemel Hempstead: Harvester Wheatsheaf.

Huntington, S. (1997) *The Clash of Civilisations and the Remaking of the World Order*, London: Touchstone.

Jamail, M. (2000) *Full Count. Inside Cuban Baseball*, Carbondale and Edwardsville: Southern Illinois University Press.

Klein, A. (1991) *Sugarball: The American Game, The Dominican Dream*, Newhaven: Yale University Press.

—— (1997) *Baseball on the Border*, Princeton: Princeton University Press.

Maguire, J. (1999) *Global Sport: Identities, Societies, Civilizations*, Cambridge: Polity Press.

Mann, M. (1986) *The Sources of Social Power*, Vol. 1, Cambridge: Cambridge University Press.

Miller, T., Lawrence, G., McKay, J. and Rowe, D. (2001) *Globalisation and Sport*, London: Sage.

Morishima, M. (1982) *Why has Japan Succeeded?*, Cambridge: Cambridge University Press.

O'Connor, W. (1994) *Ethno-nationalism*, Princeton: Princeton University Press.

Reischauer, E.O. (1995) *The Japanese Today*, London: Harvard University Press.

Robertson, R. (1990) 'Mapping the global condition: globalisation as the central concept', *Theory, Culture and Society* 7(2–3): 15–30.

Smith, A. D. (1995) *Nations and Nationalism in a Global Era*, Cambridge: Polity Press.

——(1998) *Nationalism and Modernism*, London: Routledge.

Sugden, J. and Tomlinson, A. (1998) *FIFA and the Contest for World Football: Who Rules the Peoples' Game?*, Cambridge: Polity Press.

Whiting, R. (1989) *You Gotta Have Wa*, New York: Macmillan.

Wieber, R. (2000) 'Imagined communities, nationalist experiences', *Journal of the Historical Society* 1(1): 33–64.

3 Theorising spectacle

Beyond Debord

Alan Tomlinson

Introduction

High-profile sport events, with their intensified media profile, provide some of the most observed, screen-watched, live-spectated and commented-upon events in history. In the contest in the stadium, the raw power of the athletic competition or the sporting rivalry conveys not only its own internal dynamic, but also meanings, values and ideologies from the wider culture and society. The sports event also prompts the mobilisation of spectator passions and, as such, is a forum for the expression of various levels of identity and affiliation. Sport and the sites at which high-profile events take place can therefore be seen as prominent contemporary forms of spectacle.

Particularly prominent are the opening and closing ceremonies of the Olympic Games. These have escalated in their media profile since the Los Angeles Olympic Games of 1984, when the Cold War riposte of the USA to the boycotted 1980 Moscow games was combined with a showbiz extravaganza, a remaking of the political economy of Olympism, and a media celebration of the US's perception of its own role in rescuing Olympism for the Free World. Since 1984, and the inflation in the television and sponsorship rights around the Games, a major element of the justification for this level of media and corporate expenditure on buying and being associated with the event has been that the Olympics, and its framing ceremonies, provide the biggest audience for a regular cultural spectacle transmitted on the media, in the history of humankind. I have attended several such events since LA '94, and all them try to outdo the immediate predecessor. But, as I have argued (Tomlinson 1996), there is a persisting rhetoric in these ceremonial spectacles, playing to pseudo-universalising rhetoric and, simultaneously, narrowly nationalistic born-again themes of parochial pride. World-historical figures, such as Muhammad Ali, may be brought into the cast list of such spectacles, but their world-historical significance is dissolved into the melting-pot of the recurrent Olympic ideology (Tomlinson 2000a).

At Olympic Games, and increasingly at football/soccer World Cups, extravagant shows are staged, claiming to hold the global audience's attention. I sat on the drizzly terraces of the Place de la Concorde in Paris 1998, the night before the opening of the France '98 World Cup, and, along with global commentator Juliette Binoche, sought to make sense of the sustained expectation of the French and world media as to the scale and significance of the giant humanoids that cornered us from the four points of the compass. *L'Équipe* (Wednesday, 10 June 1998: 7) wrote of an atmosphere of madness and carnival pervading the streets and squares of the city, for a spectacle that brought the city to life and launched the World Cup 'in the most beautiful fashion imaginable', 'astonishing' the city's 'strollers'. The four giant figures, over twenty metres high, dwarfed many of the city's ancient monuments. Pablo the American Indian, Ho the Asiatic, Moussa the African, and Romeo the European paraded the streets of Paris for three hours, at the tortuously slow average pace of 1.4 kilometres per hour, watched by close to a quarter of a million people. Their colours symbolised the continents represented in the forthcoming tournament, their forty-metre robes were designed by Yves Saint-Laurent. Eighty thousand awaited their arrival in the Place de la Concorde. Binoche soon ran out of superlatives in her television commentary, and the spectators in the Place de la Concorde soon tired of the lumbering figures as the event brought in countless hundreds of children around the replica of the World Cup situated in the centre of the Concorde. But sports bodies ignore such gripes, arguing for their high-impacting global profile at such moments.

For the Parisian press especially 'spectacle' could say it all for this kind of public festival. Perhaps a little less effusive, but equally guilty of an interpretative shorthand, are academics – including myself – who have taken such events for granted by labelling them as spectacles without any fully developed sense of the conceptualisation of the spectacular. In this chapter I take the opportunity to offer a corrective to this a priori form of thinking, especially a lazy anarcho-political adaptation of Debord, and attempt a problematisation of the very notion of spectacle. I emphasise, too, not just what might go on 'before our very eyes' at the spectacle, but what may well be going on behind the gloss of the spectacular event. Thus my emphasis in the following section. I also review some general ways in which sport has been seen in this fashion as spectacle, and subject the most influential theorisation of spectacle – in the work of Debord – to a critical re-evaluation. This is intended as an intervention and a call for a fundamental re-conceptualisation of spectacle. In doing this, I emphasise the ethnographic (drawing upon fieldwork in Europe and Australia), the etymological (reviewing the semantics of the concept) and the exegetical (presenting what Debord actually said).

Guy Debord published his polemic – or some might say theoretical treatise – *The Society of the Spectacle* in 1967. In 1994 he killed himself with one gunshot through the heart, acting out his claim that suicide was 'the purest critique of the "spectacle"' (Hussey 2001a; 2001b: 3). The fame, impact and, in some circles, notoriety of his tract were confirmed during the political disturbances of 1968. An unaltered second edition was published in

1971 and regularly reprinted until 1991. A third edition, though newly translated, was published in 1994, identical to the 1967 edition. In no edition, then, were changes made. As Debord himself states with no hint of ambiguity or irony: 'I am not someone who revises his work' (Debord 1995: 7). He has, though, deigned to comment on his own work in prefaces to new editions, afterwords (Jappe 1999) and in response to particular political and intellectual currents, and most extensively twenty years later in his *Comments on the Society of the Spectacle*, first published in 1988 (Debord 1998). Essentially, then, the same text has remained available for almost a third of a century. What accounts for the enduring life of this text – a polemic, an embryonic manifesto, a collection of prolix rather than pithy 'theses' (221 in all)? And might Debord's work inform in any way a systematic, synthesising and seriously sustained analysis of sport as spectacle in the contemporary global order?

The recognition of sport as spectacle is nothing new, but the nature of the spectacle, its changing forms and comparative cultural, social and political meanings, remain surprisingly under-emphasised. In works as important as Harvey's groundbreaking study of *The Condition of Postmodernity* (1989), the 'sensationalism of the spectacle', and immediacy of events, are seen as 'the stuff of which consciousness is forged' (*ibid.*: 54). Harvey also sees in the spectacle a revolutionary potential (*ibid.*: 88ff.). But a single question often remains unasked: what does the spectacle actually do?

In my work on spectacle, too, I have used the term in a relatively simplistic fashion, as a descriptive category for large-scale, increasingly mediated sports events and their associated symbolic and ceremonial dimensions (Tomlinson 1999). Where I have cited Debord I have done so in order to acknowledge and use what amounts to a theoretical shorthand for talking about the economic dimensions of the spectacle and the overlapping dimensions of the economic and the symbolic in such an event, talking of international football on worldwide television as:

> the construction and presentation of the wholly commodified game in a colorful, ritzy yet standardised society of the mediated spectacle: 'The SPECTACLE is *capital* accumulated to the point where it becomes image'.
>
> (Debord 1995: 24; Sugden and Tomlinson 1998: 77)

So the empirical case can be interpretively captured, theorised, in the pithy Debord quote. But that is only one dimension of the spectacle. It should not be read as a comprehensive theorisation. Real, too, has used the concept in his influential work on mega-sports events, on the mythic dimensions of the American Superbowl (Real 1975). 'Mythic spectacle', he called the Super Bowl, arguing that the event was best explained as a contemporary form of mythic spectacle, but nowhere defining or problematising the notion of spectacle itself. Spectacle he saw as an element among other elements that make up the structural and symbolic basis of the event, and also as the level at which US ideology can be collectively celebrated. In a later overview of popular cultural theorising, 'Cultural theory in popular culture and media spectacles', he reviewed the roots of the popular cultural interdisciplinary field, primarily in the US and English contexts, related this to media events such as the death and burial of Princess Diana, and reviewed three books on sport and the media. Yet the article might really have stressed 'media events', rather than 'media spectacles', in its title. The notion of spectacle remains underdeveloped in Real's discussion, and when mentioned is used as a kind of heavy emphasis:

> The sheer *scale* of popular cultural practice, technological systems, and the global media spectacle is of theoretical significance.
>
> (Real 2001: 172)

> The scale of some popular spectacles does not mean there is one uniform, multinational form of culture taking over the world today.
>
> (*ibid.*: 174)

Real also refers to spectacle as one of the 'dynamics of the popular', which 'create representation and meaning in everyday life' (*ibid.*: 174), along with technology, popular ritual, commerce and hegemony. But when more broadly contextualising the cases of spectacle he refers to the 'media event', and Dayan and Katz's (1992) influential work. His most convincing focused analytical discussion, on Diana's death, he calls 'classical mythical ritual at work' (*ibid.*: 172). The close-up analysis conceptualises ritual, the global context prioritises the media event. Spectacle is left floating, a sort of bold-face version of the global event, but also acknowledged as a dynamic. Real's useful overview would have lost nothing if all cases of use of the word 'spectacle' were simply replaced by the word 'event'.

Spectacle, as a form of descriptive labelling, has also characterised more general historical work. One overview of spectacle in history, stressing the effect of the spectacle on popular collective memory and sweeping across a range of ancient and contemporary cases, recognises sport's contribution to national prestige and propaganda as a significant emergent form of spectacle (Dumur 1965). Much work has identified the nature and continuity of the spectacle in its theatrical mode (Amiel n.d.). Public spectacle could also be used to reaffirm power and position, In pre-industrial settings executions operated as a form of public spectacle. In seventeenth- and early eighteenth-century Amsterdam, authorities encouraged the ceremonial dimensions of the construction of a new gallows: 'Often the citizenry accompanied it with pipes and drums, while musicians played' (Spierenburg 1984: 87). As late as the early nineteenth century children were still taken along to watch executions, to join in such an 'occasion for festivity' (*ibid.*). And spectacle and associated forms of pageantry could be used to mark status, as in the case of the Tudor monarchs of late fifteenth-century and early sixteenth-century England. Henry Tudor has been described as 'a moderately obscure magnate of Welsh descent', whose triumph at the Battle of Bosworth Field in 1485 was scarcely the basis for a succession of relative 'dynastic stability' (Anglo 1997). Within three or four decades, though, the trappings of power included the cultivation of the 'full scale romantic tournament' in its most spectacularly manifest form, and the young Henry VIII developed these on an unprecedented scale with associated 'pageantry and disguisings'. Henry himself competed in these from 1510 to the late 1520s: 'A tremendous figure of a man and a redoubtable athlete, he exulted in his display of his physical prowess to friends, subjects and visitors from abroad' (*ibid*.: 110). Henry had a long run of success in these jousts, tourneyings and foot combats, and there was no shortage of a stream of vanquished opponents that provided the monarch with such opportunties to display his skills and qualities.

Art, too, has historically been used to serve the interests of the dominant classes. Strong (1984: 42) has shown this relationship between art and power in renaissance festivals. To establish a cultural pedigree for the political regime, the renaissance 'was in essence a revival of the antique world ... one of its quests ... the recreation of lost festival forms of classical antiquity'. They soon became expressions of power: 'By the third decade of the seven-teenth century the themes of the Renaissance court fête had moved from a contemplation of cosmic harmony and its reflection in the state to a contem-plation of the monarch as the genesis of that earthly and heavenly harmony' (*ibid*.: 171). In this way festivals and spectacles contributed to 'what was a unique alliance of art and power in the creation of the modern state' (*ibid*.: 173). Spectacle is the expression of power in this case, and more generally it can be argued that in contemporary societies 'spectacle construction' answers the 'search for legitimating symbols' (Edelman 1988: 123).

But despite the interpretive lessons that could be learned from such historical cases, it has been Debord to whom scholars have turned when looking for a theory of the spectacle. This chapter seeks to reassess the nature of Debord's theorisation of spectacle in the light of some examples drawn from my own work on the nature of spectacle in two of the most prominent and recurring sports forms in the modern world – international soccer and the Olympic Games. Such a task can be usefully informed by a consideration of the etymology of the term 'spectacle', which follows on from a commen-tary on a recent spectacle of soccer (drawn from Tomlinson 2000).

Ethnography: at the spectacle

On Saturday, 10 June 2000, I attended the opening ceremony of the Euro 2000 soccer tournament at the King Baudoin Stadium in the Brussels suburb of Heysel in Belgium. The old name of the stadium – the Heysel – carries with it echoes of tragedy, when many fans of the Italian soccer side

Juventus died in a crowd tragedy at its European championship final game with the English club Liverpool. The opening of Euro 2000, jointly hosted by Belgium and the Netherlands, was the ideal opportunity to show how the stadium had been revamped, that it was now a stadium fit for the new century and the demands of the globalised sports/media industry. It was a night when the ghost of the 1984 tragedy could be laid to rest. The opening ceremony ran before the first game between Belgium and Sweden. It was typical of such events (particularly their Gallic versions, which seem always to juxtapose stilts and spherical shapes in unfathomable and inexplicable permutations), combining the presence of a lumbering giant androgynous humanoid with the cavortings of smaller beings, which in this case resembled distorted figures of eight on inelegantly stilted legs, orchestrating ever-changing shapes of smaller acolytes in constantly reassembling formations. As this was a football event, at the centre of the ceremony's narrative was a little boy and his football. This was a 15-minute show, followed by the opening match of the tournament. Europe was to be diverted for several weeks, invited in by a spectacle stressing the themes of universalism, humanity and hope, and achievement for youth.

Away from the stadiums and the football action, a few days later, a transport company was being formed in the city of Rotterdam in Holland, where the final match of Euro 2000 would be played between Italy and France. The company was called Van Der Speck Transportation, perhaps hoping to be taken for a reputable Dutch truck company of almost the same name. Bizarrely, the driver of a freight lorry crossing into England on the evening of 19 June called himself Mr Perry Wacker and paid cash for a one-way ticket. His freight was a consignment of tomatoes, usually transported in a sealed refrigeration unit. The crossing was a five-hour sail from Zeebrugge in Belgium to the port of Dover in England. It was 7.30 p.m., a few games would be warming up in the European Championship. The next evening England would be up against Romania for a place in the last eight. Police and port officials would be concerned with the English hooligan problem, their eyes on potential troublemakers and on the lookout for known offenders and ringleaders. But it wasn't common for truckers to pay cash, and this other company wasn't known to customs officials. And it wasn't tomatoes that greeted the officers when they opened up a sealed unit no bigger than 16.5 metres by 2.5 metres. It was the stench and then the sight of 58 corpses, Chinese illegal immigrants who would have paid fifteen thousand English pounds each, to the notorious Snakehead gangs in China, for a dream passage to the UK. Two males survived from this human cargo of 60. Fifty-four men and four women didn't, fried to death in the switched-off unit, killed by a freak temperature that enveloped Northern Europe at 90 degrees Fahrenheit.

This bogus trucking company, registered in the name of a racketeer in his suburban flat in Rotterdam, got off the ground whilst the eyes of the continent were on the drama of the tournament, the attention of the police forces of the host nations assumed to be directed towards the problem of fan violence in the host cities. Wacker was engaged by a Turkish gang based in Rotterdam, representing the Snakeheads' interests (Kelso 2001). Within days of the opening of this festival of football, the macabre truckload revealed the real business of this new Dutch-registered company – valuable, lucrative, but now rotted human cargo, planned to be smuggled in at a quiet moment when the eyes of the authorities were drawn elsewhere. In a bizarre tragic pragmatism, Dover used its perishable goods site as a temporary mortuary. This inhuman trade was not a coincidence, a bizarre juxtaposition. It was clearly a timed plan, foiled by the unanticipated heatwave and some operational carelessness, to use the spectacle as a smokescreen. It was a tragic reminder that behind every spectacle lies another set of narratives, that the spectacle diverts, and that the meaning of the spectacle cannot be read from just the text of the spectacle itself.

Etymology

In contemporary parlance spectacle is a Janus-faced term. On the one hand, it refers to something spectated, something watched and often gaped at, to the sort of event that draws crowds and that holds the attention of large numbers. We speak of the spectacle of public hangings and executions in pre-modern European societies (indeed, in some contemporary societies where the spectacle is an integral part of the political apparatus of the particular authoritarian regime). In sport, fuelled by the Hollywood extravaganza of the movie *Gladiator*, the term reels us back to the Colosseum of ancient Rome, where the spectacle of the man against man or man against animal combined the extraordinary appetite for the bloodthirsty entertainment with the potent symbolism of the dominant order. Droves of keen undergraduates will write dissertations on the Olympics as spectacle in the wake of the Sydney Games and its no-holds-barred opening and closing ceremonies, and Greek concern about how to match the profile, scale and ambition of the spectacular Sydney shows. There is something grandiose in this conception of the spectacle. It conjures up images of the heroic or the majestic, the powerful. This sense of the term spectacle has a long-standing etymological pedigree in modern European/Western language. One 1340 usage noted 'hoppynge and dancynge of tumblers and herlotis, and other spectakils', and this was the illustrative detail for the OED's definition of spectacle as 'a specially prepared or arranged display of a more or less public nature (especially one on a large scale), forming an impressive or interesting show or entertainment for those viewing it' (OED 1971: 2951). Less neutrally, Strutt's (1841) account of popular sports and pastimes referred to spectacles as 'pompous'.

Peculiarly, we might at first think, when used of individuals the term can have a very different nuance. To make a spectacle of oneself is usually to appear the fool. There is a direct referential lineage here in the figure of the court jester. The job of this figure was to play the fool and so entertain the privileged, not always a straightforward task. If you got the tone wrong the fool could quickly become the scapegoat. If you commit an indiscretion today in public, or behave obviously out of order or line, then we speak of the individual 'making a spectacle of him or herself'. This second main sense of the term also has a distinctive etymological history, though of more recent pedigree. The OED's second definition locates the spectacle as 'a person or thing exhibited to, or set before, the public gaze as an object either (a) of curiosity or contempt, or (b) of marvel or admiration' (OED 1971: 2951). There are, then, values – that is, an everyday hermeneutic – associated with the term itself, and these need to be borne constantly in mind when considering the ways in which spectacle has been theorised.

Public cultural events are of course conducive to interpretive analysis using other terms and concepts. Ritual has its place in ceremonies around sport and religion and politics. But the ritual is usually an aspect of the bigger entity. Social anthropologists such as MacAloon have subjected festival to interesting levels of analysis (MacAloon 1984), and adaptations of his framework have been made, for instance, to the Sydney Olympic Games (Cohen 2000). Social historians have shown how apparently oppositional practices such as satirical rough music or *charivari* might simultaneously mock and assert 'the legitimacy of authority' (Thompson 1993: 478). And of course the brilliant work of Bakhtin on carnival and the carnivalesque has (whatever the complexity of the transfer of ideas from the Leninist USSR of the 1920s to just about any chosen cultural or historical context) given countless scholars the opportunity to theorise their chosen cultural form as subversive or at the very least symbolically oppositional (Bakhtin 1969). Gilmore (1998) reviews four theoretical approaches to carnival: safety-valve structural functionalist approaches; 'dynamic equilibrium' approaches stressing ritual as rebellion; Marxist approaches identifying cultures of resistance in the carnival; and interpretive-symbolic approaches (where Bakhtin and his sense of carnival as aggressive mockery is located).

MacAloon (1984) has identified four elements of the contemporary spectacle in what he claimed as the first attempt to classify distinctive features of the spectacle. First, it must be visual, comprising sensory symbolic codes. Second, it must be large-scale, characterised by size and grandeur. Third, the spectacle institutionalises the bicameral roles of actors/audience, performers/spectators. And, fourth, the spectacle is a dynamic form – movement, action and change are central to it, and such a dynamic excites spectators. But despite sophisticated classifications such as MacAloon's, the term spectacle continues to have a distinct nuance and character in contemporary cultural commentary, calling attention to the constructedness of the event and the framing of it for the mass audience. This sense of the term has quite a determinist ring and, in an increasingly mediated age of global consumerism, it has become a shorthand for ways of talking about the constructedness of the popular cultural, and, in the case of sport, the transformation of sport from a more engaged form of practice to a modern global commodity. This kind of shorthand has been helped along by the work of Debord, whose work is woefully indifferent to and even distorting of the nature of spectacle and its effects. To make that argument of course, the work of Debord must be fairly represented. In the following section I provide an exegetical account of *The Society of the Spectacle*, and in the section after that I outline my major critical reservations about his work, informed by appropriate empirical cases of the sports spectacle.

Exegesis: Debord's *The Society of the Spectacle*

(In this section, references to the Debord text are to the abbreviation of the title, *TSS*, and to both the page number of the edition cited, and the number of the thesis from which the reference is taken, as in, for example, p. 29, th. 42)

TSS comprises nine sections. The first, 'Separation Perfected', lays out the philosophical pedigree of Debord. Citing Feuerbach, he sets up a denunciation of the 'preference of the sign to the thing signified' (p. 11). In the second section, 'The Commodity as Spectacle', prefaced by a quotation from Lukács on the commodity 'in its undistorted essence when it becomes the universal category of society as a whole' (p. 25), Debord calls the commodity his 'old enemy ... in reality a very queer thing, abounding in metaphysical subtleties' (p. 26, th. 35). It is the commodity that becomes the spectacle. This is perhaps the key passage in the book:

> THE SPECTACLE CORRESPONDS to the historical moment at which the commodity completes its colonisation of social life. It is not just that the relationship to commodities is now plain to see – commodities are now *all* that there is to see; the world we see is the world of the commodity.
>
> (p. 29, th. 42)

The third section deals with 'Unity and Division Within Appearances', prefaced by a statement on the materialist dialectic from Peking's 1964 Red Flag. There are some provocative comments here on media stars, branded as 'spectacular representations of living human beings, distilling the essence of the spectacle's banality into images of possible roles' (p. 38, th. 60). Modern consumerism is said to generate pseudo-needs, life becoming dictated by a limited artificiality (pp. 44/5, th. 68). The concentrated form of the spectacle is introduced, embodied in bureaucratic capitalism (p. 41, th. 64). The diffuse form 'is associated with the abundance of commodities, with the undisturbed development of modern capitalism', in which any single form of the commodity 'is justified by an appeal to the grandeur of commodity production in general' (p. 42, th. 65).

Having established the fragmented nature of the capitalist social order, yet its overall coherence as a system of power based on the forms of the spectacle, Debord then identifies, in Section 4, the only agent of hope and change, the proletariat. This section, 'The Proletariat as Subject and Representation', is prefaced by a quote from the parliamentary enquiry into the 18 March uprising in 1968 France. Here, Debord recognises the power of Marx's supersession of the Hegelian agenda. This, at over forty pages and comprising over fifty theses, is by far the longest section of the book. It scarcely touches on the theme of the spectacle, or the commodity, and argues trenchantly for the recognition of the masses, inheriting the mantle of the revolutionary proletariat as the sole force of revolutionary change. The section is an account of Leninist and Trotskyist positions, and moves towards a description of the alienation of the workers. The section concludes with the assertion that class society has evolved into 'the spectacular organization of non-life' (p. 89, th. 123), and that (p. 90, th. 124) 'Revolutionary theory is now the sworn enemy of all revolutionary ideology – *and it knows it*'. Section 5's prefacing quote comes from Shakespeare's Henry IV Part 1 – 'O, gentlemen, the time of life is short! ... And if we live, we live to tread on kings', and here Debord speculates on the relationship between time and history – 'the temporalization of man ... is equivalent to a humanization of time' (p. 92, th. 125). There are effective aphorisms here on the basis of power enjoyed by the dominant group in a cyclical-based, pre-class-based society: 'The owners of this historical surplus value were the masters of the knowledge and enjoyment of directly experienced events ... This was the time of adventure, of war, the time in which the lords of cyclical society pursued their personal histories' (p. 94, th. 128). What then happens to time in the capitalist society? Capitalism unifies 'irreversible time *on a world scale*' (p. 107, th. 145). This unified irreversible time 'belongs to the world market – and, by extension, to the world spectacle' (p. 107, th. 145). With time established as a critical element in the spectacle, in the sixth section the theme of 'Spectacular Time' is developed. Time is led by production, it becomes commodity, it is no more than its function as exchangeability. Quoting Marx from *The Poverty of Philosophy*, time is seen as all-pervading, 'man is nothing: he is at the most time's carcass' (p. 110, th. 147). Consumable time, a category for Debord of general time, presents itself as pseudo-cyclical time, time transformed by industry, founded on commodity production. Here, Debord offers his most explicit statement on leisure:

> In its most advanced sectors, a highly concentrated capitalism has begun selling 'fully equipped' blocks of time, each of which is a complete commodity combining a variety of other commodities. This is the logic behind the appearance, within an expanding economy of 'services' and leisure activities, of the 'all-inclusive' purchase of spectacular forms of housing, of collective pseudo-travel, of participation in cultural consumption and even of sociability itself, in the form of 'exciting conversations', 'meetings with celebrities and suchlike'. Spectacular

commodities of this type could obviously not exist were it not for the increasing impoverishment of the realities they parody.

(p. 111–12, th. 152)

Time loses its natural basis, its integral human function, linked to social alienation and spatial alienation – 'a *living* alienation within time' (p. 116, th. 162). Section 7 detours into 'Environmental Planning', helped along by a quote from Machiavelli on the invading Prince's need to destroy the city. Section 8 considers 'Negation and Consumption in the Cultural Sphere', emphasising how spectacular thought is established as a general science of false consciousness (p. 138, th. 194). In his critique of Daniel Boorstin's work on the image and the way in which the image-based society creates pseudo-events he writes: 'Boorstin cannot see that the proliferation of prefabricated "pseudo-events" – which he deplores – flows from the simple fact that, in face of the massive realities of present-day social existence, individuals do not actually experience events' (p. 141, th. 199).

The final section is concerned with 'Ideology in Material Form', and identifies a schizophrenic condition at the heart of the society of the spectacle: 'The spectacle erases the dividing line between self and the world', and the individual is 'driven into a form of madness', having been 'condemned to the passive acceptance of an alien everyday reality' (p. 152, th. 219).

In his *Comments on the Society of the Spectacle* (*CSS*), Debord reiterates the main themes of his critique of the contemporary global capitalist order. Uncompromisingly, he reasserts the hold of the spectacle on contemporary consciousness: 'In all that has happened in the last twenty years, the most important change lies in the very continuity of the spectacle ... quite simply ... the spectacle's domination has succeeded in raising a whole generation moulded to its laws' (*CSS*: 7). His new theoretical emphasis is to identify a third form of spectacular power, beyond the concentrated and the diffuse: this is the extension of the more strongly established form, the diffuse, into the form of the '*integrated spectacle*, which has since tended to impose itself globally' (*ibid.*: 8). In such commentaries Debord reiterates all the elements of his earlier analysis. Domination is intact, still more entrenched. Intervention and challenge will need to be still more dramatic: 'innovation will surely not be displayed on the spectacle's stage. It appears instead like lightning, which we know only when it strikes' (*ibid.*: 88).

Towards a more comprehensive theorisation of the spectacle

TSS is an intriguing, infuriating and challenging text, and must be taken seriously for a number of reasons. Most of all, it recognises the emerging and suffocating power of the commodity form. It places cultural analysis and a kind of social psychology of the individual at the centre of political economy. It represents a metatheoretical tradition, in the spirit of Hegel, and demonstrates its persisting resonance for the cultural critic of advanced capitalism and its culture. I am not arguing that there is nothing at all there in the Debord text, rather that it is led by a closed theoretical agenda and a political project, that of the Situationist International and its place in post-Second World War French politics (see Best and Kellner 1997: ch. 3). It was a revisionist Marxist project, mediated by some of the work of Lukács on the early Marx, in which a form of philosophical universalism was linked to Marx's concern with the commodity and the analysis of capital (Lukács 1971). The spectacle symbolises – indeed embodies – the narcotisation of the whole society; as Best puts it: 'The spectacular society spreads its narcotics mainly through the cultural mechanisms of leisure and consumption, services and entertainment' (Best 1994: 47). Best and Kellner can therefore situate the Situationist as a direct predecessor of Baudrillard, as a pessimistic analyst of contemporary consumer culture.

But there are huge problems with Debord's account, which should not go unnoticed in a necessary kind of history of contemporary ideas. Here I emphasise four. First, in *TSS* Debord at best trivialises human agency, at worst denies it. There is no sense of the specific cultures that might characterise spectacular forms or practices. In Sydney the 47,000 or so volunteers of all ages and backgrounds who serviced the Olympic Games had a significant role in the staging of those Games. They might not see themselves as tools of global consumer capitalism, and there is without doubt an overarching ideological celebration of their role, but they were knowing participants aware of their contribution to a collective project. As I queued for tickets for Olympic events in Newcastle, New South Wales, several weeks before the Sydney Olympics, I asked people why they wanted to go to some events. People said that they were unfussed about what event they could acquire tickets for. Rather, they just wanted to be able to say that they'd been there for Australia's proud moment in the gaze of the world; they wanted their grandchild to be able to remember and relate that they had been taken to such an event. The identity-forming inoffensive patriotism of such human choices should not be dismissed as the inconsequential delusions of the dupe.

Second, as an interpretive framework *TSS* is staggeringly arrogant in any historical terms. The ways in which the spectacle is staged, constructed and changes under the influence of economic, political and cultural forces, cannot be accommodated in Debord's account. Pivotal moments in the history of the sports spectacle, such as the 1936 Berlin Olympics and the 1984 Los Angeles Olympics, show how the spectacle is staged on the basis of particular political and economic imperatives. Berlin, of course, elevated the sports event to the status of powerful nationalist symbolism and ideology, linked to the Nazi propaganda machine and enshrined in Riefenstahl's film of those Olympics. The Hollywood Olympics of 1984 celebrated a new market-model for the staging of the Games in the height of the Cold War. Identifying different interests in the staging of the spectacle is necessary if the changing balances and alliances of power that have framed the sports spectacle are to be understood.

Third, as a cultural critique *TSS* is sociologically incomplete. It conflates the spectacle into the central dynamic of capitalist social relations, eliding it with the commodity form. In Sydney, the spectators in the city's live-sites – at Darling Harbour, Martin Place in the CBD, watching Australian swimming victories – were heterogeneous in the extreme, but consistently united in support of the Australian presence. This had nothing to do with the commodity form. These were not passive consumers as they articulated an assertive Australian national pride. As a cultural phenomenon, the sport spectacle operates on a variety of levels of production of meaning.

And, finally, as a consequence especially of these first and third problems, *TSS* puts forward a culturally pessimistic worldview with the only antidote being a specific form of revolutionary practice. It fails to recognise any affirmative dimension of pleasure or fun in consumer culture. Spectacles of sport spawn a range of subcultural practices, and these can be positive forms of sociability and collective affirmation. As we have seen, Debord wholly ignores such possibilities. His analysis is an either/or model of history and culture. Jappe (1999: 159) rightly locates Debord alongside the young Marx, both desperate and romantic humanists of sorts, in providing 'a new foundation for the contention ... that political economy is "the denial of man accomplished"'. In this analysis you are either dominated or liberated. Human agency is robbed of the range of its potential expression in any such model. There is, in Debord's thinking, an implicit resistance to the all-pervasive nature of domination, and his political project has been cast as a call 'for a critique of daily life and a new idea of happiness that entailed profound personal change' (Bracken 1997: 88). But there is little sense in Debord of any cultural sensitivity to the possibility of any such changes, to their expression in the range of responses generated by human subjects in their experiences of the spectacle.

If we are to develop an adequate theorisation of the spectacle of sport in an interconnected and highly mediated globalised world, the revolutionary fervour and intellectual inflexibility of a committed situationist of the late 1960s is no substitute for carefully researched cases of spectacular events, analysed in adequate detail in historical, cultural, political and sociological terms. This is not a call to any kind of analytical relativism, or a slippage into atheoretical empiricism. But Debord's work, whatever its impact as critical social theory, simply does not stand up as sociological theory. Despite the longevity of its influence, it remains testimony to the revolutionary practice, rather than any cultural and analytical perspicacity, of its author; and perhaps the poverty of thought of those of us who have sought to interrogate the polysemy of the contemporary spectacle.

It might be asked that if *TSS* is so flawed, then why give it any attention at all, why construct this straw man or easy target? But the book's elusive style and at times dazzling rhetoric have meant that it has been open to a kind of drop-in use, and so in a number of cases in performance studies (Richards 2000), and in sociological work on contemporary sports (Bélanger 2000; Gruneau 1997), Debord continues to be cited as a theoretical justification and rationale for studying the spectacle. Bélanger describes the 'integration of a new entertainment economy with a new urban economy' as 'the spectacularization of space' (Bélanger 2000: 378), cites Harvey's work in support of the general theoretical point and notes too that 'Harvey's argument ... draws heavily on the work of the French situationist Guy Debord' (*ibid.*: 381). Here again Debord's presentation of spectacle as the intensified passivity of human agency then overdetermines the overall analysis. In such cases the analysis would lose nothing at all if Debord was not cited and if the multi-faceted dimensions of the spectacle were allowed to speak for themselves.

Kellner has drawn upon Debord in an analysis of Michael Jordan and his sponsor Nike. He sees spectacle, along with images and commodities, as key aspects of a media and consumer society:

> Spectacles are those phenomena of media culture that embody contemporary society's basic values, serve to enculturate individuals into its way of life, and dramatise its conflicts and modes of conflict resolution. They include media extravaganzas, sports events, political happenings ... sports is a largely untheorised and underrated aspect of the society of the spectacle that celebrates its dominant values, products, and corporations in an unholy alliance between sports celebrity, commercialism, and media spectacle.
>
> (Kellner 2001: 38–9)

Undeniably, the spectacularisation of sport, led by the media, promotes 'values, products, celebrities and institutions of the media and consumer society' (Kellner 2001: 38). But the spectacle is not solely the prop of global consumerism. Kellner's eloquent and sophisticated analysis confirms one dimension of the spectacle, its symbolisation of the commodity form. But there are other dimensions, as my critique of Debord has highlighted. Spectacles serve the state as well as the global market, for instance (McGillivray 2000; Tomlinson 1996). The production of a fuller critique of *TSS* remains necessary ground-clearing work for those of us interested in the questions of who produces the sport spectacle, how and why the spectacle is staged and performed, and what the spectacle both means and masks.

Acknowledgements

I am grateful to all who attended the panel on sport and spectacle at the annual conference of the North American Society for the Sociology of Sport, in Colorado Springs, USA in November 2000, where an earlier version of this chapter was presented and circulated. I would also like to thank Ben

Carrington and Richard Gruneau, who directed me towards useful and important sources where Debord's work, and especially his Situationist agenda, are discussed.

Thanks, too, to my co-editor of this volume, John Sugden, for his editorial promptings and continued professional and intellectual support, and to Anna Kiernan for her incisive copy-editing response.

References

Amiel, D. (ed.) (n.d.) *Les spectacles à travers les ages – théatre, cirque, music-hall, cafés-concerts, cabarets, artistiques*, Paris: Aux Éditions du Cygne.

Anglo, S. (1997) *Spectacle, Pageantry and Early Tudor Policy* (2nd edn), Oxford: Clarendon Press.

Bakhtin, M.M. (1969) *Rabelais and his World*, Cambridge MA: MIT Press.

Bélanger, A. (2000) 'Sport venues and the spectacularization of urban spaces in North America: the case of the Molson Centre in Montreal', *International Review for the Sociology of Sport* 35(3): 378–97.

Best, S. (1994) 'The commodification of reality and the reality of commodification: Baudrillard, Debord, and postmodern theory', in D. Kellner (ed.) *Baudrillard: A Critical Reader*, Oxford: Basil Blackwell.

Best, S. and Kellner, D. (1997) *The Postmodern Turn*, New York: Guilford Press.

Bracken, L. (1997) *Guy Debord: Revolutionary*, Venice, California: Feral House.

Cohen, M. (2000) 'Performing the nation [-state]: Spectacular identity in Olympic arts', paper delivered at annual conference of Australasian Drama Studies Association, on *Performance and spectacle*, Newcastle, New South Wales, 4 July 2000.

Dayan, D. and Katz, E. (1992) *Media Events: The Live Broadcasting of History*, Cambridge MA: Harvard University Press.

Debord, G. (1995) *The Society of the Spectacle* (trans. Donald Nicholson-Smith), New York: Zone Books.

—— (1998) *Comments on* The Society of the Spectacle (trans. Malcolm Imrie), London: Verso.

Dobie, I. (1978) *The Role of Wrestling as a Public Spectacle: Audience Attitudes to Wrestling as Portrayed on Television*, London: IBA Audience Research Department.

Dumur, G. (ed.) (1965) 'Histoire des spectacles', in *Encyclopédie de la Pléiade*, Paris: Éditions Gallimard.

Edelman, M. (1988) *Constructing the Political Spectacle*, Chicago: University of Chicago Press.

Gilmore, D. (1998) *Carnival and Culture: Sex, Symbol and Status in Spain*, London: Yale University Press.

Gruneau, R. (1997) 'Canadian sport in the society of the spectacle', paper presented at 'How can sport change the world?', annual conference of Japan Society of Sport Sociology, Kyoto, Ritsumeikan University, Japan, 27–8 March.

Harvey, D. (1989) *The Condition of Postmodernity: An enquiry into the Origins of Cultural Change*, Oxford: Basil Blackwell.

Hussey, A. (2001a) *The Game of War: The Life and Death of Guy Debord*, London: Cape.

—— (2001b) 'Situation abnormal', *The Guardian (Saturday Review)*, July 28: 3.

Jappe, A. (1999) *Guy Debord* (trans. Donald Nicholson-Smith, Foreword by T.J. Clark, new Afterword by author), Berkeley: University of California Press.

Kellner, D. (2001) 'The sports spectacle, Michael Jordan, and Nike: unholy alliance?', in D.L. Andrews (ed.) *michael jordan, inc.: Corporate Sport, Media Culture, and Late Modern America*, Albany: State University of New York Press.

Kelso, P. (2001) 'Trucker "shut air vent and let 58 migrants die" ', *Guardian*, 1 March: 7.

Lukács, G. (1971) *History and Class Consciousness: Studies in Marxist Dialectics* (trans. Rodney Livingstone), Cambridge MA: MIT Press.

MacAloon, J.J. (1984) 'Olympic Games and the theory of spectacle in modern societies', in J.J. MacAloon (ed.) *Rite, Drama, Festival and Spectacle: Rehearsal Towards a Theory of Cultural Performance*, Philadelphia: Institute for Study of Human Issues.

McGillivray, G. (2000) ' "Do not forget that you are mortal!": The suppression of theatricality in the staging of stage spectacles', paper delivered at annual conference of Australasian Drama Studies Association on 'Performance and Spectacle', Newcastle, New South Wales, 6 July 2000.

Merback, M.B. (1999) *The Thief, the Cross and the Wheel: Pain and the Spectacle of Punishment in Mediaeval and Renaissance Europe*, London: Reaktion Books.

Montgomery, M.E. (1998) *Displaying Women: Spectacles of Leisure in Edith Wharton's New York*, New York: Routledge.

Oxford English Dictionary (OED) (1971) *The Compact Edition of the Oxford English Dictionary* (Complete text produced micrographically, Vol. II, P–Z), Oxford: Oxford University Press.

Real, M. (1975) 'Super Bowl: mythic spectacle', *Journal of Communication* 25(1): 31–43.

—— (2001) 'Cultural theory in popular culture and media spectacles', in J. Lull (ed.) *Culture in the Communication Age*, London: Routledge.

Richards, A. (2000) 'Pseudo-events and pseudo-elites: Olympics, audiences and spectacle', paper delivered at annual conference of Australasian Drama Studies Association on 'Performance and Spectacle', Newcastle, New South Wales, 4 July 2000.

Spierenburg, P. (1984) *The Spectacle of Suffering: Execution and the Evolution of Repression: From a Pre-industrial Metropolis to the European Experience*, Cambridge: Cambridge University Press.

Strong, R. (1984) *Art and Power: Renaissance Festivals 1450–1650*, Suffolk: Boydell Press.

Strutt, J. (1841) *The Sports and Pastimes of the People of England, Including the Rural and Domestic Recreations, May Games, Mummeries, Shows, Processions, Pageants and Pompous Spectacles from the Earliest Period to the Present Time*, London: Thomas Tegg.

Sugden, J. and Tomlinson, A. (1998) *FIFA and the Contest for World Football: Who Rules the Peoples' Game?*, Cambridge: Polity Press.

Thompson, E.P. (1993) *Customs in Common*, Harmondsworth: Penguin.

Tomlinson, A. (1996) 'Olympic spectacles: opening ceremonies and some paradoxes of globalization', *Media, Culture and Society* 18(4): 583–602.

—— (1999) *The Game's Up: Essays in the Cultural Analysis of Sport, Leisure and Popular Culture*, Aldershot, UK: Ashgate.

—— (2000a) 'Carrying the torch for whom? Symbolic power and Olympic ceremony', in K. Schaffer and S. Smith (eds) *The Olympics at the Millennium: Power, Politics and the Games*, New Jersey: Rutgers University Press.

—— (2000b) 'Bigger, glitzier, better? Comments on Olympic spectacle and ceremony', paper/article based upon plenary address delivered at annual conference of Australasian Drama Studies Association on 'Performance and Spectacle', Newcastle, New South Wales, 4 July 2000.

4 Network football[1]

John Sugden

Sport spaces have become increasingly lucrative commodities in a time of the expansion of global spaces. The media and local and global governing bodies have driven such trends, with, in many cases, severely dislocating effects on the cultural product in question. This has not been a seamless and uncontested process, but one of struggle among those who seek to overwhelm sport for largely corporate and/or personal gain and between them and those others who want to protect sport as a popular domain of civil society. For the most part, for the final quarter of the twentieth century and the early years of the twenty-first, it is the latter who have lost out, and nowhere has this been more pronounced than in the world of association football. Based around ongoing archive research and investigative fieldwork carried out in and around world football's corridors of power, this chapter offers an account and interpretative theorisation and framework for understanding some of the key features of these power struggles.

Using the concept of sportisation, Maguire (1999: 79–89) views the development of modern sport in general in terms of Robertson's five-stage model of modern world history (Robertson 1990). In their books, on the growth, development and politicisation of the world governing body of football FIFA (La Fédération Internationale de Football Associations), Sugden and Tomlinson (1998, 1999) likewise argue that this organisation's development, since its inception in 1904, can be usefully understood, at least at the level of historical periodisation, in the context of Robertson's third, fourth and fifth stages. The global history and development of a significant cultural product like football provides the opportunity for applying and evaluating stage theories such as Robertson's. The following are brief summaries of Robertson's five phases and illustrations of how they can be applied to football in general and to FIFA in particular.

The first dimension of Robertson's typology of globalisation, the Germinal Phase pre-dates the establishment and codification of association football in Britain, and will not be considered here. The second, Incipient Phase, pre-dates the internationalisation of the sport and will be largely ignored. However, it is worth noting the significance of the fact that what was to become the world's most popular and most commercially attractive sport was conceived and nurtured in Britain, the most advanced crucible of commercial and industrial capitalism. Modern football was a concomitant of a new industrial culture based upon radical reconceptualisations of time, space and labour, generating new and rapidly expanding urban centres of fluid populations, often devoid of any anchorage in traditional sources of cultural identity. From its earliest days football helped to fill this void by becoming a focal point for collective identity and local pride. In this regard, its followers have always regarded football as 'their' game.

The third phase – Take Off Phase – which lasts from the 1870s until the mid-1920s sees a dramatic increase in international contact and communication between nations. The medium for this internationalisation combines elements of political economy with significant cultural transfers. The most powerful engine driving this phase was imperialism whereby, in competition with each other, first the major European powers, and later the United States, the former Soviet Union, Japan and China, sought to extend political authority, economic domination and cultural influence. It is during this industrial–colonial period that football becomes professional in Europe and is established as a commercial entity. It is also when international competition develops, and FIFA is set up by Britain's colonial rivals, in some ways, acting as a counter-weight to Britain's global domination in the sport on and off the field.

The Struggle for Hegemony Phase, which lasts from the mid-1920s to the late 1960s, witnesses the continuing struggle for political, economic and military supremacy between nations and blocks of nations. It also sees the gradual dismemberment of Western European empires, the emergence of super powers and their confrontation in the cold war and the introduction of less obvious but equally binding chains of dependency between first, second and newly independent third world nations. It is during this period that FIFA comes of age, expanding dramatically as newly independent countries seek to reaffirm their national status through membership of global sporting bodies like the IOC and FIFA. European hegemony over world football begins to be challenged by representatives of the 'second' world (South America) backed by the growing political power of the 'third' world (Africa and Asia). It is also during this epoch that television develops as a global medium and football begins to be shaped as an armchair spectacle.

Robertson characterises the final quarter of the twentieth century as a Phase of Uncertainty as long-established lines of co-operation, rivalry and ways of doing business begin to break down. This period sees the West, championed by the United States, victorious in the cold war, culminating in the collapse of the Soviet Union and the disintegration of the Soviet Bloc. Old alliances and antagonisms are replaced by new social movements, redefined nationalism and nationalistic missions and less boundaried forms of collective identity, most notably, Islam. In this phase the sovereignty of the nation-state and, with it, the state's capacity to control events both within and without its borders is increasingly challenged, changed and transformed

(MacClean 1999: 187). There is the highly accelerated development of communications technologies and capacities and a marked expansion in the 'off-shore' sector of international business. It is during this phase that world football expands into new constituencies, most notably in the Far East and the United States (Sugden and Tomlinson 1998: chs 7 and 9). The mediation and commercialisation of the game accelerates dramatically and FIFA's operations are increasingly targeted, co-opted by and integrated with transnational business interests.

These summaries of Robertson's model and Maguire's adaptations contain more references to political economy than either might like. For them, globalisation is a multi-layered, multi-textured affair that includes the economic sphere, but certainly not as a determining dynamic. That globalisation is multidimensional is not in dispute, but, as Castells (1996, 1997) argues persuasively, the current phase of global development is not as uncertain as Robertson's model suggests, or as Maguire (1999: 78) argues in his own elaboration of it. Rather, we live in an age when the power and influence of the nation-state is being overridden by a network of international financial interests enmeshed through global communication networks. As Sklair (1991) recognises, the most important aspect in understanding the nature, scale and scope of change in world society is the position of the global capitalist class who continue to have the power to dictate economic, political and cultural-ideological transnational practices. Unlike in earlier phases of capitalist development, when the capitalist class was more anchored in the nation-state and labour intensive industrial production, their diffuse nature in this period of high-tech globalisation makes them more difficult to identify, pin down, and oppose.

Globalisation is bound together by what Castells refers to as 'the network society', which is yet another metamorphosis in the life of capitalism:

> The network society, in its various institutional expressions, is, for the time being, a capitalist society. Furthermore, for the first time in history, the capitalist mode of production shapes social relationships over the entire planet. But this brand of capitalism is profoundly different from its historical predecessors. It has two fundamental distinctive features. It is global and is structured to a large extent around a network of financial flows.
>
> (Castells 1996: 47)

Castells goes on to argue that capital is invested, globally, in all sectors of commercial activity. He provides a long and diverse list of examples of the kind of markets of production and consumption penetrated by network capitalism. Sport features prominently in this list (*ibid.*: 472). Empirical evidence gathered in and around FIFA's corridors of power supports Castells's thesis and strongly suggests that, in its current phase of development, big business networks are the overriding influence in the global development and political control of world football. Shifting alliances of marketing companies, media alliances, multinational corporations and opportunist technocrats have gained access to and, for all intents and purposes, control of the commanding heights of world football. Despite rhetorical proclamations that would have us believe otherwise, this they have done for the purposes of accumulating profit and prestige and not, to use FIFA's own motto, 'For the Good of the Game'. In short, the peoples' game (i.e. the game of the peoples of the world) is in the process of being transformed into Network Football.

What are the main constituencies of Network Football and how does Network Football work? One dimension (see Figure 4.1) contains the multi-national and transnational companies, which have come to view sport in general, and football in particular, as an ideal vehicle for introducing and sustaining their products and services in a global market place. In return for a massive financial investment, blue chip (highly successful and high status) sporting goods companies, drinks manufacturers, automotive industries, high-tech suppliers, fast food chains, credit cards and the like, have, in the language of FIFA-technocrats, become FIFA's 'partners'. These partnerships are mutually dependent relationships whereby the market reach of the brand has been extended through the expansion of brand FIFA.

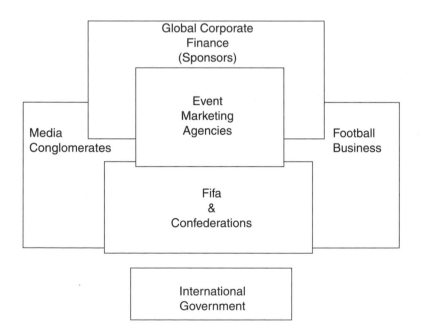

Figure 4.1   Network football

To illustrate this it is worth dwelling briefly on the Under 17 World and World Youth (under 20) Championships. Advised by Adidas boss and the founder of ISL (International Sport and Leisure) Horst Dassler, and aided and abetted by his general secretary and protégé, Sepp Blatter, when he came to power in 1974, Joao Havelange, FIFA's president until 1998, initiated these tournaments and was able to strengthen his organisation's otherwise slender financial base through allowing the US soft drinks company Coca-Cola to have its name associated with them. In return FIFA saw to it that these competitions regularly took place in regions of the world where Coca-Cola's profile and market penetration was less than complete, such as the Soviet Union, China, Japan, the Middle East and Africa. Nobody understands or explains this process better than Havelange himself:

> At that time, twenty or so years ago, Coca-Cola didn't exist in China or the Soviet Union or in the Arab countries. It was largely thanks to the FIFA Coca-Cola Cup and the obligation of host countries to accept Coca-Cola into their territories that Coca-Cola got their foot in the door.
> (Sugden and Tomlinson 1998: 237)

Horst Dassler was the key animator who accelerated the corporate take over of world sport. Likewise, Sepp Blatter, the man Dassler handpicked and parachuted into FIFA House to work alongside Havelange, understood this relationship and the key role played by the founder of Adidas:

> He (Dassler) was an extraordinary man, a man of courage, of initiative, a visionary. He went at the age of 20, in '56, with a small suitcase, the first to try to make well-known athletes identify with the brand name Adidas ... He was the father of sport sponsoring ... It is he who said that one must associate the product, develop the product, with the sport, and equally to increase the sales of sports equipment.
> (Sugden and Tomlinson 1999: 66)

Dassler died in 1987 but his legacy is indelible. Whether it is through shirts, bill-boards, blimps, or superimposition on the field itself, it is no longer possible to watch a major football competition without the eye being distracted by the brand imagery of some of the world's biggest corporations. While there is some merit in the argument that football needs such sponsorship in order to survive and thrive, the scale of corporate intervention, what impact this has on the control and administration of the game, and, what happens to the money are issues that require some investigation. What is certain is that FIFA itself gets a significant share of the spoils. It was through making corporate deals that Havelange, aided and abetted by Blatter, during his 24-year reign, was able to fill, using his own words 'substantially FIFA's cash box with four billion (US$)' (*ibid.*).

Mutually dependent relatives of these blue chip sponsors are the international media industries, responsible for projecting brand football throughout the world. Time Warner, Disney, Bertelsman, Viacom, News Corporation, Universal, NBC and TCI are the major transnational media conglomerates within the embrace of which a complex webbing of merged and partnered cartels monopolise the global mediation of cultural production, including sport (Held *et al.* 1999: 356–60). These media industries likewise are characterised by FIFA as its 'partners' and among them television is king. According to Pierre Bourdieu, 'sport visible as spectacle hides the reality of a system of actors competing over commercial stakes' (1999: 17). In this regard he refers to television as 'the veritable Trojan horse for the entry of commercial logic into sport' (*ibid.*: 16). Football, argues Bourdieu, is a very popular game, the playing and watching of which requires relatively little 'interpretative capital' (*ibid.*). Unlike, for instance, opera, ballet or other elements of high culture that may require the gaze of the connoisseur to be appreciated, viewers do not have to know too much to be able to watch, understand and enjoy a game of football – particularly the way the game is packaged and presented today. As such, more than any other global sport, the game has been appropriated by the media as spectacle and targeted by commerce for selling and marketing.

Bourdieu's observations were made on the basis of his experience of the World Cup Finals in France 1998 for which the presence and impact of the media industries could be witness on a previously unimaginable scale. In France 98, over 33 days, 32 teams played between them 64 games for which more than 12,000 members of the media were issued with accreditation passes. This number included 3,000 print media journalists, 850 photographers and 8,500 rights holding and host broadcasting television and radio reporters and technicians. This was not a press core, this was a media army, the big battalions of which were provided by the television industry. It is estimated that an unprecedented 5,760 hours of television broadcasting was consumed by the largest ever global audience – a cumulative figure in excess of 37.5 billion viewers (this figure is hotly disputed by the IOC which likes to claim that the Olympic Games is the biggest media showcase). The numbers of column inches in newspapers, magazines and books devoted to France 98 was immeasurable, but is also likely to have set new records.

The International Media Centre (CIM) was massive. It covered 33,000 square metres, which approximates to the size of 33 Wembley-size football pitches. It consisted of three areas. Firstly, the Main Press Centre which was dominated by a huge editing room with hundreds of desk-top computers, an internet suite and a giant television screen on which all of the games and events associated with the World Cup were broadcast live. It also had facilities for photocopying, faxing and film development, as well as an area for video viewing and editing. Away from the editing room were the suites of offices occupied by the major press agencies and some of the bigger newspapers, from where the action was reported. The race into print meant that for some attendance at the match was an expendable luxury. Secondly, there was the even bigger international Radio and Television Centre (CIRTV) which handled the editing and relaying of all of the broadcasts from the eight venues. An accreditation centre administered the final processing of accreditation and the dispensing of media passes. For five weeks, the CIM was the nerve centre of France 98, and some journalists covered the World Cup from France without ever leaving the media centre, apart from crossing the street to a hotel to sleep.

The awesome scale of the mediation required for the World Cup has huge implications for those who host the Finals. The size, cost and technological sophistication of the media infrastructure demanded by such a tournament means that it is highly improbable that any other than a handful of rich, first world countries, or conglomerates thereof, will be allowed to host future competitions. Months before France 98, Issa Hayatou, the President of the African Confederation had talked candidly about the obstacles facing Africa in its attempt to persuade FIFA to hold the World Cup Finals on that continent (Sugden and Tomlinson 1998). It was not, he believed, that an African country was incapable of hosting a football tournament. The successful hosting by impoverished Burkina Faso of a 24-team African Cup of Nations in 1998 demonstrates this. South Africa had also successfully staged the 1996 African tournament, using established rugby grounds as well as some specialist soccer stadiums. However, the scale of the mediation of the World Cup Finals, coupled with the high demands of FIFA's marketing partners with their sights fixed firmly on consumer demand and television audiences, meant that no country in Africa could promise an infrastructure to match those of USA 94, France 98, and Japan/Korea 2002. So long as the communications infrastructure and not the games themselves is prioritised, then the third world will never host football's most prestigious tournament. The decision made by FIFA in 2000 to award the 2006 World Cup Finals to Germany at the expense of South Africa would seem to bear this out.

A critical component of the Network comprises the brokers, the key animators, who package and tie up the deals between sponsors, the football business, the media and FIFA. These are the multi-media Event Marketing agencies such as ISL (International Sport and Leisure), TEAM (Television Event and Media Marketing) and IMG (International Management Group). The Event Marketing agencies are the cement of network football: the go-betweens who line up the corporate and media 'partners' and stage-manage the football spectacle itself. They also walk away with a sizeable share of the profits generated by Network Football. Like FIFA itself (and the IOC), these organisations usually have their headquarters and bank accounts in unaccountable money's main haven, Switzerland.

This brings us to the official commanding heights of the Network and the football bureaucrats themselves. These are the technocrats who have facilitated the takeover of professional football by network society. In doing so, many have adopted the culture of the global market place. Castells includes among network capitalism's managerial class the managers of state-owned companies, 'who, for all practical purposes, follow the same logic, and share the same culture, minus the risk for losses underwritten by the taxpayer'. These are, he continues, 'the controllers of capital assets on behalf of shareholders. These managers still constitute the heart of capitalism under informationalism, particularly in multi-national corporations' (Castells 1998: 342). This aptly sums up the roles played by the Fifacrats, an alliance of 'elected' and appointed officers and senior administrators who occupy the apex of FIFA, including representatives of world football's six confederations and, slightly off-centre but very influential within the network, the more powerful among the national associations.

FIFA has not been passive in the takeover of world football by big business and the network society; rather it has facilitated it. In his analysis of the staging of the 1998 World Cup Finals, Geoff Hare argues that football's global expansion has been driven by 'FIFA's own adoption of a business approach in its running of football and its early initiative to commercialise its key asset, the four-yearly World Cup tournament'. He then begs the question, 'whether its (FIFA's) two functions, of custodian of the sport's self regulatory integrity and of agent of the games commercialisation are compatible?' (Hare 1999: 123). When England hosted the World Cup Finals in 1966 it was the only serious global football tournament (outside of the amateur version within the Olympic Games) and comprised 16 finalists out of less than 50 nations that entered the tournament. In France 32 teams qualified for the finals via a series of qualifying tournaments involving close to 200 national associations. Consider also the growth in the number of competitions other than the World Cup in FIFA's portfolio. This now includes the men's and women's Olympic competitions, the Women's World Cup, the World Youth Championships (under 20), the Under 17 World Championships, the Futsal (Indoor Football) World Cup and, most recently, the World Club Championships and the Confederations Cup. At France 98 FIFA even had sand shipped into Paris and introduced beach football as an exhibition sport, with a view to launching a new global competition in it in the near future. To a greater or lesser extent, all of FIFA's six confederations have followed suit by expanding regional international competitions for both clubs and countries. In Europe, for instance, the indisputable epicentre of professional football, there has been huge expansion of intra-continental club football in response to immense pressure from network society. As we have seen, this has expanded the old European Cup into the UEFA Champions League, with a cast of more non-champions than champions.

One interpretation of this – also FIFA's own favourite explanation – is that this level of expansion has been necessary to accommodate demand from FIFA's expanded membership, particularly in Africa and Asia. Certainly those who speak for FIFA like to characterise this expansion as a case of the world body accelerating development of football in the third world. But this is only partially true. While there can be no doubt that Africa and Asia are deservedly better off for places in the 32-nation format of the senior competition, this must also be viewed as pay back for providing political support (i.e. votes) for FIFA's network-dependent technocrats. FIFA's constitution and administrative structures were developed in and for the age of empires. This was an era when Europe, in general, and Britain, in particular, dominated the world map either through direct political and military authority (colonialism) or related commercial and cultural influences. When there was only a handful of countries that were members of FIFA and the overwhelming majority of them were European, the one nation one vote principle underpinning the organisation's constitution could not threaten Europe's custody of association football. The potentially powerful North Americans had little interest in the world game. Resistance to Eurocentrism traditionally came from the South Americans, but with a static regional membership of 10 countries, they were always going to be outvoted by the Europeans.

Europeans' natural majority ended with the progressive dismemberment of their political empires from the 1950s onward when more and more newly independent countries became voting members of FIFA. This was noticed and understood by Horst Dassler and exploited to great effect by Havelange, the Brazilian who harvested third world votes to win the FIFA presidency from Englishman Stanley Rous in 1974. Havelange's nominated successor, Sepp Blatter, used the same tactics when he was victorious in FIFA's presidential elections in Paris 1998. In both cases after their electoral victories there were promises to keep and this led the drive to expand FIFA's competitive portfolio at every level.

Of course, as the Coca-Cola illustration above exemplifies, this expansion suited the media and FIFA's corporate partners as it gave them more events and more countries to embrace within their marketing strategies. As Blatter proudly proclaimed of the post-Rous FIFA:

> The success of the game virtually throughout the world ... Its social ramifications and its economic impact make of it a phenomenal force. The figures alone speak for themselves: 200 million persons actively involved and an estimated 1.2 billion directly or indirectly, an annual turnover of some 200 billion Dollars, far larger than corporate leaders such as Mitsubishi or General Motors. And the end is not yet in sight.
>
> (Sugden and Tomlinson 1998: 223)

World football's expansion is also connected to power struggles taking place within the heart of FIFA itself. In terms of the number and quality of clubs and competitions and the amount of money generated by football, Europe is peerless. As such, of FIFA's six confederations, UEFA, European football's governing body is, by some distance, the most powerful. It is from this quarter that the most serious challenges to FIFA's (i.e. Havelange's and Blatter's) authority have come. By expanding the portfolio of world competitions, FIFA has been seeking to broaden its power base. This is one of the main reasons that shortly after his inauguration as president, Blatter initiated both the World Club Championships and the Confederations Cup. It is also why he proposed that the World Cup Finals should be played biannually rather than every four years. Thus, in the post-Rous era, apart from paying off political debts, the expansion in world football has had as much to do with the market-led demands of the media-commercial nexus and internecine power struggles within the hierarchy, as it has with championing the cause of the oppressed.

Of course, without a clothes horse – football itself – FIFA's media and marketing partners would have nothing through which to display and sell their products. However, to borrow David Conn's (1997) pithy descriptor, the 'football business' is not a passive player within the network. Rather, it is a proactive and increasingly aggressive stakeholder. The football business consists of those most directly responsible for producing the regular raw material of organised professional football: the matches and competitions. Key personnel include the chief executives and directors of the main professional leagues and big professional clubs, the club managers, coaches, agents, the players themselves, and last, and always least, the fans. With the notable exception of the agents, this cast of characters has been integral to the development of grass-roots professional football for more than a hundred years. However, for most of the century they all, more or less, operated from the common principle of football first, business second. Not any more, and as Conn laments, top-level football in England, in recent decades, has become an industry given over entirely to moneymaking:

> For a century the game muddled through, crying out for unity, planning, some reform, some investment in the grass roots and distinguished fabric of the game. The disgrace is that now, the time of the greatest ever wealth, is the time of least distribution. Football has fallen to the dogma of its day. 'Market forces' ... Like much else in Britain, football needed to become more businesslike, and it ended up no more than a business.
>
> (Conn 1997: 175–6)

The establishment of the G14 offers a good case study that illustrates how those who produce the game – the clubs – have emerged as big power players within Network football. The G14 are a self-styled elite of clubs who in 2000 established an exclusive lobbying cartel and set up offices in Brussels. The G8 group of the world's most powerful national economies inspired the name and the G14 is comprised mainly of Europe's richest clubs from Italy, Spain, England, Germany, Holland, Portugal and France. Like the Cosa Nostra, the exact formula for membership is a mysterious combination of money, success and potential television audience. G14 portray themselves as nothing more than a group of like-minded football club owners and administrators, but the fact that they head-hunted UEFA's fixture co-ordinator to head up their Brussels operation suggests that their ultimate aim is the establishment of a super league outside of UEFA/FIFA jurisdiction. What sets the G14 apart from previous failed breakaway attempts, such as the Murdoch-backed Media Partners initiative of 1998, is the fact that G14 is comprised of organisations that are the leading producers of the European football industry.

The rationale behind the G14 has less to do with democratic reform and more to do with greed. It is estimated that globally football generates in excess of $250 billion of which more than 75 per cent is generated in Europe (Sugden and Tomlinson 1998). The G14 argue that it is they who provide the facilities, fans, and muscle and blood without which none of this cash would flow, and therefore they should have more say in how the spectacle is produced and where the money goes. (This is the very argument that G14 club presidents decry most when it comes from players and agents, accusing *them* of being too greedy!) The G14 also object to the way UEFA taxes the rich to feed the poor, top-slicing Champions League revenue, ostensibly to prop up weaker European clubs and leagues, but also to finance its own lavish operation in Switzerland. If G14 set up competitions independently of UEFA, transfer payments such as these would be unnecessary. Such a system may irreparably damage smaller leagues and clubs, but, after all, business is business in Network Football.

In response to earlier threats of secession, in order to ensure that as many of the big clubs as possible qualify for the Champions League, UEFA relaxed the criteria for inclusion, allowing entry for up to three clubs from the strongest leagues and two from the weaker countries. As illustrated by Barcelona's untimely exit from the Champions League during season 2000–2001, however, there can be no guarantee that the big clubs will always get through to the lucrative final stages of the competition. With massive wage bills, impatient and success-hungry shareholders, sponsors and fans, 'maybe Europe next season' is not good enough for the business planning and projections of Europe's top clubs.

UEFA's initial reaction to the establishment of G14 was bellicose. With the backing of most national football associations, UEFA threatened to expel G14 members from all European football, domestic or otherwise. But clubs like Manchester United, Barcelona, Real Madrid, Inter Milan and Bayern Munich cannot be brushed aside so easily. UEFA's threat was dismissed by the ex-West German international, Karl-Heinz Rummenigge, who, speaking on behalf of G14 pointed out, 'twelve of these 14 clubs are Champions League Clubs. The same day that they kick us out of UEFA they can close their Champions League Shop'.

To make matters worse for UEFA the exclusiveness of G14 led outsiders to propose the Atlantic League, a transcontinental, weekend competition for clubs who have significant local and continental followings, but who play most of their football in relatively minor domestic leagues. The proposal for the Atlantic League was put forward by clubs from six nations who feel they are being left behind financially by those from England, France, Germany, Italy and Spain, a situation which could only get worse if/when a G14 league or its equivalent is set up. The clubs involved were AFC Ajax, Feyenoord and PSV Eindhoven of the Netherlands; RSC Anderlecht and Club Brugge KV of Belgium; Brøndby IF and FC København of Denmark; Portugal's SL Benfica and Sporting Clube de Portugal; Sweden's AIK Solna and Scottish sides Celtic and Rangers.

The odd derby match notwithstanding, these clubs cannot sustain big enough television audiences to attract the massive media-sponsor contracts that inflated the football cash bubble elsewhere in Europe. Proponents of the Atlantic League argued that combining would give them a potential TV audience of 60 million. Of course such a league would require participating clubs to withdraw from existing domestic leagues, virtually guaranteeing the collapse of professional football, particularly in smaller countries like Scotland.

Faced with a second, Atlantic, front UEFA's general secretary, Gerhard Aigner, conceded that, 'the Champions League in its current format has reached the end of its life. We must find a new formula in which there will be fewer matches, but the proposal to install a special league for a limited number of clubs is not the solution'. This is the same argument that led to the development of the Champions League in the first place and its subsequent expanded format. The Champions League was always a business concept and never a football development. From day one it has been driven hard by a favoured network of media and commercial interests held together by TEAM, UEFA's media-marketing partner. Indeed research shows that the whole concept of the Champions League was developed by TEAM and adopted by UEFA, and not vice versa (Sugden and Tomlinson 1998).

Finally, of crucial significance to the arguments developed at the end of this chapter, there is governance, both of the nation-state variety, and its increasingly important international dimension. One of the defining features of the twentieth century was the acceleration in the range and extent of international government organisations (IGOs) and their non-governmental equivalents (INGOs). In 1909 there were only 37 IGOs and 176 INGOs (including FIFA), while in 1996 there were 260 IGOs and a staggering 5,472 INGOs (Held *et al.* 1999: 53). In part, the growth in the number and reach of IGOs has been a response to the dramatic expansion of INGO activity. Whether they be charitable organisations such as OXFAM, political lobbyists such as CND, or global organisations of criminals and terrorists, national governments have collaborated, through bodies such as the United Nations and its satellites, or the European Union, to monitor and exert a degree of influence over INGOs' activities. Hitherto, sport, in general, and football, in particular, have been exceptional to this rule.

Up until now, the formal political presence of government in Network Football has been limited, usually, to token and largely ceremonial functions

– royalty, presidents, and prime ministers attending opening ceremonies of World Cup matches or hosting lavish dinners for Fifacrats and their retinues are among the roles routinely adopted by government representatives within the Network. Interaction between national governments and FIFA tends to become more pronounced only when world football is perceived to have a bearing on the national interest. Typically this occurs around the bidding for and hosting of major international tournaments, particularly the world cup finals. Mega-events in sports are staged for corporate profit, personal aggrandisement and for state-driven national pride. For instance, as Dauncey and Hare point out, 'the 1998 World Cup was staged for external consumption. It was to celebrate France's position as one of the major economic and political powers' (1999: 1).

Otherwise, FIFA's engagement with state politicians usually only happens when it seeks to help one or more of its member associations prevent political interference into its affairs by its national government. Herein lies a clue that helps us to understand why up until now FIFA has operated largely beyond the reach of any international and democratically accountable legal framework. FIFA, like the IOC, was established by a class of people who thought themselves to be selfless, well-meaning and right-thinking gentlemen, and who believed in the separation of sport from politics as a sacred principle. According to this view, politics and politicians could only violate sports integrity. People like Jules Rimet, Arthur Drewry and Sir Stanley Rous felt duty-bound to protect football from the overt interference of politicians, and the organisation that they helped to mould has continued to operate according to the same principles. This is a position that has, for the most part, been respected by mature democratic governments who rarely, if ever, meddle in the affairs of sports' governing bodies (Tomlinson 2000).

Of course, such a stance was naively self-serving from the outset, and is even more so now. It is a confidence trick that has been made easier to carry off because of the façade of democracy under which FIFA operates. As we have seen, when it comes to making major decisions, such as electing a new president, every member association has one equal vote. Thus, when it comes to the equity of representation, FIFA seems to occupy the moral high ground. However, usually, those who cast votes are not themselves elected and neither are they accountable to any broader constituency. Furthermore, as has been revealed elsewhere (Sugden and Tomlinson 1999), because FIFA elections operate a secret ballot, they can and have been rigged to ensure that those who are best suited to serve the business interests of the rest of the Network are elected. In this way, without any genuine democratic accountability – as Andrew Jennings and others have also shown with regard to the Olympic movement – self-styled sporting aristocrats and autocrats have manipulated and exploited global sport for their own financial and vainglorious purposes (Jennings 1996, 2000; Simson and Jennings 1992). Likewise, successive generations of Fifacrats have used the traditional separation of sport from politics as a veil behind which they have abused power and used and abused the game for their own personal and sectarian interests. In short, they have control without accountability, and it is for this reason that the profile of national governments in the Network is such a low one. In the conclusion to this chapter I will argue that, for the good of the game, this needs to be reconsidered and rectified.

The model outlined above provides us with an approximation only of the structures within which world football's power games proceed. As the elaboration of its components suggest, the real world of global football's political economy is even more complex and fluid than that implied by this ideal type. This confirms the point made in the earlier discussion of Mann (in Chapter 1) that societies 'are much messier than our theories of them' (Mann 1986: 4). Network Football, despite FIFA's persistent rhetorical invocation of kinship metaphors, is not an extended family, co-existing in harmony and wedded to a mutually supportive corporate strategy. There is in fact a considerable amount of conflict both within and between the key elements of the Network. UEFA and FIFA are in a constant state of conflict over how world football should be developed and administered. Likewise, the big sponsors struggle with one another to get the most global exposure, just as huge media corporations battle for broadcasting rights, and marketing agencies fight among themselves for the most lucrative contracts. At the same time, alliances of media interests, sponsors, marketing companies and the big clubs attempt to undermine the authority of governing bodies by proposing varieties of super-leagues. Closer to the grass roots, chairmen, managers, players and their agents, and fans dispute the day-to-day production of the football business itself.

While there is conflict, there is also correspondence, co-operation and merger among the elements of the Network. Media conglomerates and marketing companies are gaining significant stakes, both in one another – for instance, Kirsch/ISL – and in top football clubs in Europe's and South America's premier leagues. Also, several big clubs now run their own television companies. To further muddy the waters, some Fifacrats have developed very cosy relationships with their Network partners. The close relationship between Adidas, ISL and FIFA embodied through Dassler, Havelange and Blatter has been noted here and well documented elsewhere (Sugden and Tomlinson 1998, 1999). In 1997 Traffic, South America's biggest media-marketing company, brokered a controversial deal between Nike and the Brazilian football association (CBF) that gave the sporting goods giant unprecedented control of the Brazil national team for an estimated $US20 million per year. In 2001 the same company oversaw a transaction whereby the North American investment fund HMTF (Hicks, Muse, Tate and First) bought Brazil's biggest soccer club, Corinthians, while at the same time buying 49 per cent of Traffic's shares. The involvement of Havelange and his former son-in-law and CBF president Ricardo Teixeira in the affairs of Traffic compound an impression of sharp practice at the heart of the

Network. The bankruptcy of FIFA's marketing partner ISL in 2001, amid accusations that Sepp Blatter had personal interests in that company and that a senior member of the FIFA Executive and close Blatter ally, Jack Warner, had been allowed to purchase lucrative television rights to the World Cup Finals in 2002 in the wake of ISL's demise, did little to ameliorate worries that, in addition to conflict and co-operation, collusion, conspiracy and corruption also characterise the nature of the relationships through which Network Football operates. Nevertheless, irrespective of which relationship or combinations thereof lubricate the Network, the overriding result usually works to the advantage of big business.

Conclusion

Can, or indeed should, anything be done to address the way world football is governed? Let us address the 'can' question first. Returning to Robertson's (1990) stages of global development, his fifth or 'uncertain' phase – characterised herein as one dominated by the activities of network capitalism – may be drawing to a close. Held *et al.* (1999) observe that, in the latter part of the twentieth century and the early part of the twenty-first, the democratic regulation of globalisation worked its way onto and up the political agenda.

> At issue is the nature of a political community – how should the proper boundaries of a political community be drawn in a more regional global order? In addition, questions can be raised about the meaning of representation (who should represent whom and on what basis?) and about the proper form and scope of political participation (who should participate and in what way?).
>
> (Held *et al.* 1999: 446–7)

They go on to argue that such debates necessarily involve serious reconsideration of the nature of democracy within SICAS (States in Advanced Capitalist Societies) and between SICAS and a wide range of IGOs and INGOs:

> Some of the most fundamental forces and processes determining the nature of life chances within and across political communities are now beyond the reach of nation states. The system of national political communities persists of course; but it is articulated and rearticulated today within complex economic, organisational, administrative, legal and cultural processes and structures which limit and check its efficacy. If these processes and structures are not acknowledged and brought into the political realm they will tend to bypass or circumvent the traditional mechanisms of political accountability and regulation. If the most powerful geopolitical forces are not to settle many pressing matters

simply in terms of their own objectives and by virtue of their power, then the current institutions and mechanisms for accountability need to be reconsidered.

(ibid.: 447)

The authors go on to suggest that such reconsideration, both intellectually and through the application of policy, is well underway. They use evidence of the growing number of structures, empowered through democratic bodies like the UN and the EC, to regulate the global governance of business, the military, the environment, population and its mobility, and a wide range of cultural entities, including popular music, cinema and the whole telecommunications industry. Sport is notable, but only through its absence. This should not be the case. After reviewing the state of the global governance of sport, Sunder Katwala concludes that, 'it is difficult to find anything in the world quite so badly governed as international sport' (2000: 90). He goes on to say:

Reform of international sporting governance is not inevitable but it is possible. Sporting governance is in a state of extreme disequilibrium – the tensions between the global revolution and unmodernised governance must eventually bring change of one sort of another. But change is likely to come from an uncertain combination of different forces – change from within, pressure from outside and change through collapse and crisis.

(ibid.: 91)

In 1998 FIFA had a clear opportunity to 'change from within' and recover its position as the guardian of the world game when Lennart Johannson, the Swedish president of the European confederation, put himself forward as a reform candidate. His manifesto proposed, 'an international democratic network based on trust, transparency, loyalty and solidarity' (Sugden and Tomlinson 1998: 250). That, in deeply suspicious circumstances, Johannson suffered a humiliating defeat at the hands of the continuity candidate and Havelange protégé, Sepp Blatter, suggests that as presently constituted, FIFA is incapable of reforming itself.

Hitherto, because of sport's protected status as a politics-free zone, FIFA (like the IOC) has proven itself to be relatively impervious to 'pressure from the outside' for political reform. This, in the view of this author, has to change. Elsewhere, along with Alan Tomlinson, I have argued that organisations like FIFA need to have their foundations relaid in democratic earth:

FIFA itself must be brought within the embrace of an accountable international organisation such as the United Nations, perhaps under the wing of this organisation's cultural framework, UNESCO. Under such an arrangement, FIFA's off-shore financial status would have to end. All of its important decisions would be scrutinised by officials, themselves accountable to a broader electorate and within a wider legal framework.

(Sugden and Tomlinson 1999: 88)

This is not to suggest that politicians should run world football, and here it is important to distinguish between political control and political account- ability. Control suggests uncontested domination whereas accountability alludes to representation based on transparency and the capacity for reform. In this regard, while FIFA is right to continue to protect its member associa- tions from the political interference of those who would seek to control football, it is wrong to continue to protect itself from outside scrutiny and accountability.

As the 1998 FIFA presidential elections illustrated, turkeys do not routinely vote for Christmas. However, the democratising of FIFA may yet come about 'through collapse and crisis'. The bankruptcy of ISL in 2001 and the implication of senior FIFA officials, including the president himself, in this debacle shook the organisation's foundations and renewed calls for democratic reform. Of potentially more significance than the alleged corrupt practices of individuals within or close to FIFA are the financial causes of ISL's demise. The company imploded because it had over-bid for the televi- sion rights for a range of sporting events around the world, including and especially the World Cup Finals in 2002. Put simply, ISL had paid more for the rights than the sponsors were willing to pay for media exposure. As ISL was being wound up in a Swiss court, FIFA also had to face the humiliation of having to cancel the World Club Championships in Spain at the last minute because the South American media company, Traffic, who had bought the rights to this event, had been unable to attract sufficient spon- sorship to make the event viable.

This may be evidence that media and marketing interest in football, at least at the world level, has peaked or even gone into decline. Without the huge financial surplus that accrues to FIFA from such arrangements, it is unlikely to be able to operate on the same lavish scale in the future. Without the 'cash box' brim-full and overflowing, the deals and alliances that have maintained FIFA as a fiefdom and kept the likes of Havelange and his protégé, Blatter, in power for nearly three decades, will no longer be able to be made. If this comes to pass then calls for democratic reform, both from within and without, may become irresistible.

Finally, it is necessary to address the 'should' question and respond to criticisms of the above arguments that have been raised repeatedly on the several occasions that versions of this chapter have been presented at confer- ences and seminars. 'Why', it has been regularly asked, 'should we make a special case for football? After all, isn't it just like any other object of production/consumption and shouldn't it too be subject to the forces of a global economy?'

Leaving aside the issue of whether or not any sphere of industry and/or culture should be exposed to unbridled global commercialisation, football is a special case in as much as it is one of a number of realms of cultural production that have considerable meaning beyond straightforward consumption. Theatre, opera, ballet and other dimensions of 'high' culture would have died out long ago had it not been for high levels of state and private protection and patronage. Indeed, the French have long since battled to preserve distinctiveness for French cinema in the face of Hollywood's relentless quest for global dominance. Early in 2000 the impresario, Andrew Lloyd Webber, bought a number of prominent theatres in London's West End which had been threatened with closure. In announcing his takeover, Lloyd Webber claimed that it was important that these theatres did not fall into the hands of 'pen pushers and number crunchers' who had less regard for their artistic value and more interest in real-estate and profit (*Independent*, 10 January 2000: 3). The rationale for such protectionism is that certain aspects of culture are so deeply connected to community and national identity, and of such critical importance to local and/or world heritage, that to allow them to be radically altered, or even destroyed, by market forces would be seriously damaging to the quality of life for people today, and for unborn generations.

There is no reason why such arguments cannot be extended to cover other aspects of popular culture, including football. As exemplified by the chapter in this volume by Magee, it is precisely these kinds of arguments that national governments, national football associations and European football's regional governing body, UEFA, have been using in an attempt to thwart the European Union's plans to subject football to the same employment legislation as other industries.

In Europe, South America and Africa, football, perhaps more than any other area of popular culture, captures the collective imagination and animates the discourse of citizenship. Yes, football matches are widely consumed by live audiences and, increasingly, through television, and large quantities of football-related apparel and memorabilia are bought worldwide. But football clubs and national teams carry meanings beyond the moment of consumption. They stand for things such as community, tradition, social solidarity and local and national distinctiveness. Such attributes may not be easy to package and sell, and may even stand in the way of profit-driven 'progress', but they are deeply significant in the non-utilitarian enrichment of existence for uncountable millions of people. While accepting that these 'attributes' can also, under certain circumstances, lead to less socially constructive manifestations such as nationalism, racism, sexism and hooliganism, football still needs to be protected from the more avaricious and predatory ways of unregulated global capitalism. FIFA, as currently constituted, is patently obviously incapable of providing this protection. For this reason, they, and global sports organisations like them, should not escape the attention of those activists who are dedicated to the democratic reform of the global political economy.

Notes

1 This chapter draws upon material from a paper of the same title co-authored with Ben Carrington and Alan Tomlinson and presented at the North American Society for the Sociology of Sport annual conference in Cleveland, Ohio, November 1999.

References

Bourdieu, P. (1999) 'The state, economics and sport', in H. Dauncey and G. Hare (eds) *France and the 1998 World Cup: The National Impact of a World Sporting Event*, London: Frank Cass.

Bromley, S. (1999) 'The space of flows and timeless time: Manuel Castells's *The Information Age*', *Radical Philosophy* 97 (September/October): 6–17.

Castells, M. (1996) *The Rise of Network Society*, Oxford: Blackwell.

—— (1997) *The Power of Identity*, Oxford: Blackwell.

—— (1998) *The End of the Millennium*, Oxford: Blackwell.

Conn, D. (1997) *The Football Business. Fair Game in the 1990s?*, Edinburgh: Mainstream.

Dauncey, H. and Hare, G. (eds) (1999) *France and the 1998 World Cup : The National Impact of a World Sporting Event*, London: Frank Cass.

Hare, G. (1999), 'Buying and selling the World Cup', in H. Dauncey and G. Hare (eds) *France and the 1998 World Cup: The National Impact of a World Sporting Event*, London: Frank Cass.

Held, D., McGrew, A., Goldblatt, D. and Perration, J. (1999) *Global Transformations*, Cambridge: Polity Press.

Hirst, P. and Thompson, G. (1996) *Globalization in Question: The International Economy and the Possibility of Governance*, Cambridge: Polity Press.

Jennings, A. (1996) *The New Lords of the Rings: Olympic Corruption and How to Buy Gold Medals*, London: Pocket Books/Simon & Schuster.

Jennings, A. and Sambrook, C. (2000) *The Great Olympic Swindle: When the World Wanted its Games Back*, London: Simon & Schuster.

Katwala, S. (2000) *Democratising Global Sport*, London: Central Books.

MacLean, J. (1999) 'Towards a political economy of agency in contemporary international relations', in M. Shaw (ed.) *Politics and Globalisation: Knowledge, Ethics and Agency*, London: Routledge.

Maguire, J. (1999) *Global Sport: Identities, Societies, Civilizations*. Cambridge: Polity Press.

Mann, M. (1986) *The Sources of Social Power. Vol. 1: A History of Power from the Beginning to A.D. 1760*, Cambridge: Cambridge University Press.

Robertson, R. (1990) 'Mapping the global condition: globalization as the central concept', *Theory, Culture and Society: Explorations in Critical Social Science* 7(2–3): 15–30.

—— (1992) *Globalization, Social Theory and Global Culture*, London: Sage.

Simson, V. and Jennings, A. (1992) *The Lords of the Rings: Power, Money and Drugs in the Modern Olympics*, London: Simon & Schuster.

Sklair, L. (1991) *Sociology of the Global System*, London: Harvester Wheatsheaf.

Sugden, J. and Tomlinson, A. (1996) 'What's left when the circus leaves town? An evaluation of the 1994 USA World Cup', *Sociology of Sport Journal* 13(3): 236–54.

—— (1998) *FIFA and the Contest for World Football. Who rules the Peoples' Game?*, Cambridge: Polity Press.

—— (1999) *Great Balls of Fire. How Big Money is Hijacking World Football*, Edinburgh: Mainstream.

Tomlinson, A. (1994) 'FIFA and the World Cup: the expanding football family', in J. Sugden and A. Tomlinson (eds) *Hosts and Champions: Soccer Cultures, National Identities and the USA World Cup*, Aldershot: Arena/Ashgate.

—— (2000) 'FIFA and the men who made it', *Soccer and Society* 1(1): 55–71.

5 Leading with the left

Boxing, incarnation and Sartre's progressive–regressive method

Leon Culbertson

> Then a big projectile exactly the size of a fist in a glove drove into the middle of Foreman's mind, the best punch of the startled night, the blow Ali saved for a career. Foreman's arms flew out to the side like a man with a parachute jumping out of a plane ... All the while his eyes were on Ali and he looked up with no anger as if Ali, indeed, was the man he knew best in the world and would see him on his dying day. Vertigo took George Foreman and revolved him ... He started to tumble and topple and fall even as he did not wish to go down. His mind was held with magnets high as his championship and his body was seeking the ground. He went over like a sixty-year-old butler who has just heard tragic news, yes, fell over all of a long collapsing two seconds, down came the championship in sections and Ali revolved with him in a close circle, hand primed to hit him one more time, and never the need, a wholly intimate escort to the floor.
>
> (Mailer 1975: 208)

This is a classically romanticised account of one of the most famous fights in the history of boxing, the World Heavyweight Championship fight between George Foreman and Muhammad Ali, held in Kinshasa, Zaïre in 1974. It is also broadly representative of popular representations of boxing in film, television, literature and the press. Such accounts tell us little about boxing as a synthetic totality. They focus on that which heightens the tension and excitement of the spectacle, only hinting at the complexity of the event.

Boxers are individuals, each with a unique biography and, therefore, a unique situation within any specific event. Who are Foreman and Ali? What is the significance of Foreman's acceptance of boxing as 'the vindication of the American dream' (Sugden 1996: 191), and Ali's use of boxing as a platform for political activism from which he 'turn[ed] his back on America, Christianity and the white race' (Marqusee 1999: 10)? To what degree did Foreman and Ali see themselves as representatives of their nation, their religion or their race, and in what way did this influence their actions? What was the influence of external factors such as the media, promoters, spectators, the venue, the boxing community, the American public and the Nation of Islam on this unique event and the actions of the two fighters? These are only a few of the questions that are not answered by a simple description of one man hitting another, no matter how evocative the language used. The most pressing question, however, is how do the various issues that arise come together in a synthetic account of the historical event?

Sociologists have attempted to give us a more detailed understanding of the practices and processes which combine to produce specific fights and the boxing world as a whole. Existing theoretical and methodological approaches have hitherto proved at best incomplete, and often inadequate. Attempts to characterise sport, and boxing, in particular, as part of a civil-ising process (Elias and Dunning 1986; Sheard 1990) have attempted to compress the diversity of history into a model that has far less explanatory power than it is often accorded. Such work has been critiqued in some detail in relation to boxing elsewhere (Sugden 1996: 174–80) and repetition of such arguments need not detain us here. Both Sugden (1996) and Wacquant (1992, 1995, 1998) have attempted to apply a synthetic approach to the study of boxing, yet both have failed to provide more than a sum of accounts of various aspects of boxing. Here, we will explore how the work of Jean-Paul Sartre can assist in the development of a method which can provide a true synthesis. This will be done through a discussion of boxing, and will therefore help us to clarify some of the theoretical and methodological issues which will help render boxing intelligible.

In the final lines of *Class, Sports and Social Development*, Richard Gruneau tells us that 'progress in the sociology of sport depends primarily upon our capacities to make the critique of sport a part of the much broader attempt to discern the alternatives within which human reason and freedom can make history' (Gruneau 1999: 112). Reference to 'the much *broader* attempt' leads us back to the opening pages of that text, where we encounter a discus-sion of what Gruneau sees as 'one of the basic problems' (Gruneau 1999: xix) facing the sociology of sport. Gruneau laments the demise of concerns with 'classical' research questions and the accompanying style of analysis. He cites favourably a description of early sociology as *synthetic* in character, and proceeds to chart the break up of this synthesis as a result of the institution-alisation of sociology. He claims that institutionalisation led to the setting of specific tasks for the discipline which brought a move away from synthetic encyclopedianism. This also meant a move from political philosophy and the philosophy of history, which was seen as ideologically laden, to a positivist emphasis on logic, analytical reason and empirical analysis.

Despite doubts as to whether Durkheim and Weber can be regarded as partly responsible for the shift in emphasis which led to a neo-positivist structural functionalism, Gruneau argues that this was, nonetheless, the general trend, particularly in North American sociology through the 1940s and 1950s. C. Wright Mills may have been the first notable voice of dissent in relation to this trend. The 1960s and 1970s saw something of a return, albeit a partial return, to the synthetic character of classical sociology, along with new theoretical developments. Gruneau concludes, however, following Giddens, that this return to the synthetic approach has led to little new insight. This is not just the result of a persistence of the 'theoretical ortho-doxies of the forties and fifties' (Gruneau 1999: xxiii), but, more importantly, it is a consequence of the fact that the new theoretical and methodological directions which have been adopted since the 1960s have failed to provide the insight that they promised.

In addition to claiming that the move away from a synthetic approach led to a fragmentation of sociology into many subsociologies which concentrate on narrow problems and often employ an equally narrow empiricism, Gruneau also argues that the domination of Stalinism and the inclination to dogmatic interpretations of Marx, even in Western Europe, has meant that Marxism has not given satisfactory solutions either, despite its obvious promise. This leads Gruneau to argue that, in looking for a solution to the problems facing sociology, it is necessary to return to the concerns of clas-sical sociology and preserve a unity of the critical, the empirical and the interpretative. In addition, he stresses the significance of questions relating to human capacity and the restrictions on that capacity in changing social environments (agency and structure by another name). Finally, Gruneau warns against the uncritical application of abstract theoretical models.

Gruneau raises four issues that frame the problem which will be explored here. First, there is the advocacy of a synthetic methodology. This is closely linked to the second issue, resistance to positivism, analytical reason and empiricism. The third factor of importance here is the inadequacy of the new theoretical and methodological directions that have been adopted since the 1960s. Finally, there is the problem of dogmatic interpretations of Marx as a result of the domination of Stalinism. Taken together, these issues frame a problem but do not necessarily suggest an answer. Gruneau offers one approach, but we shall explore another far more wide-reaching approach to these issues and the accompanying problem of an historically sensitive synthetic method, suggesting new theoretical and methodological directions for the study of sport.

Both Giddens and C. Wright Mills approach a synthetic method but ulti-mately fail to provide anything which conforms to the requirements of such a method. The same is true of Gruneau. Giddens sees the sociological imagi-nation as consisting of 'an historical, an anthropological and a critical sensitivity' (Giddens 1986: 13). By recovering 'the world we have lost' (*ibid.*: 14), we are able to appreciate the difference between the lives that we live today and those of our immediate predecessors. This may be true, but far more significant is the fact that historical analysis is essential if we are to grasp the process involved, as any form of praxis is a response to existing circumstances in light of a projected future, yet is deviated in this process. Giddens does not grasp the role of individual historical action, or the restric-tions and deviations of that action. He may have been closer to the formulation of a productive synthetic method had he broadened his meaning of the term 'anthropological' beyond that which allows us to eradicate ethnocentrism.

C. Wright Mills appears to be approaching a synthesis when he refers to

> the capacity to shift from one perspective to another – from the political
> to the psychological; from examination of a single family to comparative
> assessment of the national budgets of the world; from the theological
> school to the military establishment; from considerations of an oil
> industry to studies of contemporary poetry.

> (Mills 1959: 7)

He claims that 'it is the capacity to range from the most impersonal and
remote transformations to the most intimate features of the human self' –
and to see the relations between the two 'that constitutes the superiority of
the sociological imagination as an approach to the study of the social world'
(*ibid.*: 7).

The advance that we find in Mills is the concern with the individual and
the personal. Mills claimed that 'social science deals with the problems of
biography, of history, and of their intersections within social structures ...
these three – biography, history, society – are the co-ordinate points of the
proper study of man' (Mills 1959: 143). Flynn (1997) points to the simi-
larity between the approaches of Mills and Sartre, claiming that 'Mills
echoes ... the ideal of Sartre's approach and anticipates his subsequent characterisation of his massive "biography" of Flaubert' (*ibid.*: 149). The subject
of that biography (*The Family Idiot*), which Sartre claims is a sequel to *The
Problem of Method* is 'what at this point in time, can we know about a man?'
(Sartre 1981: ix). Flynn suggests that both Mills and Sartre may have been
influenced by *verstehende Soziologie*, and more specifically, Dilthey and Weber.

Mills, however, maintains a distinction between the personal, or individual, and the public, or social, and grossly oversimplifies our task by
failing to recognise the role of the social in the individual and the individual
in the social. Despite Mills's reference to biography, the issue of individual
praxis is as far from his concern as it is from that of most other sociologists
and it is this which prevents Mills, Giddens or Gruneau from formulating
an adequate synthetic method. It is also this issue which makes the work of
Sartre worthy of exploration in relation to this issue.

It is necessary to be not only more specific, but also more discerning
about what are the requirements of our synthetic method. The very nature of
our problem suggests that we should begin by rejecting artificial disciplinary restrictions. The problems outlined by Gruneau are not problems
facing sociology, but problems facing any attempt to understand the social
world. Sartre recognises that there are many layers of signification to be
uncovered in the historical event. Each signification has its own level. He
gives the example of attempting to explain the First World War. He identifies a number of levels of signification such as the economic ('rivalry between
German and English imperialisms') (Sartre 1999: 294); Pan-Germanism and
the hegemony of Prussia at the level of the 'more purely historical significa-

tion' (*ibid.*: 294); a diplomatic level (failure of alliances with Russia and Austria) and 'Emperor William's court, his government, his counsellors and his personality' (*ibid.*: 295). Sartre warns that 'a common error of historians is to put these explanations on the same level, linking them by an "and" – as if their juxtaposition ought to give rise to an organised totality with ordered structures, which would be the phenomenon itself enfolding its causes and various processes. In fact, the significations remain separate' (*ibid.*: 295). Aron, following Weber, adopts a position whereby the various accounts that emerge are each true of the event when it is assessed from different perspectives. Sartre's objection is to the fact that there is no convergence of these varying accounts of the event. They become a form of what Hegel (1977) called the 'bad infinite', as a result of the fact that there is no synthesis of the accounts. Sartre argues that all levels of signification are human and claims that the meaning of the historical situation is given by human agents. It is human choices which bring those situations to be. This means that the unity of the different levels of signification lays in the fact that human reality 'historializes itself'.

This is our first problem. We require a *synthesis*, not a sum of the many accounts that can be given of an event. This suggests a second requirement of an adequate synthetic method. Such a method must be able to render individual praxis intelligible and account for wider structures as constituted by individual praxis. In short, we must adopt a dialectical nominalism (avoiding abstract universalising) and only grant an existence to individual entities, while regarding wider structures such as class and society as constituted, rather than constitutive.

A third, and final, requirement is that a synthetic method display a temporal sensitivity. This does not simply mean that it must be historical. From Heidegger we get the notion of consciousness as spread over three temporal dimensions or *ekstases*. Sartre concretises this by arguing that praxis is temporalising. Consciousness always entails a response to a past and projection towards a not yet existing future. The principle of identity does not apply to conscious beings in that they are not perfectly at one with themselves, but spread over the past, the present and the future. In this sense, we are never wholly present, but rather, 'presence-to-self'. There is an inner distance which allows the nihilations (bringing to be of nothingness) that enable us to experience ourselves, the Other and objects in the world. The significance of this is clarified by Sartre's claim that 'man is free because he is not himself but presence to himself. The being which is what it is can not be free' (Sartre 1958: 440). In other words, inanimate objects are not free because they have a perfect identity. Conscious beings, however, are free to act and project futures, albeit under factical, or given, restrictions, as a result of the inner distance or 'nothingness' which consciousness brings to be. Our actions are, therefore, temporalising. We act on the world and alter it. Future action encounters the world as already altered by previous historical action or praxis. If we are to provide a synthesis rather than a sum we must take account of the temporal nature of human experience and action.

Mills was correct to claim that 'no social study that does not come back to the problems of biography, of history and of their intersections within a society has completed its intellectual journey' (Mills 1959: 6). It seems remarkable how often this point is ignored, although when one considers the full consequences of such a claim for a synthetic approach to the study of the social world, it is less surprising because it opens a theoretical debate which greatly complicates our problem as we have identified it. It is in the exploration of these complications that Sartre can be of assistance and, conveniently for those interested in the study of sport, it is through a study of boxing that Sartre elaborates the key idea that forms the link between biography and history. This is essential to the formulation of a synthetic method.

Comprehension, totalisation and the progressive–regressive method

Sartre draws a distinction between analytic and dialectical reason, claiming that 'the bourgeois class conceals the operation of the dialectic under the atomising rationality of positivism, whereas a theorist of the proletariat will demand explanations in the name of the dialectic itself. Thus, at one level of abstraction, class conflict expresses itself as a *conflict of rationalities*' (Sartre 1991a: 802). Sartre's position in *Existentialism and Humanism* (Sartre 1997: 55) implies the distinction between analytic reason and synthetic reason, which is prominent in the *Critique*, but the issue is clearly addressed for the first time in *Anti-Semite and Jew* (Sartre 1995a: 71). Here, Sartre argues that analytic reason creates a social atomism, it 'resolves collectivities into individual elements' (*ibid.*: 55) and does not grasp 'synthetic realities' (*ibid.*: 56). For Sartre, there is a determinism and an atomism to analytic reason. In addition, analytic reason is atemporal and, as such, the form of reason proper to structuralism, which succeeded the 'existentialism' of Sartre and a number of his contemporaries in French intellectual vogue. Sartre claims that analytic reason is unable to grasp historical events as it is unable to totalise and can only offer generalised statistical summations and 'abstract causal laws' (Flynn 1997: 100). Analytical reason is contrasted with the non-deterministic, temporalising and totalising dialectical reason. At the beginning of *Search for a Method* Sartre poses the question: 'do we have today the means to constitute a structural, historical anthropology?' His first comment on this task is to claim that 'if such a thing as a Truth can exist in anthropology, it must be a truth that has *become*, and it must make itself a *totalization*' (Sartre 1968: xxxiv). This, for Sartre, is the dialectic.

Sartre follows Marx in asserting a materialist dialectic as opposed to the idealist dialectical approach of Hegel. The problem which Sartre faces in the *Critique of Dialectical Reason* is not simply that of defending the claims of dialectical reason, but one of demonstrating the existence of dialectical reason at all. Establishing the *quid facti* is further complicated by the fact that we cannot, by its very nature, prove the existence of the dialectic prior to any dialectical investigation that we may wish to conduct. Rather, the dialectic must be assumed at the outset and allowed to emerge because dialectical reason encapsulates the object of study and the individual who is conducting the inquiry. The objectivity of the inquirer which is proper to analytic reason cannot be maintained with the application of dialectical reason. Sartre does claim a role for analytic reason during the regressive stage of analyses, but it is a comparatively minor role.

In addition to the distinction between analytic and dialectical reason, it is necessary for us to grasp Sartre's understanding of comprehension and totalisation if we are to fully appreciate his progressive–regressive method. In *Being and Nothingness* Sartre had argued that humans have a pre-reflective self-awareness. In *Search for a Method* he has stripped this idea of any Cartesian associations of cognitive idealism by arguing that we should be able to comprehend the historical agents' own understanding of their own project. The fact that the self-awareness of the historical agent is pre-reflective means that there is the potential for us to reflectively understand the individual better than they reflectively understand themselves.

Comprehension of the Other is possible, according to Sartre, because 'man is, for himself and for others, a signifying being' (Sartre 1968: 152). Sartre points out that if one observes someone at work and does not understand what that person is doing, one will find clarification of the actions being observed when one is able to 'unify the disjointed moments of this activity, thanks to the anticipation of the result aimed at' (*ibid.*: 157).

He illustrates this by the example of boxing by observing that 'in boxing, one will grant to a feint its true finality (which is, for example, to force the opponent to lift his guard) if one discovers and rejects at the same time its pretended finality (to land a left hook on the forehead). The double, triple systems of ends which others employ condition our activity as strictly as our own. A positivist who held on to his teleological colour blindness in practical life would not live very long' (Sartre 1968: 157). Sartre is developing his position on the temporal spread of consciousness, which he adapted from the work of Heidegger and outlined in *Being and Nothingness* and the thesis of the intentionality of consciousness which he borrowed from Husserl. By altering his initial position to give us temporalising praxis, Sartre allows us to see how humans can be signifying beings, but also that in comprehending the praxis of the Other in terms of its terminal signification, we may be able to grasp the dialectical relationship between biography and history. It is this comprehension that is the goal of the progressive–regressive method.

For Sartre, all praxis is totalising and dialectical and he warns that 'we will lose sight of human reality if we do not consider the significations as synthetic, multidimensional, indissoluble objects, which hold individual places in a space-time with multiple dimensions. The mistake here is to reduce the lived signification to the simple linear statement which language gives it' (Sartre 1968: 108–9). The role of totalisation therefore, is to discover 'the multidimentional *unity* of the act' (*ibid.*: 111). This allows Sartre to avoid the partial relativism in Raymond Aron's advocacy of a 'skeptical moderation' in relation to the issue of a unity to history. For Sartre, individual, organic praxis is constituting of the parts of a dynamic whole, while group praxis is constitutive. There is, he claims, an ontological primacy of individual praxis despite the fact that group praxis may provide a 'synthetic enrichment'. In addition, totalisation is continually in process, and as such any totalisation would be more correctly referred to as a 'detotalized totality'.

The progressive–regressive method

The main aim of the progressive–regressive method is to achieve a comprehension of both the individual and their time. This is an aim that was first articulated by Sartre in *The War Diaries* (Sartre 1999: 294–319), where he expressed the desire to understand both Kaiser Wilhelm II, including the role of his withered arm, and the First World War. The progressive–regressive method has three phases. The first is a phenomenological description akin to that carried out in *Being and Nothingness*. This leads us into the confusing vocabulary which Sartre employs to describe the ontological status of human reality (Being In-itself, Being For-itself and Being For-others), the details of such terminology, although extremely important, need not detain us. It is sufficient here to recognise that this phase describes fundamental features of the human condition such as the ontological freedom to which we are condemned and the central role of our individual project in determining the concrete way in which that freedom is exercised.

Phenomenological descriptions are abstract and atemporal and, as such, are far from sufficient to account for the concrete temporalising praxis of historical agents. If we are to understand an individual's 'historialisation', or the unique way in which they live their times, while being conditioned by them and, in turn, conditioning them, then we will require much more than the first phase of the method.

The second phase of the method is that of regressive analysis. The aim here is to identify the 'formal' conditions of the possibility of the social environment under investigation. This is the conventional terrain of sociology. In other words, it is a search for the factors that make the whole under investigation possible, and, therefore, render it *partly* intelligible. If it were not for the fact that the term 'concept' has a specific 'technical' meaning in the work of Sartre, one might say that the regressive phase of the analysis is a conceptualising phase. This would be inaccurate due to the atemporal nature of concepts, but it is helpful if we regard the search for concepts as a 'rough equivalence' of what is achieved in the regressive analysis. Again, we encounter a whole new lexicon of terms. The regressive analysis is the identification of praxis, praxis-process, the practico-inert and mediating thirds in relation to the object of study. Praxis-process denotes the deviation of praxis by impersonal forces, the practico-inert is matter in which past praxis is inscribed, and the mediating third is each member of a group as they are witness to and totalise the reciprocity of the other members of the group. More familiar 'formal conditions' would be base and superstructure, which are not referred to often by Sartre, and class identity.

There are, however, other conditions which are identified in the regressive analysis, but these are not referred to as 'formal'. An example of these would be the milieu in which an individual spent their childhood. All the struct-ures identified in the regressive analysis are mediating factors between the individual and the social world. The danger, which Sartre identifies with Marxist economism, but might equally be regarded as a fault of most soci-ology, is that emphasis is placed solely on regressive analysis while neglecting to consider the progressive movement.

The progressive phase aims at grasping the unique 'personalisation', or 'historialisation' of an individual historical agent. It is here that the analysis reaches its most concrete. Here the individual must be studied in conjunc-tion with their times, such as Sartre's study of Stalin and the drive for 'socialism in one country' in the Soviet Union in the 1930s, or 'Flaubert in the context of the rise of the modern novel as a bourgeois art form and the social and political ambiguities of the Second Empire' (Flynn 1997: 115). The investigation will be complete when we achieve a comprehension of the individual's own comprehension of the times in which they live and their own historical action.

From a disciplinary point of view such an analysis is complex and extremely demanding. Not only are we dealing with the convolutions of Sartrean philosophy, but also uniquely Sartrean forms of psychoanalysis and sociology, and, in addition, a great deal of historical and biographical infor-mation is required. The most important difference between the progressive–regressive method and any other broad ranging synthetic method is the manner in which the information from the various auxiliary disciplines is synthesised. That aspect is not yet fully clear. As outlined here, there is a connection between the individual and the social world through constituting praxis, but we do not yet have a justification of the study of a *specific* individual as anything other than *an* example which does not contribute to our *general* understanding of that in which we are interested. It is here that Sartre's discussion of incarnation, through a study of boxing, can be of assistance.

Boxing and incarnation

Sartre begins his analysis of boxing by claiming that 'from the very outset we note that the deep truth of every individual fight is competition for titles' (Sartre 1991b: 18). There is a hierarchical arrangement to the evening as it builds toward the main fight. Sartre argues that the hierarchy is interiorised by the boxers themselves:

> These two men very much (seemingly) at their ease, who climb into the ring amid the applause in their brightly coloured robes, are in themselves 'common individuals': they contain within them the opponents they have already defeated and, via this mediation, the entire universe of boxing. In another way, you can say that the hierarchy supports them: that they are its illuminated peaks.
>
> (Sartre 1991b: 19)

Sartre therefore, argues that the movement of a particular evening of boxing is a reproduction of that of the particular boxer's life. This means that we can only understand a particular fight through all other fights and through the totality, or more properly, the detotalised totality of world boxing as a whole. Each fight produces a retotalisation of boxing by providing a new result which will either confirm or alter the hierarchy with which that specific fight began.

Sartre argues that the whole of boxing is present throughout each moment of a fight. Boxing is present at every moment as an inert condition in the technical abilities of the fighters and in the invention by which each fighter creates, with that set of technical abilities, a unique fight. In this way, there is a transcendence of the techniques which the boxers have learned, yet every action is also a realisation of the techniques which they have acquired. Sartre is arguing that each fight is the incarnation of boxing as a whole, with its hierarchical structure, governing bodies, rules, promoters, spectators and tickets, in addition to the specific techniques and training. He then extends this claim further when he argues that each fight is the incarnation of all violence.

Sartre argues that in a boxing match the urgency and fundamentality of violence, which has its foundation in scarcity, is removed. He claims that the links between such violence and scarcity, which result in urgency, are broken and there is an insertion of the mediation of the 'entire group' and something of a 'sterilisation' of the event through the introduction of a prize and judges. This removes the urgency of the violence and leads to a situation in which, he claims, there is rarely any real hatred, the fight becomes functional; it is a job. The fight is then a spectacle which acquires social values. Violence is equated with strength and therefore Good. There is, however, a reality to the spectacle of violence in the form of a boxing match. It cannot be claimed that the spectacle is the presentation of exclusively imaginary violence for the spectators. Sartre argues that contrary to the notion that the violence is imaginary, it is rather, the incarnation of fundamental violence.

Aronson (1987) notes that this is very different from Roland Barthes's treatment of wrestling in *Mythologies* (1993). Barthes treats wrestling as a performance which, as a result of the fact that it is staged, or planned violence, he is correct to do. Sartre argues, however, that this approach cannot be taken with boxing. It would not hold the status that it does were the violence fictional:

> But the spectator of that purified brawl is an actor, because it is really taking place in front of him. He encourages the boxers or finds fault with them, he shouts, he thinks he is making the event as it takes place. His violence is wholly present and he tries to communicate it to the combatants, in order to hasten the course of the fight. That violence, moreover, is not satisfied with objectively helping the efforts of each antagonist. It would not be violence without favouring, without preferring, without opting to be partisan.
>
> (Sartre 1991b: 25–6)

Sartre argues that the spectator backs one of the fighters and that in following this individual, the spectator effectively fights through the mediation of the boxer that he or she supports. Sartre even argues that, as a result of this, the spectator becomes the incarnation of violence. He notes that violence can erupt in the audience, and that the anger that is present, from both the crowd and the fighters, is dormant until the fight begins.

The spectators therefore, are correct to feel part of the fight; they are. Sartre argues that the incarnation of violence in the boxing match is a totalisation because violence stems from scarcity, so during the fight there is an expression of violence that originates outside the fight; an expression of violence that has its origins elsewhere. It is in this sense that the fight is the incarnation of *all* violence.

The fight is a totalisation because it is the event by which specific acts of violence are gathered together and expressed. Sartre is not referring to violence as a general entity, but specific acts of violence. He argues that fundamental violence is wholly present at a boxing match, but, in addition to this, he claims that it is always wholly present, and the fact that it is present in one place does not mean that it is not wholly present elsewhere. Sartre refers to *all* violence because he is attempting to reach the unifying act of the individual subject and in doing so he must resist attempts to fragment violence into its various manifestations. For Sartre, all violent acts are interconnected; to describe an act of violence, which is after all, as Aronson (1987) notes, a praxis that has its roots in scarcity, as *all* violence, is to regard it as:

> [the] re-exteriorisation of interiorized scarcity. But this scarcity is never an abstract principle, or one external to the social ensemble. At every instant, it is a synthetic relation of all men to non-human materiality and of all men among themselves through this materiality, inasmuch as the ensemble of techniques, relations of production and historical circumstances give this relation its determination and its unity.
>
> (Sartre 1991b: 28)

So, for Sartre, any violent act is the re-exteriorisation of a real scarcity that is an element of facticity shared, and interiorised by all, which is not only an important, but a conditioning, aspect of their lived experience. Sartre argues, 'it is enough to see how much oppression, alienation and misery the act of a drunken father who beats a child gathers within itself, in order to understand that all the social violence of our system has made itself into that man and his present rage' (Sartre 1991b: 28).

Sartre does not regard incarnation as the 'conceptualisation of experience' nor as the 'exemplification of the concept'. He argues that incarnation is praxis or praxis-process. Spectators create the fight in their spectating. It is therefore impossible to regard someone as an observer of violence. The act of observation is also, simultaneously, praxis. It is complicity, as is the deliberate act of non-violence. Sartre argues that we primarily have a lived, rather than a cognitive, relationship to incarnation. He claims that the fight is a life and death struggle. When the spectators call for a knockout, they are calling for death. Sartre regards this as concrete, not symbolic. Regardless of what happens to the fighter who is knocked out – whether he dies, or, as is more likely, recovers – the spectators have called for the extreme, which brings the end of the fight.

The act of incarnation is, therefore, a material process and, as such, it is totally real. In it there is a concretisation of latent violence and a realisation of the desires of both the spectators and all those in whom scarcity produces latent violence. Sartre is therefore, asserting that 'the very meaning and substance of this match, here, can only be the vast progressive totalization which is history itself' (Aronson 1987: 63).

Given that Sartre has described a boxing match as being a particular fight with temporal specificity, boxing as a whole, and all human violence, he must now go on to look more closely at the concrete universals of boxing as a whole and all human violence. In doing this he must move from immediate totalisations to 'mediated totalisations'. In moving on to look at the 'ensemble of mediations' which are features of the reciprocal production of an event (in this case, a boxing match), and the various actors involved in such an event, Sartre must look at institutions and social structures. He notes that boxing is an exploitative, bourgeois institution that is economically driven and draws its labour force from the exploited and then proceeds to inflict an additional form of exploitation on them. He claims that, as most boxers are members of the working class, they are conditioned in violence and when they fight they incarnate the violence inflicted on the working class by the ruling class in the form of scarcity. Sartre argues that such violence can serve revolutionary and class purposes, but only when 'absorbed in social praxis'. When violence that incarnates the violence of scarcity takes the form of individual violence it is counterproductive. Rather than working for the interests of the exploited class, it works against them. By becoming a professional boxer, the individual is attempting to break free of his class. The structural violence of scarcity requires a collective response; the individual incarnation of such violence is, for Sartre, a diversion which serves the ruling class.

The individual boxer, therefore, is working against his own class. Sartre claims that the same process is in operation when, as Fanon (1990) noted, natives of colonial nations are violent towards each other, or when members of the exploited class are further exploited in their mobilisation as members of paramilitary groups of the right. Sartre regards such acts not only as a transcendence of facticity or given situation, but also as attempts to escape one's class. Sartre claims that through training, the psychological approach to the sport, the required strength and the notion of the 'art' of boxing, the sport 'produces its man'. He refers to the point an individual becomes a boxer as 'the contractual moment'. At this point the fighter pursues the project of escaping his class through the commodification of his violence. This is contrasted with the project of those who purchase that violence as a means of profit. This is the 'decisive instant of incarnation' (Sartre 1991b: 37). The boxer is, therefore, socially defined by his alienated violence. Boxing becomes a transcendence that aims at the universal and which is the individual's chosen manifestation of their original alienation. It also preserves the particularity of the fighter.

Sartre emphasises the importance of the particular within the general to the event. He argues that the individuality of the fighters is essential; they could not be the human equivalent of robots. Each fighter must have individual characteristics and features which *signify* them to the spectators. It is the individuality of the fighters which concretises the event for the spectators. Sartre regards necessity and contingency as having an internal link; they are not in opposition to each other. He is arguing that chance is dialectically intelligible. Contingency is necessary, and, as a result, events such as a punch during a boxing match are both singular and universal. This contingency and singularity of the event leads, for Sartre, to the singularisation of all boxing and all violence.

For Sartre, the boxer is a worker whose violence is mediated by capitalist institutions. He notes that the boxer as worker makes money for entrepreneurs and is selling his labour to make a living. He also notes that fighters are treated like machinery while in preparation for a fight. This alienates the boxer from his body. While it would be possible to restrict the number of fights to limit the damage to the fighter, this is rarely the situation because of the fact that the market demands that boxers are as productive as possible, and the fighters themselves know that it is only through fighting that they can advance their careers. At all but the highest level, therefore, they are unable to reduce the frequency of the fights, which maintains the degree of exploitation.

The liberating potential of the fighter's violence is lost by the fact that he is taught to save his violence for the fight and to be passive when he is not fighting. The violence of the boxer serves the ruling class, while the boxer attempts to escape his class. Sartre notes that there is only class movement in a small minority of cases. The fighter remains exploited in the act of selling his violence and finds himself in a similar situation to the worker, but the boxer is isolated, unlike the workers who have at least established a degree of class solidarity. The violence which the boxer inflicts on members of his own class is the same violence which is inflicted on oppressed groups by the ruling class through capitalist exploitation and, vice versa, in class struggle. The fact that a successful fighter will be able to sell his labour for a higher price following an important victory means that we are no longer faced with the situation of worked matter mediating between human beings, but rather humans are themselves the worked matter. It is the alienation of the violence of the oppressed, which is incarnated in the specific event, that is a particular boxing match. It is incarnated because it is alienation in this form that is present in the actions of all oppressive regimes.

There is a derealisation of the violence in a boxing match in the sense that that which is temporary is represented as permanent. It is a mystification of the real nature of the violence in the fight. This is present in the notion that the solution to the conflict is in the fight, which is, of course, false. Sartre argues that along with the derealisation there is a simultaneous 'breaking out' of this mystification. The fight presents the derealisation, but simultaneously all those involved with the fight, in whatever capacity, are pulled towards the reality of the situation. The antagonism is that of the competitive market, and the fighters are both products and victims of capitalism despite the fact that workers are involved in class struggle against capitalism. Sartre places great emphasis on the fact that the spectators are witnessing a *real* incarnation of conflict in the working class, not a symbolic representation of it. The fact that the fighters have sold their labour (their violence) means that the violence is not revolutionary, but, rather, the source of profit that is organised by the capitalist to maximise profitability.

Incarnation is therefore, for Sartre, the 'totalization of everything' which is irreducible to abstractions, it is an 'oriented totalization' which is concrete. The specific event of a punch gives everything; it is the singularisation of everything that is contained in the social whole. If anything in the social whole were different, the specific concrete reality that is this punch would not be possible.

How does this analysis of boxing compare to some of the major studies conducted by sociologists? Wacquant (1995) reduces the explanation of the boxer's own view of their action to general perceptions shared by many boxers, such as the view that boxing is an art, involving skill, rather than simply violence. There is also the view that boxing is a way of earning a living that is somehow superior to the other work available to the lower working class. In addition, Wacquant cites the respect with which boxers are held within their own community (even by drug dealers), and a widespread loathing of the sport on the part of the fighters themselves. This, however, is inadequate. There is no individual (real) biography in either the work of Wacquant or the work of Sugden (1996). Both Sugden and Wacquant limit themselves to naming the boxer and, at most, giving the briefest account of that boxer's background. This approach does not allow us to progress to a point of synthesis, but leaves us stranded without an 'inner relation of comprehension' (Sartre 1999: 301) between the various accounts which are each on different levels. This leaves Wacquant (1992) discussing the role of 'pugilistic folklore', which is really an aspect of the practico-inert encountered by boxers, but failing to recognise the proper significance of the discussion because of his inability to produce a synthetic account grounded in praxis. The same point could be made in relation to the work of Sugden (1996). In his account of 'the farm system', he sets out to produce a synthetic unification of biography, history and society in the mould of Mills. Like Mills, however, he does not develop his analysis far enough and struggles to explain boxing as a detotalised totality.

A progressive–regressive account of boxing would have to be temporally specific and consider the praxis of an individual. If we take the example with which we began, the 'Rumble in the Jungle' would be analysed (following a detailed phenomenological description) by conducting a regressive analysis to explore the role of praxis, the practico-inert, mediating thirds, group identity and other 'formal' conditions, such as economic base and ideological superstructure. Praxis would include Ali's political action, the way he dealt with the media and his preparation, tactics and actions during the fight. The practico-inert would include the venue, 'pugilistic folklore', gym life, Ali's fame and any role that was perceived for him as a representative of his race, his religion, or the nation of Islam; there would also be the fact that Ali had been stripped of his title and endured a period during which he could not fight, the fact that Ali was no longer World Champion, and the violence and possibility of death that exists in boxing. The role of spectators, the media and Ali and Foreman themselves as mediating thirds would have to be analysed. In addition, issues of racial, class and religious identity, the role of big business, governing bodies and the media, and the various ideological positions adopted by those watching, organising and participating in the fight would feature in the regressive analysis.

The regressive analysis would also look at existential structures such as the details of Ali's early childhood. The progressive analysis would identify evidence of a fundamental project, or an original choice of the manner in which Ali lives his facticity or historialises his times. Flynn summarises the motivation for this when he points out that

> without an existentialist hermeneutic of the signs of an original choice (the progressive movement), we would have to be satisfied with such 'general particularities' as 'the Soviet bureaucracy' or 'the petit bourgeoisie' – terms Sartre associates with Marxist economism. Biography would be dissolved in impersonal history. But without the dialectical interplay of micro- and macrototalization (the regressive movement), history would shrivel into biography.
>
> (1997: 115–16)

By conducting both the regressive and the progressive movements we are able to provide a synthetic account of the unique totalisation that is the specific incarnation of boxing in the fight between Ali and Foreman. It is in the preservation of the personal and the impersonal aspects of the event that a synthesis is made possible.

Conclusion

There are three areas which we should briefly discuss by way of a conclusion. First, the role of incarnation in linking the regressive and progressive elements of Sartre's method; second, the issue of the general and the particular in relation to the progressive–regressive method; and, finally, the relationship between Sartre's discussion of boxing and work conducted by sociologists of sport.

The progressive–regressive method is threatened by the problem of synthesising the details of the individual biography with the wider social and historical context in which the individual exists. It would be comparatively simple to link the two 'with an and' to produce a sum of the significations of an event, but, as we have argued, this is inadequate. The notion of incarnation and the accompanying emphasis on individual praxis as constitutive allows us to recognise that the individual action incarnates the social whole while being altered by that whole and, in turn, altering and retotalising it. As a result, it is through the study of the individual and their comprehension of their time that we reach the most concrete level of socio-historical analysis. It is here that a synthesis, rather than a sum, can be achieved.

A major criticism which can be levelled at Sartre is that he is overly negative in relation to the general plane while continually employing it to great effect. This point is stressed by Aronson (1987), yet Aronson is more critical of Sartre's tone than his actual pronouncements on the issue. Incarnation is at the heart of this problem. Sartre claims that there are two approaches to dialectical analysis. The first is that of 'decompressive expansion' which involves movement from the object to the whole (or the concrete to the abstract, or the particular to the universal). This involves understanding the specifics to form a picture of the whole. Sartre argues for a reversal of this process (totalising compression), claiming that each of the specifics is present in the whole and is a contributing factor to the singularisation of that whole, such as the boxing match. Sartre is not claiming that the general does not exist, simply that it is incarnated in the particular and that, as a result, it is more abstract and therefore not the terminal point of any analysis. Incarnation effectively removes anything other than a conceptual distinction between the general and particular. This is a corollary of dialectical analysis.

The role of boxing here has simply been to illustrate incarnation, yet the discussion provides an interesting contribution to debates within the sociology of sport relating to boxing. Sugden (1996) constructs a telling argument against Elias and Dunning's (1986) attempt to characterise sport as part of a civilising process. Yet Sugden barely escapes essentialism by regarding as persuasive the view that boxing is a 'parody of the human condition' which captures the 'timeless human struggle for survival and mastery' (Sugden 1996: 177). What seems to be overlooked by both Elias and Dunning and Sugden is the possibility that the appeal of boxing has persisted over time because of a number of factors which differ through time. The alienating nature of capitalism may allow the incarnation of fundamental violence through boxing in its modern form, yet what appears to be the same appeal of boxing may require a different explanation if we turn our attention far enough back in history. Sartre's discussion of boxing allows us to clarify and make sense of observations such as the claim that, 'through both participation and spectatorship, sport provides opportunities for people to express repressed potentials and feel basic human urges in settings which do not pose a threat to a given social order' (Sugden 1996: 178). We must ask what these 'repressed potentials' are; why are they repressed? And what are the 'basic human urges' referred to? The discussion of incarnation provides some possible answers to these questions.

Finally, we have argued that the sociology of sport tends to concentrate on regressive analysis to the exclusion of the progressive movement. This means that although there is much to be drawn from studies of boxing, such as those conducted by Sugden (1996) or Wacquant (1992, 1995, 1998), they must be regarded as providing a contribution to the regressive analysis rather than synthetic accounts in their own right.

References

Aronson, R. (1987) *Sartre's Second Critique*, Chicago: University of Chicago Press.

Barnes, H.E. (1981) *Sartre and Flaubert*, Chicago: University of Chicago Press.

Barthes, R. (1993) *Mythologies*, London: Vintage.

Catalano, J.S. (1974) *A Commentary on Jean-Paul Sartre's Being and Nothingness*, Chicago: University of Chicago Press.

—— (1986) *A Commentary on Jean-Paul Sartre's Critique of Dialectical Reason. Vol. I: Theory of Practical Ensembles*, Chicago: University of Chicago Press.

Dunning, E., Maguire, J. and Pearton, R. (eds) (1993) *The Sports Process: A Comparative and Developmental Approach*, Champaign, Illinois: Human Kinetics.

Elias, N. and Dunning, E. (1986) *Quest for Excitement: Sport and Leisure in the Civilizing Process*, Oxford: Blackwell.

Fanon, F. (1990) *The Wretched of the Earth*, trans. C. Farrington, Harmondsworth: Penguin.

Flynn, T.R. (1984) *Sartre and Marxist Existentialism: The Test Case of Collective Responsibility*, Chicago: University of Chicago Press.

—— (1992) 'Sartre and the poetics of history', in C. Howells (ed.) *The Cambridge Companion to Sartre*, Cambridge: Cambridge University Press.

—— (1997) *Sartre, Foucault and Historical Reason. Vol. I: Towards an Existentialist Theory of History*, Chicago: University of Chicago Press.

Giddens, A. (1976) *New Rules of Sociological Method*, London: Hutchinson.
—— (1986) *Sociology: A Brief but Critical Introduction*, London: Macmillan Education.
Gruneau, R. (1991) 'Sport and "esprit de corps": notes on power, culture and the politics of the body', in F. Landry, M. Landry and M. Yerlès (eds) *Sport: The Third Millennium*, Sainte-Foy: Les Presses de l'Université Laval.
—— (1993) 'The critique of sport in modernity: theorising power, culture, and the politics of the body', in E. Dunning, J. Maguire and R. Pearton (eds) *The Sports Process: A Comparative and Developmental Approach*, Champaign, Illinois: Human Kinetics.
—— (1999) *Class, Sports and Social Development* (new edn), Champaign, Illinois: Human Kinetics.
Hegel, G.W.F. (1977) *The Phenomenology of Spirit*, trans. A.V. Miller, Oxford: Oxford University Press.
Heidegger, M. (1992) *The Concept of Time*, trans. W. McNeill, Oxford: Blackwell.
—— (1996) *Being and Time*, trans. J. Stambaugh, Albany: State University of New York Press.
Howells, C. (ed.) (1992) *The Cambridge Companion to Sartre*, Cambridge: Cambridge University Press.
Landry, F., Landry, M. and Yerlès, M. (eds) (1991) *Sport: The Third Millennium*, Sainte-Foy: Les Presses de l'Université Laval.
Mailer, N. (1975) *The Fight*, Harmondsworth: Penguin.
Marqusee, M. (1999) *Redemption Song*, London: Verso.
Mills, C.W. (1959) *The Sociological Imagination*, New York: Oxford University Press.
Sartre, J-P. (1958) *Being and Nothingness: An Essay on Phenomenological Ontology*, trans. H.E. Barnes, London: Routledge.
—— (1963) *The problem of method*, trans. H. E. Barnes, London: Methuen.
—— (1968) *Search for a Method*, trans. H.E. Barnes, New York: Vintage.
—— (1981) *The Family Idiot: Gustave Flaubert 1821–1857*, 5 vols, trans. C. Cosman, Chicago: University of Chicago Press.
—— (1991a) *Critique of Dialectical Reason. Vol. I: Theory of Practical Ensembles*, trans. A. Sheridan-Smith, London: Verso.
—— (1991b) *Critique of Dialectical Reason. Vol. II: The Intelligibility of History*, trans. Q. Hoare, London: Verso.
—— (1992a) *Notebooks for an Ethics*, Chicago: University of Chicago Press.
—— (1992b) *Truth and Existence*, Chicago: University of Chicago Press.
—— (1995a) *Anti-semite and Jew*, trans. G.J. Becker, New York: Schocken.
—— (1995b) *The Psychology of the Imagination*, London: Routledge.
—— (1997) *Existentialism and Humanism*, trans. P. Mairet, London: Methuen.
—— (1999) *The War Diaries: Notebooks from a Phoney War 1939–40*, trans. Q. Hoare, London: Verso.
Schilpp, P.A. (ed.) (1981) *The Philosophy of Jean-Paul Sartre*, La Salle, Illinois: Open Court.
Sheard, K. (1990) *Boxing in the Civilising Process*, unpublished DPhil dissertation, Council for National Academic Awards, Anglia Polytechnic: Norwich.
Sugden, J. (1996) *Boxing and Society: An International Analysis*, Manchester: Manchester University Press.
Wacquant, L. (1992) 'The social logic of boxing in Black Chicago: toward a sociology of pugilism', *Sociology of Sport* 9(3): 221–54.

—— (1995) 'The pugilistic point of view: how boxers think and feel about their trade', *Theory and Society* 24(4): 489–535.

—— (1998) 'A fleshpeddler at work: power, pain, and profit in the prizefighting economy', *Theory and Society* 27(1): 1–42.

6 Critical social research and political intervention
Moralistic versus radical approaches

Ian McDonald

Good sociology is often radical. A sociology which is not good, cannot be radical in any larger sense.

(Becker 1986: 85)

Introduction

In 1999, the England and Wales Cricket Board (ECB) published its racial equality strategy, *Clean Bowl Racism*. This was a significant development for a sport in which a culture of denial about racism was deeply entrenched within the governing body and amongst its leading commentators in the media. In publishing the report, the ECB had succumbed to persistent and mounting political pressure to recognise its responsibility for removing racial inequality in the game. Not least important in securing this commitment from the ECB were the activities of the lobbying group Hit Racism for Six (HR46), combined with the publication in 1998 of an academic research report, *Anyone for Cricket?*, which concluded that a culture of racial exclusion existed in local league cricket (McDonald and Ugra 1998a). There were many other important factors that also lay behind the shift in the ECB's position. I have provided an analysis of this elsewhere, as well as a critique of the document *Clean Bowl Racism* (Carrington and McDonald 2002). However, in this chapter I will draw on my experiences in the four years from 1995 to 1999, as the secretary of Hit Racism for Six and as the co-author of *Anyone for Cricket?*, to discuss the relationship between critical social research, political intervention and political activism. I will use the different 'speaking positions' (Back and Solomos 1993) that I, as political activist and as social researcher, adopted during the four years from 1995 in order to articulate and argue for a distinctive relationship between critical social research, political intervention and political activism.

Critical social research is characterised by a concern to interrogate and expose relations of social power, not merely as a disinterested academic exercise, but as part of a broader project of progressive social transformation. It is the 'unity of theory and practice', summarised in the Marxian concept of 'praxis' that distinguishes critical social research as a sociological paradigm. As Harvey (1990: 20) writes, 'not only does [critical social research] want to show what is happening, it is also concerned with doing something about it. Critical social research includes an overt political struggle against oppressive structures.' So, researchers not only seek to highlight forms of inequality and injustice, but also view the research act itself as constituting a challenge to the status quo. It produces knowledge that is intended to 'empower the oppressed' by enabling them 'to come to understand and change their own oppressive realities' (Lather 1986: 261–2). Clearly then, critical social research sits in stark contradiction to common-sense understanding of scholarly research as a process of disinterested information gathering, based on the concept of value-neutrality.

However, the relationship between theory and practice, or more specifically between research and political struggle, is complex. For example, what forms of articulation are embedded in this 'relationship' and in what ways is the 'unity' of theory and practice conceptualised? Further, is it possible to reconcile a commitment to progressive political change with sound sociological scholarship, or is the concept of academic integrity itself ideologically charged? These are some of the issues I want to tackle in this chapter. I will present a twofold typology of the different relationships between research and anti-racist political struggle within the critical social research approach. I have labelled these: 'moralistic' and 'radical'. Although both of these can be located as examples of critical social research, they each offer distinctive ways of conceiving the relationship between research and political struggle. In terms of reconciling the transformational aspirations of critical social research with scholarly integrity, I will argue that the moralistic approach is most problematic and that the radical approach is most fruitful. Before looking at each of the approaches in more detail, I will outline the critical social research approach as it has developed within the sociology of sport. This is not merely a necessary contextual preamble to the discussion on moralistic and radical social research, but I also offer a critique of the critical sociology of sport that bears directly on the issue of research and political interventions. The nub of my critique is that the critical sociology of sport is characterised by a theory of agency that denies the possibility of fundamental social change and therefore militates against the carrying out of research that is politically interventionist.

The problem of agency in the critical sociology of sport

The critical sociology of sport is a broad term that is made up from a range of theoretical perspectives and research methodologies. Antecedents of the critical approach can be found in particular schools of thought, from the neo-Marxist multi-disciplinary analysis of culture and ideology developed by the Frankfurt School, the Weberian-influenced interpretive work of the Chicago School, to the Gramscian inspired analyses of identity and cultural

power developed by the Centre for Contemporary Cultural
CS), Birmingham, England. More recent developments in social
have also been claimed for the critical sport sociology tradition
including, for example, feminist and post-structuralist perspectives (see relevant chapters in Coakley and Dunning (2000) for an overview of these
perspectives). The critical sociology of sport can therefore be conceptualised
as theoretically eclectic, multidisciplinary, and dynamic: it is associated but
by no means theoretically reducible to Marxism; it draws on contributions
from disciplines ranging from history to pyschoanalysis; and it is constantly
developing in responses to theoretical, political and social challenges.

However, critical sport sociology is also an institutionalised form of
knowledge that, like all sociology, is itself a constitutive element of what
Bourdieu (1994) refers to as the 'intellectual field', which in turn is inscribed
by relations of power. So the decision to publish or not, to be invited to speak
at conferences, to edit key journals and to shape the field in terms of its key
concepts and legitimate areas for inquiry are all aspects of power relations in
the discipline. Following Bourdieu's logic, we can say that, although it has a
degree of autonomy, this 'intellectual field' of the sociology of sport, institutionalised in the academy, and more specifically in the form of associations
like the North American Society for the Sociology of Sport (NASSS), is partly
encompassed by the wider 'meta' field of power (Bourdieu 1994: 140–9).
That is, depending on the material conditions of existence and the political
orientation of critical sport sociology, it can serve dominant interests and
therefore be more encompassed by the wider field of power, or it can expose
dominant interests and secure a greater degree of autonomy for itself. Critical
sport sociology, armed with 'hegemony' as a concept and a strategy, claims,
almost by definition, to be concerned with the latter and committed to 'radi-
cally-transformative' praxis. However, as I now outline, this is a commitment
that exists only in the abstract as the operationalisation of hegemony is less
about identifying the conditions for social transformation and more about
theorising resistance, identity and difference.

In the historiography of sport sociology, the term 'critical' has meant, to a
very great extent, Marxism, or rather a particular appropriation of Marxism.
Writing in the early 1980s, John Hargreaves (1982) identified three types of
approaches within the Marxist tradition – namely, correspondence theory,
reproduction theory and hegemony theory. The first two were rejected
because they gave reductionist accounts of sport that left no space for the
creative possibilities and the emancipatory potential of sport which could be
accounted for in Gramscian or hegemony theory; the third approach was
identified and favoured by Hargreaves (in the early 1980s at least). As critical sport sociology is heavily framed by the Gramscian concept of
hegemony, I will refer to critical sport sociology and hegemony theory interchangeably.

However, Morgan (1994) has delivered a telling critique of the role of
agency in hegemony theory as it has been appropriated by critical sport soci-

ology. He argues that its conceptualisation of agency fails to live up to the emancipatory and transformative task set by itself. The privileged agents of social change, the working class, have been deemed by hegemony theorists to have failed in their historical role. Dominant myths about sport have been largely successful in securing both their individual and collective accommodative agency. Individual and collective oppositional agency exhausts the limits of possibility, with radical-transformative agency effectively a redundant category (1994: 94–114). Indeed the lexicon of critical sport sociology resounds with terms like 'resistance', 'appropriation' and 'contestation'; it speaks of the politics of consumption and style (Tomlinson 1990) and of the subversive power of pleasure (Whannel 1993). Of course, this line of argument need not cast any doubt over the richness and importance of the nuanced interrogations of the negotiated nature of cultural power, structure and agency that characterises critical sport sociology at its best. But it is the realm of 'negotiation', as the end of the process rather than the step towards practical change, that tends to frame the range of possibilities. The problem is that theoretically critical sport sociology is without an agency for fundamental radical transformation.

The roots of this dilemma can be partly found in the particular appropriation of hegemony. Hegemony theory emerged as a reaction against class-based Marxist analyses, which identified the working class, located at the point of production, as both the object and subject of social transformation. Essentially it was a disillusionment with this so-called economistic framework, widespread amongst left academics during the 1970s, that paved the way for an alternative reading of Marxism, via a particular Eurocommunist interpretation of Gramsci's concept of hegemony, which stressed the importance of cultural struggle. This interpretation juxtaposed Gramsci's 'war of manoeuvre', which was deemed inappropriate for conditions prevailing in advanced Western capitalist societies, with the necessity for a 'war of position' requiring long-term ideological struggle for hegemony in the realm of culture (Hoffman 1984: 150). Popular cultural forms and practices, it was argued – principally by those working at the influential CCCS, could be viewed neither as an unambiguous site for class-based ways of life nor as the ideological support of capitalist social relations of production. They were shaped by a complex and often contradictory set of limits and pressures. By the 1980s, the 'Gramscian' concept of hegemony was fashionable. Popular culture and therefore sport were viewed as a site for hegemonic struggle. However, the degree of fit between the material conditions of existence and academic fashion was not lost on Gruneau who felt that, 'the historical coincidence of the later tendency [privileging resistance through culture] with the successes of Thatcherism and Reaganism in the 1980s is discomforting' (1988: 25), and he warned against a 'celebratory optimism about the autonomous nature and oppositional possibilities of almost all forms of "pleasurable" popular cultural practices' (*ibid.*).

Whilst for Gramsci the concept of hegemony does not obviate the need for struggle, it was interpreted as a way of moving from a ruptural transformation towards the gradual modification of society. Furthermore, in privileging culture as a realm of strategic intervention, it legitimised a politics of intellectual production in the academy as a form of 'praxis'. Theory and practice could mean theory as practice. From this perspective the working class would inevitably disappoint as its subjective cultural power has historically been heavily circumscribed by its own internal differences and by dominant class interests. But by rejecting the centrality of class in the analysis of social power, it is a short step to questioning both the desirability and the viability of transformation, which in fact is precisely the position articulated by Gruneau in his reflective postscript to *Class, Sports and Social Development*:

> New critical theories of power and difference call into question the possibility of achieving any kind of 'universal' emancipation or freedoms in and through sport.
>
> (Gruneau 1999: 121)

The danger here is that research as a form of political intervention becomes at best a contingent rather than a necessary aspect of critical sociology. But the importance of any form of concrete progressive political engagement is that it acts as a bulwark against the debilitating effects of institutionalisation and professionalisation. As Gouldner remarked (1973: 61):

> The development of professionalization among sociologists deserves to be opposed ... It means the substitution of a routine and banal code of ethics for a concern with the serious kind of morality on which alone objectivity might rest.

Critical sport sociology's vulnerability to these effects are compounded because of its commitment to a form of praxis that is social democratic – that is a political position that seeks to analyse dominant social relations, rather than critique and fundamentally transform them. The disjuncture between an abstract radicalism and a critical practice leaves the door open for political opportunists like Jon Entine to moralise with NASSS about their lack of anti-racist credentials (see the correspondence on the NASSS Server List, 1, 3 August 2000) and less gallingly for liberal political philosophers like Morgan to steal the critical mantle. Morgan's abstract invocation of the logical integrity of sport itself, coupled with an idealistic call to what he calls 'Sporting-practice communities', fundamentally ignores structures of power in society.

Critical sport sociology may not be defined by a commitment to political intervention, but a critical sociology that denies it will soon find itself occupying a privileged position in the 'meta' field of power that it claimed and claims to oppose. The key issue that is then raised is the relationship between the research process and political intervention. As I outline below, there are two approaches that can be identified, the first of which is what I have called moralistic social research.

'Moralistic' social research: political activism as research

The methodological point of departure for critical social research is a damning critique of 'value-neutrality'. The belief in value-neutrality stemmed from the influence of positivist interpretations of natural science, where it was believed that the application of scientific (objective and politically 'detached') knowledge, could be applied to practical problems in society. However, as Hammersley laments in a defence of value-neutrality, 'in recent decades the balance of opinion has swung to the point where few would defend that principle' (2000: 1). Critics of value-neutrality argue that it acts more as an ideological device to obscure the value-commitment of the researchers, the effects of their work and the social functions that it performs.

Howard Becker's article, 'Whose side are we on?', originally published in 1967, was one of the earliest and certainly most influential arguments against value-neutrality. Becker asserted that political partisanship was not only inevitable but also desirable in social research. In defending his affiliation to the perspective of the 'underdog', Becker declared, 'the question is not whether we should take sides, since we inevitably will, but rather whose side are we on?' (Becker 1971: 123). As a starting point, this is not necessarily a problematic stance. Indeed, arguing against claims that sociological research into institutional structures of power can hide behind a protective ideological shield of political neutrality, Bourdieu contends:

> By uncovering the social mechanisms which ensure the maintenance of the established order and whose properly symbolic efficacy rests on the mis-recognition of their logic and effects, social science necessarily takes sides in political struggles.
>
> (1992: 51)

For Becker, one of the reasons he feels that the sociologists should reflexively make their value-system explicit is also to do with creating a level playing ground by which all research can be judged. While 'the sociologist who favours officialdom will be spared the accusation of bias' (*ibid*.: 128) siding with subordinate groups will invite accusations that 'the sympathies of the researcher have biased his [*sic*] work and distorted his findings' (*ibid*.: 124). However, Becker is less persuasive in suggesting how the researcher can defend the scholarly integrity of the research findings. Ultimately he concedes that all we can do is try to prevent our sympathies leading to methodologically invalid techniques and accept the one-sided or partial nature of our findings. Thus we are presented with an account of social research wherein the quest for objectivity is sacrificed on the altar of partisanship.

An example of partisan anti-racist research, where bias is positively embraced and pretence towards objectivity abandoned, can be found in the *Local Politics of Race* (Ben-Tovim *et al.* 1986). The authors examine how race policy is formed in the English cities of Wolverhampton and Liverpool during the mid-1980s, focusing in particular on the role of pressure group politics. The authors are explicit in their dismissal of value-neutrality, which they see as an implicit defence of the status quo, and that the purpose of their research is to inform future political struggles. They follow the position of Lather (1986: 67) who declared that:

> Once we recognise that just as there is no neutral education there is no neutral research, we no longer need to apologise for unabashedly ideological research and its open commitment to using research to criticize and change the status quo.

Ben-Tovim *et al.* place themselves unequivocally on the side of the 'underdog' – that is, the black ethnic minority groups who find themselves excluded from the formal political arena – and they consciously involve themselves in the political arena as activists. The purpose of research is to serve the political struggle and so advance their political cause. Ben-Tovim *et al.* adopt a form of advocacy where they claim, by virtue of their role in political struggles, to speak for the unrepresented minorities. However, Back and Solomos have argued that they fall back into a form of 'radical credentialism which is justified by the researcher's participation in political struggles' (Back and Solomos 1993: 184). The distinction between academic and political activist is collapsed and with it a methodologically transparent and defensible account of their fieldwork. The claim to authority comes from a speaking position as researcher-activist, in which the criterion of validity is defended by reference to their involvement in political struggle, rather than scholarly integrity.

In their book *Race, Politics and Social Change* (1995), Solomos and Back also analyse the politics of race policy in a local authority setting. In a reflective analysis of the research process, they discuss the articulation between research and political intervention, and how they found themselves negotiating different speaking positions. Unlike Ben-Tovim *et al.*, Solomos and Back's study was on those who influence and determine race policy and political outcomes. Their aim was to 'examine processes whereby the structures of racial inequality were maintained' (Back and Solomos 1993: 185). They provide some invaluable guidance to future researchers on the importance of reflexivity in locating the researcher in the research process, in particular viewing interviews with actors as 'interactional samples'. However, a problematic formulation of the relationship between research and political intervention emerges in the course of their discussion of the research process.

As Becker warned in 'Whose side are we on?' (1967), accusations of bias by the authorities towards research that exposes dominant relations of power and vested interests is to be expected. While Back and Solomos attempted to gain the insights and perspective of the more powerful figures in the policy process, they accept that their involvement as activists seeking to capitalise on their research findings led them into compromising situations. They report how they were accused by the then sitting MP, the late Denis Howell, of misrepresentation. Back and Solomos responded to this accusation by writing to the MP to reassure him that they had tried to be fair to all sides of the debate. As they then admit:

> There are obvious contradictions between this and what we have written about in the early part of this paper. There are however, two points to make here. This example shows quite clearly a situation where a particular speaking position may be politically appropriate in the context of a particular political struggle. The point that follows from this is the simple fact that as researchers we give accounts of our work that are dependent upon the context in which our speaking positions are being evaluated. We are not arguing here that anything goes. We are simply saying that as researchers involved in political struggles we may find it necessary to take on strategic academic identities ... The fundamental lesson here is that it is complete folly to believe that our research will be read and evaluated according to its content.
>
> (Back and Solomos 1993: 194–5)

Of course, Back and Solomos are right to recognise that different interested political tendencies will use academic research for their own ends. And it may be necessary – indeed, it is desirable – that social researchers disseminate their research to a wide audience using the appropriate language, and they must always be prepared to enter the political fray to defend their work from distortion. But it is important that researchers do not undermine the academic integrity of the research process by adopting speaking positions out of political expediency. The problems highlighted here go to the heart of the dilemma facing critical social researchers. What is meant by political intervention? What form of engagement is legitimate? Arguably Back and Solomos, in their commitment to 'an anti-racist project that can effect change through research' (1993: 197), have allowed themselves to become sucked into the role of political activists. Apart from the politically 'disengaged' scholarship, there is a crucial distinction that can be made in the understanding of research and political intervention. On the one hand, we can conceive of research that will then be used by the researchers in the political arena to effect change. On the other hand, we can conceive of research as creating the possibility and the conditions for change, and, as such, is a form of political intervention but recognises that political activism exists outside the legitimate realm of scholarly activity. As Becker wrote in an article called 'Radical politics and sociological research', first published in 1972:

> Good sociology is sociological work that produces meaningful descriptions of organisations and events, valid explanations of how they come about and persist, and realistic proposals for their improvement or removal.
>
> (Becker 1986: 85)

Critical social research is concerned with the production of knowledge, while political activism is concerned with securing practical changes. The symbiotic relationship between the two tasks is based on a division of labour, as the ethics of producing sociologically valid research are not always complementary with the agitational and propaganda demands of political activism. Of course, I am referring here to a functional rather than a personal division of labour. Academics can and do, maybe even should, get involved in political activism – but it should be as activists. In his article on the relationship between radical politics and sociological research, Becker also highlights the overlap between radical politics and radical sociology:

> The posture of a radical sociology overlaps considerably with that of a radical politics. Radical sociology also rests on a desire to change society in a way that will increase equality and maximise freedom, and it makes a distinctive contribution to the struggle for change. On the one hand, it provides the knowledge of how society operates on the basis of which a radical critique of inequality can be made. On the other hand, it provides the basis for implementing radical goals, constructing blueprints for freer, more egalitarian social arrangements.
>
> (Becker 1986: 88)

However, he also goes on to explain their distinctiveness:

> The radical sociologist will find that his scientific 'conservatism' – in the sense of being unwilling to draw conclusions on the basis of insufficient evidence – creates tensions with radical activists ... radical action and rhetoric are one thing, and a radically informed sociology is another. Confusing the two opens leftism to any professional opportunism of the moment.
>
> (Becker 1986: 92–3)

The sociologist and the activist are not the same. As the experience of Back and Solomos illustrated, it is not always possible to remain true to the complexity of our own research outside of the academy. However, the boundary marking off scholarship from activism has been transgressed when we depart from an accurate account of our research, no matter how politically expedient it is. Such a position places Back and Solomos closer to the unabashed ideological position of Ben-Tovim *et al.* than they would probably like to be.

Partisanship and objectivity in radical social research

Gouldner (1973) is scornful of Becker's 'underdog sociology' for its crude standpoint epistemology and its failure to reconcile partisanship with objectivity. Although he does not explicitly state it in 'The sociologist as partisan' (1968), the path towards objectivity lies in the direction of critique. In a subsequent paper called 'The two Marxisms' (in Gouldner 1973), he does give a definition of critique which opens up the possibility for the sociologist to attain objectivity:

> A critique takes a given belief system, a theory, ideology, or indeed science itself – or any cultural 'objectification' – as problematic....The aim of a critique is not simply to show a theory to be in error, formally or empirically, for the problem is not only the reliability of the theory's assertions. The 'truth' of a theory does not boil down to its reliability but also involves the nature of its selective perspective on the world. A critique is concerned with the meaning of this selective understanding, examining it in terms of the social forces that led to the focalization of certain perspectives and to the repression or rejection of others. A critique, then, is an hermeneutic.
>
> (Gouldner 1973: 427)

So one possible avenue to objectivity is to develop the ability to examine critically all perspectives, not just the one we are investigating but our own also, and to root these perspectives in their social realities, a task clearly rejected or abandoned in the moralistic approach to research. But, by recognising our own standpoint, Gouldner asserts that we will be better able to understand and do justice to the standpoints of the actors under study. Underpinning this approach is a view that there is no special virtue in those that lack power and authority, any more than in those who possess them. In particular, there is no reason to believe that the perspective of those placed at the bottom of society is more likely to be true than those at the top. Indeed, often their perspective will be the dominant ideology internalised.

And yet, this critical sensitivity, which sits neatly within the debunking tradition of sociology popularised by C.W. Mills's concept of the 'sociological imagination', is by itself insufficient in the attainment of objective partisanship. In the absence of an a priori value system, how does the researcher begin to think about critique? Hammersley identifies two main alternative sources of commitment: the political organisation, group or person, or a set of universal values (2000: 8). Whereas for Becker (*circa* 1967), and Ben-Tovim, the allegiance would lie with a political group or social grouping, for Gouldner it is clearly the latter: 'an empty headed partisanship unable to transcend the immediacies of narrowly conceived political commitment is simply just one more form of market research' (Gouldner 1973: 67). He goes on, 'It is to values, not to factions, that sociologists must give their most basic commitment' (*ibid.*: 1973: 68). The most important value identified by Gouldner is truth, which is attained when research contributes to the expansion of freedom, the equal sharing of power and the development of wholeness to the human condition. Objectivity then is defined as the unification of ideas and reality, an indication of truthful research, which ultimately will produce the possibility of a just society. So defined, partisan research is reconciled with objectivity. Objective partisanship, then, is not a matter of attachment to the personal values of the researcher, but a commitment to a set of universal values that hold out the possibility of bringing about a world in which universal values prevail and human beings are united in peace and justice. The heritage of Enlightenment thinkers such as Comte and Marx is evident here, as Gouldner comments:

> Whether objectivity is thought possible comes down then to a question of whether some vision of human unity is believed workable and desirable.
>
> (*ibid.*: 67)

Thus, Gouldner offers a vision of objectivity that is carved out of the method of critique (thereby avoiding the perils of crude standpoint epistemology) and polished by a set of humanistic values by which we can judge the objectivity of the critique. This is a formula that affirms the sociological legitimacy of partisanship while providing a universal (though still culturally specific) conception of objectivity as research that is directed towards political goals. However, such an approach departs from current postmodern orthodoxy in mainstream sociology and social research, where many people have challenged the historicist metanarrative underpinning Gouldner's conception of objectivity. Postmodern analysis argues that social critique can be no more than epistemological critique since no objective knowledge is possible: there are simply 'knowledges' from different perspectives that are equally valid. Arguably, such a position, in which the possibility of social transformation is not merely discounted as unrealistic but condemned as totalitarian, betrays a conservative political disposition that finds echoes in Callinicos's (1989) critique of the politics of postmodernism and is reminiscent of Gouldner's characterisation of the accommodative politics of Becker's epistemological partisanship:

> The new underdog sociology propounded by Becker is, then a standpoint that possesses a remarkably convenient combination of properties:

it enables the sociologist to befriend the very small underdogs in local settings, to reject the standpoint of the 'middle dog' respectables and notables who manage local caretaking establishments, while, at the same time, to make friends with the really top dogs in Washington agencies or New York foundations. While Becker adopts a posture as the intrepid preacher of the new underdog sociology, he has really given birth to something rather different: to the first version of the new Establishment sociology, to a sociology compatible with the new character of social reform in the United States today ... It is a sociology that succeeds in solving the oldest problem in personal politics: how to maintain one's integrity without sacrificing one's career, or how to remain a liberal although well-heeled.

(Gouldner 1973: 49)

Throughout the 1980s and 1990s there have been many cases in Britain where research has been explicitly linked to anti-racist political intervention. Most of these, to greater or lesser extent, draw on the work of Becker and Gouldner to justify their approach, though some accounts seem to do so in a crude manner. Perhaps the best example of critical social research which sits more comfortably in the Gouldner tradition is the work of the late Barry Troyna (Sikes and Rizvi 1997). For Troyna the fundamental principles which guided his research in education were social justice, equality and participatory democracy. Although research was undertaken as the basis for the development of strategies for social transformation, he stressed that political commitment should not lead to methodologically unprincipled research (Troyna 1993). However, merely citing the authority of these authors to justify intervention into the political field is no guarantee of scholarly integrity; indeed Troyna's work has been dismissed as 'an abandonment of research in favour of propaganda' (Foster, Gomm and Hammersley 1996: 178). Arguably, this is a harsh judgement that may reveal as much about the value position of Foster *et al.* as it does about the quality of Troyna's work. But it does raise the following critical key questions: does the commitment to assisting progressive political action through social research inevitably mean that scholarly integrity will be compromised? What is the 'correct' relationship between critical social research, political intervention and political activism? It is to my involvement in anti-racist activism and research in English cricket that I now turn in order to answer these questions.

Radical research and the case of anti-racism in English cricket

During the four years from 1995 to 1999 I was a key member of Hit Racism for Six and the co-author of *Anyone for Cricket?* (McDonald and Ugra 1998a). In other words, I assumed two speaking positions in the campaign: one as a political activist and the other as a researcher. As an activist, my anti-racist politics and goals were explicit: I was part of an organisation that called upon the ECB to take the issue of racism seriously and adopt anti-racism strategy as the necessary first step towards a developing a culture of racial inclusion rather than exclusion in the game. However, as a social researcher investigating the place of ethnic minority clubs within the structure of local league cricket, a level of scholarly detachment from the political activism of HR46 was required, and an analytical rather than a polemical engagement with the ECB was necessary. As a researcher, my role was to produce knowledge that sought to provide a coherent analysis of a complex phenomenon based on methodologically valid and sociologically sound techniques.

I became involved in the campaign from its origins in 1995 when HR46 was created in response to an article that had appeared in the *Wisden Cricket Monthly* in July of that year. The article argued that black and foreign-born players lacked the commitment to England, and it called for the Test XI to be made up of 'unequivocal Englishmen' (Henderson 1995). One of the first acts of the campaign was to issue and circulate a declaration against racism in cricket. This asked people to sign up if they agreed with the following four points: that racism has no place in cricket; that they reject any suggestion that cricketers may lack commitment to their team because of their race or country of origin; that they condemn slurs or insults aimed at cricketers or cricket fans because of their race or country of origin; and that they commit themselves to opposing all forms of racism in cricket at all levels (HR46 1996). This was hardly radical and it was difficult to think that anybody would be opposed to signing the declaration.

While many cricket fans were happy to sign up, as were many politicians, trades unions officials and anti-racist organisations, there was a refusal by the cricket establishment (including the governing body, prominent cricket journalists and – apart from a couple of notable exceptions – top Test players) both to sign the declaration or even discuss the issue. The *Wisden* article was dismissed as an aberration, and the mere mention of 'racism' and 'cricket' in the same sentence was greeted by the cricket establishment sometimes with incredulity, but more frequently with hostile indignation. Cricket was, according to the lyricist and Lords' member Sir Tim Rice, 'one of the least racist features of British Society' (Hit Racism for Six 1996: 10). It was clear from these early stages that a sustained campaign would be needed simply to force the issue of racism onto the policy agenda. The main thrust of the group in the first year was to put together a publication examining various aspects of racism in cricket. In 1996, *Hit Racism for Six: Race and Cricket in England Today* appeared with articles from a number of cricket writers, academics, and interviews with key individuals from the black and Asian cricket community. Other activities involved writing to the national press whenever a racial incident erupted in the game (as it often did during the mid to late 1990s, see Marqusee 1998), distributing leaflets outside Test matches, and organising a six-a-side cricket festival celebrating racial diversity in the game.

At the time I was employed in higher education as a lecturer in sport sociology, but I did not conceive my involvement in the campaign as related to my academic work other than in the sense of providing interesting material for teaching and research. Although the administrative home of HR46 was given as the same place as my institution, it was as a 'care-of' address, precisely to signal that the campaign and my place of work were distinct. In 1997 I was approached by social researchers from another university to put together a research project to investigate why so many black and Asian cricket clubs were not affiliated to the official regional cricket board. The research was sponsored by the Regional Cricket Board, itself an affiliate body of the ECB. As my role in HR46 was known, I was surprised that at no time during the fieldwork, or subsequently during dissemination to academic colleagues and policy makers, including the ECB, was it mentioned that I might be biased in my reporting of the findings. It was as if they had all accepted the notion of a 'hierarchy of credibility' (Becker 1970: 126) wherein academic research was deemed to be more 'truthful' and objective than the arguments of political activists. Indeed, we in HR46 were able to use the findings of the research by exploiting the acceptance of the ECB of the 'hierarchy of credibility'.

Of course, both as a political activist and as a researcher, I was not naive enough to expect the ECB to understand fully the research, let alone become supporters of anti-racism. From an activist's point of view, the research represented an invaluable resource that empowered the campaign and enhanced the position of HR46 within the policy process, while, from a research point of view, the findings needed to have academic credibility to be accepted by the ECB as 'true' and objective, which is what made it a powerful resource for HR46. The details of the aim and methodology of the report can be found elsewhere (McDonald and Ugra 1998b), but of significance here is the contrast in response from the authorities to my different speaking positions. When I was speaking as a member of HR46, my voice was ignored and discredited. However, after I had some academic evidence to present which concluded that a culture of racial exclusion existed within the game – evidence that I had helped to research and write up in my role as social researcher – the credibility of HR46 dramatically increased. For all of the actors involved in the discussion about the (non) existence of racism in cricket, my speaking positions were much more significant than my personal identity, which allowed me to play the dual role of activist and researcher during this period without any vocalised dissent from the key protagonists.

In 1998, the ECB created a Racism Study Group to prepare material that would be used for the 1999 document. Members of HR46, myself included, were the first to be invited to address the study group, and our formal submission received acknowledgement in the final report: 'The chronicled HR46 proposals, which were welcomed, were considered in detail and included, in the main, within the report recommendations' (ECB 1999: 15).

Though the publication of *Clean Bowl Racism* was of importance and a small but significant achievement for HR46, the document *sui generis* means very little. What matters is how the document is translated into real proposals leading to real changes in the structure and culture of cricket. The relevant point to make here is that it is important to recognise both limitations and also the power of radical social research, and that it is the symbiotic relationship between this radical social research and activism that offers the best scenario for social change.

In the same way that my anti-racist politics led me to get involved as an activist, it was my intellectual commitment to critical sport sociology that led to my desire to conduct research. There was a symbiotic relationship between activism and research. As an activist I knew that academically sound research could be used as powerful evidence to pressurise the ECB into action. As a social researcher I was committed to the production of knowledge that would expose and explain injustice and unequal relations of power, and thus provide the possibility for social change. Unusually in this case, I was involved in providing the evidence that I, as part of HR46, could then use politically as a resource in the campaign to implement progressive social change.

Concluding thoughts

In this chapter I have discussed the relationship between critical social research and the problem of 'taking sides'. I have drawn on the classic writings of Becker and Gouldner to outline a framework for social research that holds out the possibility of being politically engaged without surrendering academic integrity. However, achieving the appropriate relationship between research, political intervention and political activism is not easy.

I have identified two perspectives within critical social research, each shaped by different conceptions of the relationship between research, political intervention and political activism, namely, moralistic and radical. Although they all overlap in very fundamental ways – for example, in their rejection of value-neutrality, in their orientation on relations of power, and in their demystifying and de-bunking aims – they also offer distinct interpretations of critical social research.

Moralistic social research collapses the boundaries between research and activism. Researchers are involved in political struggles using their research as a political weapon to secure political goals. Little attention is paid to the conventions of sound scholarly habits, which are dismissed anyway as elitist and bogus, as the aim of the research is to support the attainment of immediate political goals. It is moralistic because it defends its integrity in accordance with the level of involvement in the struggle, rather than the intellectual rigour of the research and analysis. Understood in this way, it is possible to argue that the moralistic approach represents a move against the central tenets of critical social research.

The radical approach is best understood as a politicised application of critical social research. The agenda for radical social research is influenced to a much greater extent than critical social research by political imperatives. It is an orientation to the political situation and a desire to provide resources that can empower subordinate and campaigning groups against dominant relations of power that characterises radical social research. But unlike moralistic social research, the radical approach recognises the distinction between political intervention and political activism. Research that empowers subordinate groups or exposes dominant relations of power is a form of political intervention. It is the primary motivating force behind radical social research. Using this research as a political resource is the proper preserve of the activist. Therefore a radical sociology of sport should be seeking to assist the reconfiguration of the culture of sport by intervening against dominant relations of power. Social researchers working in the privileged spaces of the academy who claim to be radical can be expected to do no more, but no less, than this.

References

Back, L. and Solomos, J. (1993) 'Doing research, writing politics, the dilemmas of political intervention in research on racism', *Economy and Society* 22(2): 178–99.

Becker, H. (1967) 'Whose side are we on?', *Social Problems* 14: 239–47.

—— (1970) *Sociological work*, Chicago: Aldine.

—— (1971) *Sociological Work: Method and Substance*, London: Allen Lane.

—— (1986) *Doing Things Together: Selected Papers*, Illinois: Northwestern University Press.

Ben-Tovim, G., Gabriel, J., Law, I. and Stredder, K. (1986) *The Local Politics of Race*, London: Macmillan.

Bourdieu, P. (1992) *An Invitation To Reflexive Sociology*, Cambridge: Polity Press.

—— (1994) *In Other Words: Essays Towards a Reflexive Sociology*, Cambridge: Polity Press.

Callinicos, A. (1989) *Against Postmodernism: A Marxist Critique*, Cambridge: Polity.

Carrington, B. and McDonald, I. (2002) 'The politics of "race" and sport policy', in B. Houlihan (ed.) *Sport and Society*, London: Sage.

Coakley, J. and Dunning, E. (2000) *Handbook of Sport Studies*, London: Sage.

England and Wales Cricket Board (ECB) (1999) *Clean Bowl Racism: 'Going Forward Together'. A Report on Racial Equality in Cricket*, London: ECB.

Foster, P., Gomm, R. and Hammersley, M. (1996) *Constructing Educational Research: An Assessment of Research on School Processes*, London: Falmer.

Gouldner, A.W. (1968) 'The sociologist as partisan', *American Sociologist* May: 103–16.

—— (1973) *For Sociology: Renewal and Critique in Sociology Today*, London: Allen Lane.

Gruneau, R. (ed.) (1988) *Popular Cultures and Political Practice*, Toronto: Garamond Press.

—— (1999) *Class, Sports and Social Development* (2nd edn), Champaign, Ill.: Human Kinetics.

Hammersley, M. (2000) *Taking Sides in Social Research: Essays on Partisanship and Bias*, London: Routledge.

Hargreaves, J. (1982) 'Sport and hegemony: some theoretical problems', in H. Cantelon and R.Gruneau (eds) *Sport, Culture and the Modern State*, Toronto: University of Toronto Press.

Harvey, L. (1990) *Critical Social Research*, London: Allen & Unwin.

Henderson, R. (1995) 'Is it in the blood?', *Wisden Cricket Monthly*, July: 9–10.

Hit Racism for Six (1996) *Hit Racism for Six: Race and Cricket in England Today*, London: Wernham Press.

Hoffman, J. (1984) *The Gramscian Challenge: Coercion and Consent in Marxist Political Theory*, Oxford: Blackwell.

James, C.L.R. (1994) [1963] *Beyond a Boundary*, London: Serpent's Tail.

Lather, P. (1986) 'Research as praxis', *Harvard Educational Review* 56(3): 257–77.

Marqusee, M. (1998) *Anyone But England: Cricket, Race and Class*, London: Two Heads Publishing.

McDonald, I. and Ugra, S. (1998a) *Anyone For Cricket? Equal Opportunities and Changing Cricket Cultures in Essex and East London*, London: University of East London.

—— (1998b) 'It's just not cricket!', in P. Cohen (ed.) *New Ethnicities, Old Racisms?*, London: Zed Books.

Morgan, W. (1994) *Leftist Theories of Sport*, Urbana, Ill.: University of Chicago Press.

Sikes, P. and Rizvi, F. (eds) (1997) *Researching Race and Social Justice In Education: Essays in Honour of Barry Troyna*, Staffordshire: Trentham Books.

Solomos, J. and Back, L. (1995) *Race, Politics and Social Change*, London: Routledge.

Tomlinson, A. (1990) (ed.) *Consumption, Identity and Style: Marketing, Meanings and the Packaging of Pleasure*, London: Routledge.

Troyna, B. (1993) *Racism and Education*, Buckingham: Open University Press.

Whannel, G. (1993) 'Sport and popular culture: the temporary triumph of process over product', *Innovation* 6(3): 341–9.

7 'It's not a game'

The place of philosophy in a study of sport

Graham McFee

Introduction

When the world of sport is subjected to academic scrutiny, one important question one must ask (early on) is how is it to be theorised? To use an example we will return to, the Olympic Games is clearly taken by many, spectators as well as athletes, as the pinnacle of sports accomplishment, and often claimed as a celebration of all that is noble in physical culture. But the (Summer) Olympic Games now draws a huge television audience, and catapults sport into the consciousness of billions of people. How should one investigate in depth the nature of the phenomenon, locating the Games in their true context historically, politically and socially, and probing the rhetoric of Olympic ideology? It would be a mistake to think that rigorous study here can simply ignore the role of such key 'players' as past president of the International Olympic Committee (IOC) Juan-Antonio Samaranch (see Jennings 1996: 42–6); but neither can we simply explain all the features of sport just by reference to them. The world of sport cannot be caught in any simple analytical 'net'. So how such topics should be explored (McFee 1989) is an issue alongside what the precise topics here are. And these questions have a dimension in philosophy.

So what contribution could/should philosophy make to an authentic study of sport? Too often, what passes for 'philosophy of sport' is actually just the application, to sports cases, of general issues from philosophy. Of course, sport – like anything else – may be perplexing. But sport, here, is just an example: the perplexities are not essentially to do with sport. In thus showing why there cannot be a reliable philosophy of sport or philosophy of leisure (in the sense of an academic discipline), my arguments (for example, McFee 1998) might seem to preclude any role for philosophy, much less any essential role, in the investigation of sport. Rather, my point is that philosophy can offer kinds of clarification essential to the study of sport – and in ways that are revealing for philosophy. (The 'traffic' is not all one way.) The key thought is from Wittgenstein (1953: 402):

> [W]e have got a picture in our heads which conflicts with the picture of our ordinary way of speaking.

Here, such a picture might come from the theoretical presuppositions of social science. And it is this new picture that misleads us. We do not really infer, for example, that the utterance 'It is raining' is meaningless because we cannot say what the 'it' is. So care is needed before we conclude that our ordinary inferences mislead – perhaps they do, but we cannot assume so. (And, especially, we cannot assume – in advance of investigation – that advances in 'science' show this to us.) So philosophy has – or should have – a crucial conceptual role in the study of sport; a kind exemplified (although not explicitly theorised) in some of my writing.

Reference to Wittgenstein's philosophy here is relevant for three reasons: first, Wittgenstein has regularly been invoked by writers of sport – although not typically in the places I am deploying his arguments. For instance, in respect of the prospect of defining the concepts *game* and *sport*, Bernard Suits responds to Wittgenstein's remarks about the term 'game' by claiming that 'Wittgenstein himself did not follow ... [his own] excellent advice and look and see' (Suits 1978: x); had he done so, Suits thinks, he would have found a definition of the term 'game', the very one Suits himself claims to identify.[1] Second, the social theorist whose work provides our central example – Anthony Giddens – does draw on ideas from Wittgenstein, locating the resolution of some of the issues (as here) in 'the Wittgensteinian critique of traditional notions about the purposive character of human action' (Giddens 1979: 41). Third, and here more an assumption, is my own commitment to the general insightfulness of Wittgenstein's work.

General claims of the kind above (about a crucial conceptual role for philosophy in the study of sport) cannot be defended in the abstract – at least, not in my conception of philosophy. Additionally, it is implausible to think that so large a matter can be resolved briefly. Yet a worked example might both achieve some of that general task and motivate a yet wider acceptance, but within the bounds of what can be shown about this specific case (as part of a case-by-case argument). Thus here I address – as such an example – the agency side of a structure–agency divide. Thus, two funda-mental questions for my chapter are:

- What is the correct account of agency?
- What are the implications of that account for what we 'structure and agency' theorists can say about sport?

But we must also look (methodologically?) at what our mode of answering tells us about philosophy's place in investigating sport.

Structure and agency

A fundamental issue for the sociology of sport and leisure is what role (within one's account of social structure) to give to agency. As Morgan

(1994: 63) accurately notes,[2] the criticisms usually levelled at (other) Marx-inspired theories of sport come to this – that such theories:

> are guilty in one way or another of exaggerating the structural constraints (whether economic or structural) on human agency with the unfortunate result that sport is adjudged little more than a staging ground for the inculcation of the prevailing ways of life and values of society at large.
>
> (Morgan 1994: 63)

Giddens (1979: 253) equates the 'lack' within *orthodox sociology* ... [of] ... *a theory of action* with 'a failure to make power central to social theory' (*ibid.*: 253), since 'the notion of human action logically implies that of power' (*ibid.*: 256). The thought is that the 'fans' of hegemony – by virtue of their commitment to agency – do better than the 'traditional' views. Implicitly, then, Giddens equates a concern with agency with one with power; and he endorses both perspectives.[3] But exactly how does the 'agency' part play a role in respect of sport? Certainly we should not expect to find very explicit (personal) agents here.

As an example, consider 'perhaps the most sophisticated application of Gramsci's theoretical framework to the world of sport' (Sugden and Bairner 1993: 133), the writing of John Hargreaves, which was/is:

> directed towards revealing the multifaceted ways through which sport has been implicated in the achievement, maintenance and development of bourgeois hegemony in British society during the last century and a half.
>
> (*ibid.*)

There is no suggestion here of a relation of great specificity to the particular sporting activity. Rather, as they urge, Hargreaves focuses on two processes:

> the role of sport in the fragmentation of the working class ... and their reconstruction 'within a unified social formation, under bourgeois hegemony'.
>
> (Sugden and Bairner 1993: 133, quoting Hargreaves 1986: 209)

And, even at this level of generality, the situation is complex as 'there is no single, all powerful agency involved in the instrumental manipulation of sports' (Sugden and Bairner 1993: 133). So one should not look for individual agents and individual structures, but rather to see the dynamic within modern sports as involving more than simply the imposition 'from above' of values and ideas; and the preferred perspective will be all the easier if there is 'no meaningful distinction between material and cultural production' (Morgan 1994: 102). For power is not just power of economic (etc.)

forces but also of ideas/conceptions/cultural factors: this leads both to hegemony and to the state–civil society contrast. As Sugden and Bairner (1993:
131) put it, 'civil society is made up of a range of semi-autonomous institutions and activities, such as education, the church, the media, sport, leisure
and other areas of popular culture'. So action here should not (in general) be
cashed-out as the specific activities of specific individuals. Yet, once this
concession is made, the focus becomes on the varied forces that operate in
the social context of sport: the 'structure and agency' position simply offers a
richer account of these than some of its competitors.

Then a key question becomes whether sport tends to reinforce the status
quo (the existing power relations, ideological force of definition, etc.) or to
challenge it; as Morgan (1994: 72) summarises, 'does sport ... enslave or
liberate us?'. Where might part of an answer to such a question be sought?
One answer is, 'in the actual practices of sport, and – in particular – in its
history'. For here we see how in fact sport has been understood, and has
'developed' (or, at least, changed). Thus, looking for answers to the question
'liberate or enslave?' will, for such theorists, necessarily involve looking to
history.

But how is this outcome to be theorised? For Giddens, the goal might be
put as:

> orthodox sociology backed by a theory of action ... [where 'a theory of
> action' means] a conception of conduct as reflexively monitored by
> social agents who are partially aware of the conditions of their
> behaviour.
>
> (Giddens 1979: 253)

Giddens is clearly on the target here in requiring genuine agents; for
example, Giddens (*ibid.*: 254) criticises Parsons by urging that:

> *his social actors are not capable, knowledgeable agents.*

Thus the importance of 'capable, knowledgeable agents' is transparent, for
we should acknowledge 'that human beings reflectively monitor their
conduct via the knowledge they have of the circumstances of their activity'
(Giddens 1979: 254) – their knowledge of what others might term 'their
context'. In this way, Giddens (1990: 38) recognises the central role of
Wittgenstein's 'knowing how to go on' for any account of agency, but, as we
shall see later, without really understanding what this entails.

Giddens's own picture of how to assign relative roles to structure and to
agency is suggestive. Of course, social relations might be conceptualised
differently. So elaboration of Giddens's picture is best understood via an
example: here, Giddens's discussion of the (seminal) writings of E.P.
Thompson. For, in effect, Giddens's (1987) criticism is that, in his critique
of Althusser (see Thompson 1978: 193–406 [1981: 1–205]) and elsewhere,

Thompson accords too little role to structure, too much to agency – or, if this is different, fails to recognise 'the duality of structure' (Giddens 1979: 69 [also : 255]) – namely:

> that the structural properties of social systems are both the medium and the outcome of the practices that constitute those systems.

In reality (as we shall see), Thompson's account, appropriately read, is truer than Giddens's to the spirit of Wittgenstein's own writing – as a consequence, a more plausible account of agency. Making out this argument (in later sections) requires both a sketch of Wittgenstein's own account of agency, and consideration of some of its implications, showing what is really needed to characterise social practice.[4]

In criticism of E.P. Thompson

The nature of Giddens's worries concerning what account should be given of the relations between 'structure' and 'agency' is clear in his criticisms of Thompson: for (according to Giddens) Thompson's version has too great an emphasis on agency – its conception of agency does not fully recognise 'the duality of structure' (Giddens 1987: 220).[5]

So Giddens's worries in respect of Thompson's thought clarify the difficulties he would identify for a 'structure and agency' view. As we will see, the error is best seen as a misconception of the nature of 'agency', important since (a) the inclusion of agency in the picture is one of its distinctive features (in contrast to some (Marx-inspired) views) and (b) Giddens's own account of agency has an explicit debt to (what he takes to be) Wittgenstein's view – as we have noted.

Moreover, we should first sketch the conception of structure Giddens requires. As Morgan (1994: 66) puts it (in a passage specifically linked to Giddens):

> Structures are not the aggregate sum of individual acts, nor are they structurally independent and determinative of such acts. Rather, they are historically constituted actions of collectivities that bind the way we act in the social world.

This account captures well the sense in which structures cannot be reduced to individual acts (once 'individual' is construed in a certain way).

Giddens acknowledges that Thompson is right to place 'a strong emphasis upon the capability of the human agents actively to shape and reshape the conditions of their existence' (Giddens 1987: 204): as Giddens (*ibid*.: 203) puts it, this is 'something we could loosely call a sense of agency'. Moreover, he explicitly recognises the connection of Thompson's ideas to his own discussion of agency (*ibid*.: 215). However, those:

who, like Thompson, are prone to assert the primacy of agency typically
have difficulty coming to grips both conceptually and substantively with
what might be termed the 'structural constraints' over human action.

(Giddens 1987: 215)

The difficulties thus recognised are those 'involved in developing a standpoint able to adequately encompass both action and structural constraints'
(*ibid.*: 215). As Giddens (*ibid.*: 211) describes these difficulties, they turn on
Thompson's identification of 'agency with willing rather than reasoning,
with volition rather than knowledge' – a view Thompson shares with
Wittgenstein (see below).

   In fact, Thompson is recognising how easily reference to agency is lost, as
he thought it had been in much previous history, when there was little or no
conception of agency 'from below': hence Thompson's 'tendency to plump
for the reality of individuals, or at least of individual experience' (Giddens
1987: 220). So that is the methodological point here, which Giddens takes
(mistakes?) for Thompson's 'mistrust of "structural" concepts' (*ibid.*: 224).

   Instead, for Thompson, much here turns on the nature of the very structural concepts he is supposed to mistrust. Thus, as Giddens notes, in
rejecting the mechanical model of the solar system ('the Orrery') as a
metaphor for social theory, 'class is not a mechanical component of the
Orrery' (*ibid.*: 212). And it was with the inexorability, or mechanicalness, of
some accounts of structural concepts that Thompson took issue. Here
Giddens quotes in explanation:

> When we speak of a *class* we are thinking of a very loosely defined body
> of people who share the same categories of interests, social experiences,
> traditions and value system, who have a *disposition* to *behave* as a class, to
> define themselves in their actions and in their consciousness in relations
> to other groups of people in class ways. But class itself is not a thing, it
> is a happening.
>
>   (Thompson 1978: 85 [1981: 295], quoted Giddens 1987: 212)

(We should note both the relation to individuals and Thompson's refusal to
reify classes, since these are features we shall see again.) To this degree, then,
class would be other than merely structural.

   This leads neatly to what Giddens perceptively calls 'two main queries'
(Giddens 1987: 216) to be addressed by any investigation of the character of
human agency:

> What is it about agents which differentiates them from objects or from
> the operation of impersonal forces in the world of nature? What distin-
> guishes human agents from all other beings to whom agency might
> reasonably be attributed – that is to non-human animals?
>
>   (Giddens 1987: 216)

Roughly, the first is the problem of agency in a world of universal causation (not treated here: see McFee 2000a), while the second turns on the possibility, and the importance, of correctly characterising some events as actions. As we have seen, Giddens's own answer to this second query imports the thought that a nexus of normative rules (and similar) is presupposed by the very idea of agency, because agency (in this sense) is the province of 'concept-bearing beings' (Giddens 1987: 216). Thompson might agree. As a result, any conception of agency must have something to say about this background of (presupposed) normative rules. Can one begin from 'the reality of individuals, or at least of individual experience' (*ibid.*: 220), as Thompson does, and still manage this? Yet this puts the matter slightly misleadingly. For the point is not whether one begins from 'the reality of individuals', but whether (and how far) one goes beyond the reality of such individuals.

Here Giddens (1987: 217–18) accurately lists some of Thompson's themes in respect of agency:

1   Human beings actively 'make their own history' as much as they are made by it ...
2   Historical study should not ignore the underprivileged ... History should not be just written 'from the top', but from 'the bottom up' ...
3   Day-to-day events have a significance in and of themselves, which cannot [better, should not] be ignored by the historian ...
4   History is always a contingent affair. There is no overall teleology in history, apart from the purposes of individual agents; and these often have consequences which could not have been foreseen or intended.

For our purposes now, the first and last of these are the most crucial. To take them in reverse order, the lack of any overall teleology (or historical necessity) does not mean that nothing can be said or done – rather, it means exactly that things must be said and done if the individuals described in the first comment are to be mobilised to action, political and otherwise.

What sense should one make of the quotation from Marx embedded in the first comment? Giddens reports that Thompson 'is fond of alluding to both Vico and Marx in developing this idea' (Giddens 1987: 217). For the account one gives of the agents is crucial: what powers does one have to possess in order to count as an agent here? And what assumptions of a background against which agency is possible are built in? Of course, these are large questions, not to be answered here. My point here is simply to identify features of Giddens's position, and features of positions (here typified by Thompson) with which he is unhappy – in this way, as it were, to plot some boundaries of Giddens's conception of agency from outside as well as inside.

What bothers Giddens: the issue of individualism

What aspects of the notion of agency, as Giddens finds it in E.P. Thompson, is he bothered by? More strongly, what is he frightened of for his own position?

Two considerations suggest that Giddens's fear is that his own position – in acknowledging agency – will dissolve into a kind of individualism, a worry (for him) because he identifies individualism with methodological individualism. First, Giddens's objections to Thompson are just that Thompson's account of social process involves agency unconstrained by structure (or, perhaps, insufficiently constrained by structure), in contrast to Giddens's own which is – let us not forget – the thesis of the duality of structure. Thus, although posed in terms of Thompson's failure to do justice to the full extent of agency (because – for Giddens – Thompson treats agency too individualistically), the real inadequacy of such a conception of agency lies in its inability to satisfactorily address the second of Giddens's 'two main queries' above: that concerning the normative background required for the very possibility of agency. Second, when Giddens 'reads' agency in his own voice, it is as radically anti-individualist.

As a conception of social theory here, methodological individualism has three related parts:

- it is a *methodological* doctrine, aiming to locate which *kinds* of concepts are required in order to give satisfactory accounts of social phenomena;
- it is a doctrine of *individualism*, taking the basic units for analysis to be the individual persons – these are what one needs to take account of, for methodologically correct social theory;
- relatedly, it takes a *view* of individuals, as atomistic (in contrast to moral individualism: see Kukathas and Pettit 1990: 11–16).

For our methodological individualists, talk of (say) social classes would always be reducible to talk of individuals, at least in principle; and general considerations of theoretical parsimoniousness will mean that if social theory can do without talk of such collectivities, then it should do so – at least when it is being methodologically scrupulous. As a sloganised version, to give its flavour, consider:

> social entities such as institutions or associations ... [are nothing but] ... abstract models constructed to interpret certain selected abstract relations between individuals.
>
> (Popper 1957: 140)

Thus, for example, just as talk of 'the average English family' may have a place, so too may talk of other collectivities; but, as with 'the average English family', these are tools of limited usefulness.

So our methodological individualists are not denying that we are all individuals; nor that we meet in 'social groups' (we obviously do); nor that we learn from one another (again we obviously do). The point, though, is that, in the last analysis, such 'relational' properties can be analysed into my learning from you, and Joe learning from you, and Jill learning from you, etc. And parsimoniousness in theory construction is, in itself, laudable; for, clearly, we should not invoke theoretical constructs that we can avoid (or, if we do, we should gauge carefully our commitment to them, as we did with 'the average English family'!).

But, as Stephen Lukes (1973: 118) has shown, one cannot explain ('without remainder') human social behaviour by limiting one's conceptual categories to those of biology (such as genetic make-up, brain-states, conditions of central nervous system), nor those of a naive psychology (such as aggression, gratification, stimulus-response) nor even those of ethology (such as co-operation, power, esteem). For example, a study of humankind based on biology would not be social theory – the distinctive features of human life are not captured by concepts we might share with, say, the rest of the animal kingdom. Moreover, if concepts of such ethology resemble those in, say, Desmond Morris's book *Manwatching* (1977) – more accurately called 'womanwatching' – there is human interaction, right enough, but of a severely attenuated form; in particular, it is not characterised by the importance of what Harré perceptively calls 'talk' (Harré 1983: 160–1). And our negative conclusion on the adequacy of these candidate category types for genuine social analysis could agree with Giddens's own.

Giddens takes considerations such as these to deal with individualism as such. As will become obvious, my view – like Lukes's (1973: 119–22) – is that at least some 'action concepts' (such as those used to describe voting, or signing cheques) are required to characterise human behaviour; and that these concepts cannot be treated in terms of atomistic individuals. For this conception of action uses concepts appropriate to persons to analyse personal behaviour are thereby acknowledged as both (a) social, although rooted in the individual, and (b) essential for an account of human behaviour. This will be more than methodological individualism permits, but less than is required for the kind of emphasis on social structure favoured by Giddens. If this is right, there is a place for an individualism which is richer than methodological individualism, but stops short of the 'duality of structure', as I have read it.

So it identifies an alternative that Giddens does not consider: the choice here is not between methodological individualism and some form of holism – there could be forms of individualism other than the methodological sort, generated by giving up methodological individualism's conception of the individual. And this is the position of Thompson (and also of Wittgenstein, see below).

I have not, of course, shown that this conception is adequate (although that is approached in the next section). Perhaps appeal to collectivities (like social class) is essential too. Yet this is just where Thompson's account of class (quoted earlier) can seem so perceptive, since its stress does fall exactly where other considerations are asking if a theory's stress might fall – although such a conception may be problematic, of course.

How might Giddens respond? We find a hint in one of his other comments. Although Giddens (1976: 160) speaks of the 'unstable margin' between the properties of structures and those that can be analysed as intentional action:

> in respect of sociology, the crucial task ... is to be found in the explanation of the properties of structures.
>
> (Giddens 1976: 160)

Why? Because anything else won't be 'sociology'!? This might be his reply here: that meeting only the constraints implied above will not generate sociology, however fruitful otherwise. Consider, here:

> Dignity, rights and responsibilities are attributes of persons as social beings, while feelings and sensations are contents of consciousness and attributes of persons as psychological beings.
>
> (Harré 1991: 16)

But this issue concerns the nature of the differences highlighted in such a contrast; in particular, can Harré's 'social beings' be treated individualistically, given a sufficiently generous treatment of individualism?[6]

This contrast gives us a way to characterise Giddens's view here: that the only (or minimal) analytical tools for social being are tools drawn from sociology – where these cannot be provided by individualism. Equally, our position is that individualism tolerates (in Harré's terms) more than mere psychological being. But, of course, this is just the issue. And I cannot see how it could (in principle) be resolved other than by trying to think in social–theoretical terms without this additional 'baggage': that (if I am right) Thompson had already gone down this road is encouraging. But the task (the *philosophical* task) awaits completion – and will not find it here!

Wittgenstein (and Winch) on action

Later Giddens (1979: 4; 1984: 21) came to associate insights into action that he drew from analytical philosophy with the writing of Wittgenstein, granting that Wittgenstein's thought was 'exceptionally important for current problems of social theory' (*ibid.*: 4; see also p. 245). Yet originally he attributed these insights to 'post-Wittgensteinian philosophy' (*ibid.*: 44); and in particular to the writings of Peter Winch, who Giddens sees as attempting 'to apply ideas drawn from [Wittgenstein's] *Philosophical investigations* to problems of sociology' (*ibid.*: 51). Giddens stresses Winch's account of the normativity of action: the key question is 'whether it makes sense to distinguish a right and a wrong way of doing things in connection with what he does' (Winch 1958: 58, quoted in Giddens 1976: 45). For when there is a right and a wrong way, we have an action; the difference is not simply that between the movement which does happen and the one which does not – the naming of a ship, say, can misfire even if the right name is uttered – for instance, if the 'utterer' is not an appropriate namer of ships. Such normativity is clearly required by any satisfactory account of agency (as Giddens, quoted earlier, noted) – without it, we lose the key contrast between simple misfires ('the wrong words uttered') and complex ones, where something is attempted (perhaps even done) but not the right thing. For example, redistributions of the chess pieces that are not moves in chess contrast with legitimate but bad moves. But how is such normativity to be held in place?

Winch's answer appeals to 'forms of life' rooted (partly) in our self-understanding. So one's form of life invokes 'a historical group of individuals ... bound ... into a community by a shared set of complex, language-involving properties' (McGinn 1997: 51): how I see the world should not be conceptualised purely individually. As one perceptive commentator notes:

> For Weber ... as Winch observes, sociology is concerned with behaviour 'if and insofar as the agent or agents associate a subjective sense with it' (Winch 1958: 45). Weber [too] explains behaviour in terms of meaning.
>
> (Lyas 1999: 47)

But, as Giddens recognises, for Wittgenstein, there is a generalising power here:

> self-understanding is connected integrally to the understanding of others.
>
> (Giddens 1976: 19)

This conception is embedded in Wittgenstein's so-called 'Private Language Argument', to which we must return.

Yet Giddens is not uncritical of Winch (and Wittgenstein);[7] as noted, this very talk of 'forms of life' seems to him to undercut the reliability of any insight. For this reason, for Giddens, Winch's view can leave:

> in obscurity ... how one is to set about analysing the transformation of forms of life over time; or how the rules governing forms of life are to be connected to, or expressed in terms of, those governing other forms of life.
>
> (Giddens 1976: 17)

And this is why, for Giddens, 'Wittgensteinian philosophy has not led towards any sort of concern with social change' (Giddens 1979: 50). But this is not simply a misreading of Wittgenstein (especially of his views on 'forms of life'), it is a misreading of the possibility of philosophy. For Wittgenstein's work has the potential to transform how people understand their dealings with one another – it can clarify mistaken ways of thinking about action and the mind, for example.

This conception (embedded in Wittgenstein's so-called 'Private Language Argument') is complex from a scholarly point of view: what exactly did Wittgenstein say or mean? Here I simply assert, without defence, my reading of three key aspects of that argument. First, its target is not – as some writers have thought – the understanding of other minds: the position is not that, without shared concepts (a shared 'language'), I could not understand the thoughts and feelings of others. Wittgenstein is willing to grant, for the sake of argument, that a 'genius' child might arrive at a personal solution to the problem of other minds, as if by magic (Wittgenstein 1953: 257) – but then investigates its implications for knowledge of one's own mind. So, for example, Wittgenstein shows no interest in how so-and-so is learned (he is not doing social psychology), but only in the implications of its having been learned. Thus the topic concerns one's own understanding of one's own thought, feelings, etc.: this is what Wittgenstein argues would be impossible were that understanding not, in principle, shareable with others – so a logically private understanding is impossible (although this does nothing to speak to the practical difficulties of understanding one another).

This is not how Giddens reads Wittgenstein (from Winch). Instead, and second, the shared understanding required by Giddens seems best characterised in terms of induction into our 'linguistic community' (our 'form of life') of those who thereby come to understand the world as we do.[8] Such a 'community view' of meaning and understanding could generate relativism: why should our ways of talking, thinking or understanding be prioritised? As we will see, Giddens goes on to raise just this worry. But this is not Wittgenstein's position.[9]

Third, and relatedly, on Wittgenstein's own view, there is no 'foundation' here because none is needed – appeal to the logical presuppositions of understanding represents the deepest one can go at an abstract level. One implication, then, gives due weight to the agent's perspective on action – it is not (always) simply the agent's, as the Private Language considerations suggest. But, for any action, the agent will have a sense of it, explicable (often) in terms of 'why he/she did it', even when that is articulated after the fact. As our perceptive commentator observes, 'to elucidate the social is to elucidate the notion of a meaning-giving form of life' (Lyas 1999: 48). And this task is proper to philosophy, which seeks to elucidate 'what is involved in the notion of a form of life as such' (Winch 1958: 41, quoted in Lyas 1999: 48).

Making sense of an action, for Wittgenstein, is in part making sense of an agent, a person doing that; in particular, in insisting that 'in the beginning was the deed' (Wittgenstein 1969: 402; 1993: 395), Wittgenstein is denying that explanations of actions must always – on pain of falsity – follow some chain of psychological connection engaged in by the agent. As an agent, I just do certain things. When others ask for an explanation, I often do so 'after the fact', pondering how these 'doings' made sense to me.

Two features of the agent's perspective are important here: first, I cannot explain my action by reference to things I do not know – in particular, I cannot so explain it by reference to forces of which I am unaware, or to rules of which I am unaware – just as the rules of chess cannot explain the 'behaviour', faced with a chess board, of someone who does not know those rules. Such a case is, therefore, easily seen; and acknowledged when we distinguish behaviour which merely accords with a rule from behaviour done on the basis of, or for, that rule (even when it contravenes the rule). Second, I do not recognise all the forces – and especially the social forces – that have a bearing on my life; thus, my perspective alone can never fully characterise any event where forces (and especially social forces) beyond my ken are operative – and this will be very many events. So an exclusive emphasis on agency from the agent's perspective cannot be all we need. (Although, notice, this takes nothing from the point that the very characterisation of action from the agent's perspective already imports the nexus of rules.)

What principally needs explanation is behaviour different from the norm, or from what is expected: what Wittgenstein (1993: 379) calls 'reasons for leaving a familiar track'. When we deviate from the path, an explanation is needed in ways which it is not when we stick to the path. (This goes for figurative as well as for real paths.) Following signposts is a normative activity in that we can do it badly or wrongly; but that explanation will only be invoked when my behaviour stands in need of explanation, when it is not transparent – I do not have to give such explanations to myself. (In typical cases, 'explaining to myself' could only be a roundabout way of talking about my deliberating.) As Wittgenstein (1953: 217) puts it, 'it is about the justification for my following the rule in the way I do'. And the explanatory application of rules must stop somewhere; if not, we have the vicious regress with a rule needed for the application of that rule, and another rule needed for the application of the new rule, and so on. So there are actions whose explanation is rarely required, but, when it is, it need not be expected to retrieve some explicit (and prior) thought process of the agent. If this is sometimes true, it removes the need for a general account of agent motivation.

In summary, then, thus far we have:

- seen that E.P. Thompson's account of agency might consistently be adopted (although without saying enough about what this might mean for sport);
- offered some reasons to prefer this account to Giddens's, both because the reasons Giddens has offered are not sufficient to refute Thompson's view, and because Giddens's motivations in rejecting Thompson's version can be accommodated within that (Thompsonian) version;

- seen how one source Giddens draws on (namely, the philosophy of Wittgenstein) does not provide the support for Giddens's view that he assumes.

Abstract solutions and rules

Marx famously said:

> Men make their own history, but not ... under circumstances they themselves have chosen.
>
> (Marx 1973 [1869]: 146)[10]

This should not suggest that only the material situation comes down to us; rather, we are 'born into' (Cavell 1981: 64) a nexus of rules, practices and principles of which we are not the authors. Moreover, for most, neither we nor any specific set of human beings (past or present) actually chose these rules. Except where we can see the practices or principles enshrined in legal rules, humans create these contexts by their actions; but not any specific set of human beings. To speak figuratively, they were created by human history – more exactly, by the cultural history and traditions of this culture. The kinds of moral principles that, as Dworkin (1978: 72) has shown, lie behind legal decisions (and sporting ones: see McFee 2000b) should be seen this way, and they subtend a vast nexus of rules, principles and practices concerned with justice, fair treatment and the like.

Given this provenance, of course, they are 'authorless'; this tempts some (for example, Giddens) to find another author for them – in their class, or some such. And hence to treat the structure as though it were an agent. So a key mistake here takes some author as needed: since it cannot be a particular group of humans – and that is neither true nor would it be sufficient authority – another author must be sought. Then a kind of super-individual is chosen, such as a class.

But that is not a necessary move; nor one I can endorse (or see Wittgenstein endorsing). To see why, consider a kind of parallel position. Suppose another author were needed (say to provide the authority 'behind' the principles, etc.), then we should need to search for one. But how plausible a general claim is that? To bring out, in a simplified way, that no such authority is needed, consider the arguments of those who explain moral value by claiming that what is good or right is what God wills as good or right: that is, they find the relevant authority in God (compare, for example, McGinn 1992: 13–14).[11]

Now, do such thinkers believe that the actions are, say, right because God wills them? Or, instead, that God wills them because they are right? Neither option is satisfactory. If God acts as an authority in respect of moral judgement, there seems to be two related problems. First, were an authority really needed, the argument seems weak; do we not therefore require a further authority for God? (Parity of reasoning might seem to suggest this.) And, second, God's willing the action now seems arbitrary – as though God could have willed, say, that murder, or torturing the innocent, was morally OK: that is, the force of the moral prohibition seems to lie simply in God's decision. But why was that decision reached? If it was reached because, for instance, of God's goodness, we simply repeat the problem: in what does God's goodness consist? If it consists in God's choosing the (morally) right options, then those options are morally right independent of God's so choosing – and that takes us to the other version, which has two positive benefits for us: first, in locating the rightness of God's decisions in the rightness of the action itself, it does not require of us any authority here. Second, and relatedly, it does not require God as such an authority.[12] So we see here the general futility of the search for authority. As our simplified case shows, the demands of morality (and other such demands on human decisions) do not require an authority; yet, as suggested above, this was behind Giddens's insistence of the inadequacy of individualism.

There is no suggestion here of another 'source' or authority for moral principles, prohibitions, etc. These are, of course, centrally human: with no humans, there would – I should argue – be no actions to be morally right or wrong, good or bad. So that any account here must deal with human choices, decisions, and the like (and develop an account of agency, objectivity, etc. to permit this).

To return briefly to methodological individualism, discussed earlier: there, general claims about human behaviour (while permissible) should be treated like remarks about 'the average English family' – that is, as true but of an abstraction; hence as not true exceptionlessly of actual families. There is more to general claims than that. But this feature too is worth acknowledging: that there are ways of treating, say, classes or genders (for methodological purposes) which might be true of them, although (a) not exceptionlessly and (b) without treating them as super-agents.

The target is a confused one; there is a question about the authority 'behind' rules, as though that explains rule-following – or, even more so, action (recognising some action as rule-following behaviour). But this is mistaken, in ways our discussion of Wittgenstein above highlighted; first, one does not in general require to be prompted by a rule ('in the beginning was the deed') and, second, rule-following cannot itself be a matter of the application of yet more rules, on pain of regress.

Notice, one cannot simply appeal to one's rule ('thou shalt not kill'), for what does that rule amount to in this situation? Knowing the rule alone does not look promising here, for that is just a formalisation, to be applied (where possible) in the new situations faced. Is killing still as absolutely prohibited in this new context? Or was the prohibition never that absolute? The rule alone cannot decide. Equally, further rules will not help – on pain of the regress where an interpretive rule is needed for each new rule mentioned, and then one for that rule, and so on. So that, in learning morality, one does not learn a set of principles (only?), much less a set of rules – rather, one learns to make moral judgements, and one learns that first in specific contexts (Dancy 1993: 56–7). Since any such learning must take place in some particular situation, one might hope for 'learning-situations' not ones of maximum risk to life, limb, sanity or world peace. These are what sport might offer (see McFee 2000c).

Clearly, this particularist conception of moral judgement is both a specific thesis in philosophy and highly contentious. Two misconceptions seem to speak against it: first, the view of morality as a system of rules – but, as we have seen, the application of rules cannot itself be a matter of rules. So something other than rules is required. Second, the assumption of a tension between particularism and moral principles; yet particularism is only opposed to substantive moral principles, not to moral principles as such. For such 'substantive moral principles' are of precisely the kind claimed to apply clearly in one situation because applying in another. Our discussion of 'thou shalt not kill' highlighted the difficulties here. For particularists, on the contrary:

> that the moral relevance of a property in a new case cannot be predicted from its relevance elsewhere.
>
> (Dancy 1993: 57)

Here 'predicted' is the key term, for, of course, we will agree – once the plan of action is decided upon – that this case instantiates the principle. It is just that we could not know this 'before the fact'.

In summary, criticism of Thompson for failing to provide an 'author' (or a validation) of the nexus of normative rules is unwarranted, since no such author is required.

Agency in sport: some comments on Olympism

As implied earlier, we should consider the use made of the structure–agency contrast by those who employ it in discussing sport: roughly, those Morgan (1994: 63) calls 'hegemonists' or 'hegemony theorists'[13] – whether or not they would accept the name. But, of course, following the (Wittgensteinian) account of agency (gestured towards here) might be little different from following (roughly) Giddens's, for any differences will be subtle, if important.

As an example: the values of Olympism emphasise its universal (which here means 'global') possibilities. Thus De Coubertin claimed that the Olympic Movement was 'a potent if indirect factor in securing universal peace' (MacAloon 1981: 261),[14] and urged that:

> Healthy democracy, wise and peaceful internationalism, will penetrate the new stadium and preserve within it the cult of disinterestedness and

honour which will enable athletics to help in the tasks of moral education and social peace as well as of muscular development.

(MacAloon 1981: 188–9)

For only with such a global mission could Olympism claim its educational
goal. As Hargreaves (2000: 113) notes:

A species of internationalism constitutes a chief rationale of the
Olympic movement.

Yet this claim requires understanding: we may be offered an internationalist
rationale for Olympism, but are we really sold it?

Certainly, the values offered or displayed (and especially claimed by the
IOC)[15] are internationalist ones, at least primarily; if we swallow them
entire, without demur (as some BBC commentators seem to suggest we
should), the reality of the power so construed will involve our accepting all
the normative claims offered – in particular, those the IOC offers us. But, for
most observers, the experience of the Games is less than fully determinate in
this way; the national teams do not all seem to manifest the kind of commitment to sport (and especially to fair play and the minor importance of
victory) that the Olympic oath asserts, nor do all the judges (always – see
boxing: Jennings 1996: 79–92) strive to reach the standards in their oath.
An informed public, in recognising these facts, also recognises that there are
nevertheless many babies in all this bathwater. So that, without simply
adopting the version of Olympic reality thereby offered, he/she does not
simply become brainwashed about the possibilities of Olympism, rather, the
virtues asserted are recognised as virtues, and the efforts to reach them
applauded where these are genuine efforts. (And if some spectators are less
realistic – and hence less critical – than this, that should be ascribed to the
kinds of ignorance an Olympic cover-up can generate: see, for example,
Jennings and Sambrook 2000: 290–306.)

If the Olympic movement were as powerful and as adept at deploying
its powers, as might be imagined, dissent of this sort would be literally
inconceivable, both for athletes and spectators. But that was never the case;
some were prepared to doubt the claims of Olympism almost from the
beginning – and certainly by 1936, where the Workers' Olympics of 1937
stands as a concrete testimony (Riordan 1984: 106–8). Moreover, the
ability to recognise sleaze within the 'Olympic Family' is not equivalent to
recognising flaws in the Olympic Ideal. This is one consequence of our
account of the nature of agency. On individualist accounts of the sort
Giddens feared, to find the people corrupt, would be to taint the agency:
such a view identifies agency with agents. Because he cannot accept such a
conclusion, Giddens rejects individualism. But this is not our view – for
us, the moral concerns are agent-concerns without (necessarily) being the
concerns of particular agents. Hence, in our view, individualism still

permits a separation of the concept of agency from the doings of Tom, Dick or Juan-Antonio.

Conclusion

Thus far, we have given reason to prefer Thompson's picture of agency to Giddens's; and mentioned at least one place where this might make a useful intervention in the study of sport. But all of this is really our worked example, recall. My central point is made if readers can see the general value of philosophy here, even if they dispute my conclusions in this debate. Indeed, readers who join this debate with me will be making theoretical interventions of the appropriate (conceptual) kinds – they will need these even to dispute my conclusion. In thus engaging in conceptual dispute, they are entering philosophy. For me, recognising that fact makes it more likely that this foray into philosophy will be successful, because it suggests that engagement with the practices of philosophy need not be beside the point.

But it also suggests a view of philosophy perhaps less abstract than is sometimes thought.[16] In particular, it would give reason to doubt at least the full generality of the claim that 'real events can save us much philosophy' (Willis 1978: 1) – for how are these 'real events' to be understood? Instead, the 'drop of reality' is a key part of philosophy (on this conception). For we would be seeing how philosophy might work directly through concrete cases such as those considered here: that it is not abstract in one of the ways often thought. Indeed, the concreteness of even logic might be recognised. Here, our argument worked through concrete examples. But, as John Wisdom (1965: 102) rightly assured us, this is actually true of all reasoning: 'at the bar of reason, always the final appeal is to cases'. In this way, the study of sport (as I have modelled it here) could be part of a revitalisation within philosophy; thus, it might permit the kind of reciprocal role (between discussions within sport and those in general philosophy) presently so often absent.

Notes

1 Suits (1978 : 41) summarises his own definition as 'playing a game is the voluntary attempt to overcome unnecessary obstacles'. But I certainly do not appeal to this unobvious 'feature' in deciding whether or not such-and-such is a game. (Indeed, I never thought along these lines until reading Suits.) So, if I presently understand what games are, Suits is not here helping me.

2 Morgan's text is especially interesting here, since it is a philosophical text read by (some) sociologists – not a familiar kind of object.

3 Many writers on sport have taken a similar view: Morgan (1994: 61) lists 'John Clarke, Philip [Paul?] Corrigan, Peter Donnelly, Stephen Hardy, Robert Hollands, Alan Ingham, Jim McKay, Brian Palmer, Alan Tomlinson, and David Whitson', in addition to Richard Gruneau and John Hargreaves.

4 Discussion of the conceptualisation of agency might be put (as here) in terms of concept-employment; equally, it might be put in terms of language – that:

Language is the medium of social practice, and as such is implicated in all the variegated activities in which social actors engage.

(Giddens 1979: 245)

This can be puzzling, of course, if we read this claim in terms of words uttered and/or heard: in terms of language. But that is to misunderstand it. Rather, it should be read as one part of a characterisation of action as such. For the aims and goals of agency reflect the conceptualisation of those activities, (implicitly) contrasting them with others for which they might be mistaken. For example, the wedding ceremony differs from the rehearsal even were the very same people to utter the same words (in the very same order) in the same building – each constitutes a different action. Any plausible account of agency must recognise just this contrast. This is one way to bring out the connection to so-called meaning, for I cannot understand behaviours as actions unless I can make some sense of how the agents conceptualise them ('the meaning they might attribute to the behaviour' (Lyas 1999: 61)). Or, better, I can do the one only to the extent that I can do the other. Lacking the agent's perspective, I cannot see the action in this behaviour.

5 This idea is central in much of Giddens's writing: see, for example, Giddens (1979: 69–70).
6 Our examples of such generous treatment here are (a) moral individualism (Kukathas and Pettit 1990: 11–16) and (b) the requirements of Lukes's conception of normative action.
7 Thus Giddens (1976: 47–9) lists criticisms of Winch.
8 For discussion of this widely held, but mistaken, reading of Wittgenstein, see Baker and Hacker (1984).
9 See, for example, Baker and Hacker (1980: 137):
   A form of life is a given unjustified and unjustifiable pattern of human activity ... It consists of shared natural and linguistic responses, of broad agreement in definitions and in judgements, and of corresponding behaviour.
10 The full quotation is:
   Men make their own history, but not of their own free will; not under circumstances they themselves have chosen but under the given and inherited circumstances with which they are directly confronted. The tradition of the dead generations weighs like a nightmare on the minds of the living.
   (Marx 1973: 146)
11 Here, one does not need a commitment to theism to see the logical structure of the argument.
12 Which cannot be attractive to our theists.
13 Some of the crew here (see Morgan 1994: 61, quoted in note above) are familiar names in the sociology of sport (and in the index to this volume).
14 Quotations from De Coubertin are taken from MacAloon (1981), since he translates them all, and also since his references are not always complete.
15 Article VIII of the Congress of 1894 justifies the Olympic Games 'from the athletic, moral and international standpoint' (MacAloon 1981: 167).
16 Morgan might share this aspect of my view here – one of his strengths.

References

Baker, G. and Hacker, P. (1980) *Wittgenstein: Understanding and Meaning*, Oxford: Blackwell.
—— (1984) *Scepticism, Rules and Language*, Oxford: Blackwell.
Cavell, S. (1981) *The Senses of Walden* (expanded edn), San Francisco: North Point.

Dancy, J. (1993) *Moral Reasons*, Oxford: Blackwell.

Downing, T. (1992) *Olympia*, London: BFI.

Dworkin, R. (1978) *Taking Rights Seriously*, Cambridge, MA: Harvard University Press.

Giddens, A. (1976) *New Rules of Sociological Method*, London: Hutchinson.

—— (1979) *Central Problems in Social Theory*, London: Macmillan.

—— (1987) 'Out of the orrery: E.P. Thompson on consciousness and history', in *Social Theory and Modern Sociology*, Cambridge: Polity Press.

—— (1990) *The Consequences of Modernity*, Cambridge: Polity Press.

—— (1994) *Beyond Left and Right: The Future of Radical Politics*, Cambridge: Polity Press.

Hargreaves, J. (1986) *Sport, Power and Culture: A Social and Historical Analysis of Popular Sports in Britain*, Cambridge: Polity Press.

—— (1992) 'Revisiting the hegemony thesis', in J. Sugden and C. Knox (eds) *Leisure in the 1990s: Rolling Back the Welfare State* (LSA Publication No. 46), Eastbourne: Leisure Studies Association.

—— (2000) *Freedom for Catalonia?: Catalan Nationalism, Spanish Identity and the Barcelona Olympic Games*, Cambridge: Cambridge University Press.

Harré, R. (1983) 'An analysis of social activity', in J. Miller (ed.) *States of Mind: Conversations With Psychological Investigators*, London: BBC.

—— (1991) *Physical Being: A Theory of Corporeal Psychology*, Oxford: Blackwell.

Jennings, A. (1996) *The New Lords of the Rings*, London: Simon & Schuster.

Jennings, A. and Sambrook, C. (2000) *The Great Olympic Swindle: When the World Wanted its Games Back*, London: Simon & Schuster.

Kukathas, C. and Pettit, P. (1990) *Rawls: A Theory of Justice and its Critics*, Cambridge: Polity Press.

Lukes, S. (1973) *Individualism*, Oxford: Blackwell.

Lyas, C. (1999) *Peter Winch*, Teddington: Acumen.

MacAloon, J. (1981) *This Great Symbol: Pierre de Coubertin and the Origins of the Modern Olympics*, Chicago: University of Chicago Press.

McFee, G. (1989) 'The Olympic Games as tourist event: an American in Athens, 1896', in A. Tomlinson (ed.) *Sport in Society: Policy, Politics and Culture* (LSA Publications No. 43), Eastbourne: Leisure Studies Association.

—— (1998) 'Are there philosophical issues with respect of sport (other than ethical ones)?', in M. J. McNamee and S. J. Parry (eds) *Ethics and Sport*, London: Routledge.

—— (2000a) *Free Will*, Teddington: Acumen.

—— (2000b) 'Spoiling: An indirect reflection of sport's moral imperative?', in T. Tännsjö and C. Tamburrini (eds) *Values in Sport*, London: Routledge.

—— (2000c) 'Sport: A moral laboratory?', in M. McNamee, C. Jennings and M. Reeves (eds) *Just Leisure: Policy, Ethics and Professionalism* (LSA Publication No. 71), Eastbourne: Leisure Studies Association.

McGinn, C. (1992) *Moral Literacy; Or, How To Do The Right Thing*, Indianapolis, IN: Hackett.

McGinn, M. (1997) *Wittgenstein and the Philosophical Investigations*, London: Routledge.

Marx, Karl (1973) [1869] 'The eighteenth Brumaire of Louis Bonaparte' in *Surveys From Exile: Political Writings Vol. 2*, Harmondsworth: Penguin.

Morgan, W.J. (1994) *Leftist Theories of sport: A Critique and Reconstruction*, Urbana, IL: University of Chicago Press.

Morris, D. (1977) *Manwatching: A Field Guide to Human Behaviour*, London: Jonathan Cape.

Popper, K. (1957) *The Poverty of Historicism*, London: Routledge & Kegan Paul.

Riordan, J. (1984) 'The workers Olympics', in A. Tomlinson and G. Whannel (eds) *Five-Ring Circus: Money, Power and Politics at the Olympic Games*, London: Pluto.

Sugden, J. and Bairner, A. (1993) *Sport, Sectarianism and Society in a Divided Ireland*, Leicester: Leicester University Press.

Suits, B. (1978) *The Grasshopper: Games, Life and Utopia*, Toronto: University of Toronto Press.

Thompson, E.P. (1978) *The Poverty of Theory*, London: Merlin (US edn 1981).

Willis, P. (1978) *Profane Culture*, London: Routledge & Kegan Paul.

Winch, P. (1958) *The Idea of a Social Science*, London: Routledge & Kegan Paul.

Wisdom, J. (1965) *Paradox and Discovery*, Oxford: Blackwell.

Wittgenstein, L. (1953) *Philosophical Investigations* (trans. G.E.M. Anscombe), Oxford: Blackwell.

—— (1969) *On Certainty* (trans. D. Paul and G.E.M. Anscombe), Oxford: Blackwell.

—— (1993) *Philosophical Occasions 1912–1951* (eds J. Klagge and A. Nordmann), Indianapolis, IN: Hackett.

Part III

Method: case studies and ethnographies

8 Sport, power and the state in Weimar Germany

Udo Merkel

Introduction

When the first German nation-state was founded in 1871, the modern concept of sport had just emerged as a kind of by-product of the engineering, mining and textile know-how of the British, who helped to industrialise the German Empire. By that time the Germans had already developed and consolidated their own distinctive form of physical culture, *Turnen* (gymnastics). A large number of *Turner* (gymnasts) were part of a national movement that had actively promoted the political unification of the German people and democratisation of society. The conservative *Turner* reacted to the arrival of English sport(s) initially with indifference, which quickly turned into open hostility. They were, however, unable to stop this triumphal march of modern sport. Boosted by the development of public transport systems and the mass press, the momentum of modern sports proved unstoppable, and *Turnen* gave way slowly to the new forms, the latter embodying the contemporary spirit of energetic competition.

Although Germany was a relatively late developer in sport, the state encouraged physically active forms of recreation and physical education in schools for military, economic, political and ideological reasons. After the First World War, Germany finally adopted a democratic constitution which maintained the federal structures with cultural rights vested in the 25 federal states. At the same time, 'sport' became the generic term for all kinds of physically active forms of recreation. It consisted of two pillars: the first one integrating the traditional German gymnastic exercises and the other comprising team games, athletic competitions and competitive sports. By the beginning of the 1930s, however, membership data clearly show a ratio of 5:1 in favour of participation in sport organisation.

This short summary of the early development of sport in Germany sets the scene for the following analysis of sport's significant contribution to political and civil society in Germany. It will particularly focus on the relationship between sport and the German state(s), the notion of power and class relations. This form of critical analysis has been largely ignored by German scholars interested in the sociology of sport. A critical appraisal of the development and current state of the sociology of sport in Germany will be followed by a more detailed outline of Antonio Gramsci's concept of hegemony, which provides the theoretical framework for this chapter. Subsequently, the relationship between sport and the state will be explored in the Weimar Republic (1918–1933). In doing this I will make extensive use of the empirical research of other scholars (in particular, sport historians) in order to demonstrate the complex nature of sport as an object of struggle, control and resistance. I will argue that in this particular historical phase sport, as an element of popular culture with a mass appeal, was an integral and prominent part of the struggle for hegemony in German society. Neither German historians nor sociologists appear to be interested in such a perspective. Even the most recent publication (Eggers 2001) focusing upon football during the Weimar Republic is highly descriptive and restricts itself to explaining the growing popularity of football in this era without acknowledging fundamental conflicts and tensions in German civil society and sport. Finally, some conclusions will be drawn.

The first truly hegemonic conflicts emerged at the turn of the twentieth century when various forces were competing for the power to define and shape the nature and future of physical culture. This struggle found its climax when a fierce battle ensued between the traditional supporters of German gymnastics (*Turnen*) and the followers of the newly imported English sports and games. As this fight has been analysed elsewhere (see Merkel 1998 and 2000 with particular reference to football) it will be ignored in this chapter.

A harbinger of the forthcoming extensive and complex hegemonic struggles during the Weimar Republic was the lengthy and heated debate in the German parliament on 14 February 1914, in which the Social Democrats were the largest faction due to the electoral support of about one-third of the German population. At the end of the debate, a clear majority was in favour of state support for the 1916 Olympic Games. This decision meant that the German state intended to provide the funding and many other forms of support. Responsibility for top-level sport in Germany was allocated to the Home Office. Prior to this decision the discussions focused upon the merits and advantages of the modern concept of international competitive sport compared to the traditional German gymnastics and upon concerns of the working-class representatives who argued that only bourgeois sport organisations would benefit from the Olympic Games and the state's support.

This episode already highlights two important issues which were to become key features of sport's role in the hegemonic struggles in the Weimar Republic. First, never before had a central government so openly demonstrated its will to fund international representation of the state through top-level sport. Second, in contrast to the nineteenth-century power struggles, the different factions involved and their values have already become much more complex and consensus is achieved on the basis of discussions and negotiations rather than restrictive measures. There were not only the conservative supporters of traditional forms of German gymnastics arguing with the followers of the new concept of athleticism, competitive sport and team games about the most appropriate approach to physical culture, there were also the representatives of working-class sport accusing the government of neglecting and excluding them from public support, whilst the bourgeois sport organisations were keen to ensure funds for the hosting of the next Olympic Games. (The Olympics were to be held in Berlin but were cancelled due to the First World War.)

The critical and comparative study of sport

This chapter is not only motivated by my academic interest in the study of the relationship between sport, power and the state but also by my growing sense of uneasiness about the state of theory and research in the sociology of sport in Germany. There appear to be (at least) two fundamental problems from which the sociology of sport in Germany suffers. First, it is preoccupied with practical and applied questions about sport. It is only very rarely concerned with critical inquiries into the meaning of sport in society. The applied focus is often tied to positivist tendencies and structural–functionalist premises that permeate theory and research. Second, and certainly a related fundamental problem, is the general withdrawal from certain classical research questions and from the style of analysis that has most often accompanied them. The undeniable persistence of scarcity, power imbalances, gender, racial and ethnic inequalities, ideological conflicts, etc. are widely acknowledged but only occasionally investigated. There is a widespread belief that the popularisation and democratisation of sport over the last 100 years and the massive and dramatic expansion of opportunities for active and passive participation was largely a result of more facilities, cheaper equipment and caused the gradual demise of social barriers based on class, gender and racial differences. Consequently, social inequalities and conflicts are either ignored or considered to have ceased to exist. Furthermore, the very few new directions in social theory that have developed over the last decades in Germany have not contributed to a better understanding of the important social and political conflicts of our times.

Currently, the dominant theoretical paradigm in the German sociology of sport derives from Niklas Luhmann's extended Systems' Theory. Luhmann's analysis of the emergence and development of modern societies follows, to a large extent, the ideas of Herbert Spencer and Emile Durkheim. According to Luhmann, modern societies are the product of and characterised by a continual functional differentiation process leading to the emergence of subsystems which operate according to their own codes. However, he differs from them insofar as he adds the concept of stratification as an additional phase in the differentiation process of modern societies. Eventually, however, he argues that individuals are liberated from the constraints of the hierarchical structures of traditional societies. Luhmann's followers claim that his:

Systems' Theory with all its facets provides an additional important component to the theory of social differentiation whose explanatory potential goes far beyond Parsons. In contrast to Parsons, the starting point is not to preserve the existence of systems and to improve the ability of a society to reproduce itself but two guiding differences: system/environment and element/relation.

(Hartmann-Tews 1996: 22; quote translated by UM)

Luhmann's critics, however, argue that there are a number of fundamental problems with his Systems' Theory. Most frequently, from a humanist perspective, the perceived secondary role of human beings has been questioned as individuals appear to play a less important role than the actual systems themselves. From a sociological perspective:

The fundamental mistake of Luhmann's theory is the conflation of analytical and empirical, conceptual and institutional differentiation. One can construct analytically the code and the corresponding meaning of economic, political, legal or scientific action, namely taking that action which is profitable, or which increases power, or which settles conflict, or which approaches truth. Action can be guided by such a code; however, it nevertheless always involves elements of other codes. ... The collective action which takes place here and its product cannot be attributed to a single, autopoietic system; they are constituted by a multiplicity of action-orientations which can be separated analytically, but not concretely.

(Münch 1993: 54)

Despite these critical voices, Luhmann's Systems' Theory has found a considerable number of followers in general sociology, as well as the sociology of sport, in Germany. One of very few writers who is widely respected in both areas and currently one of the most prolific and sophisticated writers on Systems' Theory is Uwe Schimank (e.g. 1992 and 1996). Ulrich Beck (1986) also claims to employ Luhmann's theoretical framework and to have added a critical dimension by highlighting the growing risks through the expansion of modern technology in industrial society. Within the sociology of sport in Germany, Luhmann's work is highly regarded by a small but influential group of scholars – for example, Karl-Heinz Bette in Heidelberg, Klaus Cachay in Bielefeld and Ilse Hartmann-Tews in Cologne. Although all of them have made a number of significant contributions to the sociology of sport in Germany, they do not appear to be interested in the classical sociological issue of power. Their response to the observation of the emergence of new arenas of conflict within and between different systems is often simply to demand more efficient co-ordination mechanisms. They tend to ignore or marginalise the concept of power. Hartmann-Tews's comparative analysis of *Sport for All!?* (1996) provides a detailed insight into the development and realisation of the Sport for All policy in France, Great Britain and Germany, but hardly addresses any power issues. Although she demonstrates a thorough knowledge of the historical development of sport and the distinctive characteristics of the sport systems in these three countries, recognises the importance of different political forces in shaping sport and shows a detailed understanding of the organisational structures of sport in these societies, she does not focus upon power issues which the theme itself desperately requires as it implicitly raises questions of access, equality, equity, etc. The closest she gets to investigating this issue is her interesting but limited analysis of the tensions between inclusion and exclusion.

Whilst the followers of Luhmann's Systems' Theory form a small but influential group and are regularly engaged in constructive discussions, other colleagues with an interest in the sociology of sport display a much more dogmatic position in theoretical debates. There is, for example a widespread categorical rejection of Marxist concepts. Helmut Digel, who holds a chair in the Sport Pedagogy at the University of Tübingen, provides a good example. He explicitly rejects any understanding of sport as an entirely political phenomenon and instrument in the hands of powerful social groups as it exaggerates the political importance of sport. He claims that such an interpretation is based 'on a deficient theoretical foundation and contradicts the empirical evidence of the sporting praxis' (Digel 1988b: 138–41; quote translated by UM). In his writings, Digel explicitly acknowledges the decreasing autonomy of sport organisations and the increasing influence of the German state. He also shows through various examples how sport acts as a mediator between the individual and the state and is thus an important element of German civil society. However, his main concerns focus upon co-ordination problems between the different political tiers in Germany, the efficiency of the public administration system, the increasing dependency of sport organisations and athletes on state funding, the problematic principle of subsidarity, etc. (Digel 1988a: 60–80). Although Digel's research usually provides valuable and insightful information, his rejection of Marxist ideas is often accompanied by fairly uncritical and tame analyses. Digel considers the tendency to use sport for the purpose of national representation to be a 'problem' and a 'danger' but does not relate this development to more radical concepts of jingoism, nationalism, racism or xenophobia (Digel 1988b: 141). Nor does he offer an alternative theoretical framework for his analyses.

I can only speculate on the causes for these above-mentioned problems. They may partly stem from the fact that the reconstruction of German sociology after 1945 with considerable American support has guaranteed a direct reception of transatlantic methods and problem settings. In the sociology of sport, this found its most obvious manifestation in the work of Günther Lüschen, who is widely considered to be one of the founding fathers of this subject area in Germany. His writings clearly display the influence of structural–functionalist thoughts, which found its latest reincarnation in the work of Luhmann. Second, the academic background and socialisation of those scholars holding university chairs in the sociology of sport (many since the 1970s) could also play an important role. There are only about a dozen chairs in this subject area but a very large number of the scholars appointed to this position were not actually trained in sociology but in physical education and sport science or related fields, such as (sport) psychology. Anecdotal evidence suggests that appointment panels of Physical Education or Sport Science departments in universities have on several occasions rated academic qualification in these two areas higher than a degree in general sociology. A third reason could be the academic networks in which German scholars operate. Although a small number are regularly involved in the meetings of the International Society for the Sociology of Sport there are hardly any colleagues who appear to be engaged in (or simply in touch with) the advanced debates and discussions happening on the Anglo-American axis via NASSS (North American Society for the Sociology of Sport) or the BSA (British Sociological Association – Sociology of Sport Study Group). Fourth, from the late 1960s onwards there was a period of intense and heated theoretical discussions driven and dominated by the supporters of a 'Critical Theory of Sport' (e.g. Prokop 1971; Rigauer 1969; Rittner 1976; Vinnai 1972), which lasted for more than a decade. Subsequently, the 1980s and partly the 1990s appear to be lacking any theoretical debates. There is a sense of a general theoretical exhaustion during this period, from which the sociology of sport community in Germany has not yet fully recovered.

What the sociology of sport in Germany badly needs is a very different and innovative kind of theoretical approach leading to critical analyses which intend to get to the roots of things, challenge dominant conceptions, identify new points of departure for discussions and provide new ideas and directions for analysis. As the institutionalised and obsessive competition between the sporting and political systems of East and West Germany has now disappeared, the time for such a reorientation appears to be right, although there are, of course, still many practical, post-'reunification' problems to solve. The founding fathers of modern sociology, Comte, Marx, Durkheim and Weber, all aimed to understand fundamental processes of social change. They were particularly interested in identifying those forces that had destroyed feudal society and promoted the rise of industrial capitalism. In addition, they were deeply concerned with reconciling the new dilemmas and conflicts emerging as a result of industrial capitalism. These are, of course, grand questions, but they have not lost any of their significance. It would be very helpful if the German sociology of sport community would remind itself of these fundamental issues within sociology's classical tradition. Rediscovering such fundamental sociological concerns – for example, about social change, power and inequality – needs to be accompanied by the development of a critical sensitivity.

John Sugden and Alan Tomlinson have clearly highlighted in the introduction to this book that critical and radical approaches to the study of sport in society have been extremely fruitful for the development of the sociology of sport, and in his chapter Ian McDonald reaffirms that they are still essential for understanding and changing social and political relations. I am convinced that uniting such a critical or radical approach with empirical and interpretative analyses forms an effective strategy for the study of sport and society. Such a critical sociology of sport must be drawn inevitably to the classical sociological problem of inequality, power and domination. A focus on relational issues associated with class and power (instead of distributive aspects) will help to avoid crude categorisations, static and abstract models, and will be able to explain the dynamics of power relations much better.

Any critical sociological analysis ought to start with clearly identifying the nature of problems and issues that have led one to conduct the study. Attention must also be paid to the fundamental assumptions which usually form the base for one's orientation and chosen approach. In this sense, much of the following analysis owes its point of departure to some Marxist and neo-Marxist concerns and agendas, in particular, to the long-standing tradition of class theory and conflicts. As this chapter is concerned with physical culture and the relation of this cultural formation to political domination, Gramsci's concept of hegemony will play an important role. My analysis has also been influenced by British Cultural Studies and rejects simple notions of economically determined class domination, the traditional Marxist base–superstructure model and theorisations of the seductive manipulative powers of ideologies leading to a false consciousness.

Gramsci's concept of hegemony was certainly the most original Marxist thought of the first half of the twentieth century and has become most influential and widely used in the social sciences. Gramsci's focus is upon the role of independent civil society which allows a high degree of autonomy to private institutions, such as political parties, the church, etc. For Gramsci, the domination of one class over others is not the product of force, coercion or economic power, nor the outcome of ideological manipulation, but the result of one class establishing cultural domination and authority through economic, political, intellectual and moral leadership. Hegemony is achieved (although never complete) within civil society and the private institutions, which mediate the individual and the state. This distinction between civil and political society cannot be absolute as modern societies cannot be broken down into entirely separate and independent institutions. Sport, as an institution of civil society, is not only dependent on the state's funding and provision of facilities, but also highly prescriptive and ideologically loaded within the education system. Whilst Marx argued that the primary task of the state was to defend the economic and political interests of the capitalist class, Gramsci stresses the state's instrumental role in creating and maintaining those institutions comprising civil society. Hegemony is essentially a synthesis of moral, political and intellectual leadership by one class which has successfully developed from initially defending its own interests to unifying and directing all other social groups:

> The whole tenor of Gramsci's Marxism was against reductionism of any kind: culture was not simply class culture, the state was not merely a class state, consent was not false consciousness. Hegemony implied a democratic relation between ruled and ruler, the existence of institutions which enable the subordinate groups to articulate their own interests and defend them, to build their own distinctive culture.
>
> (Swingewood 1991: 209)

For Gramsci, the area of culture, in particular popular culture, is the arena for negotiations in which dominant views achieve and secure hegemony. These negotiations must lead to some kind of apparently genuine accommodation in order for the dominant class to achieve leadership. As hegemony is never complete there are always battles to fight, whose parameters are partly given by economic conditions, in order to win the consent of those it ultimately subordinates.

Whilst John Hargreaves has very fruitfully employed Gramsci's concept for the analysis of *Sport, Power and Culture* (1986) in Britain, George Sage (1998) clearly illustrates that sport has also been integral in the struggle for hegemony in American society. Sugden and Bairner's study of the political nature of sport in Northern Ireland (1995) shows convincingly that Gramsci's distinction between political and civil society is an extremely helpful analytical tool.

Using Gramsci for the following analysis offers a more subtle and flexible approach and helps avoid monolithic and mechanical explanations of the workings of modern class societies. The very few radical sociological studies focusing on class, power relations and sport in Germany go back to the late 1960s and early 1970s and must be seen in the context of the emergence of a New Left subsequent to the student riots. Bero Rigauer's seminal text on the relationship between *Sport and Work* (1969) was followed by Ulrike Prokop's critical sociological analysis of the Olympic Games (1971) and Gerhard Vinnai's book on *Sport in Class Society* (1972). What all these authors had in common was that they used a (neo-)Marxist theoretical framework for their studies which aimed to contribute to wider debates about sport and capitalism. Paradoxically, all of them dealt with sport without saying very much about the body. This changed in 1976 when Karin Rittner published her book on *Sport und Arbeitsteilung* (*Sport and the Division of Labour*). Gramsci's ideas, however, have so far hardly been recognised in the sociology of sport in Germany and thus not been employed as a theoretical framework for the study of sport.

Sport, civil society and class relations in the Weimar Republic

The following analysis will focus on sport, civil society and class relations in the Weimar Republic. This era plays an important role in the social and political history of Germany as it marked the end of fairly static and rigid power structures, which have traditionally been based on force, coercion and suppression, and the beginning of a more dynamic set of power relations. The new constitution made Germany a representative parliamentary democracy with universal suffrage for men and women over twenty, independent of their social status and based on the principle of strict proportional representation. Although all the political inequalities of the previous eras had been swept away by this new constitution, many aspects of the old social order had survived. However, they had seriously weakened and undermined the faith in the established order and in all authority:

> With the collapse of the Empire, three ultimately irreconcilable political tendencies emerged. The first comprised those who resented all democratisation and any loss of their political or social privileges. ... At the other extreme were the revolutionaries, who hoped not only for political democracy, but the abolition of capitalism. ... Between these two forces were those politicians and social groups for whom the avoidance of chaos was the primary concern.
>
> (Pulzer 1997: 103)

Although the First World War had certainly interrupted, and had a negative impact on, the development of German society and the growth of sport, the roots for any further developments reach back to the period between the foundation of the first German nation state and the war. A short summary of the main trends in the relationship between sport and class relations will therefore be provided before discussing the state-supported growth of modern sport during the Weimar Republic and sport's role in the fragmentation, recomposition, missionising and disciplining of the working class in this period. The concluding comments will focus on the achievement of hegemony.

From repression to reform of popular leisure activities

Despite the political unification in 1871, German society continued to show very clear divisions between the aristocracy and the middle class, farmers and the workers, monarchists and republicans, liberals and socialists, rich and poor, conservatives and modernists, educated and those who did not have any access to education and cultural capital. The old and still dominant aristocratic elites clung to political power, whilst the new middle class and the workers movement with its political parties and unions demanded more political participation and rights.

Even after the Anti-Socialist Laws had been repealed in 1890, working-class leisure activities often provoked a negative response from those concerned with maintaining the relatively new social order:

> Traditional fairs and festivals were suppressed and curtailed. Drinking was made illegal in factories, outlets for the purchase of alcohol were closely monitored and tavern opening hours were continually interfered with. The streets were gradually cleared of irksome entertainers, small-scale theatrical entertainment was strictly controlled and even dancing was frowned upon ... And when workers joined associations to pursue their interests collectively they were accused of neglecting their family lives.
>
> (Abrams 1992: 139)

The driving force behind these repressive actions was not the central state, which appeared to be less concerned about the nature of working-class leisure, but rather the local authorities often combining law enforcement with paternalistic attitudes to maintain the established social order. Towards the end of the nineteenth century, a number of local and regional middle-class organisations emerged whose primary concern was positive improvements in the provision of leisure and recreation. Due to the lack of central legislation regulating working-class leisure, these groups were able to develop some considerable influence. Consequently, a large number of local authorities got involved in welfare schemes and introduced social reform measures. Larger employers started to provide their own company welfare systems for their workforce. Although both company as well as public welfare paternalism was double edged and combined social reform with social control, the latter often being more prominent than the former, there was also an increasing concern with creating and promoting harmony between the classes.

During the first decade of the twentieth century, social reform groups and organisations concentrated their efforts on improvements in the provision of parks and libraries as the proletarian body and mind became the central focus of the concept of rational recreation (cf. Abrams 1992: 139–68). In the long run, both parks (which often provided playing fields) and libraries (which promoted the reading of various kind of literature including sport reports in the mass press) had a significant impact on the growth of modern sport, particularly during the Weimar Republic. At the same time, the urban industrial working-class developed a distinctive class consciousness, which found its most explicit expression in the foundation of a dense network of educational, recreational and sporting organisations affiliated to either the SPD (Social Democratic Party) or the KPD (Communist Party).

From socially exclusive to fragmented mass sport: the role of the Weimar state

In contrast to the pre-war period, the central German state, as well as local authorities, assumed a much more active and positive role in regulating and promoting leisure. Instead of repressing the popular leisure activities of the working class, there was now a much stronger emphasis on channelling proletarian energies into more rational, beneficial and healthier forms of recreation. Their changed attitude and input contributed significantly to the development and massive growth of sport in the twentieth century. During the Weimar Republic, the central government and the 25 federal states, as well as local authorities, began systematically to plan for leisure and recreation. Although the war had impoverished Germany, fairly generous funds were provided for the building of sport facilities and spaces allocated for recreational purposes. This very often happened with the support of local capital and industry.

In 1922, Bochum already had a football stadium with a capacity of 70,000. The match between Germany and Hungary marked the international inauguration of the new ground which had been built by the Gymnastics and Sport Club (*Turn- und Sportverein (TSV)*) and was heavily subsidised by the local council. The multi-functional stadium in Cologne was opened in 1923 and only two years later, in November, the building of the Westfalenhalle in Dortmund, a large multi-purpose indoor facility, was completed. Its playing area is almost as large as a football field and is surrounded by a bicycle racetrack. This venue had a flexible seating concept which ranged from 5,000 seats at cycle races to a capacity of 15,000 spectators for boxing fights. Only a few hundred metres away and seven months later, in June 1926, the new stadium *Rote Erde* (Red Earth) – comprising a football field, a 400-metre running track and other athletic facilities – was opened. In July 1926, the similarly designed stadium in Duisburg with a capacity of 40,000 was opened. Whilst one of the town's largest steel companies provided a large part of the 750 acres of land needed for the new multi-functional *Wedau-Stadion*, the building costs were taken over completely by the local authority.

Other local authorities were less generous but yet supportive in other ways. As the crowds following the football club Schalke 04 in Gelsenkirchen in the mid-1920s regularly exceeded the capacity (5,000) of their stadium, the club decided to build a new, bigger stadium. This happened with the support of a large industrial company and the local council. The former let very cheaply an adequate area to the club while the latter functioned as a creditor to the banks. Although this was a very risky project for such a small club as Schalke 04 with only about 800 predominantly working-class members, the *Glückauf-Kampfbahn* was finished in 1928.

The often very generous public support for the building of new facilities – despite inflation and economic crisis – had a clear rationale. Whilst in the nineteenth century gymnastics were primarily promoted in order to create a powerful army for Germany's liberation from French occupation, the military aspects of physical exercises had become less important in the Weimar Republic, though not obsolete. There was a much stronger emphasis on health benefits of regular physical exercises and the impact on the economic productivity of the nation. Government papers of the 1920s repeatedly highlighted the expected positive benefits of physical exercises for the world of work. Consequently, previously neglected groups, such as young people and women, were particularly encouraged to join sports organisations during the 1920s. However, there was also a general consensus that active participation in sport meant that the male population was physically better prepared for a potential war. This was particularly relevant as the Treaty of Versailles confined the German army to a total of 100,000 soldiers.

Other measures taken during the 1920s in order to promote sport involved:

1   In 1921, the Sport Badge (*Sportabzeichen*) was introduced for men, women and young people. It came in gold, silver and bronze and was awarded according to age and achievements in five different disciplines. It became very popular and still exists.
2   The education authorities introduced annual school championships for boys and girls promoting mass participation and the striving for top-level performances in a wide variety of track and field events.
3   Tax reductions and certain allowances were introduced for sport organisations.
4   Members of sports clubs travelling to competitions were entitled to reduced public transport fares.

(Ueberhorst 1986: 109–16)

In addition, sporting issues were important elements in the political and public discourse of the time. Although neither the proposed introduction of a *'Turnen* and Sport Duty Year'* (as a substitute for the banned compulsory military training) nor the Sports Space Bill (demanding the provision of 5 square metres of outdoor space for each citizen by local authorities) became law, the public debates about these initiatives had their impact.

Consequently, many sports experienced an enormous boom during the 1920s, as the following figures clearly show: several tens of thousands watched the 'Essen Grand Prix' in 1920, a professional cycling race; 35,000 spectators witnessed the above-mentioned goal-less football match between Hungary and Germany in 1922 in Bochum and two years later 40,000 people had gathered in Duisburg to see Italy beat Germany 1–0. Moreover, people were not only interested in watching sports but also in participating. The gymnastic festival in Cologne in 1928 was attended by about 200,000 active and passive participants and the Workers' Olympics in Frankfurt in 1925 attracted 150,000 spectators.

In comparative European perspective, there is no doubt that such a degree of state involvement and intervention in sport at all political levels was unique for the 1920s. It is also important to stress that sport's expansion to a mass participation base opened new avenues for the development of class relations and widened the network of paths for hegemonic struggles. 'Mass sport' provided the dominant groups in German society with a large and rich cultural resource for the consolidation of their position and the spread of their norms, values and ideas. Due to sport's popularity and its ability to attract large numbers of spectators, it became quickly integrated into consumer culture. The commercialisation of leisure, in general, was not a new phenomenon. The widespread availability, acceptance and popularity of commercial leisure products had already commenced before the war (Abrams 1992). However, the 1920s saw the emergence of a new consumer ideology which manifested itself quickly in the world of (spectator) sports. Due to the general increase of disposable income, workers were now able to attend cinemas, dance halls and football grounds. The middle-class-domi-nated mass media – in particular, the press, film industry and later the radio – also 'contributed to the emergence of a mass culture by transmitting the same message to readers, viewers and listeners belonging to all classes, nationalities, religions and regions' (Abrams 1992: 180). Although leisure priorities were mainly class specific – the middle class continued to enjoy the socially still very exclusive theatres, opera, cafes and restaurants – the world of sport provided a number of opportunities for direct and indirect encounters.

However, as the new German constitution contained a long list of basic rights for all citizens, such as freedom of speech and association, the already dense network of working-class organisations under the split leadership of the SPD and the KPD grew considerably. Part of this network were strong and autonomous Social-Democratic and communist sport bodies. The umbrella organisation for working-class sport clubs was the *Zentralkommission für Arbeitersport und Körperpflege* ((ZK) Central Committee for Workers' Sport and Physical Hygiene), which had already been founded in 1912. A key element of the ZK's statutes was the objective to combat the class enemy's attempts to gain the allegiance of workers through sport. The majority of the ZK's members derived from the *Arbeiter- Turn und Sportbund* ((ATSB) Workers' Gymnastics and Sport Association), which had about 840,000 members in 1922 and was closely associated to the SPD. Another influential member body of the ZK was the cycling organisation 'Solidarity' with about 350,000 members. The organised working-class sport movement did not only reject any co-operation with its bourgeois equivalent but regularly appealed to the class consciousness of proletarian athletes to leave bourgeois organisations. However:

> the earlier discrimination had long-lasting effects. So many young people ... who had joined middle-class clubs and who had made friends there were reluctant to give all this up ... because of ideological consid-erations.
>
> (Gehrmann 1988: 187; quote translated by UM)

When it became obvious to those striving for hegemony that there was a considerable opposition to dominant groups organised around sporting activities many middle-class sport clubs started to develop marketing strategies in order to undermine the popularity of the working-class sports movement. Whilst some focused on very few sports and attempted to develop a distinctive profile and better services for their members, others widened the spectrum of sports on offer, introduced various forms of competitions and championships and developed different sets of rules and regulations to suit different age groups. The aim was to attract new and, in particular, younger members and to increase the already existing fragmentation of working-class sport.

Sport and the fragmentation, recomposition and disciplining of the working class

The general fragmentation of working-class sport was clearly reflected at grass roots level. The involvement of the industrial working class in the Ruhr area, a region dominated by coal mining and the steel industry in North Rhine Westphalia, clearly demonstrates this situation. Whilst initially – that is before the First World War – a large number of working people joined existing clubs of the German middle class to participate in sport, later, during the Weimar Republic, they also founded their own voluntary organisations, which caused a number of tensions and conflicts.

Already, before the First World War, a small group of very affluent middle-class individuals had started to appropriate the role of sport patrons supporting various teams. Since involvement in sport was perceived to have a positive impact on productivity and to generate an emotional bonding to the workplace, many industrialists supported already existing clubs or encouraged their foundation, morally and financially:

> Gyms, pitches, all kind of equipment and sports clothes were all provided by the companies, coaches were employed ... members of the clubs had to pay only very small membership fees – if at all – transport to away matches was provided by the companies and they also paid for social events.
>
> (Gehrmann 1988: 191; quote translated by UM)

Furthermore, middle-class clubs managed to present themselves successfully in the media as responding to the need for heroes and glamour in a world weary of war. At the same time, reports in the print media promoted the emergence of stars and role models due to the strong emphasis upon individual achievements. Proletarian newspapers, however, hardly ever mentioned the names of specific players. Instead they referred to players' positions and stressed the team performance.

The interest of the German working class to establish their own football clubs rose dramatically, however, after the successful fight for the 8-hour working day in 1919, the further mechanisation of industrial production and the decrease of the average family size in the early 1920s. In addition, the new constitution of the Weimar Republic had ended the state suppression of socialist, communist and working-class organisations and provided a liberal legal framework and opportunities for self-organisation. However, the role model and established template for a voluntary organisation was the private club. Whilst in the past they were very exclusive and often socially extremely homogenous institutions, they now started to function more and more as mediators between the state and the individual.

Already, in the early 1920s, it became very obvious that the new working-class football clubs, such as Schalke 04 based in Gelsenkirchen in the Ruhr area, were going to dominate the soccer scene. A number of outstanding players quickly became local heroes. Although their supporters did not reject their status as stars, they modified this bourgeois concept and made them into representatives of a very distinctive working-class culture by allocating nick names, such as 'Hammer' or 'Iron Foot', which clearly referred to industrial qualities and derived from their familiar world of industrial work.

At the same time, the West German Football Association decided in 1923 to introduce a policy entitled 'The New Way'. This policy suspended any promotion and relegation for two years. Officially, the rationale behind this measure was to counteract the increasingly unfair and violent behaviour on and off the pitch resulting from the growing competitiveness among the teams. The aim was to improve the standards of behaviour of both players and spectators. Although newspaper articles frequently reported violent outbreaks during football matches, for many 'The New Way' was a policy taken to secure the dominant position of bourgeois clubs whilst stopping the proletarian clubs and players on their way to success and fame (Gehrmann 1988: 95–6).

There is also historical evidence that the middle-class-dominated governing body, the German Football Association (DFB), excluded some working-class football clubs from organised competitions as they were considered to be 'wild'. This affected two groups of football clubs: first, those comprising members from the unskilled and rougher sections of the working class, in particular miners, who had formed clubs without proper statutes, middle-class guarantors and without joining an appropriate regional or national governing body; second, those who had decided in the spirit of egalitarianism not to have any official leaders in the form of a board of directors. In contrast, the skilled members of the working class did not hesitate to accept bourgeois notions of respectability and to adopt middle-class models of social organisation. The non-compliance to the prescribed bourgeois organisational framework and legal arrangements was, however, also disapproved by the Social Democratic and communist sports movements which were very keen to recruit these voluntary associations and to commit them to their respective political programmes. The continuous efforts to integrate these 'wild' clubs into one of the organised working-class sports movements displays a fundamental weakness of both the Social Democratic and communist parties in Weimar Germany; they did not really understand the full complexity and all the subtleties of the social and cultural development of the working class and their attempts to integrate this class were consequently restricted to exclusively organisational issues.

The concept of amateurism also played an important role in the hegemonic struggles between dominant groups and working-class organisations. The statutes of the governing body for football, DFB, clearly stated that only those football clubs whose players were amateurs could join it. Professionals were defined as those players who received money or goods as rewards, broken-time payments, who taught football in order to earn a living or who accepted reimbursements for travel expenses which were beyond the actual costs incurred. Although already at the beginning of the twentieth century a few clubs had started to charge admission fees, the question of amateurism and professionalism became a pressing issue only in the 1920s when spectator sports, such as boxing and football, experienced an enormous boom. The increasing popularity of football as a spectator sport clearly undermined the amateur ethos as players started to demand their share of the gate money. Although it was no secret that many received illegal payments, the DFB was not prepared to move away from the rigid amateurism clause. Instead, professionalism was publicly denounced as a modern disease undermining the cultural and national mission of German football. The DFB saw this debate as another welcome opportunity to show the wider public how distinctively different German football was from the English game. As a competitive amateur game it was perceived to be a continuation of genuine German physical culture, played in the pure and holistic spirit of physical and mental improvement instead of for material gains. As a consequence, rules, regulations and lists of punishments became more extensive, detailed and draconian:

> The German version of amateurism was an ideology, which denounced professionalism as decadent alienation, a particularly nasty form of materialism, an expression of an ill-fated spirit, and positioned professional athletes – in a way – close to prostitution.
>
> (Schulze-Marmeling 1992: 53; quote translated by UM)

In 1930, Schalke 04 became a prominent victim of the DFB's crusade against professionalism as an enquiry found evidence of illegal payments, gifts and loans to many of its first team's players and declared them to be professionals. This meant that they were excluded from participating in any DFB competitions and, as almost all of them had working-class origins, were driven into unemployment. In addition, they had to pay large sums of money as a fine and Schalke's board of directors was urged to retire.

Subsequently, Schalke's treasurer committed suicide. However, the pressure on the DFB to ease the draconian punishment meant one year later most of the players were rehabilitated and allowed to play again (Gehrmann 1988: 99–101). The first match of the reinstated first team of Schalke 04 was only a friendly against Fortuna Düsseldorf, but when it took place on 1 June 1931 it attracted 70,000 spectators.

The fierceness of the conflicting local patriotism surrounding this match was even picked up by the print media and clearly demonstrates an additional and new quality of fragmentation. In contrast to the period before the First World War when a clear class consciousness among German workers did not exist as their identities were based on religious, ethnic and occupational divisions, in the years after the war the German working class became more homogenous, lost many of its divisive features and was subjected to a far-reaching standardisation process ranging from work arrangements to commercial leisure products. However, this growing class solidarity was clearly undermined by two sets of divisions: those caused by membership in bourgeois and proletarian clubs, and those expressed in the celebration of local and regional loyalties.

Conclusion: Sport, working-class culture and the struggle for hegemony during the Weimar Republic

The Weimar Republic was chosen as the focus for this analysis because of its social and political significance for the development of German society, sport and the relationship between sport and the power network. This era marks an important turning point in Germany's history as it questioned and transformed the established, pre-First World War social order. In this process, sport became increasingly implicated in the interaction between dominant and subordinate groups.

The rapid adoption and remarkable scale of expansion of organised sport was a major cultural achievement of Weimar Germany, which laid much of the foundation for the country's future developments in sport. It was particularly the Weimar state, in conjunction with industrial and commercial capital, which allied itself with the working-class demand for exciting leisure activities against the remaining protagonists of rigorous (local) state control and suppression – an alliance which allowed the proletariat in the first instance to gain greater access to physically active forms of recreation and, in a later stage, to compete with members of the middle class on equal terms. Without the state's direct and indirect support sport could not have penetrated and become part of working-class culture.

Sport has contributed to the hegemonic project during the Weimar Republic in (at least) three different but nevertheless related ways:

1   The state-supported growth of sport led to the emergence of a rich cultural formation. Although large numbers of workers were organised

in the social democratic and communist sport movements the total adoption of dominant norms and values, such as the principles of individual achievement, competition, division of labour and specialisation, the concept of top-level sport and the corresponding model of vertical stratification in the form of league tables, clearly shows that the project of hegemony through sport was successfully achieved by the Weimar State and its allies within civil society, and the emerging commercial sector.

2   Organised sport provided the dominant classes with access to those whose consent they were seeking and with the opportunity to retain a relatively high level of control and influence at the cultural level and to discipline the working class into conformity with bourgeois norms of respectability. This found its most explicit expression in the way workers were organising themselves as they chose the sports club as their preferred organisational framework. This model of a voluntary association had a long tradition in German (middle and upper class) history, was regulated by the state and formed the basis for an organisationally, fairly standardised civil society.

3   When the working class began to lose its marginal position in urban society and developed into a much more homogenous social group, sport (as an intentional, conscious project of the state) contributed significantly to its fragmentation. The most obvious internal divisions occurred between men and women, old and young, the respectable and rougher sections, those in social democratic or communist sport organisations, and between different local and regional loyalties.

As the process of achieving hegemony is hardly ever complete, it is often accompanied by unresolved conflicts, contradictions and confusions. The non-compliance of some working-class organisations to the bourgeois amateur ideal is one good example of such a tension. The celebrations for the new football and athletics stadium 'Red Earth' in Dortmund also show this convincingly as it experienced two inauguration ceremonies, one on 6 June and the other on 13 June 1926. As the bourgeois and the proletarian sport organisations were unable to agree on the format of the opening ceremony, they decided to have two. Whilst no media coverage could be identified for the first occasion, the working-class baptism of 'Red Earth' was widely reported and appreciated in the local newspapers – in particular, the colourful procession of 6,000 participants through Dortmund and the staging of a living chess game, in which the white figures represented the French aristocracy and the black figures the workers and farmers of the French revolution. The latter won.

References

Abrams, L. (1992) *Workers' Culture in Imperial Germany: Leisure and Recreation in the Rhineland and Westphalia*, London and New York: Routledge.

Bade, K.J. (1994) *Homo Migrans: Wanderungen aus und nach Deutschland*, Essen: Klartext.

Beck, U. (1986) *Die Risikogesellschaft*, Frankfurt/M.: Suhrkamp Verlag.

Cachay, K. (1990) 'Versportlichung der Gesellschaft und Entsportung des Sports: Systemtheoretische Anmerkungen zu einem gesellschaftlichen Phänomen', in H. Gabler and U. Göhner (eds) *Für einen Besseren Sport: Themen, Entwicklungen und Perspektiven aus Sport und Sportwissenschaft*, Schorndorf: Verlag Karl Hofmann.

Dann, O. (1996) *Nation und Nationalismus in Deutschland 1770–1990*, München: Beck.

Digel, H. (1988a) 'Die öffentliche Sportverwaltung in der Bundesrepublik Deutschland', in H. Digel (ed.) *Sport im Verein und Verband*, Schorndorf: Verlag Karl Hofmann.

—— (1988b) 'Sport als Interessenobjekt nationalstaatlicher Politik', in H. Digel (ed.) *Sport im Verein und Verband*, Schorndorf: Verlag Karl Hofmann.

Dixon, J.G. (1986) 'Prussia, politics and physical education', in P.C. McIntosh, J.G. Dixon, A.D. Munrow and R.F. Willetts (eds) *Landmarks in the History of Physical Education*, London: Routledge & Kegan Paul.

Eggers, E. (2001) *Fußball in der Weimarer Republik*, Kassel: Agon Sportverlag.

Eisenberg, C. (1999) *'English Sports' und Deutsche Bürger: Eine Gesellschaftsgeschichte 1800–1939*, Paderborn: Schöningh.

Fischer, G. and Lindner, U. (1999) *Stürmer für Hitler: Vom Zusammenspiel zwischen Fußball und Nationalsozialismus*, Göttingen: Verlag Die Werkstatt.

Gehrmann, S. (1988) *Fußball-Vereine-Politik. Zur Sportgeschichte des Reviers*, Essen: Reimar Hobbing Verlag.

—— (1996) 'Symbol of German resurrection: Max Schmeling, German sports idol', in R. Holt, J.A. Mangan and P. Lafranchi (eds) *European Heroes: Myth, Identity, Sport*, London: Frank Cass.

Gramsci, A. (1971) *Selections from the Prison Notebooks*, London: Lawrence & Wishart.

Hargreaves, J. (1986) *Sport, Power and Culture: A Social and Historical Analysis of Popular Sport in Britain*, Cambridge: Polity Press.

Hartmann-Tews, I. (1996) *Sport für Alle!?*, Schorndorf: Verlag Karl Hofmann.

Heinrich, A. (2000) *Der Deutsche Fußballbund: Eine Politische Geschichte*, Köln: Papy-Rossa.

Krüger, A. (1996) 'The German way of worker sport', in A. Krüger and J. Riordan (eds) *The Story of Worker Sport*, Champaign, IL: Human Kinetics.

Mann, G. (1996) *The History of Germany Since 1789*, London: Pimlico.

Merkel, U. (1998) 'Sport in divided nations: the case of the old, new and "re-united" Germany', in A. Bairner and J. Sugden (eds) *Sport in Divided Societies*, Aachen: Meyer & Meyer.

—— (2000) 'The hidden social and political history of the German Football Association (DFB) 1900–1950', *Soccer and Society* 1(2): 167–86.

Münch, R. (1993) 'The contribution of German social theory to European sociology', in B. Nedelmann and P. Sztompka (eds) *Sociology in Europe: In Search of Identity*, Berlin/New York: Walter de Gruyter.

Prokop, U. (1971) *Soziologie der Olympischen Spiele*, Munich: Carl Hansa Verlag.

Pulzer, P. (1997) *Germany, 1870–1945: Politics, State Formation and War*, Oxford: Oxford University Press.

Reulecke, J. (1982) ' "Veredelung der Volkserholung" und "edle Geselligkeit": Sozialreformerische Bestrebungen zur Gestaltung der arbeitsfreien Zeit im

Kaiserreich', in G. Huck (ed.) *Sozialgeschichte der Freizeit. Untersuchungen zum Wandel der Alltagskultur in Deutschland*, Wuppertal: Peter Hammer Verlag.

Rigauer, B. (1969) *Sport und Arbeit,* Frankfurt/M.: Suhrkamp Verlag.

Rittner, K. (1976) *Sport und Arbeitsteilung: Zur Sozialen Funktion und Bedeutung des Sports*, Bad Homburg: Limpert Verlag.

Sage, G.H. (1998) *Power and Ideology in American Sport: A Critical Perspective*, Champaign, IL: Human Kinetics.

Schimank, U. (1992) 'Größenwachstum oder soziale Schließung? Das Inklusions-dilemma des Breitensports', *Sportwissenschaft* 22: 32–45.

—— (1996) *Theorien Gesellschaftlicher Differenzierung*, Opladen: Leske & Budrich.

Schulze-Marmeling, D. (1992) *Der gezähmte Fußball: Zur Geschichte einer subversiven Sportart*, Göttingen: Verlag Die Werkstatt.

Sugden, J. and Bairner, A. (1995) *Sport, Sectarianism and Society in a Divided Ireland*, Leicester: Leicester University Press.

Swingewood, A. (1991) *A Short History of Sociological Thought*, London: Macmillan.

Ueberhorst, H. (1986) 'Sport, physical culture and political action in Germany during the Weimar Republic', in G. Redmond (ed.) *Sport and Politics*, Champaign, IL: Human Kinetics.

Vinnai, G. (1972) *Sport in der Klassengesellschaft*, Frankfurt/M: Suhrkamp Verlag.

9 Contest, conflict and resistance in South Africa's sport policies

Marc Keech

Introduction

Andre Odendaal and 'Cheeky' Watson were two of a kind – although not at first sight. Andre was a cricketer, tall, angular, but after meeting the newspaper editor Donald Woods at the age of twelve,[1] thoughtful and analytical – 'different from the other kids in my class'.[2] 'Cheeky' was a rugby player, strong, powerful and defined by his family's values. Andre lived in the Western Cape; 'Cheeky' was from Eastern Province. However, both were white and both defied the South African Government by playing sport with non-white teams. Andre Odendaal played provincial cricket, but in 1977 he became the first white player to play in multi-racial cricket leagues, and thereby defy the Group Areas Act, forsaking first-class facilities at Stellenbosch University for what he terms 'a life-changing experience':[3]

> When I joined to play for SACBOC (South African Cricket Board of Control, the non-racial cricket federation), I had no other contact with the cricket world. That was how polarised our world was. It was a choice you made that affected your entire existence … you couldn't go back from that into your apartheid enclave.[4]

'Cheeky', along with his brothers, Gavin, Valance and Ron, left the Eastern Province Rugby Union to play in the non-racial KwaZakhele rugby union in Port Elizabeth. They were found guilty of entering an African township in 1977. The former Springbok rugby captain Morne Du Plessis met the Watsons long after the episode:

> To play sport under permit was an action of one's own volition; a sportsman's collaboration with the system. The Watson brothers gave up almost everything to make their point. It was a tremendous sacrifice; one that can now only be admired and make others humble. I asked them why they did what they did. They could only reply that it was the right thing to do.[5]

As part of its multinational sports policy the South African Government extended its permit system, which prohibited interaction between the races in African townships to sport.[6] Those wishing to visit a part of a township not demarcated for one's own race were required to request permits. In order to counter the emergence of the non-racial sports movement during the mid-1970s, applications to stage sporting events between races were to be made via the Department of Sport and Recreation. The state's intention was threefold: first, to inhibit the growth of the non-racial sports movement by organising the non-racial sports movement along racial and class lines; second, to strengthen collaboration between African federations (and thereby nullify collaboration with white federations); and third, to break up attempts to initiate alternative sports programmes (Roberts 1988: 29). The actions of the Watsons and Odendaal are but two illustrations of the extent to which sport served to highlight apartheid practices and brought critical international attention to human rights being denied through the apartheid system.

This chapter argues for a reconceptualisation that shows how sport, at both domestic and international levels, intensified the cultural struggle against apartheid and challenged the structures of the apartheid system. This reconceptualisation requires the blending of hegemony theory as applied to internal South African politics, with a pluralist recognition of the nature of international relations, and acknowledgement that these spheres impact reciprocally one upon the other. The academic study of South Africa's unique political framework has often been documented in terms of the 'domestic' or the 'international'. In international relations the dividing lines between different perspectives tend to be firmly drawn with academic studies usually located clearly within one perspective or another. As an international issue the politics of the anti-apartheid movement could be substantially encapsulated within a pluralist framework. However, to rely on such a framework to explain the domestic politics of apartheid and the international anti-apartheid campaign would risk failing to capture the multi-layered nature of the conflict over apartheid. There is often a general reluctance to attempt to build explanatory models which draw upon concepts and theories from more than one perspective or integrate analysis within the domestic frameworks of political struggle. In order to provide a satisfactory explanation of both domestic and international politics of apartheid it is necessary for a process of theory building to take place that combines the explanatory strength of hegemony theory and the organisational understanding permitted by pluralist theory. Eclecticism in theory building is often seen as an indication of indecision and theoretical confusion. However, some case studies in international relations require substantial analysis, drawing upon more than one conceptual framework, to illuminate both the international and domestic levels of interaction. South Africa is one such case.

International sport and domestic political change in South Africa

Culture is a constant dynamic in the domestic politics of South Africa and in incidences where the issue of cultural struggle around the issue of apartheid overspilled into the international arena, significant international interaction took place. Culture emerged as a prominent arena for conflict and contestation between dominant and subordinate classes as political repression and rigorous control over the means of production denied the non-white population the political and economic resources required for a viable counter-hegemonic strategy. Changes in hegemonic relations occur through struggle, resistance and accommodation, although the respective weighting of such factors would appear as yet, difficult to determine accurately. However, it is possible to see South Africa during the apartheid era as one social formation where the theory accounts particularly well for the intensity of the struggle at a cultural level. One must be careful not to uncritically overextend the use of hegemony as an explanation of change. The problem is to specify the conditions under which it is an appropriate explanation. A possible answer to this is to identify hegemony as a model of transformation where culture is a central site of conflict. A further contention is that hegemonic transformation can also be a component of global processes wherein local forces shape global processes beyond the boundaries of a nation-state and vice versa.

Thus, the challenge is to theoretically entwine the 'domestic' and the 'international' in order to provide a more sensitive awareness of the power dynamics concerning the domestic and international anti-apartheid movements in sport. At the heart of a discussion that involves international moves against South Africa lies the extent to which domestic policies shaped global processes, and the consequent responses of the international community to supporting movements that aimed to challenge hegemonic processes. Identifying the precise nature of the contact between agencies and extent to which political change occurred as a result can illustrate the international contribution to domestic counter-hegemonic struggle. To identify where this occurred most effectively it is necessary to concentrate on elements of social and cultural change that occurred within sport, and on the part played by them in changes to political practices.

The international anti-apartheid movement was a social movement bound by a desire to work toward a change in a single society's system of values. It was reflective of other international social groups which are bound together, not by any formal organisational contact, but by a sense of shared value and flows of information that are fluid and transcend both national and organisational boundaries. Elements of a common cultural ethos and collective values were at the heart of the international anti-apartheid movement. They became shared by an increasing number of individuals and organisations who adopted a sense of communal opposition to a system identified as morally wrong. Media and personal/organisational communication channels were used as vehicles for the diffusion of information regarding South Africa. International protest against South Africa took on a variety of different organisational forms in a number of cultural spheres. Consequently, organisational activity against apartheid varied in size, composition and forms of action. It is the precise nature of these interactions that provides the examples of how domestic and international protest reciprocated resources so as to put pressure on the apartheid system.

One impetus for the growth of such a forceful movement was the continuous contact between counter-hegemonic organisations in South Africa and their international counterparts. The notion of international solidarity with oppressed communities inspired non-white South Africans to continue to supply foreign colleagues with information that could be utilised to galvanise diplomatic pressure against the South African government. In theorising the entwined responses of domestic and international sports protest against apartheid, one can position the domestic politics of a country's sports policy within a network of international relations, provided the background to the formulation of the policy is understood. Thus, whilst culture emerged as a prominent arena for conflict and contestation in the domestic politics of South African sport, significant developments in international and domestic power relations enabled the promotion of strategies that could use sport to challenge sociocultural practices representative of the apartheid order. As the dominant ideology within South African sport was controlled and moulded by the political legitimacy given to apartheid it became necessary at times, to go beyond the reaches of that dominant ideology in order to initiate strategies that would counter its effects.

Sport, hegemony and South Africa

The concept of hegemony attempts to crystallise the processes of cultural resistance and domination. The possibility of the concept explaining sports resistance is established if one accepts that sport is an integral part of a social formation, as sport is a cultural practice within that social formation. In South Africa, sport was defined along strict racial and class formations because of apartheid structures and legislation. Gramsci's work is characterised by a concern with the problems of culture and the relation of cultural formations to political domination (Jarvie and Maguire 1994: 108). For Hargreaves (1986), the relationship between sport, power and culture is based on an understanding of hegemony and its centrality to comprehending the methods by which a class achieves leadership over the rest of society. Furthermore, Hargreaves (1986) asserted that civil society and the state each in their own manner are implicated in the achievement of changing patterns of hegemony; that the state is increasingly active in the process where sport is concerned. In addition, hegemony is not simply a question of ideological domination but also of how processes develop whereby social agents actively and consciously accommodate each other in pursuit of their perceived interests. Coercion and the threats of coercion are important aspects of the process (Hargreaves and Tomlinson 1992: 211).

In examining the roots of the anti-apartheid movement in sport, Jarvie (1985, 1993), Roberts (1988) and Booth (1995, 1998) cite the Gramscian concept of hegemony as one that is particularly valuable. To Gramsci (1971) hegemony meant:

> The permeation throughout civil society ... of an entire system of values, beliefs, attitudes and morals that is in one way or another supportive of the established order and the class interests that dominate it.
>
> (Gramsci 1971: 39)

Williams (1977) saw hegemony as always being an active process. For this reason, hegemony can never be taken for granted. There is a need to constantly reinforce the ideology behind it that requires the dominant culture to attempt to maintain and strengthen their social authority. The process is illustrated when the hegemony of the dominant culture is challenged. Accordingly, a period of instability and transition occurs during which time the alliances that form the basis of hegemonic rule undergo changes, and at times restructuring in order to survive. Callinicos (1981), Saul and Gelb (1981) and Wolpe (1983) all suggest to varying degrees that the crisis in South Africa from 1948 is best conceptualised within the organic and conjunctural sense of the word crisis. Gramsci (1971) distinguishes between the two:

> A crisis occurs sometimes lasting for decades. This exceptional duration means that incurable structural contradictions have revealed themselves (reached maturity) and that despite this, the political forces which are fighting to preserve and conserve the existing political structure itself, are making every effort to cure them within certain limits and overcome them. These incessant and persistent efforts form the terrain of the conjunctural and it is upon this terrain that the forces of the opposition must organise themselves.
>
> (Gramsci 1971: 177)

In this respect, conjunctural means the passing and momentary period of crisis in which the contesting political forces struggle for state power. The organic aspect refers to the long-term contestation for ideological hegemony. Hall (1981) reinforces Gramsci's argument by suggesting that what defines the conjunctural, the immediate terrain of the struggle, are the incessant and persistent efforts made to defend the status quo. By accepting this contention, it is possible to argue that if the crisis is deep (i.e. organic), these efforts are not defensive but formative, leading to a new balance of power as a consequence of the challenges to the efforts of maintaining the existing status quo.

The crisis that existed in South Africa was organic in nature and was manifest along four dimensions: firstly, the structural contradictions which characterised the accumulation process under racial capital; secondly, the innate political struggle in the ruling National Party between the *verkramptes* and the *verligtes*;[7] third, and perhaps most importantly, the escalation of resistance from a number of liberation forces internally and externally; and, finally, the conjunctural response of the ruling political party (Jarvie 1985: 23). The relationship between the conjunctural and the organic is dialectical in that a reciprocal interaction exists between the two. For this reason the conjunctural is not just a response to the organic but a reflection of the crisis itself.

The Gramscian concept of hegemony can be used to explore contestation between dominant and subordinate groups. Viewing sport as a component of social formation permits the location of sport within an overall war of position in establishing an alternative hegemony. For Gramsci (1971), wars of movement, in relation to political struggles, may include the valuable use of counter-insurgent tactics such as violent unrest. Politics creates the possibility for wars of movement, which should be viewed as tactical rather than strategic functions. In politics, the war of movement subsists so long as there is a need for winning positions which are not decisive (Gramsci 1971: 232–5). In contrast, the war of position demands enormous sacrifices by infinite masses of people, and, once won, is definitively decisive (*ibid.*: 239). It is worth noting here that in the international arena, the international anti-apartheid movement was essentially engaged solely in a war of position, whereas within South Africa itself the war of position was fought simultaneously with the war of movement. Thus it is possible to surmise that only those internal, and more central, to the struggle can be engaged in both wars. For Gramsci, a distinction between the coercive framework of the state and the state's role as an organiser of consent was essential. The state is viewed as the entire complex of activities with which the ruling class not only maintains its dominance but also manages to win consent from subordinate classes. Gramsci asserted that the state was a composite of political society and civil society, or, put another way, hegemony protected by the armour of coercion. It is therefore possible to observe the coercive element of the state withering away as ever more conspicuous elements of regulated (civil) society make their appearance. The nature of power in this discourse is critical. Power is embodied within the state through coercion, but can also be used in political struggle to win hegemony of civil society (Gramsci 1971: 243–63). Because of the complexities of state power, Gramsci viewed it as necessary that battle be waged in every arena in which capitalist power was exerted, as the authority of power relied upon mass consent.

Framing the domestic–international axis

Clearly, a plurality of forces and alliances was required to initiate a war of position based on a mass movement and the political party (the ANC) that represented such forces must have the interest of the masses at heart. Thus, international non-state actors such as international sports organisations, or domestic organisations which coalesced to form the broader anti-apartheid movement, have a significant role to play in adjudicating on the legitimacy of disputes arising from the (mis-) use of power by other international actors. As a result of pressure applied, the targeted actor may make sub-optimal decisions, purportedly designed to reaffirm the former's power base. The comparatively recent modernisation of the international system is reflected in the increasingly porous nature of domestic boundaries. Houlihan (1994: 42) likens this process to the establishment of a cobweb, which has a multitude of connections, linking not only states but also a variety of inter-national actors.

In shaping their contribution to political struggle non-racial sports organisations, supported by domestic and international agencies alike, devel-oped implicit internal relations between previously divided communities that would formulate the origins of a democratic society. Sports-based protest within South Africa precipitated a broader movement which pres-surised established sporting and cultural struggles and also formed the location for a high-profile prototype for alternative forms of political protest in the transformation to democracy. Sport, as an integral component of South African social formation, was subject to the laws of apartheid and affected by the many contradictions of legislative and discriminatory policy. The authorities used sport as a tool to maintain their political ascendancy.[8] As a reaction to this, the non-white sporting communities had their sporting aspirations frustrated. Apartheid was used to widen the inequality of provision in sport as well as in other walks of South African life. Sport was falsely propagated by the South African government as an arena of apolitical ideology, and thus provided an accessible opportunity for non-racial sport federations to prove that there was an alternative to segregation and racial subordination. The pattern of international relations prompted by the emer-gence of sport as an arena for anti-apartheid protest provided part of the practical stimulus through which hegemonic struggle generated a contested terrain, and, therefore, potential support within South Africa. The gradual recognition by organisations within South Africa of the need for a plurality of forces through which to challenge apartheid structures ensured that the principles of the non-racial sports movement were in complete contrast to those of apartheid. As a result, the non-racial sports movement was political in its character, predominantly charged with establishing principles of unity and equity. It is to this area that the chapter now turns.

SACOS: political struggle in sociocultural practices

The formation of the South African Council on Sport (SACOS) in 1973 was a response to the limits of multinationalism and the government's with-drawal of concessions to the non-white sporting community once international pressure had softened slightly. Co-operation with white sports bodies was negated in favour of a tougher stance, which aimed to unify non-racial federations under one banner and push to gain international recognition for the cause of non-racialism. It was essential for SACOS to establish an international mandate for the lack of black majority support would not allow SACOS to completely dominate the non-racial sporting terrain. According to former SACOS treasurer Harry Hendricks, 'it was important to spend time structuring the organisation democratically. The concept of regional affiliation permitted the development of sport nationally along the same policy lines.'[9] In turn, policy objectives would be located around exposing the camouflage perpetuated by the South African government's sports policy. It was clear that the non-racial sports movement had touched a nerve within the non-white populations as, in principle, non-racialism could transcend barriers of class and race in order to expose the barriers erected by the imposition of the multinational sports policy.

More pragmatically, the SACOS leadership realised from the outset that their organisation was involved in a political struggle,[10] although it took some time before SACOS adopted politically sensitive tactics and the organisation remained politically non-aligned for much of the apartheid era. Non-racialism was exposed as no more than an aspiration, because of the rigidity of apartheid structures exemplified by the Watsons and Odendaal. 'Race' could not mix with 'race' under the Group Areas Act and the use of permits reinforced the stratification of the social formation. Unless the political system within South Africa changed, SACOS could not enforce a non-racial sports structure and non-racialism could not legitimately exist within the apartheid system. Yet, with their power delimited by the dominant ideology of the government, SACOS fought to establish the practice of internal sports-based protest and created a terrain which would later be occupied by the forces of the majority and gained instant recognition from the international sporting community.

Initially, SACOS's position within the struggle was that of a pressure group prepared to use conciliatory tactics to achieve unity through negotiations with establishment sports federations (Roberts 1988: 25–6). The negotiations were manipulated by the white federations and the reiteration of the policy to prevent mixed sports clubs by then Sports Minister, Dr Piet Koornhof, coincided with the influx of the politically conscious into SACOS. According to Roberts, dominant among the newcomers were militant activists from the 1940s and 1950s who proposed policies of non-collaboration with any pro-apartheid organisation. Whilst Roberts argues that the mobilisation traditions that resurfaced were to the detriment of the non-racial sports movement (Roberts 1988: 27–8), former SACOS secretary Reg Feldman contends that such strategies were a necessary element in SACOS shedding its political naivety.[11]

The Soweto uprisings of 1976 and associated disturbances in Cape Town coincided with the adoption of a more militant standpoint within SACOS and regionally within WEPCOS (Western Province Council on Sport), the strongest provincial member of SACOS. From 1977, provincial councils were permitted one seat on the Executive Committee of SACOS in recognition of their work in organising non-racial sport in the provinces and providing communication between players and administrators. The links between WEPCOS and SACOS were augmented through the location of the SACOS executive in the Western Cape, as both regional and national constituencies were, to all intents and purposes, the same. SACOS adopted its more militant standpoint through the principle of non-collaboration – an ideology designed to oppose the immorality of apartheid. The government's response to SACOS's formation was to propagate images of integrated sporting structures. A notable consequence of the South African government's decision to attempt to reform sports policy within the framework of apartheid structures was the creation of a climate wherein the profile of domestic sport became an issue for international actors. This created the complex axis through which a domestic issue took on an amplified international significance. The first consequence of this process was that the prevailing relationship between apartheid and sport focused on specific issues for the first time. Two examples of this relationship are now presented.

The Double Standards Resolution (DSR): creating and delimiting contested terrain

In 1977, SACOS demonstrated its shift in political focus through the formulation of the Double Standards Resolution (DSR). In essence, the DSR prevented non-racial federations and sports persons from belonging to SACOS whilst also belonging to any organisation not organised along non-racial lines, and held at its root the principle of non-collaboration. Any member who practised double standards would face expulsion from SACOS. The President of SACOS, Norman Middleton, did not endorse the adoption of the DSR. Hassan Howa immediately replaced Middleton and committed the organisation to the slogan 'No Normal Sport in an Abnormal Society'. The intention behind the DSR was to purify membership, rid SACOS of members not committed to the principles of non-racialism and prevent negotiations with establishment sports bodies. Whilst reaffirming SACOS's commitment to non-racialism, this was perceived by some within the organisation as a hard-line stance that could cause more problems than it would solve.

The DSR posed a number of issues for the Executive Committee. Members of SACOS from non-racial sports federations were responsible to their organisations, but members representing the provincial councils were not responsible to the federations, as the councils were responsible for the promotion of all non-racial sports within their areas. With hindsight the differing aims of the federations and councils can be seen as the cause of many tensions. The issue for SACOS was that it presented itself as a vehicle for co-ordinating and unifying non-racial sport, as a forum for discussion, and as a mouthpiece for non-racial sport. The DSR served to create divisions within SACOS between the federations responsible for organising their members' sport and provincial councils who were seemingly more aware of, and involved in, the wider political struggle. The resolution was issued in the context of the relationship between SACBOC and its establishment counterpart: a relationship which encouraged mixed competitions between teams of different racial origins, and organised the league in which Andre Odendaal played. Conversely, the implementation of the DSR further highlighted SACOS's developing profile as a symbol of the anti-apartheid movement in sport and garnered support from around the globe.

SACOS's Executive Committee revised the Resolution in October 1978, in order to have total control over whether clubs and affiliated federations were non-racial. The move gave the Executive Committee power to exclude clubs or federations without right of appeal. At the Biennial General Meeting of 1979, the resolution was further amended to incorporate the moral obligations of members to the policy of non-collaboration and was extended to all establishment institutions including universities. The meeting agreed that the quality and character of contacts would determine the non-racial principles involved. Furthermore, it was determined that the amended resolution would now provide clear and unambiguous guidance for non-racial sports persons and would bring the sports struggle into line with the rest of the anti-apartheid movement.[12] The Double Standards Resolution can be viewed as an extension of the widespread policy of non-collaboration that led up to the Soweto riots in 1976 and the accompanying political tensions. In addition, it served to sharpen the image and awareness of SACOS internationally. In contrast, the benefit of hindsight demonstrates that the DSR also strengthened the hand of the radical faction within SACOS and prevented SACOS acquiring a stronger hold on the terrain of sporting struggle. Universal adoption of the resolution's principles was not always possible. By law, black Africans were not able to satisfy the principles of the resolution because of their enforced separation from other non-white population groups. To play sport with or against other population groups represented collaboration. If the resolution was enforced to the letter, black Africans could not join SACOS. A problematic area regarding the resolution was the method by which it was implemented as an Executive Committee decision and imposed on rank and file membership. Despite the difficulties, SACOS managed to effect an increased level of international understanding about the prevailing situation. The internationalisation of counter-hegemonic struggle originated from SACOS having adopted a policy of non-collaboration which characterised other organisations outside the realm of sport and effectively highlighted the susceptibility of sports policy to both domestic and international protest.

The position of SACOS within the liberation struggle: 'domestic' pressure group and 'international' symbol

Despite the dilemmas posed by the DSR and the permit restrictions, SACOS provided non-racial sport with a far more aggressive and militant platform on which to put forward the case of non-white sporting culture. The appeal of SACOS lay in its policy of non-negotiation and a declaration of solidarity among non-racial movements. Such a platform was used to bring attention to the struggle against apartheid sport and identify their principles with international colleagues:

> SACOS in a declaration of solidarity with the Supreme Council for Sport in Africa hereby rejects all forms of racialism in sport and accepts a complete moratorium on sports tours to and from South Africa until all the trappings of apartheid have been removed from South African sport (and society).
>
> (Ramsamy 1982: 14)

This aggressive approach however worried some of SACOS's members and supporters, who felt that an inflexible approach and strict adherence to radical policies could sever the movement from the mass of South African sportsmen and women. Internal squabbling hindered SACOS's progress and the cause for debate was non-collaboration. When Hassan Howa suggested a possible return to negotiations with white sports federations, he lost the presidency of SACOS. But as Hunter (1980) points out, SACOS became so closely associated with the struggle for non-racial sport that, both within and outside South Africa, the concepts of non-racial sport and the political struggle it attempted to support, became combined. Yet throughout the late 1970s and the 1980s there were repeated calls from the banned ANC and from sports organisations for SACOS to call on its international counterparts to maintain sanctions to enforce isolation against South Africa:

> SACOS gained great credit for exposing the dishonesty of multi-national sport and became internationally recognised as the champion of non-racial sport. We can only continue to champion this cause if the outside world maintains the suffocating isolation of South Africa.[13]

SACOS's policy of non-collaboration may have gained the organisation a high profile in the debate concerning sports protest and it continued to provide internal and external sports protest with a rallying point against apartheid. But SACOS had trouble in promoting the practice of non-racial sport outside of apartheid structures as it lacked the facilities and resources to encourage widespread participation.

During the first half of the 1980s SACOS maintained its position as the standard bearer of non-racial sport. Following the state repression of organised political resistance in the late 1970s and early 1980s, SACOS occupied a central position in the political terrain amongst oppositional politics. The first SACOS Sports festival in 1982 not only represented a significant event, in the staging of a single co-ordinated effort in the non-racial fraternity; moreover, it was a 'symbolic gesture within (which) the seeds of unity (were) beginning to form' (Naidoo 1982: 2). The perception of unity was not the same within different groups within SACOS. It was clear that despite its location, SACOS had not achieved an overarching leadership role in domestic liberation struggle for sport. Its constituency was too narrow and concentrated in the Western Cape. The politics of the leadership, mainly Coloured and Indian intellectuals, were too narrow for mass appeal and mobilisation. Its support therefore derived mainly from the Coloured and Indian population groups (Roberts 1988: 42). Despite this, it is difficult to counter any contention that the organisation was not a significant socio-political force. It was involved with schools, church groups, community organisations, trade unions and sports organisations as well as co-ordinating the sports campaign and, in doing so, created a terrain which a mass-based sports movement could occupy more forcefully.[14]

The convergence of sports persons in the non-racial struggle successfully exposed state strategies of 'window-dressing' through the use of multi-national sports policies. SACOS presented a version of non-racial sport to the international community and vigorously countered the state's utilisation of sport as a tool for propagating apartheid. In establishing contacts with the United Nations, the Supreme Council for Sport in Africa (SCSA) and SAN-ROC (South African Non-Racial Olympic Committee), SACOS formed a global network of communication that could be relied upon to maintain international protest through the use of information generated from the terrain of struggle itself. Because of the exchange of information between these bodies, South Africa became largely ostracised from the international community and provoked high profile attempts by the Government and white sports bodies to break isolation. Despite this, opposition to apartheid sport was not the form of mass resistance engendered through Black Consciousness. To the most oppressed communities sports, even the more prevalent such as soccer, were not particularly popular activities because of the lack of access afforded to them. Young black communities were exceptionally politicised and community, workplace and political protest, not sports based protest was their primary concern.[15] The recognition of SACOS by the international sporting community did not, in itself, engender a coherent strategy against established sporting power relations but it permitted the international community to focus upon an arena of contested cultural terrain and highlight hypocrisies in the apartheid system.

A leadership seeking to advocate a coherent political strategy, but failing to take full account of regional differences, provoked predictable resistance from SACOS. The principles and policies of the organisation, especially the DSR and policy of non-collaboration, limited the potential structural development of SACOS into a mass-based organisation. Decision-making became hierarchical, leaving rank-and-file membership relatively inactive and passive recipients of organisational policies. The leadership comprised doctors, teachers, engineers, solicitors and like-minded professional people. Intelligent, articulate and informed, they attracted a large membership through affiliation of non-racial sports bodies. WEPCOS was the strongest regional affiliate,[16] but largely consisted of Coloured and Indian sports people. WEPCOS found it difficult to penetrate the large African townships of Langa, Guguletu and Khayletisha around Cape Town.[17] The Transvaal (TRACOS) and Natal (NACOS) Councils had smaller memberships that in part reflected the smaller Indian and Coloured communities in these areas. TRACOS found it very difficult to attract support from the huge townships around Johannesburg.[18] A possible reason to explain the lack of attraction was that sporting non-collaboration deprived black Africans more than other population groups because they still suffered the most severe deprivation in terms of facilities and resources. Non-collaboration held little potential for the most oppressed population groups. Thus, in isolation, it is difficult to imagine that domestic resistance to apartheid through sport would have had a particularly significant impact. However, once connected to the international theatre, a different picture emerges.

International sport and the intensification support for internal protest: the consequences of the 'Gleneagles Agreement'

In 1977, the 'Gleneagles Agreement' further focused international attention on sport in South Africa and contributed to a climate wherein SACOS could avoid repression and continue to campaign for the cause of non-racialism within South Africa. By threatening to make disruptive statements and to boycott the Edmonton Commonwealth Games scheduled for 1978, the affiliate members of SCSA had little trouble in persuading most Commonwealth nations to support their calls to continue the intensification of pressure on South Africa. Canada, after the African-led boycott of the Montreal Olympics, and whose policy toward South Africa was generally supportive of the anti-apartheid movement (Kidd 1990), was determined at the time to ensure that their second major sporting festival within such a short space of time would not be ruined (Ramsamy 1982). The motive behind the threatened boycott was to discourage the continued sporting contacts with South Africa by New Zealand and Britain. Commonwealth Secretary-General Shridath Ramphal received information from SACOS, via SAN-ROC and the organisation's Executive Chairperson, Sam Ramsamy, who had been formally appointed by SACOS to speak on its behalf internationally.[19] Ramphal was instrumental in finding a solution to the growing discontent among the African members in particular, at the Commonwealth's failure to take effective action against South Africa. The success of the Gleneagles agreement depended on its acceptance by New Zealand's new Prime Minister, Robert Muldoon, who had come to power supporting his country's rugby contacts with South Africa. By early 1977, the Muldoon government still had not confirmed its support for the sports boycott. It countenanced individual and non-tour contact and held out the prospect of 'merit' teams from South Africa being seen as acceptable. Its readiness to state opposition to particular contacts was spasmodic and it continued to subsidise sports contact with South Africa (Trainor 1978: 66). The efforts of Jamaican Prime Minister Michael Manley were crucial in gaining acceptance of the agreement. The Gleneagles agreement was in essence only a press statement, agreed upon by the Commonwealth heads of government. Nothing was signed, yet it was the first and most stringent political declaration against apartheid in sports from the Commonwealth, as it asked governments to use all available means to prevent any form of sporting contact with South Africa. Although it could easily be circumvented, the statement began to lead to decreased levels of contact in sport (Payne 1991: 420–21).

The Commonwealth's contribution to international sport is broadly related to the adoption of two main principles that were reflected by SACOS – democracy and non-racialism. The majority of states that hold Commonwealth membership had thrown off their colonial status and therefore strongly identified with the protests against white minority rule. Furthermore, many Commonwealth nations suffered, like the front-line states, from a paucity of international resources and found that sports sanctions and adherence to boycotts were possibly the only effective weapon with which to make statements against apartheid. Because of the strong African composition of the Commonwealth it is not surprising that the South African question was at the forefront of the organisation's diplomatic activity during the years of apartheid.

The contact between states through the Commonwealth demonstrates the utility of such a forum to promote foreign policy objectives. The sporting boycott was critical in its effect. It was a powerful punitive force creating the sense of isolation that South African sport felt, especially because of white South Africa's obsession with sport: '[it] set an international benchmark; it was the starting point for inter-governmental commitment and inter-governmental understanding' (Ramphal in Bose 1994: 114). Six months later the United Nations adopted a declaration that called upon all member states to isolate South Africa through the cessation of all sporting exchanges with the country.

Accordingly, Gleneagles was the most significant declaration produced by the international sporting community against apartheid. Its effect (if unintended) was to lessen the threat of overt repression on SACOS as it cast a spotlight on the plight of sport in South Africa and drew international attention to organisations that were involved in the liberation struggle. Gleneagles served as the catalyst for the intensification of South Africa's international isolation. In response, the international sporting community began to develop a more sensitive awareness of what SACOS was trying to achieve in its struggle

White administrators had been active on an international basis, trying to gauge opinion on the possibility of readmission. In 1978, government representative Rudolph Opperman reported to the Minister of Sport regarding his visit overseas that attempted to 'establish more effective international liaison.' Opperman's brief was to ascertain the prospects of arriving at some basis of co-operation or consensus with South African sports' most active opponents within or outside South Africa. Opperman met with Norman Middleton, the President of SASF, but now ostracised from SACOS, and initiated correspondence with the SAN-ROC executive as he believed SAN-ROC to be more than just a 'spokesman' for SACOS. One of the most common responses Opperman encountered was that 'there comes a time when you can offer a lot but when you do not possess any bargaining power'. [20] The implication of such a response is that the required leadership was now beyond the domain of sports administrators. The politicisation of SACOS and the role of governments in Gleneagles had weakened attempts by sports administrators to maintain their position through negotiations based on sports issues alone.

The solution, as Opperman saw it, was to accede to demands made in secret meetings with SAN-ROC members and Peter Hain. Passport restrictions on, and harassment of, SACOS officials had to stop and the multi-national sports policy had to be officially abandoned. Lord Killanin, President of the International Olympic Committee at the time, admitted that the IOC had become powerless to do anything regarding readmitting South Africa because of international politics. Killanin commented that 'considering the internal situation in South Africa following the Soweto riots, the discussion of South Africa's readmission to the IOC was pointless'. [21] Opperman recommended that discussions with all parties, in particular SAN-ROC and SACOS, be initiated. The response to non-collaboration served to highlight the value of the principle, preventing white sports administrators gaining any credibility in light of the political situation prevailing in South Africa during the late 1970s. It reflected another instance of the complex interplay between domestic and international protest in that counter-hegemonic strategies had forced the South African government to go to key figures in exile in an attempt to break the stranglehold of isolation. Non-collaboration, quite simply, perpetuated the suffocation of white sport in South Africa. [22] It is worth acknowledging here that sports people and, moreover, sports administrators are frequently and heavily influenced by their own very specific set of priorities. Historically, this is a recognisable pattern in the emergence of the axis of domestic-international sports based protest against South Africa (Keech and Houlihan 1999; Keech 2001). In this instance it can be argued that there was an unwillingness by Opperman to acknowledge the blinkered effect of his desire to see South Africa fully readmitted to international sport. Indeed, given the clandestine and government-initiated nature of his duties, his responses, whilst permeated by political conservatism, perhaps reflected the privatised world of the sports administrator. Only when taken into the more powerful and explicitly political domain of the government did Opperman's report take on a more (c)overt political tone.

SAN-ROC's role in raising and maintaining the profile of the principle of non-collaboration should not be discounted or discredited. Working with the SCSA and its parent organisation the Organisation of African Unity (OAU), SAN-ROC was able to broaden the influence of African states united by their opposition to apartheid, yet unable to take any internationally significant action individually. SAN-ROC had ensured that the issue had become one of international policy, but African nations needed provoking to maintain their action in light of SACOS failing to acquire black majority support. In an attempt to reinvigorate the African boycott, Ramsamy tried to persuade Major-General Joseph Garba, Chair of the UN Special Committee Against Apartheid, to use his influence in his home country of Nigeria. However, the 1980s witnessed little unity of action from the SCSA, and Ramsamy was left to pursue other avenues of protest through organisations such as ICAAS (International Committee Against Apartheid in Sport), a UN sponsored committee designed to facilitate wider debate about international sport and South Africa. The ICAAS was organised by the SCSA in conjunction with SAN-ROC and ANOCA and built upon the repeated call from SACOS for the sporting boycott to be maintained. This marked the origins of a 'two-track' strategy that attempted to invigorate international protest whilst maintaining a policy of non-collaboration with establishment sports bodies. The incorporation of international protest and action into protest against internal policy signalled a redefinition of the focus of the sporting protest movement.

The development of SACOS's actions within South Africa, combined with the wide variety of organisational influences that brought about Gleneagles, represented the formation of a cohesive internal and external sporting protest movement. The fact that the movement remained relatively solid was indicative of the successful continued exchange of information by SAN-ROC, SACOS, the SCSA and more prominent international organisations such as the United Nations. The continued lobbying of governments represented the attempts of pressure groups, without any significant resources, to maintain their profile and the profile of sports protest against apartheid. The flow of information involving this issue took on a reciprocal nature with SACOS feeding SAN-ROC, in particular, about many events within South Africa. SAN-ROC used the international mass media as an important vehicle in maintaining the continuous flow of information into the public eye. An increasingly worldwide consensus against apartheid had some origins within this movement, as in many countries anti-apartheid organisations were able to develop tactics in their country designed to increase and maintain awareness of the situation in South Africa.

Conclusion

If one were to begin at the domestic level, then a Gramscian model of hegemony captures the centrality of cultural politics to South Africa and locates
that cultural struggle within the broader politics of apartheid. In order
though to provide a satisfactory explanation of both domestic and international politics of apartheid it is necessary for a process of theory building to
take place that combines the explanatory strength of hegemony theory and
the organisational understanding permitted by pluralist theory. Sports-based
protest within South Africa was the stimulus for a broader based movement
that maintained the international profile of the relationship between
apartheid and sport. It was because of SACOS that sport continued to have a
high profile within the internal political struggles during the 1970s and
1980s. The subsequent pressures upon establishment sports practices in
South Africa were symbolic prototypes for methods utilised in more
complex fashions during the ensuing transition to democracy. Hence, sports-
based protest contributed to the development of global consciousness
against apartheid in particular, and racism in sport in general, thus influencing the values of sport and many other forms of sociocultural activity.

The concept of hegemony can be employed in the domestic socio-political
context of any state as well as in the context of any dominant mode of
production that cuts across boundaries of states, nations and regions.
Hegemony allows scholars the opportunity to unveil how the subordinate
class or group, along with its coalition of forces, national as well as transnational, organises its challenge to society and the dominant culture, both
within and across states. An exploration of the strength of the state's political structures can be used to demonstrate that diverse forms of political
struggles can be enhanced by challenging entrenched mechanisms of
control, many of which may be transnationally orientated. Apart from the
political and diplomatic ties between states there exists a vast terrain that
brings societies together through bilateral and multilateral transactions in a
broad spectrum of economic, cultural and technological activities. The
increasingly rapid exchange and flow of information through developments
in communication technologies have reduced distances between people and
perpetuated opportunities for organisations to co-ordinate strategies with a
greater degree of efficiency.

Many international organisations involved in the South African question
were concerned explicitly with the politics of culture and cultural responses
to policy implementation. The development of a range of domestic and
international anti-apartheid sports organisations, plus non-sports organisations who contributed to fostering the profile of sports-based protest, often
competed with each other to acquire degrees of influence and control over
anti-apartheid sports policy. Spurred by the rich and fluid flow of information between organisations on the domestic and international levels of
international relations, the international politics of sport and apartheid can
be effectively accounted for within a pluralist framework. However, if one is

to explain the power dynamics of political change the use of a process of theory building must be utilised with hegemonic processes explaining the domestic politics of apartheid and sport's location therein. Each approach enriches the other in that pluralism supports hegemonic analysis within South Africa, and hegemony permits one to explicate the impact of the domestic context on international debate regarding policies against apartheid. Rather than trying to force the analysis of apartheid into established theoretical frameworks, it is important to accept that the unique characteristics of the anti-apartheid campaign in sport require a degree of theoretical development and fusion. As such, this is not promoted as an example of theoretical indecision or weakness but rather it is a necessary requirement for a satisfactory historical analysis.

Notes

1   To understand more about Donald Woods, see Woods (1981, 2000). His friendship with black activist Steve Biko, and subsequent escape from South Africa can be seen in the film 'Cry Freedom'. For an account of Woods's association with multi-racial cricket, see Bose (1994: 101–5).
2   Andre Odendaal, interview, 22 August 1997, interviewee's home, Cape Town.
3   For a more detailed account, see Odendaal (1977). Andre Odendaal is now Professor of History at the University of the Western Cape and curator of Robben Island museum.
4   Andre Odendaal, interview, 22 August 1997, interviewee's home, Cape Town.
5   Morne DuPlessis, interview, 17 August 1997, Newlands Rugby Stadium, Cape Town.
6   For a detailed account of the multinational sports policy, see Archer and Bouillon (1982: 206–27); Booth (1998: 100–4); Keech (1999: 109–15); Lapchick (1975); Ramsamy (1982).
7   The *verkramptes* were the traditional supporters of apartheid, recognising force as the primary means of maintaining their power base. The *verligtes* were reformist in nature, not in the sense of wanting to repeal apartheid but with the express aim of modernising racial domination to take account of the limited utility of forceful coercion.
8   Indeed, it was five years after its introduction when the multinational policy was formally implemented. When Andries Treurnicht became chairman of the Broederbond, the semi-clandestine Afrikaner society, he used his influence to delay the introduction of multinational sport as he feared that mixing between players and spectators would generally condition whites toward integration (Wilkins and Strydom 1978: 247).
9   Interview: Harry Hendricks, 18 August 1997, interviewee's home, Kuils River, Cape Town.
10 Interview: Reg Feldman, 12 August 1997, interviewee's home, Johannesburg.
11 Interview: Reg Feldman, 12 August 1997, interviewee's home, Johannesburg.
12 SACOS, Minutes of 3rd Biennial General Meeting, Cape Town, 1979.
13 Frank van der Horst, presidential address, 7th Biennial General Meeting, SACOS, Johannesburg, 4–5 April 1987.
14 Interview: Frank van der Horst, 24 August 1997, interviewee's home, Cape Town.
15 Interview: Peter Jones, 22 August 1997, Cape Town.
16 Interviews: Harry Hendricks, 18 August 1997, interviewee's home, Kuils River; A.E. Fortuin, 19 August 1997, interviewee's home, Paarl.

17 The WEPCOS sports person of the year nominations for 1982, 1983 and 1984 provide circumstantial evidence of this with no black nominees.
18 Interview: Reg Feldman, 12 August 1997, interviewee's home, Johannesburg.
19 Letter from Hassan Howa, President of SACOS, to Ramsamy, 14 June 1977. For a detailed account of the role of Ramsamy in South Africa's re-admittance to international sport, see Keech (2000a, 2000b).
20 The Information about Opperman's visit is taken from a strictly confidential report by Rudolph Opperman to the Minister of Sport, 7 March 1978, DSR 4/2. Direct quotations are Opperman's own words.
21 *Ibid.*
22 *Ibid.*

References

Archer, R. and Bouillon, A. (1982) *The South African Game*, London: Zed Press.
Booth, D. (1995) 'United sport: an alternative hegemony in South Africa', *International Journal of the History of Sport*, 12(3): 105–24.
—— (1998) *The Race Game: Sport and Politics in South Africa*, London: Frank Cass.
Bose, M. (1994) *Sporting Colours: Sport and Politics in South Africa*, London: Robson.
Callinicos, A. (1981) *Southern Africa after Zimbabwe*, London: Pluto Press.
Gramsci, A. (1971) *Selections from Prison Notebooks*, London: Lawrence & Wishart, reprinted 1998.
Hall, S. (1981) 'Moving right', *Socialist Review*, No. 55.
Hargreaves, J. (1986) *Sport, Power and Culture: A Social and Historical Analysis of Popular Sports in Britain*, Cambridge: Polity Press.
Hargreaves, J. and Tomlinson, A. (1992) 'Getting there: cultural theory and the sociological analysis of sport in Britain', *Sociology of Sport Journal* 9(2): 207–19.
Houlihan, B. (1994) *Sport and International Relations*, Hemel Hempstead: Harvester Wheatsheaf.
Hunter, M. (1980) 'The United Nations and the Anti-Apartheid sports movement', *Canadian Journal of History of Sport and Physical Education* 11(1): 19–35.
Jarvie, G. (1985) *Class, Race and Sport in South Africa's Political Economy*, London: Routledge & Kegan Paul.
—— (1993) 'Sport, politics and South Africa', in E. Dunning, J. Maguire and R. Pearton (eds) *The Sports Process: A Comparative and Developmental Process*, Champaign, IL: Human Kinetics.
Jarvie, G. and Maguire, J. (1994) *Sport and Leisure in Social Thought*, London: Routledge.
Keech, M. (1999) *International Sport and the End of Apartheid*, unpublished PhD thesis, Staffordshire University.
—— (2000a) 'Sam Ramsamy', in E. Cashmore (ed.) *Sports Culture: An A–Z Guide*, London: Routledge.
—— (2000b) 'At the centre of the web: the role of Sam Ramsamy in South Africa's readmission to international sport', *Culture, Sport and Society* 3(3): 41–62.
—— (2001) 'The ties that bind: South Africa and sports diplomacy 1958–1963', *Sports Historian* 21(1): 71–93.
Keech, M. and Houlihan, B. (1999) 'Sport and the end of the apartheid', *Round Table: Commonwealth Journal of International Affairs* 349: 109–21.

Kidd, B. (1990) 'From quarantine to cure: the new phase of struggle against apartheid sport', in C. Roberts (ed.) *Challenges Facing South African Sport*, Cape Town: Township Publishing Co-operative.

Lapchick, R. (1975) *The Politics of Race and International Sport*, Westport, Conn.: Greenwood Press.

Naidoo, M. (1982) 'Presidential message', *SACOSSPORT*, Durban: SACOS: 2–4.

Odendaal, A. (ed.) (1977) *Cricket in Isolation: The Politics of Race and Cricket in South Africa*, Cape Town: published by author.

Payne, A. (1991) 'The international politics of the Gleneagles Agreement', *Round Table: Commonwealth Journal of International Affairs* 320: 419–31.

Ramsamy, S (1982) *Apartheid: The Real Hurdle*, London: International Defence and Aid Foundation.

Roberts, C. (1988) *SACOS 1973–1988: 15 Years of Sports Resistance*, Cape Town: Township Publishing Co-operative.

Saul, S. and Gelb, S. (1981) *The Crisis in Southern Africa*, London: Monthly Review Press.

Trainor, L. (1978) 'The primacy of internal policy: national sport and external relations 1975–78', *Political Science*, 30(2): 62–76.

Wilkins, I. and Strydom, H. (1978) *The Super Afrikaners*, Johannesburg: Ravan.

Williams, R. (1977) *Marxism and Literature*, Oxford: Oxford University Press.

Wolpe, H. (1983) 'Apartheid rule', *Marxism Today*, February.

Woods, D. (1981) *Black and White*, Dublin: Ward & River Press.

—— (2000) *Rainbow Nation Revisited*, London, André Deutsch.

10 *Sport, Sectarianism and Society in a Divided Ireland* revisited

Alan Bairner

Introduction

One of the main issues that has exercised the minds of sport social scientists in recent years has been the relationship between sport and social division and how that relationship interacts with relations of power in the wider society. This has led to a vast academic output concerned with such topics as race, social class, gender, sexual orientation, and so on. When the phrase 'divided society' is used, however, it is to slightly different sources of cleavage that discussion tends to turn. Thus, the study of sport in divided societies is likely to focus on themes that include national identity, ethnicity and religious belief (Sugden and Bairner 1999a). A relatively early contribution to that particular debate came in the form of a book written by John Sugden and myself and published in 1993 – *Sport, Sectarianism and Society in a Divided Ireland*. The aim of this chapter is to examine how sport in Northern Ireland and also the study of Northern Irish sport have developed since the publication of that work. This involves more than simply bringing the story (or the two partially related stories) up to date. The chapter also contains an element of self-criticism to the extent that I propose to interrogate aspects of the analysis which John Sugden and I developed in the 1993 publication. In particular, there will be more discussion than has been previously attempted of the ways in which developments in the world of sport both reflect and impact upon the power relations that currently operate within the Northern Irish context.

It will be argued that there have been changes in the manner in which sport is played, watched and administered in the north of Ireland in the relatively short period since our book was published. Some of the changes are clearly linked to an evolving political situation in which people have actually dared to use the word 'peace'. Others are arguably more influenced by external developments which have also affected sport in other societies. In addition to examining these perceptible changes, however, the chapter also highlights what are thought to be important omissions in the earlier study and considers ways in which the academic study of sport in Northern Ireland has also evolved in particular by drawing upon a broader range of theoretical approaches. The chapter concludes with a series of recommendations concerning further developments within the real world of sport in the north of Ireland together with some reflection on possible new research directions. It is hoped that these concluding comments have a relevance that extends well beyond the confines of Northern Ireland itself and could certainly have some analytical application to the links between sport and the relations of power that exist in other divided societies.

Sport, Sectarianism and Society in a Divided Ireland: the background

Sport, Sectarianism and Society in a Divided Ireland emerged from a very specific political and personal context. As incomers to the region, we recognised that sport in Northern Ireland was (and remains) an extremely popular pastime, particularly for men. We could see that sport was (and still is) linked to the construction and reproduction of different identities in Northern Ireland. We saw little or no evidence that sport in Northern Ireland had been subjected to any real social scientific analysis. We also sensed, and were increasingly made aware, that our attempts to develop a sociology of Northern Irish sport were unpopular, particularly with administrators and representatives of governing bodies who were keen to argue the case for sport's autonomy and to make claims about the ways in which their activities provided people with places of sanctuary away from the political conflict, rather than arenas in which the fundamental antagonisms around which the conflict centred could be further played out. I suspect that some of the ill-feeling towards us was prompted not by weaknesses in our analysis (of which, as I shall argue, there were a few). Indeed these failings were seldom mentioned by our local critics. Instead it may well be that we were simply regarded as meddling outsiders with no appreciation of the complexities of Northern Irish life. I would argue that this was unfair given that we had grown up in parts of Britain, Merseyside (Sugden) and central Scotland (Bairner) where ethno-sectarian division has been a prominent feature of social, political and cultural life. Our social scientific antennae were already attuned to the kind of issues which we would encounter in Northern Ireland although we could not deny that in this new context sectarian divisions had assumed even greater significance.

Sport, Sectarianism and Society in a Divided Ireland: a reminder

The basic argument which we presented in *Sport, Sectarianism and Society in a Divided Ireland* is that in all societies, but particularly ones that are deeply divided along racial, ethnic and/or national lines, the various ways in which sport is played, watched, administered and presented are reflective of the most significant divisions. As we argued, 'in a region where sport and politics are both pursued with passion, it is inevitable that the two worlds will collide' (Sugden and Bairner 1993: 1). In addition, we observed that sport may also serve to exacerbate these divisions. Commenting, for example, on the violent repercussions that followed a football game between Linfield and Donegal Celtic which was played in Belfast in February 1990, we noted that 'the character of the two clubs involved and the nature of the support they attract can only be explained with reference to the politics of division' (*ibid.*). We conceded, however, that from time to time sport may actually help to bring people together. For example, with reference to community relations programmes involving sport, we argued that 'practical, grass-roots experiments in social engineering can have some impact on the relatively small numbers of individuals who experience them' (*ibid.*: 109). Indeed, we reported that 'the view taken by many of those who are involved in the development and supervision of such initiatives is that after a quarter of a century of serious sectarian violence and in the absence of any impending political panacea, this very gradual grass-roots work is the only way forward' (*ibid.*). In general, however, as we have argued more recently, we believe that sport 'possesses the capacity to transcend division but it is just as likely to highlight and exacerbate division and to provided an important forum for the celebration of difference, often with damaging consequences' (Sugden and Bairner 1999b: 10).

In support of these basic arguments, we suggested that the sports which are played in Ireland belong to three broad categories in terms of their socio-cultural and political implications. We assigned cricket, hockey, rugby union, etc. to the category of British (or anglophile) games. We identified Gaelic games, which are played under the aegis of the Gaelic Athletic Association (GAA), as forming a separate and distinct category of sporting activity. Finally, we identified what we called universal games, most notable amongst them being association football (or soccer). These were sporting activities which, although they may have originated in Britain and, without doubt, established themselves in Ireland as a direct result of the close relationship (however that is conceptualised) between Britain and Ireland, have become so universally popular that they are increasingly less culturally specific in terms of nationalist rivalries within Ireland.

We argued that Gaelic and British games are deeply implicated in those processes through which nationalist and unionist identities respectively are constantly being reproduced in Northern Ireland. 'Gaelic sport in Northern Ireland', we wrote, 'is more than a game and has come to be recognised by both sides as a reservoir of Irish identity' (Sugden and Bairner 1993: 37). As for British games, we asserted that 'as surely as the GAA provides a network for the development of nationalist sentiment in the Province, cricket, rugby and hockey clubs are part of the social fabric of Northern Irish Protestantism and as such have an important role in maintaining the status quo' (*ibid.*:

66–7). Finally, we claimed that, as the Linfield–Donegal Celtic confrontation had all too graphically revealed, universal games, especially association football, despite having the potential to unite the warring factions by virtue of their cross-community appeal, are in fact just as likely and arguably more likely to contribute to an escalation of inter-communal conflict. Indeed, we argued that 'despite an active commitment to integration at the level of youth football, the administrators of the game in Northern Ireland give the impression that at senior levels, far from being interested in allowing their sport to help the process of community reconciliation, they may actually have a vested interest in maintaining its capacity to divide' (*ibid.*: 91). Our overall assessment, therefore, was that sport's influence in terms of the politics of division in Northern Ireland had tended to be negative rather than positive, although certain cross-community initiatives had met with a degree of success at least in terms of individual experience.

We also looked at the roles of both the British state and the Sports Council for Northern Ireland as regards the political functions of sport in the region. Using an essentially Gramscian perspective, we argued that the British state has used sport in Northern Ireland primarily as a means of lessening civil disorder and also as a basis for the promotion of popular consent, whether active or, more commonly, passive. To begin with, this approach had concentrated on providing leisure opportunities as a means of simply getting troublemakers off the streets. However, the focus quickly changed, partly as a direct response to the changing character of the conflict itself, and sport was increasingly used as a vehicle for establishing and developing cross-community understanding.

We argued, however, that at the same time as sections of the British state were pursuing consent through sport, its other arms were still actively engaged in coercing sports people, most notably members of the GAA as well as soccer fans, especially those following 'nationalist' teams. The objective was to prevent sport from being successfully used as a vehicle for counter-hegemonic resistance. We believed that the state in Northern Ireland was faced with a dilemma. As we argued at the time, 'it has an ideological commitment to and responsibility for encouraging and facilitating widespread participation in sport and leisure' (Sugden and Bairner 1993: 136). However, sport itself, as has been increasingly recognised, provides scope for division and cultural contestation. Thus, 'the state in its traditional coercive guise finds itself policing those divisive areas of popular culture which, in its welfarist role, it helps to sustain' (*ibid.*).

We believed that the Sports Council for Northern Ireland (SCNI) had worked alongside and in support of the British state's rational recreation policy above all by seeking to promote an essentially British ethos. Indeed, we argued that 'in promoting a particularly middle-class and apolitical view of sport in a society within which all significant aspects of social behaviour in one way or another are bound up with the politics of division, the SCNI is covertly advancing the political objectives of the British government to prompt an image of normality, thereby helping to counter nationalist attempts to depict the region as being on the brink of civil war' (Sugden and Bairner 1993: 101–2). As a consequence, the SCNI was seen by many nationalist members of the sporting community as being, at best, unsympathetic and, at worst, downright hostile to their interests. In conclusion, our assessment of sport's capacity to assist in the creation of a more peaceful Northern Ireland was largely pessimistic.

Sport in Northern Ireland revisited

It is clear that there have been significant developments in the world of Northern Irish sport since 1993. Furthermore, these have taken place, not necessarily coincidentally, within the context of a peace process which, although it has not yet reached ultimate fruition, has already become part of a more general transformation of life in the region. A more recent account of the situation already exists (Bairner and Darby 1999), but the full implications of what has occurred since 1993 have still to be examined in depth. For example, the three separate categories of sport which we suggested in 1993 appear less analytically secure than they were in the past. Arguably the best example of this is provided by increased Catholic interest in and, to a more limited degree, direct involvement with rugby union, a British game still perhaps, but one that has the potential to win some acceptance on the part of nationalists, not only in the south of Ireland where this has traditionally been the case, but even in the north. It would be wrong to exaggerate this change and to create the wholly false impression that rugby in the north of Ireland is well on the way to becoming a cross-community sport. Much was made of the level of nationalist interest in the achievements of the Ulster rugby team that won the European Cup in 1999. Certainly, as I have suggested elsewhere, 'as the northern nationalist middle class has grown … inevitably the interest of Catholics in middle-class activities, including rugby, has also increased' (Bairner 2000: 72). Moreover, by consistently supporting a sport that is organised on an all-Ireland basis together with an Irish national team which plays all of its home games in Dublin, the unionist rugby fraternity has shown that, although its political identity may be indivisible, its sporting allegiances are characterised by greater flexibility. Nevertheless, 'even if substantial sections of the northern middle classes can set aside their differences, working-class members of the rival traditions may find it less easy, or indeed desirable, to do so' (*ibid*.: 73). Thus, 'when all is said and done, a triumph for the Irish rugby team still offers as little cause for celebration on the unionist Shankill as does a victory for the Ulster rugby players or the Northern Irish soccer team on the nationalist Falls' (*ibid*.).

Within the categories there have also been important developments. For example, while Gaelic games remain essentially exclusive in terms both of ethos and of popular appeal, since 1993 they have been subject to far more public scrutiny from within the nationalist community in the north than was ever previously the case. Discussions have centred on the GAA's ban on British security force members (Rule 21) and its continued protectionism vis-à-vis 'foreign' games. These culminated at the end of 2001 with the removal of the ban in response to the formation of a new police service in Northern Ireland. The fact that only one of the six county boards in Northern Ireland voted for this move does not alter the fact that the move itself has potentially positive implications for the north.

It is also apparent that commercial pressures have been partly responsible for internal debate within the GAA. The formation of the Gaelic Players Association is a clear response to the greater demands being put on players and the increased revenue accrued by Gaelic games. With sponsorship already a regular feature of both Gaelic football and hurling, it seems only a matter of time before 'shamateurism' gives way to professionalism at least at county level.

As regards the universal game of soccer, perhaps one of the more interesting developments has been the signing of an increasing number of Catholics by Linfield Football Club, traditionally regarded as the loyalist side par excellence. Although this development has had little appreciable impact upon the way in which the club is regarded either by its own fans or by the outside world, the fact that it has taken place without serious controversy is important. In addition, the Irish Football Association (IFA), for so long regarded by nationalists as a defender of unionist football interests, has developed a community relations programme aimed at making the game more inclusive. Cynics might argue that this is essentially an exercise in public relations and that the association has little real interest in promoting a different culture. Moreover it could also be argued that no matter how successful the programme is, for example, in terms of removing loyalist imagery from Northern Ireland international games, Catholics will still refuse to support the 'national' team for largely political reasons. Nevertheless, the fact that the IFA is addressing such issues is in itself a major advance, one that is linked to more general changes in the administration of sport in the north of Ireland.

Indeed, perhaps the most significant development that has occurred since the publication of the book concerns the role of the Sports Council for Northern Ireland. The organisation's ethos is far less British now than in the past. In addition, it has embarked on equity and anti-sectarian policies which would have been unthinkable only a few years ago. It is worth noting, however, that although individual clubs and sports people have reacted relatively favourably to the council's prompting in this regard, governing bodies, apart from the IFA, have been considerably more resistant (Sugden and Harvie 1995).

The British state has been primarily concerned since 1993 with supporting community relations initiatives in sport. In one sense, this policy represents little more than a continuation of the hegemonic strategy which we noted previously. However, given the growing involvement of the

Dublin government in Northern Irish affairs, it could be argued that the overall approach now has more to do with stable government as opposed to British rule. Certainly the harassment of GAA members which took place on a regular basis in the past would be far less likely to occur under the present constitutional arrangements.

Sport, Sectarianism and Society in a Divided Ireland revisited

It is my feeling that the book itself was flawed in a number of respects, both empirical and theoretical. The use of the three categories as the basis for our discussion was helpful, but it may have hidden more than it managed to illuminate. Although the developments outlined in the previous section of this chapter are of relatively recent origin, even when the book was written there were overlaps and nuances in Northern Irish sport which this kind of crude categorisation inevitably missed. We concentrated too much on the major team sports, particularly the various codes of football. Sugden's more recent work on boxing (Sugden 1996) offers insights into Northern Irish society which were not provided by our examination of soccer, rugby and Gaelic games. It would have been valuable, for example, to take more account of the fact that 'while boxing is an intrinsic part of Belfast's inner-city culture, to some extent the boxing fraternity manages to remain apart from those forces which promote cross-community conflict' (*ibid*.: 127). Even more significantly, perhaps, it has also managed through its own efforts to acquire a reputation for political neutrality. Other activities, such as motor cycling and motor car rallying, which are also popular in Northern Ireland were similarly ignored. Indeed, the list of significant omissions could go on and on.

We failed to say much about the role of the media in relation to sport in the case of Northern Ireland, a weakness that Gruneau (1999) has also identified in his own work, looking back at the first edition of his *Class, Sports and Social Development* (1983). We should have noted, amongst other things, that Gaelic games had been all but hidden from the wider public gaze by certain sections of the media throughout most of the post-partition era. This observation in turn prompts the need to examine whether the increased prominence of Gaelic sport on local television is a reflection of the growing popularity of the games themselves, or of the greater self-confidence of the nationalist community, or both. Alternatively, it could be that the local television companies recognised a potentially lucrative niche market and, as a result, actually helped to stimulate an interest in Gaelic games, together with a growing sense of security in their own identity amongst nationalists.

It is in terms of theorisation, however, that I believe our study could have been more robust, not least in an effort to outline more clearly the ways in which sport both reflects and impacts on the relations of power in Northern Ireland. Our focus on a single power relationship – that between the

majority unionist population and the minority nationalist community –
whilst understandable in terms of main dynamics of the ongoing conflict,
ignored other power loci. In this respect, I would argue that our understanding of sport in Northern Ireland could have been greatly assisted by a
more robust Marxist perspective and by the judicious use of concepts located
in theories of postcolonialism and gender. What follows is an attempt to
justify these assertions and to establish new parameters for research into the
socio-political significance of sport in Northern Ireland.

With reference to our overall theoretical approach, I feel that we were too
seduced by Gramscianism or hegemony theory. There were good reasons for
this, not least the fact that I had written my doctoral thesis on Gramsci's
theory of the state and we were both impressed by the contribution of hegemony theory to the analysis of the socio-political significance of sport.
However, if as we claimed, we hoped to produce a radical analysis of
Northern Irish sport from a Marxist or neo-Marxist perspective, then it
could be argued that we should have shown more interest in political
economy. Without wishing to endorse his overly deterministic approach, it
is still worth remembering Hoffman's critique of the so-called theory of
praxis as constructed by Gramsci's followers amongst others. According to
Hoffman (1975: 153–4), 'the world is governed by real causes, by natural
laws, and human creativity is only possible if it acknowledges the independent existence of this universal necessity'. I would agree with Manners
(1998: 38) when he argues that 'the objection that the Marxist conception of
determination is reductionist is necessarily predicated upon a particularly
mechanistic interpretation of the explanatory claims advanced by it'. Indeed,
as Gramsci and others revealed, Marxism relies on a far more multidimensional explanatory theory than many of its critics would allow. Nevertheless,
any radical analysis of society which purports to have Marxist credentials
must recognise the fundamental importance of the economic realm of
human activity. However, while Sugden and I made regular references to
middle-class and working-class people and their activities in our 1993 study
of sport in the north of Ireland, at no stage did we offer anything of real
substance to explain the economic context within which various sports were
being played and watched. For example, we offered little or no empirical
evidence of social exclusion and its impact on the capacity of people to
engage in leisure pursuits. Arguably, this was a highly significant failing. As
Gruneau (1999: 117) comments in his own exercise in intellectual self-criticism, 'it was too much to say that capital alone provided the rules and
resources that shaped the dominant structures of the field of sporting practice, but capitalist class structures, and the relentless expansion of
commodification, were immensely important'. These remarks, which were
made with specific reference to Canada in 1983, apply with almost equal
force to the north of Ireland during the 1980s and early 1990s. Also highly
apposite is Gruneau's subsequent comment that capitalist class structures
and the like are even more relevant today. Indeed, in the case of the north of

Ireland, it would appear obvious that many of the developments which have taken place since 1993, both in sport and in the wider society, have been largely prompted, if not wholly determined, by economic transformations, including deindustrialisation, rampant consumerism, the rapid expansion of the Catholic middle class, and so on.

An example of the latter is the growing interest of Catholics in the traditionally British sport of rugby. Rapidly increasing consumerism together with the power of the media, above all in the form of satellite television, have been largely responsible for massive changes in the way in which association football is accessed by people in Northern Ireland. At one stage, and even as recently as the 1980s, Irish League clubs could attract reasonably large crowds to their games and the main alternative attractions were Glasgow's Old Firm of Celtic and Rangers. Today, however, with the Glasgow clubs still exercising a powerful hold on local football fans and with English clubs such as Manchester United exerting an even greater pull, interest in the Irish League and its relatively low-key rivalries has reached rock bottom. Whether or not this development has any positive implications in terms of the transcendence of sectarian division remains to be seen. The fact is, however, that Catholics and Protestants from the north of Ireland do embark on regular football pilgrimages, not just to Glasgow where their sectarianised identities are largely consolidated, but also to Manchester United's Old Trafford, Liverpool's Anfield and Arsenal's Highbury. In between and during visits moreover they spend large sums of money on club merchandise.

Those who are left behind in this pursuit of fandom as a form of conspicuous consumption include many of the men who have been most deeply affected by changes in the local society brought about by deindustrialisation and its consequences for employment patterns, particularly within working-class Protestant communities. I have argued elsewhere that it is precisely in these material circumstances that particularly strident expressions of hegemonic masculinity have been able to maintain a presence at Irish League grounds (Bairner 1997, 1999a, 1999b).

In addition to limitations in our employment of Marxist categories, we made no reference to alternative theoretical approaches or tools of analysis. In my view, theories of postcolonialism might have assisted our analysis. This does not mean that I regard theories of postcolonialism as unproblematic. As Moore-Gilbert (1997: 11) comments, 'such has been the elasticity of the concept "postcolonial" that in recent years some commentators have begun to express anxiety that there may be a danger of it imploding as an analytic construct with any real cutting edge'. Furthermore, in the case of Ireland, north and south, it is particularly contentious. Indeed, it has been suggested that Ireland can be described as both 'imperial' and 'colonial' (Jeffery 1996). According to Kibberd (1997: 97), 'only a rudimentary thinker would deny that the Irish experience is at once post-colonial and post-imperial'. Nevertheless as Howe (2000: 2) admits ıot only has this European country become the focus for many of the most intense international debates about colonialism, culture and anti-colonial/postcolonial nationalisms, but the particular mixture of postmodernism, poststructuralism and postcoloniality which has made its mark on North American, Indian, African and Middle Eastern cultural–political disputes has found a profound recent resonance in Ireland.

Howe himself is unimpressed by attempts to apply postcolonial theory to Ireland and there are good reasons for scepticism. Nevertheless, the implications of this entire debate need to be followed through if our understanding of the role of sport in the construction of identities in the north of Ireland is to be fully developed.

For example, the fact that patriotic Catholic Irishmen (and women) play rugby, albeit predominantly in the Irish Republic and not in Northern Ireland, might be taken as evidence of the extent to which the colonial legacy lingers on. Alternatively, one might regard this evidence as reflective of the extent to which members of the Irish ruling classes were themselves part of the imperial project which brought British rule as well as British games to Ireland. Or, finally, one might simply wish to consider in the light of theories of nationalism, colonialism and anti-imperialism, the fact that there are numerous ways in which sport can be used as a vehicle for promoting national identity. While playing Gaelic games represents an essentially purist and, therefore, ultimately exclusive and protectionist approach, games such as rugby offer the Irish the opportunity to enter into the sporting world. That both forms of sporting nationalism are open to Irish nationalists says much about the peculiar nature of Ireland's experience of empire, and any worthwhile study of sport in contemporary Ireland, north and south, undoubtedly requires a theoretical perspective that is capable of relating recent developments to their historical context.

We said little or nothing in the book about gender except insofar as to point out that most of our comments would refer to a realm dominated by men. We did not explore the implications of that domination either in terms of the experience of feminist resistance or the issue of hegemonic masculinity and its potential to cause harm not only to women but also to non-hegemonic men. As mentioned above, I have tried to remedy this omission to some extent in subsequent work on sport and the construction and reproduction of masculine identities in Northern Ireland (Bairner 1999a, 1999b). However, my work has been mainly concerned with men and, specifically, with Protestant working-class men. Much needs to be done if we are to form a clearer picture of the representation of maleness in nationalist communities and, above all, if we are to understand the relationship between women and sport in the north of Ireland.

As well as borrowing from these important theoretical traditions, we could also have entered into other intellectual debates such as that centred around the concepts of modernity and postmodernity. For example, an inter-esting research area that we might well have considered is the role of the GAA in contemporary constructions of Irishness. It is one thing to argue that the GAA is a repository of a particular version of Irish national identity. It is dangerous, however, if one creates the impression that this is the only possible representation of Irishness and that Irish national identity is uncontested both in the world of sport and elsewhere. In addition, it is worth analysing the suggestion that the version of Irishness which the GAA is partially responsible for reproducing is either pre-modern or at best modern and that it has little relevance to a society that has become postmodern. Alternatively, one might wish to consider the possibility that the GAA is linked today not to an outmoded reading of Irishness but simply to a different modern version of national identity from that which is promoted by a self-proclaimed cultural elite based primarily in south Dublin.

Another debate which could have featured far more prominently in our work was that concerned with globalisation. Arguably the relevance of glob-alisation to the study of sport was only emerging, for example, in the work of Maguire (1993a, 1993b, 1994), when we were preparing our study. Also, like many other commentators on Northern Irish politics and society at the time, we were almost certainly convinced that the conflict possessed its own intrinsic integrity which made it almost immune from external cultural influences. As a consequence, we failed to account, in adequate depth, for how we understood the ways in which the rival political identities were (are) constructed. Furthermore, although I would be reluctant to accept that our analysis of Northern Ireland was simplistic, it is undeniable that much of our narrative centred around the existence of two separate tribes whose distinctiveness was in part reflected by the sports that they played and whose differences could be either exacerbated or, from time to time, tran-scended and perhaps even resolved, by way of sporting engagement. As a consequence, we tended to write about two monolithic blocs and ignored intra-communal division. In addition, we did not say enough about the actual theorisation of Northern Ireland as a place (real and/or imagined), a disputed territory or a political entity.

In sum, therefore, there is considerable scope for the expansion of research into the socio-political importance of sport in Northern Irish society. However, before outlining what directions that research might take, it is worth briefly considering how sport in Northern Ireland may itself evolve in the foreseeable future.

Future developments in sport in Northern Ireland

Just as it is difficult to predict with any degree of certainty how the Irish peace process will develop, so it is hard to anticipate the ways in which the organisation and overall character of sport in the north of Ireland will evolve in the future. As a consequence, most of my comments at this point are necessarily speculative. However, it is certain that all governing bodies will be required to take anti-sectarian and equity policies seriously. In addition, it is a distinct possibility that the GAA's conservatism will weaken in response to political change and, more importantly, the pressures of commercialism. All-Ireland competitions will flourish perhaps even in association football, although it is almost certain that the latter will continue to be administered separately from Belfast and Dublin. It is not inconceivable, however, that the level of control currently exercised by the existing governing bodies might be challenged as a consequence of wider trends in European football, including the formation of an Atlantic League with members from Belfast and Dublin by no means out of the question. Women's sports will also develop significantly at least in terms of participation figures if not of status. It is unlikely, however, that the hegemonic masculinity that dominates sport in Northern Ireland at present will be threatened in the near future.

Even more speculatively, based at the new Odyssey Centre which has been constructed on the banks of the River Lagan in Belfast, the Belfast Giants might yet help to make ice hockey a sport which engenders massive cross-community sport. It has the distinct advantage of not being seen to belong to either of the main traditions. Moreover, the venue at which the Giants are playing their games and the marketing strategies which are deployed to support their efforts both fit neatly into the new Belfast – part real and part imagined – in which images and signs linked to consumption are rapidly replacing the old ideological concerns in all but the most hard-line and impoverished districts. Indeed, it is not impossible that Belfast could become home to other franchises, both in traditional areas of activity such as soccer and also in imported games (basketball, American football?) as European sporting experiences in general move, superficially at least, in the direction of commercially driven Americanisation (Bairner 2001). Let's hear it then for the Belfast Bigots and/or the Belfast Believers depending upon one's views on matters theological.

The traditional sports will continue to be played, of course, and they will still possess the capacity to engender both hegemonic and counter-hegemonic values and attitudes. As the lines between them become more blurred, however, and as other sporting activities and leisure pursuits enter the space that was previously dominated by a handful of major games, the role of sport as an arena for socio-political and cultural contestation may be greatly diminished.

Research strategies

It is to be hoped that the focus of future research into sport in Northern Ireland can go beyond the pioneering work of John Sugden and myself so as to tackle issues which we ignored and to make use of different conceptual frameworks. In a variety of papers, articles and chapters, I have tried to introduce gender into the debate. More work is needed in this area. For example, there needs to be a greater feminist involvement in the study of Irish sport, and women's games, including rugby union and Gaelic football, must be examined.

In terms of theory, and in addition to recognising the importance of feminist interventions, it is certainly important to make more use of Marxist categories other than hegemony and to take more account of postcolonial and postmodern theories. As regards other theoretical concerns, it is hoped that my book, *Sport, Nationalism and Globalisation* (2001), will complement Cronin's attempts to tighten up the use of concepts such as nationalism, nationality and national identity with specific reference to the study of sport in Ireland (Cronin 1999).

There is a real need for more research into the relationship between sport and intra-community rivalry within both the Ulster unionist and Irish nationalist traditions, not least in order to reveal that the contestation for positions of power is in no way confined to disputes between the two traditions. Why, for example, is there such bitter rivalry between the predominantly Protestant fans of Glentoran and Linfield or between fans of those clubs and the loyalist supporters of Glenavon and Portadown, and how do these sporting rivalries reflect and impact upon political divisions within unionism as a whole? Why do some unionists feel happy to represent Ireland at sport and to involve themselves in all-Ireland sporting bodies whilst others eschew contact with their southern counterparts, and, once again, what do these differences of opinion tell us about the general condition and philosophical outlook of Ulster unionism?

In similar vein, I would contend that sport offers interesting insights into differences of substance and emphasis within the nationalist community. Why do so many nationalists choose to play and watch so-called foreign games, particularly soccer? To what extent does the GAA, despite its all-Ireland remit and its nominal desire for a 32-county republic, reflect in its day-to-day existence the fact that northern nationalism and southern nationalism are, by and large, very different doctrines? In addition, far more work needs to be done on the specific Gaelic games, in order to explain, for example, the strength of hurling in certain parts of Ulster and the relationship between hurling and football in those clubs which are involved with both games. In terms of identity politics, furthermore, we might wish to consider the extent to which Irish sporting nationalism of an exclusive type is dependent on the future success of hurling. Would the failure of hurling to maintain a significant presence in Ulster represent a real blow to Irish nationalism, not least because Gaelic football possesses far less intrinsic historical purity and is far more susceptible to encroachment from other codes? Finally, more attention also needs to be paid to the impact of commercialism and globalisation on the GAA.

Furthermore, as suggested earlier, scholars must go beyond the main team sports if we are to arrive at a more comprehensive understanding of the social significance of sport in the north of Ireland. It is naturally tempting for social scientists to focus on those activities that are most closely bound up with the construction and reproduction of cultural identities. The fact remains, however, that many individuals devote their leisure time to sports which have little or no political resonance and which should be all the more interesting for that very reason.

Conclusion

Sport, Sectarianism and Society in a Divided Ireland was an important book which contributed not only to the study of the Northern Ireland conflict but also more generally to our understanding of the socio-political significance of sport in the modern world. I hope that research into the relationship between sport, sectarianism and society in the north of Ireland will continue to develop not only in the directions signposted in this chapter but many other ways besides. I am slightly more hopeful than was once the case that sport can play a positive role in underpinning initiatives directed at cross-community reconciliation. This assessment, however, owes little to any confidence that I might have in the vision and ability of those who administer sport in the north of Ireland. Rather, I believe that those same social forces which have been of vital importance in creating the conditions in which the peace process has been able to develop are equally capable of making the world of Northern Irish sport a less contentious, albeit also a less interesting and culturally challenging, arena.

What remains undeniable, however, is that no matter how peaceful the adjoining worlds of politics and sport in Northern Ireland might come to appear in the years ahead, beneath the surface both will continue to be characterised by power relationships that are ultimately rooted in political economy. These may well differ in detail from those that have dominated the scene in the past. For example, as the preceding discussion has revealed, certain sections of the nationalist population will almost certainly enjoy more power than ever before. Their growing self-confidence, however, like the peace process itself and accompanying developments in the sporting culture of Northern Ireland, is in large part propelled by material improvement. The brutal fact is that as regards both politics and sport, and for many of the same reasons, women, the poor and non-hegemonic men amongst others continue to be marginalised, discriminated against and locked within a sectarian environment which the peace process has failed to eradicate and, in the short term at least, may actually have served to maintain. It is on the causes of the relative powerlessness of the socially excluded that the social scientific study of Northern Ireland in general as well as the social science of sport specifically should focus.

References

Bairner, A. (1997) ' "Up to their knees?" Football, sectarianism, masculinity and protestant working-class identity', in P. Shirlow and M. McGovern (eds) *Who Are 'The People'?*, London: Pluto Press.

—— (1999a) 'Soccer, masculinity and violence in Northern Ireland: Between hooliganism and terrorism', *Men and Masculinities* 1(3): 284–301.

—— (1999b) 'Masculinity, violence and the Irish peace process', *Capital and Class*, 69: 125–44.

—— (2000) 'Sport and peace: An uneasy dialogue', in E. Slater and M. Peillon (eds) *Memories of the Present. A Sociological Chronicle of Ireland 1997–1998*, Dublin: Institute of Public Administration.

—— (2001) *Sport, Nationalism, and Globalization: European and North American Perspectives*, Albany NY: State University of New York Press.

Bairner, A. and Darby, P. (1999) 'Divided sport in a divided society: Northern Ireland', in J. Sugden and A. Bairner (eds) *Sport in Divided Societies*, Aachen: Meyer & Meyer.

Cronin, M. (1999) *Sport and Nationalism in Ireland: Gaelic Games, Soccer and Irish Identity since 1884*, Dublin: Four Courts Press.

Gruneau, R. (1983) *Class, Sports and Social Development,* Amherst: University of Massachusetts Press.

—— (1999) *Class, Sports and Social Development*, new edition, Champaign, Illinois: Human Kinetics.

Hoffman, J. (1975) *Marxism and the Theory of Praxis*, London: Lawrence & Wishart.

Howe, S. (2000) *Ireland and Empire: Colonial Legacies and Irish History and Culture*, Oxford: Oxford University Press.

Jeffery, K. (1996) 'Introduction', in K. Jeffery (ed.) *'An Irish empire?' Aspects of Ireland and the British Empire*, Manchester: Manchester University Press.

Kibberd, D. (1997) 'Modern Ireland: postcolonial or European?', in S. Murray (ed.) *Not On Any Map. Essays on Postcoloniality and Cultural Nationalism*, Exeter: University of Exeter Press.

Maguire, J. (1993a) 'Globalization, sport and national identities: the empire strikes back', *Society and Leisure* 16: 293–322.

—— (1993b) 'Globalization, sport development, and the media/sport production complex', *Sport Sciences Review* 2: 19–30.

—— (1994) 'Sport, identity politics and globalization: diminishing contrasts and increasing varieties', *Sociology of Sport Journal* 11: 398–427.

Manners, J. (1998) 'Marxism and meaning: towards an immaculate conception of determination', *Studies in Marxism* 5: 37–54.

Moore-Gilbert, B. (1997) *Postcolonial Theory: Contexts, Practices, Politics*, London: Verso.

Sugden, J. (1996) *Boxing and Society: An International Analysis*, Manchester: Manchester University Press.

Sugden, J. and Bairner, A. (1993) *Sport, Sectarianism and Society in a Divided Ireland*, Leicester: Leicester University Press.

—— (eds) (1999a) *Sport in Divided Societies*, Aachen: Meyer & Meyer.

—— (1999b), 'Sport in divided societies', in J. Sugden and A. Bairner (eds) *Sport in Divided Societies*, Aachen: Meyer & Meyer.

Sugden, J. and Harvie, S. (1995) *Sport and Community Relations in Northern Ireland*, Coleraine: Centre for the Study of Conflict, University of Ulster.

11 The sports star in the media

The gendered construction and youthful consumption of sports personalities

Gill Lines

Gendered power games across the media field of play

The 'Summer of Sport '96' offered a proliferation of imagery and icons surrounding contemporary sport throughout the media events of the European Soccer Championships (Euro '96), Wimbledon and the Atlanta Olympics. Sport stars during these events represented the diversified, contradictory and dissonant elements in the sporting discourse. They offered representations legitimating and reinforcing popular beliefs about cultural values and behaviour and confirmed the nature of the gendered power games at play across sporting fields of play within the media.

This chapter analyses the naturalised representations of sport personalities and the common-sense assumptions of their place and influence in the lives of a group of young people aged fifteen. The functions of sport stars as characters within sporting narratives are scrutinised in the light of young people's perceptions of stars as celebrities and role models. Dyer (1991a) and Whannel (1998a) identify how textual analysis across film, and media sport star analysis have relatively ignored meaning and power between text and audience interaction. Yet this is significant, for whilst textual meanings can reflect the hierarchical mobilisation of power in gender sporting relations, the articulation of varied interpretations provides the context for considering the extent to which the audience is empowered or enslaved by the messages it receives. Fiske's (1987: 5) comment that 'all meanings are not equal and the activation of any one set of them does not occur at the unmotivated whim of the reader' reinforces the complexity of social, political and economic relations across media production, texts and audiences.

Issues of power are articulated in four ways in particular in this chapter. Firstly, although sportswomen are becoming increasingly successful across a range of different sports, ideological strategies operate through sporting narratives to construct gendered meanings that confirm the acceptability and dominance of male sport stars whilst marginalising women. An heroism—villainy continuum provides a basis for the discussion of the social function of sport stars as inspirational role models for young people. The continuum also reinforces social values and connections between masculinity and sporting prowess. The multiple symbolism of national, gender and ethnic identity evident in the construction of sports personalities reflects ideological power struggles across different social groups and consistently emerges across varied media textual analysis (Blain, Boyle and O'Donnell 1993; Boyle and Haynes 2000; Rowe 1999; Wenner 1998; Whannel 1998b, 1999). Procedures of omission and selection that work to prioritise or marginalise personalities in the sporting discourse form a key framework of this textual analysis.

Secondly, and this is a key focus, is how young people respond to or sometimes may resist dominant ideological readings of the texts. Common sense assumptions intimate that young people are vulnerable and gullible to the commodified and objectified star images they receive; 'No-one has more powerful influence than sport stars. They are eulogised and emulated' (*Daily Mail*, 7 October 1998: 11). Yet it is too simplistic an assumption that young people will adopt the most highly profiled stars and imitate on and off field behaviour. [1]

Thirdly, production practices can construct gendered audience positioning, and corresponding responses can confirm or dispute these constructions. The patriarchal media sporting domain positions women readers as outsiders (Whannel 1998a). This research reveals how young people enter the field, use it and adopt their own positioning in relation to the signification of the texts. It considers how boys learn about masculinity and form modes of identification with their heroes. Conversely, it raises concern about the ways in which girls are virtually excluded and sportswomen are represented as 'other'. Yet such gendered divisions are not so rigidly imposed and both girls and boys negotiate the texts far more fluidly than has often been recognised.

Finally, within this methodological framework, power issues between the researcher and the researched come into play. Decisions had to be made about the levels of analysis, the nature of the case study group, the media products and events and the interaction and reflexivity of the researcher in the process. Lines (2000a) argues that the researcher role as female, insider and outsider enhanced the on-going sequential stages of analysis.[2]

Methodological framework: articulating power through text and audience interaction

The appropriateness of varying methodological frameworks for analysing audience experiences and the media's ideological impact attracts widespread and persisting debate. The increasing cultural and reception-focused approaches have highlighted the significance of pleasures and meanings, reception contexts and cultural backgrounds (Morley 1992; Hermes 1995; Gillespie 1995; Buckingham 1993). Post-structuralist celebration of the audience, whilst rightly identifying the importance of the reader in the analytical process, has been criticised for allowing celebration of audience power outside of textual positioning, socio-historical, ideological and political economy contexts inherent in the processes of production and consumption (Kellner 1995, 2001b; Bordo 1993; Underwood 2001). A critical emphasis on media sport audience analysis cannot simply celebrate the power of the audience to make their own meanings, but should account for how these meanings are made within the ideological constructs of the texts. Buckingham (1993: 14) suggests power should be perceived as embedded in the relationship between the audience and text. Morley (1992) and Fiske (1987) also acknowledge that the power stakes cannot be so easily dismissed.

Welcome though the growth in textual analysis of media sport has been (Wenner 1998; Rowe 1999; Boyle and Haynes 2000), the phenomenal audience appeal of sporting events requires a more interpretative response incorporating audience voices in the research process (Kinkema and Harris 1998; Whannel 1998a). For, as Lye (1996: 5) indicates, deconstruction is more than decoding; 'it is a matter of entering into the thoughtful play of contradiction, multiple reference, and the ceaseless questioning of conclusions and responses'.

Effects, semiotics and audience analysis, whilst divergent and lacking an integral approach, have all contributed to a greater understanding of the media experience. Thompson's (1990) approach to media analysis provides for a systematised and integrative framework that offers the researcher a reflexive approach to interpretation and a rich opportunity for description, articulation and explanation. Thompson seeks to overcome criticisms of individual methodological approaches to media analysis by arguing for 'depth hermeneutics'. This framework allows for the combination of varying analytical tools within levels of analysis whilst affording critical consideration of relations of power within the ideological constructions (Underwood 2001). Willis (1980: 95) advocates multi-method approaches to enhance accounts of the complexity of the media experience and reveal contradictions across layers of analysis. Tomlinson (1992: 45), in defence of Thompson's (1990) tripartite framework, argues for a methodological approach, combining 'social history and sociology; discourse analysis and ethnography'. Kellner (2001a: 8) also pursues the need for critical integrated perspectives 'linking cultural studies ultimately to social theory and politics'.

Driven by the strengths of these arguments, the methodological approach of this investigation focused on an integrated approach combining textual analysis from the Summer of Sport 1996 with audience interpretation. The first stage within the framework combined quantitative and qualitative newspaper and television analysis. This identified the most highly profiled sportsmen and women and ways in which they were signified as stars and role models. A case study group of twenty-five young people completed daily diaries and group and individual interviews. Discussions focused on identifying which sport stars were most appealing and why. These revealed how young people made sense of the gendered constructions of sports personalities and the extent to which sports personalities were adopted, appraised and rejected as role models (Lines, 1999b).

The sport star as hero(-ine): textual contradictions in the patriarchal construction of sports personalities

Sporting representations provided key themes articulating celebratory and contradictory tales of sporting heroism. Each of the events covered a wide range of personalities, although amplified images reflected the higher news value of national male heroes and villains. This reinforced the primary importance of the male hero in the sporting narratives and the signification of the female as outsider and other.[3]

Euro '96 discourse initially portrayed tales of 'laddish behaviour' reflecting contemporary concerns of masculinity (Whannel 1999). Criticism gave way to heroic war rhetoric and stars represented as ancient warriors. Successful traditional heroism equated with sportsmen as social role models and privileged, in the English press, the soccer stars of the English national side; 'Every boy wants to score goals like Alan Shearer, tackle like Stuart Pearce, curl free kicks like Paul Gascoigne and save penalties like David Seaman' (*Daily Mail*, 21 June 1996: 3).

The multiple imagery and ideological contradictions of Paul Gascoigne, highly profiled during Euro '96, offered potential for differentiated audience responses. Textual constructions reveal him as embodying two distinct social trends. The traditional working-class football hero, skilful and patriotic, is superseded increasingly through the 1990s as he depicts the 'New Lad' – gorgeous blondes, childish pranks, boozy exploits, laddish friends and an affluent lifestyle become alternative and central characteristics of his image:

> Gazza inspired the nation by blubbing like a child. He belched into microphones, turned up on a formal occasions wearing a pair of plastic breasts, was paired in headlines with 'sexy Miss Whiplash', produced a book called 'Daft as a Brush', made a rash tackle. And was never the same again.
>
> (Simon Barnes, *The Times Euro '96* pullout, 3 June 1996: 3–4)

Whilst Gascoigne's fluctuating fortunes 'From prat to paragon in an instant' (*Daily Mail*, 21 June 1996: 78) afford him newsworthiness, this behaviour is criticised as unbecoming of a national sport star. The immense emphasis placed by contemporary media sports culture on the desire for 'heroic' sports personalities is contradictory. For sport stars such as Pete Sampras, who epitomise the 'sporting gentleman', are often reproached for being 'dull'. Another is Tim Henman, the British tennis player who emerged during 1996 as a focal point of audience identification:

> He does everything he can to keep his emotions bottled up. He mixes immense theatricality with almost painful diffidence. He would die rather than make a public exhibition of himself in the way that Jimmy Connors did ... watch those odd little mannerisms, the funny little skip

he does when walking back to the baseline, the rarer skip when he is especially pleased ... But he is English and this is Wimbledon. All the passion has to be expressed in that little skip.

(The Times, 29 June 1998: 32)

It is the stereotypical 'Englishness' of Henman, combining national identity with potential for success, that works to sell his image. For initially he does not have the charisma of 'Agassi', the clowning of 'Gazza' or the idiosyncrasies of 'Eric the swimming Eel' in the Sydney Olympics, that work to create both sport star and celebrity. The contrasting yet highly profiled images of Gascoigne and Henman provide a central feature of the discussions with young people.

The Summer of Sport '96 proved no exception in its textual representation of sportswomen (cf. Duncan 1990; Duncan, Messner and Williams 1990; Daddario 1994; Davis 1997). The relative omission of successful sportswomen highlights their questionable status as 'heroines' and reflects patriarchal power and control in the nature of the selected female representations. Stories of sexuality and vulnerability, accompanied by images of 'women on display', confirmed the masculine–feminine duality of representations and the 'otherness' of women in the sporting world.

Firstly, the under-representation of female sports stars identifies ways in which their invisibility acts to assert patriarchal dominance of the sporting terrain. The lack of star names and the criteria for news value provides an illusory picture of the number of women taking part and their reasons for doing so. During Wimbledon for example, the *Sun* devoted just 15 per cent of coverage to women's tennis. The focus upon three of the four players headlined accentuated their vulnerability:

Stabbing made me a recluse ... I put on 2 1/2 stone by bingeing.

(Sun [on Monica Seles], 15 June 1996: 20–1)

Wrist injury for Arantxa Sanchez-Vicario.

(Sun, 29 June 1996: 42)

In the past Graf has broken her thumbs, sprained wrists and torn ligaments. She has had bone spurs, stress fractures and chipped bones.

(Sun, 2 July 1996: 31)

Individual features on Graf and Seles reinforced problems caused by sporting involvement (injuries, emotional and personal trauma) and their early dependence on their fathers. Photographic space prioritised glamorised, sexualised images of them. Mary Pierce's feminised news value afforded high profile despite the player's limited success in the tournament:

Glamour girl Mary Pierce cruised through the first round ... and promised a brand new outfit. Mary was a sensation at the French Open with her all black dress.

(*Sun*, 25 June 1996: 27)

Similarly, women's beach volleyball and gymnastics during the Atlanta Olympics afforded definitions of femininity, sexuality and vulnerability (Lines 2000b). In Kuhn's (1985: 43) terms, this further reinforced a patriarchal selection of female sporting imagery and a 'masculine definition of femininity'.

Power games at play in the Summer of Sport '96 texts revealed processes of omission and selection which reified the importance of masculinity, bravery and heroism on the sports field. Feminine attributes and sexualised images sought to articulate sportswomen as distinctly different from their male counterparts and to deflect attention away from their sporting prowess.

Youthful interpretations: negotiating the contradictions – 'A true hero-showing courage in the face of adversity'

Ways young people perceive sports stars as admirable, heroic, or trivialised (Harris 1994; Vande Berg 1998; Whaunel 1995) reveal the multiplicity of the media messages that they receive about them.

Consumption patterns and pleasures (Lines 1998) indicated that footballers dominated the thoughts of the young people, asserting the power of high profile representations and the media hype given to the successful run of the England team during Euro '96. Preference for watching male sports personalities was evident – as during Wimbledon when men's singles matches monopolised the viewing. Of the third who tuned in to women's tennis, all of them watched at least part of the singles final. Only three adolescents watched any other women's matches. Despite a vast number of performers, the lack of British success offered a distinct lack of Atlanta Olympic heroes. Steve Redgrave and Roger Black, two of the most successful performers, lacked the 'celebrity' status to capture the imagination of the young people.

In discussing traits they most admire, for young people, the complexity of the male sporting hero becomes evident. Most frequently, their articulation of heroic characteristics conjured images of the importance of excellence, dominance and sheer genius in sport. Confirming Harris's (1994) findings, the characteristics identified located the hero as representing a traditional standpoint – excellence at sport accompanied by social and moral virtues of determination, hard work, coping with pressure, courage in the face of adversity and the love of the game.

Young people articulated social expectations and values about legendary perceptions of the hero as someone unattainable, with supernatural qualities; someone with 'an aura about them, a mystique and inspirational'. The particular criteria that young people use to indicate who stands out as a rare and special person, beyond mere celebrity status, are difficult to determine. Some of the young people's interpretations below suggest that the Michael Jordan image is successful by the way he is seen to enforce moral codes of conduct, the work ethic and social mobility:

> There are stars worth looking up to, like Michael Jordan, because he hasn't done anything bad, and he's good at his sport, and working with children and stuff, and that's someone you look up to.
>
> (Male, aged 15)

> He's such a character, he just sticks in your mind. He's worked really hard to get where he is, so I think I admire that ... in a sense he is a hero to young people, more of an inspiration actually. They get inspired about how hard he worked and where he came from because he came from downtown America.
>
> (Male, aged 15)

Michael Jordan has featured across my longitudinal research since 1990, and his longevity and popularity as a sports hero is confirmed by Vande Berg (1998), Harris (1994) and McDonald (1996). His overseas base has meant that the British press has made a less critical, probing investigation into his private life, for the young people in this case study seemed unaware of his alleged dealings with the gambling and fights referred to by Harris (1994).

Muhammad Ali's sporting career and continued media visibility are significant features. Whilst Ali receives mixed receptions from American youth (Harris 1994), his portrayal during the Atlanta Olympics produced a wave of sympathy and praise. For, as several boys indicated, his courage to take a particular political stance and overcome his current ill health were applauded:

> He was a great geezer. He came back to the Olympics like nothing had happened, he put it all behind him. He's got Parkinson's now, it made it all special and they gave him his medal back and he accepted, so he was a hero coming back after it happened.
>
> (Male, aged 15)

> He's the world's best ever boxer, I know about when he threw the medal in the river, he stood up for his race and showed that nothing was more important and that made loads of people love him.
>
> (Male, aged 15)

> He showed great courage, he was an inspiration as well. I think he has done a lot for his community and his race.
>
> (Female, aged 15)

He's got determination and he keeps on with whatever he is doing and even now with his disease he's still fighting all the way and I think that is a true hero to show courage in the face of adversity.

(Male, aged 15)

Long-term memories and dramatic imagery of Ali lighting the Atlanta Olympic flame evoked a nostalgic and mythical impact of Muhammad Ali as a true hero, alongside contemporary sports stars. Whilst some commentators (Tomlinson 2000) have argued that Ali's act demeaned his myth and his world-historical legacy, the admiring voices of these young people – however much influenced by media discourses – must nevertheless be acknowledged. Similar comparisons can be drawn with the Jordan persona, for Ali, too, whilst admired for his sporting expertise, also embodies issues linked to racial identity and overcoming social disadvantage and adversity.

Whilst young people do make positive readings of role models, including the heroic, media messages can also tarnish such reflections. Aspects of the coverage raised issues about how the media affords hero status too readily, and trivialises the concept. The ways in which some English footballers were reconstructed from villain to hero after a singular moment of success, supports this point. Henman, similarly, after one Wimbledon victory, was positioned as the 'All England Hero'. The media, arguably, can be credited with the amplification of such characteristics in order to draw consumers into the sporting spectacle.

Opposition to the construction of Henman as 'a hero' during Wimbledon 1996 indicated that young people, by emphasising sustained achievements, were less inclined to trivialise aspects of the heroic. A number of them had little awareness of him and were reluctant to be judgmental about his hero status: 'I think Tim Henman has a long way to go yet. I don't think they see him as a hero yet because he hasn't achieved anything really major'.

Young people found it difficult to identify with Henman's lack of charisma. They wanted him to laugh and make stimulating conversation during interviews. The media's attempt to portray him as an idol for the girls was refuted: 'Tim Henman – he's like ugly ... ugly. He's good but I don't think he's nice looking or anything.' Whilst young people do not wish to trivialise the heroic concept in their regard for level of achievement, they do place importance on sports stars' personality and appearance alongside their sporting prowess.

Villains: 'all geniuses have something wrong with them'

Young people were also able to reflect upon weaknesses. This caused a contradiction for them, for although they desired a traditional hero, they also realistically acknowledged that sports stars were likely to exhibit everyday behaviour just like everyone else. They were discriminating and perceptive about the lives and roles of sport stars with statements such as:

'they are only in it for the money, they were letting their country down and they should have more pride'. Similarly, there were references to individual sports personalities as 'aggressive, big-headed, a psycho and an idiot'.

Young people articulated concern about the behaviour of sport stars and questioned conflicting issues encompassing morality and sport. As Whannel (1995) also suggests, sporting discourse does provide a channel for young people's development of attitudes, towards aspects of morality and acceptable social behaviour.

One group of young people raised concern about the ways in which footballers play for financial gain rather than the love of the game. A surprising raising of the 'professional versus amateur debate' by a group of fifteen year olds brought up in the commercial world of sport, showed the currency of an old-fashioned, yet lingering, ideal. One discussion developed in this way: 'I think you should be prepared to play for your country and a club without getting paid at all'; 'I'd be happy to play for any team for next to nothing, a fiver a week would do me'. One boy confirmed powerful images across newspapers of footballers with beautiful girls on their arms by suggesting that other perks could compensate for low financial rewards: 'Can you imagine how many birds you'd get if you played for a premier league club?' The argument focused on young people's perceptions of the ways in which wealth and status was more of a priority than playing the game for its own sake. Whilst for some this depreciated hero status, several adolescents offered fortune and wealth as an admirable characteristic of their favourite players.

Despite public concern for the impact of violence in sport on the young audience, a clear disdain was shown for violent traits displayed by sport stars such as footballers Paul Gascoigne and Eric Cantona. Responses to Gascoigne show how young people's interpretations of the footballer become more derogatory and critical as the media reveal aspects of his personal life and behaviour. Rather than idolise him as the media suggested, many young men actively expressed their disdain for such behaviour. One disillusioned boy, following the revelation that Gazza had beaten his wife, suggested: 'After Euro '96 everyone was saying how brilliant he was and then he spoilt it. And he let his country down. There must be someone who likes him, but after what he's done … '. The responsibility of sports stars as national representatives was evident as several instances of bad behaviour were cited as letting down the country, rather than fans or the player.

Gascoigne and Cantona, whilst criticised for bad behaviour, both receive acclaim as geniuses. A realistic appraisal by one boy supports the ways in which young people are able to accept stars at both ends of the hero–villain continuum: 'But when you think about it, all geniuses have got something wrong with them'. Another pursued the point: 'But people should know that, that sport stars aren't exactly brilliant, they're really human'.

The media, it appears, has eroded notions of the superhuman sports stars for, in their quest for scandal, sensationalism and an ever-changing star system, the news and sports agendas are quick to discredit celebrities for their own ends. Young people acknowledge the difficulty, in the contemporary world, of remaining unblemished. For young people, whilst admiring traditional ideals, are tolerant in their recognition that today's sports star embodies current social problems and, as such, acknowledge that the star does not have superhuman qualities.

Role models: young people as wannabes or realists?

It was clear that the 'Gazza' myth was in decline as contrasting media representations of hero and villain had led some young people to decode the sportsman as an ageing star, lacking in responsibility as a role model for younger children. Whilst appreciating some of the finer points of his sporting performance, they were judgmental, yet realistic, about his personal lifestyle and behaviour.

Whilst a few boys engaged with Gascoigne's character, humour and skill, there was little evidence of him being hero-worshipped. Positive pleasures mostly revolved around his physical skill: 'Gascoigne is good, I mean that goal he did where he flipped it over'. There was limited evidence of emulating Gascoigne, apart from imitating his skill level on the pitch: 'You go over the park and you try and copy what they all do'.

A number of comments reflected their realistic appraisal of stardom:

> It was Paul Gascoigne's birthday and he had a drink. Exactly, everyone does. It doesn't matter how old you are, you go out, everyone gets slaughtered when they go out and have a drink. And it's like because they're idols, they shouldn't be doing it, they should be toning it down, have a quiet meal and a drink, which is stupid because no one does it.
>
> (Male, aged 16)

Recurring interpretations show a moral stance and resistance to the values portrayed by his image. Comments about his drinking exploits and home life such as: 'I've gone off Gazza because of all that thing with his wife. I'm not into all that wife bashing stuff – big sport stars have got an obligation to set a good image', and 'Don't like the way he treats women though. Especially that beautiful blonde bird', reflected that boys were judgmental of violent masculine behaviour.

Concern about the 'effects of Gazza' on young people is far removed from the reality of their interpretations:

> Perhaps we should discuss the fate of the boys for whom Gazza was and will remain an icon … don't cry for Gazza, a has-been at 31, the real tears should be shed for the wannabes who are still genuinely too young to know any better … Unfortunately it doesn't take much to be classified as an all round good guy, one of the lads, a real geezer.
>
> (*Independent*, 3 June 1998: 21)

Yet there is little support for the claim that Gascoigne is perceived as a 'real geezer' by the group. They are not 'Gazza wannabes', but are conservative in approach and express moral concern about players' responsibilities.

They reject the notion that they, or their peers, would seek to emulate Gascoigne, although they acknowledge that others might. Concern rested with young children, who they perceived were less able to make mature judgements. There was a strong and coherent argument from young people that they were able to make prudent decisions about modes of imitation, and that they were not readily fooled. Although they identified with and admired certain stars, there was in many cases an emphatic denial of wanting to be like them.

They made significant statements about the function of a sports star as someone people would look up to and who has a social responsibility. One argument developed as follows: 'sport stars say they are not role models but they are, it comes with the job, if you are good at sport you have a responsibility to behave because young children are going to look up to you because they need someone to inspire them'. Yet they also acknowledge that the stars themselves have not necessarily asked for that role: 'I think they are role models when they are playing football but they don't ask to be role models'. This shows young people do not assume that the social and moral responsibility required by players on the pitch does or should transfer into everyday life.

Yet, though they readily accept that sporting behaviour and responsibility on the field is distinct from everyday reality, they see sport stars as behaving according to the same standards as everyone else. Realism and cynicism about the 'superhuman' status of sport stars was revealed by interpretations such as: 'Just because they're idols, they shouldn't be doing it ... which is stupid cos no one does it'. Young people were not necessarily gullible – as one boy indicated: 'People like to have heroes when they are our age, but they can see them with a touch of reality, but when you are that bit older, you know people they don't seem as good as they were, they don't have that mystique anymore'. Comments such as, 'I suppose other young people my age don't see him as a hero 'cos they know all the stories that have been going around in the papers but I think younger kids probably do because they don't pay as much attention ... they don't see him as the real person', suggest that these young people believe that adulation is more likely from younger children who are not as media literate as themselves. Whilst girls believed that 'blokes, boys and younger children' would adopt sporting role models, boys suggested it would most likely be younger children and those who wanted to be athletes.

This tendency to question the ways in which sports stars could, and should, be positive role models for others indicates the ways in which young people were able to identify flaws in sports stars, and shows their awareness of public arguments about role models for young people. Whilst they voiced concern about the responsibility of sports stars to set examples for others to follow, they firmly suggested that as adolescents they were able to make their own judgements about acceptable behaviour, and would not necessarily need a sport star to lead them astray. This highlights several points: the stage of adolescent development in their search for their own identity, the unconscious awareness of modes of imitation and the desire to express themselves as their own person. This provided a general counter to perceptions that young people saw themselves as gullible. However, the ways in which they easily dismissed how they themselves might be persuaded, but cast aspersions on the vulnerability of those other than themselves, suggests that they did perceive elements of power in media messages.

Sports stars provide audience identification with the sporting spectacle. Young people desire the 'social–moral exemplar' of sporting myths, and reject some stars that move beyond these boundaries. This could silence critics' suggestions that the youth of today adopt undesirable role models. For young people assert their own power to read textual contradictions, and so make realistic appraisals of sport stars.

The marginalisation of female sports personalities

The previous section revealed how the male sporting personality dominated 'sports talk' and confirmed naturalised constructions of patriarchal dominance. Young people failed to significantly acknowledge female sports stars, and generally perceived women's sport as inferior to men's. The nominal discourse about women ensured the virtual exclusion of females as either sporting heroines or role models.

The pleasures and meanings of the sporting narratives showed that although male dominance was significant it was not complete, for young people did accord some praise to female sport stars. However, clearly, women's sport was not taken as seriously and male sport was seen as the benchmark for comparison and was bounded in terms such as these: 'I do admire female stars it's just that they are not given as much importance as the males': 'It doesn't appeal to me at all, especially rugby with women playing. I think because you expect the skills of the men's game and you just don't see it there, there's no charisma or anything, it's not as appealing'.

The marginalised discourse surrounding women's sports stars was a point pursued through interview questioning. Relatively few young people selected female sports stars, or raised comments about female sport unless specifically questioned, suggesting that their low profile on the news agenda means that they are neither taken seriously, nor featured in the sporting discourse of these young people.

Of the handful of female stars mentioned, those such as Steffi Graf, the German tennis star, and Sally Gunnell, the British athlete, had received long-term coverage. The young female gymnasts from the USA, Romania and China reflected the intensive coverage of the women's gymnastics at Atlanta. Female beach volleyball, identified in the textual analysis as a highly profiled media sport showing sexualised and trivialised images of sports women, was not dominant in the thoughts of the young people. This indicates that the media researcher may identify or focus upon an issue which is of little significance to an audience and indicates the importance of the audience–text interaction.

Young people lacked detailed knowledge about specific female sports personalities, as indicated by references to 'that girl' rather than by name, or references to ethnic characteristics – 'that black girl' or 'She was a Chinese person'. Central memories revolved around negative images of vulnerability. These included the injuries to Sally Gunnell, Kelly Holmes, Kerrie Strugg and Arantxa Sanchez-Vicario, the ageing Sally Gunnell, the failed come-backs (Tessa Sanderson) and the fall in the floor exercise by Dominique Dawes, the black American gymnast. Both vulnerability and lack of detailed recall are visible in the following comment: 'then there was the one whose leg all swelled up and she had to have an injection'.

Such incidents, highlighted by the press, did successfully deflect atten-tion and recall away from more positive aspects of female sporting success. Surprisingly, the Atlanta bronze medal won by British heptathlete, Denise Lewis, was not recalled by the group. Steffi Graf, despite some admiration, was blamed for making women's tennis boring by her sustained dominance at the top.

Negativity and invisibility confirmed the marginal place of women in the sporting texts. There was an acceptability that, inevitably, sport is a male-dominated world, and relatively little concern was expressed about it. When asked why they had not mentioned any female sport stars in their diaries, in many cases there was a general lack of realisation of this omission, reflecting the conventions in production practices. The omission of women from the sporting texts carried over, it seems, into everyday 'sports talk'.

Heroes, body watching and the gaze

Theoretical approaches to the gaze and voyeurism in film studies (Mulvey 1989; Van Zoonen 1994; Tasker 1993; Shroeder 1998; Chandler 1998) have identified and confirmed connections between 'the gaze' and the articulation of power. As they indicate, the gazer signifies power and status over the object. Whilst notions of female athletes for the male gaze provide a forum for discussion, the focus of the male sporting body as a marketing potential for the gaze of the female audience is relatively unexplored (Rowe 1999: 130).

Preoccupation with body image, looks and youthfulness of selected stars supports the importance of style and appearance in consumer culture, and the ways in which young people, especially girls, are drawn in by the phys-ical and visual appeal of a star. One of the discussions followed this point. Some admire sports stars 'because of how good they are', but 'some people admire sports stars because of the way they look'.

Boys were more interested in the physicality, skills and tactics of male sport than with the opportunities to 'gaze' at female bodies in action. Comments about female stars were often unflattering, such as; 'Then there's some of the women. How big are they? They're 6' 4".' Apart from several asides about looking 'at fit birds' and 'Mary Pierce wearing those little all in one things', the sexualised image of female sport stars was not mentioned.

Girls, on the other hand, do openly admit their use of sports viewing as an opportunity to 'gaze' at male bodies. Whether such pleasure can be defined as resistance to patriarchy, giving them power over men, as desire or fantasy, or simply as accepting consumer positioning in the way that producers draw women into the sports media from a feminine perspective, is uncertain. For, as sport is not idealised as an appropriate activity for girls, then they are instead positioned to admire masculinity, male power and dominance across the sports terrain.

Pin-ups of male athletes were the main sporting features found in girls' magazines during the summer. Watching male footballers was significant for 'with the girls it was more did you see so and so, it wasn't so much the game, it was more the players'. When asked if it was important for a sports star to be good looking: 'No, but it does help a bit though. It makes you want to watch them more'. The significance of 'male body watching' revolved around references to 'sexy legs, looks and their bodies' and comments like, 'Yum!' and 'Oooh he's nice', articulated their view of sport stars as sex symbols and 'heart throbs'. The number of girls who stopped watching the tennis following Andre Agassi's defeat at Wimbledon showed that the event became meaningless without opportunities to 'gaze' at their favourite player.

This is reminiscent of ways in which film and pop stars are identified as heart-throbs for the female audience, and it could be argued that this is neither oppositional nor empowering, for the physicality of the sports media ensures that visual pleasures focus on images of action, strength and masculinity. In Mulvey's terms (1989), the 'sports gaze' still operates within patriarchal boundaries as images of 'active' male sportsmen are distinct from the more prevalent, passive, sexual images of feminine sporting heroines.

Subject positioning with regard to the masculine and feminine gaze in this field requires further interpretative work as it is clear from the ways in which young people articulate their pleasures that they see potential within media sports viewing for the sexual objectification of both male and female sports personalities.

Revisiting the levels of analysis: empowerment or enslavement?

This chapter has identified four key methodological emphases in studying power within the field of media and sport. Figure 11.1 illustrates these around the hub of the theme of power and its mobilisation and articulation.

The hermeneutic approach advocated here provides a framework that supports integrated levels of textual and audience analysis affording the potential to explore varied power relations. It encourages the reflexivity of the researcher, reflecting on how their own power and knowledge comes into play in the process of reinterpreting the voices of the audience.

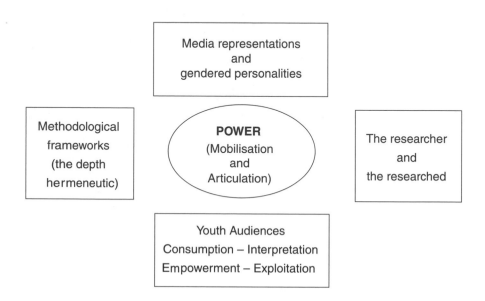

Figure 11.1   Deconstructing the mediation of a summer of sport

By revisiting the interplay between textual construction of sport stars and youthful interpretations, conclusions can be drawn as to how meaning and power are mobilised and articulated. It demonstrates elements of control, diversity and empowerment in the reading of sport stars. Audiences' 'talk' about the texts they consumed reflected ways in which they made sense of media imagery and messages. The four main conclusions below identify the extent to which young people did buy the ideological attractions of the sport personalities on display and were enthralled by the dominant images of masculinity, heroism and villainy.

First, patriarchal control was visible and dominant. Young people's sports discourse revolves around men. They generally buy the bond between masculinity and sport. They virtually exclude sportswomen from their sports talk, legitimising the sports field as essentially male. This confirms that omissions from the texts carry over into everyday life and shows how such procedures work to control and shape ongoing discourse beyond the media events themselves. It controls the extent to which successful sportswomen are seen to provide enduring sporting memories and questions the place and value of girls and women across sports participation and media sport. Selection strategies of stereotypical sporting roles, and the amplification given to sexualised and feminised attributes, questions the extent to which either sportswomen or the female youth audience were empowered through these constructions.

Yet patriarchal power is not complete as some young people did mention women and, when encouraged by the researcher to reflect on omission or selection strategies, were surprised that they had not noticed it themselves. This could be seen to empower the audience for it made them question the representations and offered potential for reinterpretations as the young people were encouraged to reflect on their experiences and articulate processes of identification and assimilation that are more frequently taken for granted in everyday media interaction. As Kinkema and Harris (1998: 50) suggest: 'Empowering subject positions are especially important because they ultimately offer possibilities for social change'. The research reported in this chapter highlights ways in which young people are media literate. Yet it provides the potential for exploring ways in which PE practitioners and sports policy makers can work together to develop greater public awareness about the procedures of omission and selection, which affect both the representation and acceptability of sportswomen as heroines and role models. It can also provide a stimulus for PE professionals to use sports media products and events to enhance discussion, reinterpretation and greater critical media sports literacy amongst young people in their classes. Sports inclusion policies regarding gender distinctions in attitudes to sport and physical education have too readily ignored the constructions and constraints for girls inherent across media and sporting ideologies. Utilised in this way, the research framework discussed here provides potential for developing strategies which can seek to transform power relations and empower audiences. Research such as this can provide opportunities for intervention in audience–media power games, confirming Kinkema and Harris's (1998) optimistic projection.

Second, young people articulated desires for sport stars who embody traditional values and who recognise their social responsibility as role models. Adherence to moral codes of conduct, the work ethic, amateurism, social mobility and overcoming adversity suggested elements of power and control over young people's values and behaviour. Yet elements of diversity in their readings of sport stars suggest they can read and negotiate the complexity of meanings and the celebratory yet contradictory discourse around heroism and villainy. They do not necessarily admire or identify with the most highly profiled, trendiest or most badly behaved sports stars, nor do they accord hero status as readily as the media might appear to.

On the other hand, some articulate a sense of realism and fail to see why sports stars can or should be expected to behave differently from the general populace. The ways in which media representations probe the lives of stars, making visible the flaws in their lifestyles suggests that fans may be disillusioned, rather than inspired, by stardom.

Gender diversity in the pleasures and meanings derived from the texts offers a sense of empowerment. Girls and boys use the sports media for different purposes and reflect on them from their own social positioning. For boys, affiliation with sports personalities assures a bombardment of powerful masculine images. Talk about sports personalities offers boys close associations between masculinity, sport and physicality, affirming the 'naturalness' of their place in the sports world.

Third, not all girls read the hegemonic exclusivity of the male sporting domain and do enter in. This opportunity to penetrate the male sporting stronghold affords them power by allowing them access into male peer group culture and gossip. A number of girls were articulate, knowledgeable and enthralled by the world of sport and its personalities in the same way as were many of the boys. Yet, for many girls, their involvement with sport stars reflected dominant ideals about the female consumer as admirers of males rather than as sporting experts or fanatics. Whilst it could be argued that this reflected patriarchal control and dominance and enslavement to consumer culture, the ways in which girls chose to 'gaze' at muscular bodies afforded a rethinking about aspects of power and subject positioning of the female audience. For the extent to which the female audience might perceive themselves as empowered as 'the gazer' in their readings of the sexualised male body was unclear.

Fourth, in general conclusion, the interpretative practices of young people show that they can actively define their own experiences and articulate certain pleasures that they gain from participation in mediated sports events. They show that young people are not passive and readily enslaved, but capable of making lucid and critical judgements of the images that they receive. Whilst there is evidence that gender relations are strategically mobilised and sustained through media representations and ongoing audience discourse, the precarious nature of the field of play remains as young people do negotiate the contradictions and acknowledge some elements of the power games being played.

Notes

1   Aspects of this research were driven by a desire to inform the teaching of physical education to young people. Lines (1999a), in documentation for physical education teachers, argues that the role of the media as a sport socialising agency has been virtually ignored. The increasingly high media profile of sport stars and their function as role models for young people provides public discourse concerning behavioural responses and the power of the media. The dissemination of information from this research about ways in which young people are engaged with the sporting texts can provide a forum for discussion within the PE and sports profession about the nature of the partnership between young people and media sport.

2 Whilst the role of the researcher cannot be discussed in depth here, Lines (2000a) provides a more detailed and reflexive methodological account of the researcher's positioning in the field.
3 This section provides an overview of key themes that emerged from the textual analysis. A more detailed account of sport stars as heroes, villains and role models during the Summer of Sport '96 can be found in Lines (2000). Several core newspaper sources are quoted in both that article and this chapter.

References

Blain, N., Boyle, R. and O'Donnell, H. (1993) *Sport and Identity in the European Media*, Leicester: Leicester University Press.

Bordo, S. (1993) 'Feminism, Foucault and the politics of the body', in C. Ramazanoglu (ed.) *Up Against Foucault: Exploration of Some Tensions Between Foucault and Feminism*, London: Routledge.

Boyle, R. and Haynes, R. (2000) *Power Play: Sport, the Media and Popular Culture*, Harlow: Pearson Educational.

Buckingham, D. (ed.) (1993) *Reading Audiences: Young People and the Media,* Manchester: Manchester University Press.

Chandler, D. (1998) 'Notes on the gaze', www document, URL: http://www.aber.ac.uk/media/Documents/gaze/gaze.html (last visited 25 October 2000).

Creedon, P. (ed.) (1994) *Women, Media and Sport: Challenging Gender Values*, London: Sage.

Daddario, G. (1994) 'Chilly scenes of the 1992 Winter Games: the mass media and the marginalisation of female athletes', *Sociology of Sport Journal* 11(3): 275–88.

Davis, L. (1997) *Hegemonic Masculinity on the Hot Seat: Sparring with Sports Illustrated Over Its Swimsuit Issue*, Albany: State University of New York Press.

Duncan, M. (1990) 'Sports photographs and sexual difference: images of men and women in the 1984 and 1988 Olympic Games', *Sociology of Sport Journal* 7(1): 22–43.

Duncan, M., Messner, M. and Williams, L. (1990) *Gender Stereotyping in Televised Sports*, Los Angeles: Amateur Athletic Foundation of Los Angeles.

Dyer, R.(1991a) 'Charisma', in C. Gledhill (ed.) *Stardom: Industry of Desire*, London: Routledge.

—— (1991b) 'A star is born and the construction of identity', in C. Gledhill (ed.) *Stardom: Industry of Desire*, London: Routledge.

—— (1993) *The Matter of Images: Essays on Representation*, London: Routledge.

Fiske, J. (1987) 'TV: Re-situating the popular in the people', *Australian Journal of Media and Culture* 1(2): http://Kali.murdoch.edu.au/~continuum/1.2/Fiske.html (consulted 12 October 1999).

Gillespie, M. (1995) *Television, Ethnicity and Cultural Change*, London: Routledge.

Gledhill, C. (ed.) (1991) *Stardom: Industry of Desire*, London: Routledge.

Hall, S., Hobson, D., Lowe, A. and Willis, P. (eds) (1980) *Culture, Media and Language*, London: Hutchinson.

Hargreaves, J. (1994) *Sporting Females: Critical Issues in the History and Sociology of Women's Sports*, London: Routledge.

Harris, J. (1994) *Athletes and the American Hero Dilemma*, Champaign, IL: Human Kinetics.

Hermes, J. (1995) *Reading Magazines*, Cambridge: Polity Press.

Keech, M. and McFee, G. (eds) (2000) *Issues and Values in Sport and Leisure Cultures*, Aachen: Meyer & Meyer.

Kellner, D. (1995) *Media culture: Cultural Studies, Identity and Politics Between the Modern and the Postmodern*, London: Routledge.

—— (2001a) 'Critical theory and the crisis of social theory', http://www.uta.edu/english/dab/illuminations/Kell5html (last consulted 24 April 2001).

—— (2001b) 'Communication vs. cultural studies: overcoming the divide', http://www.uta.edu/english/dab/illuminations/Kell4html (last consulted 24 April 2001).

Kinkema, K.M. and Harris, J. (1998) 'Mediasport studies: key research and emerging issues', in L. Wenner (ed.) *MediaSport*, London: Routledge.

Kuhn, A. (1985) *The Power of the image: Essays on Representation and Sexuality*, London: Routledge.

Lines, G. (1998) 'A case study of adolescent media consumption during the Summer of Sport 1996', in U. Merkel, G. Lines and I. McDonald (eds) *The Production and Consumption of Sport Cultures: Leisure, Culture and Commerce*, Eastbourne: Leisure Studies Association.

—— (1999a) 'Setting the challenge: creating partnerships – young people, P.E., sport and the media', *British Journal of Physical Education* 30 (2): 7–12.

—— (1999b) 'Young people and mass-mediated sports events: Consumption, impact and interpretation'. Unpublished Phd thesis, University of Brighton.

—— (2000a) 'Media sport audiences – young people and the Summer of Sport '96: revisiting frameworks for analysis', *Media, Culture and Society* 22(5): 669–80.

—— (2000b) 'The media spectacle of women at the Olympics: Dissimulation, legitimation and issues of patriarchy', in M. Keech and G. McFee (eds) *Issues and Values in Sport and Leisure Cultures*, Aachen: Meyer & Meyer.

Lines, G. (2001) 'Villains, fools or heroes? Sport stars as role-models for young people', *Leisure Studies* 20 (4): 285–303.

Lye, J. (1996) 'Deconstruction: some assumptions', http://www.brocku.ca/english/courses (last consulted 9 April 2000).

McDonald, M. (1995) *Representing Women: Myths of Femininity in the Popular Media*, London: Arnold.

McDonald, M.G. (1996) 'Michael Jordan's family values: marketing, meaning and post-Reagan America', *Sociology of Sport Journal* 13: 344–65.

Morley, D. (1992) *Television Audiences and Cultural Studies*, London: Routledge.

Mulvey, L. (1989) *Visual and Other Pleasures*, London: Macmillan.

Rowe, D. (1999) *Sport, Culture and the Media*, Buckingham, Open University Press.

Roy of the Rovers Annual (1992) London: Fleetway Publications.

Shroeder, J. (1998) 'Consuming representation: a visual approach to consumer research', in B. Stern (ed.) *Representing Consumers: Voices, Views and Visions*, London: Routledge.

Tasker, Y. (ed.) (1993) *Spectacular Bodies: Gender, Genre and the Action Cinema*, London: Routledge.

Thompson, J. (1990) *Ideology and Modern Culture: Critical Social Theory in the Era of Mass Communication*, Cambridge: Polity Press.

Tomlinson, A. (1992) 'Whose game is it anyway? The cultural analysis of sport and media consumption', *Innovation* 5(4): 33–47.

—— (2000) 'Carrying the torch for whom? Symbolic power and Olympic ceremony', in K. Schaffer and S. Smith (eds) *The Olympics at the Millennium: Power, Politics and the Games*, New Jersey: Rutgers University Press.

Tomlinson, A. and Lines, G. (1996) 'Gender, consumption and the "popular media" interests of 14/15 yr olds', in J. O'Neill, E. Murdoch and S. Fleming (eds) *Physical Education: A Collection of Working Papers*, Brighton: University of Brighton Chelsea School Research Centre, Topic Report 7.

Underwood, M. (2001) *Reception Studies – Criticisms*. http://www.witsock.ndirect.co.uk (last consulted 20 November 2001).

Vande Berg, L.R. (1998) 'The sports hero meets mediated celebrityhood', in L. Wenner (ed.) *MediaSport*, London: Routledge.

Van Zoonen, L. (1994) *Feminist Media Studies*, London: Sage.

Weidman, L. (1997) 'In the Olympic tradition: sportscasters' language and female athleticism', unpublished paper presented to annual meeting of North American Society for the Sociology of Sport (NASS), Toronto, 7 November.

Wenner, L. (ed.) (1998) *MediaSport*, London: Routledge.

Whannel, G. (1992) *Fields in vision : Television sport and cultural transformation*, London: Routledge.

—— (1995) 'Sports stars, youth and morality in the print media', in G. McFee, W. Murphy and G. Whannel (eds) *Leisure: Cultures, Values and Lifestyles*, Eastbourne: Leisure Studies Association.

—— (1998a) 'Reading the sports media audience', in L. Wenner (ed.) *MediaSport*, London: Routledge.

—— (1998b) 'Individual stars and collective identities in media sport', in M. Roche (ed.) *Sport, Popular Culture and Identity*, Aachen: Meyer & Meyer.

—— (1999) 'Sport stars, narrativization and masculinities', *Leisure Studies* 18: 249–65.

Willis, P. (1980) 'Notes on method', in S. Hall, D. Hobson, A. Lowe and P. Willis (eds) *Culture, Media and Language*, London: Hutchinson.

12 Shifting balances of power in the new football economy

Jon Magee

Introduction: the new football economy

> Blair leads fight to keep transfer fees
>
> Tony Blair is seeking to assemble a powerful coalition of European political leaders, including the French president Jacques Chirac and the German chancellor Gerhard Schroeder, to protect football from the European Commission's plans to outlaw transfer fees.
>
> (*Guardian Unlimited*, 7 September 2000)

The structure of European football (of which England is a key associate) was literally at a breaking point in 2001. Despite the intervention of some of Europe's political leaders the transfer market, synonymous with the professional era, was scheduled to be dissolved and replaced by a compensation scheme. Commenting on significant employment modifications to European football in the mid-1990s, former professional footballer Garry Nelson (1995: 278) warned with prescience that in the future 'the transfer market across the entire European Union could be altered beyond recognition. Indeed, it could become obsolete'. Nelson was right. The deregulation of football's labour market changed the economics of the game. Financial figures for the Premier League and the three divisions of the Football League indicate a growth in overall performance:

> Overall, the ninety two clubs generated £1,078 million of income in 1999/2000 – up an impressive £128 million (13%). Premier League clubs generated 15% more income (up £103 million to £772 million). The seventy two Football League clubs generated 9% more income (up £25 million to £306 million).
>
> (Boon and Jones 2001: 5)

On the surface, then, the finances of English football looked healthy. But shifting balances of power within the game, and threats to the redistributive financial effects of the transfer system, told another story. Despite the buoyancy of the overall financial figures, the worries of commentators such as Nelson were to be confirmed, and the professional game in England was in crisis.

In August 2000 the European Union·(EU) ruled that the European football transfer market was in breach of EU employment regulations and the EU ordered UEFA, the European football governing body, to modify employment regulations and bring them in line within the legislative framework that applies to labour in general. Implementing the EU request to end the transfer market in Europe subsequently made the rulings of FiFa, the global governing body, unworkable and threw the football world into chaos. Consultation between the EU, the football authorities and national governments brought about the negotiation of a more employment-friendly compensation scheme to replace the transfer system. Rather than receive a transfer fee for a player, clubs would receive a set compensation figure to cover the nurturing process and lost services of that player, though in most cases it was expected that this figure would be likely to be considerably less than a fee commanded on the free transfer market. Thus a significant income generator for clubs was lost in this new football labour market.

Also, as part of the new football market, it was expected that players would be able to serve a minimum period of notice to their club before taking up a transfer-free move to another club. This was a compelling move for professional footballers in their quest for equal employment status and gave players freedom similar to the free agency situation in American professional sports. Cashmore (2000b: 146) depicts free agency as the 'ability of sports performers to negotiate their own contracts with clubs without being subject to trade restrictions'.

Football clubs, having once commanded total control and hold over playing contracts, would soon find that contract power rests firmly with the increasingly mobile and relatively emancipated player. Without the ability to sell their assets/players on the transfer market, some clubs would inevitably find their operating position too weak to survive without transfer revenue. In England, with top clubs experiencing a boom period of unprecedented proportions, many clubs were reliant on survival through transfer dealings and some lesser clubs would be likely to be forced out of business without the safety net of transfer revenue. It was recognised, too, that the proposed notice of employment clause could be used by players as a mechanism to raise salary scales in moving from one club to another, or indeed as a reward for showing contract loyalty and remaining with a club. Also, top clubs could use the notice clause to tempt Premier League stars with exorbitant wages as a powerful magnet to lure them away from their present clubs and contracts.

In England, in particular, the danger in this sort of spiral of inflation of the football economy would be that some clubs, especially in the Premier League, might seek to compete for top players by offering salary packages that they would not be able to sustain in the long term. The changes to the football market were in this sense likely to spell the beginning of bust for some involved in the football business.

With an economic platform founded upon the Sky Television money, Premiership football in England hit the ground running and gathered up a relentless pace, quickly recovering the lost ground on its European competitors. The business had entered a new world and the once bedevilled English game enjoyed such a meteoric rise that it quickly became a global product, benefiting from its immense popularity and mounting commercial capacity. The hooligan-ridden 1980s gave way to a more classy, spectator-friendly, 'Europhiled' 1990s sport:

> By the middle of the 1990s football embodied the central features of a modern high-profile sport, as much a mediated spectacle and vehicle for insatiable consumerism as a forum for physical pleasure, cultural affiliation and playful creativity. New breeds of entrepreneur had moved into the game, making fortunes in share and property deals as top clubs became public limited companies, and the football business expanded to meet the needs of shareholders and accountants rather than members and administrators.
>
> (Horne, Tomlinson and Whannel 1999: 52–3)

English football was in boom time and placed itself alongside Italy and Spain at Duke's (1994) apex of the opulent forces of European football.

In this climate, Manchester United secured a ten-year £300 million kit sponsorship with Nike, which began in July 2002. Cashmore (2000a: 323) observes that 'the trademark swoosh, as Nike call the tick or checkmark that is its logo, is everywhere'. Not content on teaming up with the global power of Nike, Manchester United also struck a deal, in early 2001, with the world's premier baseball team, the New York Yankees, to promote a joint corporate and merchandise entity. Never before had such a cross-Atlantic, cross-sport partnership been formed. MUFC, NY, and the swoosh of Nike would complete a powerful triumvirate set to conquer the global sports market place. The context for this chapter is this fast changing political economy of English football and the key developmental changes that have transformed the sport into a modern day spectacular, popular, and highly rich yet potentially fragile form. Football, in the last decade of the twentieth century, underwent an unprecedented boom making the game more popular and affluent than at any other time in its long history. In England, this high-speed commercial development lacked an element of regulation, structure and planning. In particular, the game struggled to deal with a revolutionised political economy and an increasingly volatile marketplace that saw transfers spiral in number and cost, and player wages rapidly soar. As a consequence, power struggles within and between the main stakeholders in football became increasingly evident, and changes to the transfer system could only exacerbate these.

Whilst there was phenomenal change to English football business in the 1990s and, despite alterations to the transfer system which allowed greater numbers of players to achieve millionaire status, the football labour market was still not without its problems. Commenting from within the professional game, former professional footballer Garry Nelson (1995: 277) described the transfer fee demanded by a club for an out-of-contract player as a 'ball and chain ... shackled to his [the player's] leg'. Modifications to the labour market, whilst welcome, were still restrictive and the transfer fee situation denied true occupational freedom to football players in similar manner to baseball's famous reserve system (Cashmore 2000b: 146; Horne, Tomlinson and Whannel 1999: 247). This could be regarded as exploitation, a view supported by Maguire (1999: 102) who described the transfer market as a 'slave system', while Horne, Tomlinson and Whannel (1999: 249) commented that because of the transfer system 'support remains for the argument that a modern form of slavery still exists in British football'.

The denial of occupational freedom within football was ultimately to prove important in the 1990s as the transfer system was successfully challenged by Jean-Marc Bosman, a little-known out-of-contract Belgian player. Upon contract completion with his Belgian club RC Liege, Bosman was offered reduced terms on a new contract and also prevented from taking a transfer to FC Dunkerque in France because of a dispute over the transfer fee. Unlike in Britain, Belgium did not have a tribunal system to settle transfer disputes and a disgruntled Bosman actioned court proceedings with a restraint of trade case. After a four-year legal battle that involved depositions from the European body UEFA and the global body FIFA, in 1995 the European Court of Justice ruled in favour of the player. The court ruled that the transfer fee retention system at the end of a player's contract was illegal and 'effectively ended the necessity for soccer transfer fees and opened the way for freedom of employment. Players were permitted to move from club to club as soon as their contracts had expired' (Cashmore 2000b: 54). EU players were granted freedom of contract to move freely between EU member states at the end of a contract, though movement within European member nations still required a transfer fee at this stage.

Cashmore (*ibid.*: 53) notes that 'the court brought the contracts of employment in soccer into alignment with those of any other industry ... Post-Bosman, a player was free to move to any club with whom he could agree personal terms'. The contract shackles were loosened and players started to utilise their contract freedom to become more mobile and alter recruitment patterns across Europe. Bosman facilitated increased traffic of football labour across European borders, and Maguire and Stead (1997) have documented that the growth of the foreign legion in England was one of the most tangible changes in the transformation of English football.

European football was also transformed post-Bosman as players utilised their new freedom to criss-cross the continent in search of inflated salaries in the wealthy core leagues. The Premier League became a core European league and owed much of this to substantial investment from Sky Television. Premier League wealth has continued with further deals with Sky Television of £670 million (1996) and £1.1 billion (2001) for coverage rights of English football. The Sky Television money influenced change to the English game in a number of ways.

First, clubs quickly used their new financial muscle to buy the top players and the domestic transfer market escalated, triggered by the £7 million transfer of Andy Cole from Newcastle United to Manchester United in early 1995. This figure was soon surpassed by other transfers, but became dwarfed by the transfer of the then England captain, Alan Shearer, from Blackburn Rovers to Newcastle United in 1997 for £15 million – at that time, a world record fee. Cashmore (2000b: 55) reports that transfer fees in the Premiership reached a record level of £105 million in season 1996/7, a graphic indicator of how much money the transfer market can accrue as well as the level of spending power English clubs had at the time. Despite uncertainty over the future of the transfer market, in season 2000–2001 Leeds United paid £18 million for English international Rio Ferdinand. Manchester United spent the same to secure Dutch international Ruud Van Nistelrooy and £27.4 million on Argentinian Juan Sebastian Veron. The dissolution of the transfer market would prevent this type of trade and while buying clubs would benefit due to removal of the transfer fee, selling clubs would lose out on this and would place heavy reliance on other income generators, particularly television.

Secondly, football grew more spectacular in the 1990s and player salaries increased significantly as the economic platform of clubs expanded and clubs began to offer greater financial rewards to secure the top players. The Bosman case added a further boost to the earning capacity of players by offering a transfer-free clause. To fend off the Bosman case clubs began to improve the terms of already contracted players as a measure, 'especially for bankable players', to keep them at their clubs (Cashmore 2000b: 55). Players were now able to use the threat of seeing out a contract and taking a transfer-fee move as a lever to negotiate improved terms on their present contract. This was a powerful position for players to assume, especially the top ones, as clubs could not afford to lose a player without a transfer fee reimbursement. Increased television money and the lubricant of 'Bosman' free transfers have given players, especially the top ones, significant bargaining power and control to increase their earnings greatly as well as to manage their career destination. Longer-term contracts have become the normal practice as clubs wish to tie down their players and fend off Bosman in the process. However, it has started to become a regular procedure where some top players are looking to renegotiate their terms despite being tied to a longer term contract. If the club refuses, then the player threatens a transfer and a player-versus-club battle ensues. The most notable example of this was in the summer of 1999 when French star Nikolas Anelka, unhappy at Arsenal's refusal to renegotiate the terms of his contract, instigated a dispute with the club, threatened strike action and secured a transfer to Real

Madrid in Spain. This was a clear example of player power, but Arsenal's bitter experience at being powerless to prevent a top player from leaving was mildly tempered by the £19 million transfer fee.

By 2000, soccer millionaires were common, with a Premier League average wage of £409,000 (Professional Footballers' Association/*Independent* survey, April 2000). Thirty-six per cent of top flight players earned more than £500,000 per season from football with at least 100 topping the £1 million mark (*ibid.*). Forty years after Johnny Haynes of Fulham became the first £100 a week footballer, the highest paid player was Roy Keane, the Manchester United captain, with a weekly salary of £52,000. Keane became a soccer millionaire every fifth month and this comparison shows the marked contrasts between the modern-day player and his less than affluent predecessor. The evolution of the modern-day footballer into a high earning superstar saw the pendulum of power over labour rights shift away from the clubs/authorities and rest with the player and his agent.

Third, with greater value contracts on offer, as well as more out-of-contract footballers seeking to maximise their career potential through Bosman, there has been a significant increase in players using agents in contract negotiations (Horne, Tomlinson and Whannel 1999: 248). Out-of-contract footballers provided greater opportunities for agents to get involved in football negotiations where they 'came to occupy key roles in the negotiation of performer's contracts' (Cashmore 2000b: 144). It is arguable that the agent has become the most important figure in the football market and more have become involved in the English football business, fuelled by the large commission fees available from negotiating contracts that could be worth millions of pounds. Agents are able to manoeuvre and act by inhabiting the space that occurs between player and club, coming to occupy a key role in football trading.

Fourth, and perhaps the most tangible of all, was the consequential increase in foreign player migration to England. The Sky Television-led wealth in the Premier League allowed English clubs to compete with clubs in Italy and Spain for the top players, reordering Duke's (1994) model based on European football wealth. On top of the increased riches in England, transfer-free Bosman movement across Europe lubricated the mobility of players and, with an increasing network of agents trading in players, foreign players were able to access the wealthy Premier League. In the early days of the Premier League it was only a trickle of foreign players who arrived but, following the success of the German international Jürgen Klinsmann at Tottenham Hotspur in season 1994/5, the trickle became a steady stream. By July 1997, 218 foreign players were registered in England (*Express*, 22 July 1997: 1), a number that was to quickly grow. The figure almost doubled by the opening day of the 2000/1 season, when 400 foreign players were registered with English professional clubs.

Another, though arguably less tangible, change within the English football business was the shift in the balance of power between players, managers (clubs) and agents. The principal aim of this chapter is to focus on these shifting power relations and conflicts between the main stakeholders within the network. A significant feature of 1990s football was the increasing hold players, with the help of their agents, gained over their trade and its value, making the prohibitive pre-1960s period seem a distant memory. The business acumen of the agents allowed players to take greater control of their athletic labour value, significantly boosting their bargaining power in the process.

Considering that English football had never had such a boom period before, it is difficult to comprehend that with such monies flowing around the game, bust has become a real possibility for some professional clubs. English football now nestles close to the centre of the football world and global business marketplace, but two concerns show that the boom may be fragile. First, long-term sustainability of the market product is under threat and, despite the Sky Television-led wealth in the Premiership, the proposed changes to the transfer market along with the dramatic spiral of player salaries may prove to be ultimately damaging. Second, it appears that Premier League chairmen have been willing to sacrifice lower league clubs in their incessant clamour for increased riches. As Horne, Tomlinson and Whannel (*ibid*.: 52) put it, the 'breakaway phase in the history of football might have revitalised the economic fortunes of the top clubs', but one consequence of this has been that the top clubs have got richer whilst the lesser clubs have got poorer. Lower league clubs have struggled to survive on a trickle of television money as well as diminishing transfer money due to the Bosman ruling. Changes to the football market raise, as well as an over-reliance on television revenue, serious questions about the future security of some clubs.

Fragility exists as the football network has struggled to cope with its meteoric transition and use the large cash injections to stabilise the English game. At present English football finds itself in a complex state of flux where boom and potential bust are viewed as close relatives. In his article 'Is the bubble about to burst?', concerning the health of the English game, journalist Roy Collins commented that:

> beneath the surface gloss there are signs of decline in popularity ... It might sound healthy enough, but the [financial] report's authors – Deloitte and Touche – were still moved to include a warning that the trend [of needing rising profits to sustain player wages] was 'unsustainable in the long term'.
>
> (Collins 1999)

The removal of transfer fees and the potential severance notice allowed players and their agents greater bargaining power to demand increased wages without the necessary contract commitment that was a feature of the transfer system. Clubs may find it difficult to maintain spiralling salaries without the reimbursement safeguard that would have come from transfer revenue. Players will no longer be regarded as marketable assets given their ability to serve a period of notice. Cashmore (2000a: 375) describes the European Champions League as 'the richest sports league in the world' but warns that, with increasing player wages and transfer fee inflation, to survive 'soccer is going to be in serious need of money' (*ibid*.: 375). For all its riches, the English Premier League has been laying a foundation for crisis, if not bust, in its inflationary spiral.

Research findings

Examination of the combined issues of Premier League wealth, increased player salaries, increased labour rights through the Bosman case, the use of agents and the consequential increased trade in foreign players are of central importance to this chapter. To do this, a sample of the foreign legion cohort of overseas players in England will be used as an empirical basis and supplemented with data acquired from managers and player representatives/agents.[1]

In my student years I enjoyed a successful semi-professional football career during which I was capped for Northern Ireland at every level to Under 21, represented Northern Ireland, Ireland and Great Britain Universities, as well as competing in three World Student Games. Thus, by securing a network of gatekeepers acquired through my two-pronged career in football and academia, I have been able to gain insider access to a key group in the football business, namely, the foreign legion of overseas professionals.

Dandelion (1997: 181) constructed a typology for insider research and I was able to use my position as a fellow football labour migrant to gain access to the foreign legion as a member to the context. Interviews were conducted with a sample of the foreign legion of varying nationalities, but during the initial stages of this fieldwork, further contacts within professional football were established and additional gates were opened that granted access to other important figures in the business. The following analysis of the processes that structure the cohort allows this chapter to cast a critical gaze on the football business and the examination of the key actors and agents in the football labour mobility process. Thus, the insider research position offers the capacity for critical insights into the football business and teases out some of the major power contests currently taking place within English football. What follows is structured around the more salient themes that emerged from the interview data.

In relation to the boom that hit English football in the 1990s, Don Howe, former manager of Arsenal and current Director of Youth Coaching at the club, described the changes to football in the 1990s as 'wholesale' and commended the growth in profile and popularity of Premier League football. He was keen to acknowledge however that 'since the advent of *Sky*

Television commercialism within football has just spiralled ... it's all come through television ... it's just exploded ... television has got a lot to do with it. Football on *Sky Television* has stimulated the crowd'. Roy Evans, the former Liverpool and Fulham manager, was not surprised to see commercial involvement from someone like Rupert Murdoch as Evans believed that English football 'usually follows America in terms of how things develop'. Evans described the 1990s changes of subscription television, Monday night football, split kick-off times, season pattern changes and increases in the amount of live coverage as part of the 'Americanisation of English football'.

Howe concurred with Evans's assessment of television developments in football when he said:

> we [English football] are going that [American] way ourselves with *Sky's* three tv [sport] channels ... all the channels are starting to realise the viewing figures of football ... where will it end? Pay-per-view, like in boxing, they are trying that in Scotland [football coverage] this season, so you never know.

Further, and also like in America, the competition between television companies for television rights has significantly increased as the sport has gained popularity and the contract price for Premier League rights has risen from a then extravagant £304 million in 1992 to the present £1.1 billion. Howe reckoned that this is because:

> all the channels are starting to realise the viewing figures of football and that brings money to the sport ... this can only be good for football ... Mind you the money *Sky* is offering, 1.1 billion pounds or thereabouts doesn't bear thinking about. It's frightening but it's the way football has gone.

Whilst £1.1 billion is a significant amount of money with the British sports coverage market, it is dwarfed by the television deals secured by some sports in America. Global markets and international exposure are delivered by the Sky Television/Premier League alliance in a relationship that sees financial wealth maximised for all involved. With continued involvement of Sky Television one can only expect further Murdochisation of English football with pay-per-view coverage expected. Television has allowed the top English clubs to become powerful on the European stage but, in return, the football authorities have allowed television, especially Sky Television, to become powerful in determining the delivery of the football package.

Expanding the television debate, Howe pointed out that since the involvement of Sky Television commercialism within 'football has just spiralled ... it's all come through television ... it's just exploded'. The result is that, according to Blackpool and former Swindon Town manager Steve

McMahon, 'a few years ago people were saying English football was the worst. Now they are saying it is the best. It's only the best because of the money ... It's the best because it's paying the most'. Whilst it is difficult to be able to gauge what league is the best in the world, it is apparent that since its inception the Premier League has become a powerful league in the world and is able to pay comparable salaries to rival leagues in Italy and Spain. Mick McGuire, Deputy Chief Executive of the Professional Footballers' Association, argued that 'our [English football] wages are right up there above the best. Italians can't compete anymore with us. In the last five years wages over here have gone through the roof'. Certainly the commercial spurt experienced by the Premiership has allowed English clubs to apply different operating procedures and become a force within the European football market. Greater freedom of movement across European frontiers, particularly since the Bosman case, and extended patterns of global recruitment have impacted greatly upon England. Most Premiership clubs have their share of foreign players in their squads with the likes of Liverpool, Arsenal and Chelsea having as much as 75 per cent foreign representation.

The immediate task at hand is to go beyond the statistics and examine the factors behind foreign player mobility by addressing two significant questions. Firstly, what drew the foreign players to England? Obviously individual cases were different but two dominant responses figured: money and ambition. To deal with money first, it was clear that some players were drawn to the Premiership by its new-found wealth and the clubs' willingness to spend it. During the interview with Anders Limpar and Andrei Kanchelskis, it quickly became evident that finance was their chief motivating factor in coming to England (and also in playing football). Both players had arrived at Everton (the club at interview time) from another English club, had benefited financially in the transfer, and were among the top-paid players in the country at the time. Post-interview informal conversations with some of the coaching staff confirmed that both players were motivated and centrally concerned by money.

Pontus Kaamark, interviewed when at Leicester City, was swayed to come to England rather than accept a move to Portugal because of the superior money, but defended this by saying that as a divorced parent he had his daughter's welfare in mind. Stig-Inge Bjornebyë, with Liverpool at the time of interview, pointed out that foreign players were now attracted to England because of its financial health. He was particularly keen to stress that the Sky Television money had instigated a new willingness 'of the top players' to place England on their career destination map. English Premiership clubs have attained significant ability through television investment enabling them to attract some of the premier global stars, though salaries have also increased in the Nationwide Division One and allowed clubs in that league to develop their foreign recruitment policy.

Steve McMahon, manager of Blackpool, had forthright comments on the motives of top foreign players seeking to come to England:

> You get them, the likes of Kluivert [top Dutch player at Barcelona], bandying about 'I'd like to play in the Premier League'. It's nothing to do with the Premier League, it's to do with cash ... English football is paying bundles, more so than anyone in Europe.

Mick McGuire of the PFA lent support to this view and linked rising salaries with increased traffic of foreign players to England, describing the rate of foreign imports in the last five years as 'going through the roof'. The reason for this, in McGuire's opinion, is that the 1996 Sky Television deal allowed English clubs to strengthen their activity on the continental transfer market and offer salaries as competitive as, if not greater than, their rivals. Greater numbers of foreign players have come to England, particularly those reaping the benefit of Bosman. With £1.1 billion on offer in the new television deal and changes to the labour market, one can expect more foreign players to come to England.

The debate surrounding foreign players is a useful signifier of the type of power struggles currently existing in English football as there is a contentious and forceful issue at play regarding quality-versus-quantity in relation to foreign recruitment. In support of what he termed 'the quality, cream players', Mick McGuire related the PFA's 'admiration for the technical skills of the top quality foreign player'. Don Howe of Arsenal defended the work ethic and dedication of the foreign players at Arsenal and praised them as 'raising the standards of the game here', citing the example of top Dutch player Dennis Bergkamp as a 'wonderful example of the true professional player'. Few respondents involved within club football questioned the logic of recruiting top foreign players, but there was a general feeling that too many foreign players were not of sufficient quality, were restricting the progress of indigenous players and were recruited because they were cheaper, not better.

Roy Evans made the point that Premiership clubs used their increased budgets from the Sky deal to 'open the door to the continent, something that was not possible before'. Television provided the stimulus for English clubs to become powerful operators on the continent, but too much use of this power resulted ultimately in damaging levels of recruitment to the future of English players. Joe Royle, former manager at Everton and Manchester City, outlined the initial attraction of the foreign player, 'the English player has made himself expensive in comparison and I suppose these [foreign] players are cheap. A lot of clubs take cheap foreign imports just for the sake of them being cheap'. Mick McGuire of the PFA supported this view as in his opinion 'the vast majority are cheaper and not better than what we have got'. Cheaper is again a reference to the Bosman-type foreign players and further recognition that the domestic player has become too expensive in comparison to his foreign counterpart.

Steve McMahon, manager of Blackpool, was critical of how clubs used the television money to recruit from the foreign markets and did not offer enough opportunities to develop English players, 'those managers who go foreign are stumping the growth [of English football and its young players] by the big teams in the Premier League buying all the foreigners'. Don Howe of Arsenal did accept the difficulties of recruiting large numbers of foreigners because 'you have to be realistic and say these foreign players are going to cut out the chances of young players in England. Shortly we may ask, where are England going to get their players?'. Slaven Bilic of Croatia, when he was at West Ham – where there was then a large number of foreign players – felt that 'we have too many foreign players which cannot be good for West Ham or English football'. However, Bilic defended his recruitment to West Ham arguing that because he was a recognised international he was worthy of his place, although he pointed to lesser foreign players in the squad who he felt should be replaced by young English players.

Roy Evans, despite being responsible for signing foreign players during his reign as Liverpool manager, also expressed his fear for the national side – perhaps unfounded, after England's 5–1 drubbing of Germany in a World Cup qualifying match in Munich, on 1 September 2001, when all five goals were scored by Liverpool players. Evans pointed to his success with the progression of the local youth players (and now England internationals) Robbie Fowler, Michael Owen, Jamie Carragher and Steven Gerrard even though 'the squad was full of foreigners ... I preferred it when there was a limit. I never tried to get more than five or six as I didn't want to upset the balance of home players and foreign ones'. Without a limit clubs have been given a free hand on the continental market and Evans was critical of Chelsea who have fielded a non-English team in the past; he warned that 'with so much foreign players the progress of our kids will be disadvantaged if the likes of Chelsea continue'. Evans understood the reasoning behind the top clubs recruiting from abroad as 'I don't think you can be just English anymore. Otherwise the competition swamps all over you', but it was the lesser clubs that he criticised for developing too much foreign recruitment.

In light of this criticism, Joe Royle defended his own position of foreign recruitment because 'Bosman has changed the way you recruit now and you cannot afford to discount the foreigner'. He cited Liverpool and the progress of the local players identified by Evans as a good example of not having to worry about the influx of foreign players being too great: 'look, it doesn't matter how many foreign players are here, if you [English player] are good enough you'll get through'. As someone who has had mixed dealings with foreign players, Royle comically adds 'so if you're good enough, whether you are black, white, blue, British, purple or polka dot, you'll get there if you are good enough'. Despite this there is a reality that opportunities at the very top clubs are restricted for English players because of the seeming preference of managers to recruit high numbers of players from abroad. Although participants in this research identified that the number of successful foreign players was rather limited and that the quantity of foreign players greatly outweighed their quality, no one expected the traffic to slow down. The new labour market will further lubricate the mobility of players and one can expect more foreign players to come to England, even if it is to the detriment of the national team.

With regard to foreign players coming to England, not every foreign player is able to join a top-level club and earn a large salary, and not all are centrally motivated to do so. Some of the respondents wanted to play in England because of its historical reputation as the home of football, particularly those who were from countries that had regular coverage of the English game. Roy Evans confirms that 'most foreign players coming to England would say it's an ambition which is fair enough. It's the most high profile league at this moment in time'. Players with Australian and Scandinavian backgrounds specifically held strong desires to play in England having been brought up on a television diet of English football. In fact, some of the Australian players came to England in the hope of securing a professional contract after a trial period. Such is the determination to succeed that Australian Frank Talia spent a year of his life on a trial basis before securing a contract at his thirteenth trial club. With the success of fellow Australians in England, notably Harry Kewell at Leeds United, one can expect more Australian players to be recruited and follow a similar path.

Other players, such as Shaun Goater of Bermuda and Sasa Ilic of Yugoslavia, were mainly driven by their ambition to play professional football and England was the place that offered the career opportunity. Ilic is an interesting case as he played semi-professional non-league football for eighteen months and used his time in the non-league to utilise the football network and arrange trials through Serbian playing colleagues. Eventually, after much perseverance – he 'literally went knocking on doors of clubs', he joined Charlton Athletic on a non-contract basis and this successfully led to a professional contract and the fulfilment of his professional football dream. It is acknowledged that even though some of this group came to this country primarily as opportunists, some were able to fulfil their ambition *and* be well paid for it in the process, especially at Premier League level. Players such as Bjornebyë, Thomsen, Ilic, Goater and Bilic were able to combine ambition with finance and, in some cases, also gain transfers to better clubs. Such players could be classed as career movers as, once established in England, they seek to enhance their careers in both football and monetary terms.

There is little doubt that the mixture of English history and Premiership fortunes is a powerful magnet for foreign players. It is possible to outline a financial motivation continuum in operation based on types of players and also because professional football is a livelihood with varying financial rewards. The continuum looks like this:

←————————————————————————————→

Money motivated   Career mover   Career opportunist

At one end is the career opportunist (hopeful/emerging professional), in the middle is the career mover (established professional), and at the upper end is the money motivated player (top/established international). The continuum is fluid and players' positions are dependent on factors such as form, injury, market value, contract position and international career. Mick McGuire of the PFA defended players on the issue of earning maximisation and argued that people should 'never criticise a player for trying to maximise his eight year career span'. Ultimately knowing your career position on the continuum and acting upon it, or having an agent to act upon it, is important for earning maximisation and this was not lost on some in the foreign legion group of this research.

The second significant question regarding foreign recruitment is how do these players get recruited to English clubs? It is obvious that recruitment has become internationalised and the subject group in question indicated the varied and available methods as well as the internationalisation of the process. For instance, Isidro Diaz and Roberto Martinez were sponsored by Dave Whelan, owner of JJB Sports, to move to Wigan Athletic, the club of which Whelan was a director. It was through a contact in the JJB factory in Spain that the club became aware of the players and Whelan effectively sponsored the transfers.

In other cases, players were able to use the football grapevine of contacts to instigate moves. As an example, Claus Thomsen's move from Denmark to Ipswich Town began when 'one of my colleagues from my former club in Denmark came to me and asked whether I fancied a move to England'. That playing colleague had heard that Ipswich Town was looking to recruit a player like Thomsen and passed on his name. Both Bart Griemink and Toddy Orlygsson also had former playing colleagues as the first point of contact regarding a move to England, whilst Franck Rolling came to Scotland (and to England from there) because a former playing colleague was managing a club there at the time. However, it is fair to comment that neither sponsor nor grapevine are popular or, indeed, reliable methods. There are two more dominant methods in this process– namely, scouting and agent intervention.

Scouting is the traditional main method of recruiting players and it involves a club representative (scout) reporting back to the manager about the performance of a certain player who may be useful to the club. Until very recently, English clubs rarely scouted beyond the Celtic fringes, but in the last decade football has become so much more international and the globalisation of scouting is testament to this. For instance, Jürgen Sommer was invited to Luton Town, his first English club, having been spotted playing for an American side at a youth tournament in Holland. Likewise, Shaun Goater was first scouted by Manchester United, his first English club, when the club was on a pre-season tour of Bermuda. In Mauricio Taricco's case, Ipswich Town's chief scout and manager flew to Argentina to watch him and then signed him post-match.

The managers interviewed confirmed that scouting was central to their success in the job and building a scouting network crucial. Roy Evans elaborates:

> as a manager you need a network to get you the information about players so that when they become available, or you know they are available you can watch them and then move in or not move in as the case is sometimes.

Joe Royle placed emphasis on his scouting network, but did insist that 'the signing of players is down to me so I want to see a player two, three times to be sure of him'. The expanding international calendar has been a key factor in developing the migration of football labour across the globe. Marc Hottiger (Switzerland) and Andrei Kanchelskis (Russia), for instance, first attracted English clubs when on international duty. It was clear they saw international football not just as a pinnacle achievement but also as a global showcase in which to parade their talent. This international showcasing has given the club scout an increasing global role, especially given the incessant twelve-month international football calendar, as well as regularly putting the player in the international shop window.

The other recruiting role is that of the agent, and players repeatedly identified the significance of the agent in the trajectory of their careers. As identified earlier, agents represent their clients – in this case, professional football players – in contract negotiations as well as in managing their careers. Significantly, the agent needs to understand his client's position on the career continuum and act accordingly to maximise the revenue potential for both the player and the agent. It could be argued that even though the player has gained significant control from the clubs in recent times, it is the agent who ultimately controls and potentially exploits the player. The wealth of the Premiership, combined with the expanded recruitment horizons of English clubs and their ability to operate in a Continental/global market, has attracted an increasing number of agents who trade in the movement of professional football players. In a sense, it is possible to observe that the agent has in some ways replaced the role of the club scout in the football recruitment market, and a notable example identified in this research was how Tranmere Rovers relied on the agent network and video material of players instead of appointing a chief scout at the club.

Formal player representation emerged as a significant force for players' collective interests in the 1960s, but it was in the 1990s that the agent became a central figure as the economics of football altered and English football became more powerful. However, the sport was unprepared for the increased involvement of agents, their business approach and their rapid centralisation in the transfer and contract process. Joe Royle accepts that with regard to agents, 'they are here now and it's something we have to deal with', and Steve McMahon, manager of Blackpool, agrees that 'agents are part of the game now and we have to deal with them'.

Following a series of high profile and damaging scandals surrounding certain transfer dealings in the mid-1990s – notably the case of Norwegian agent Rene Hauge and an unsolicited payment of £400,000 to the then Arsenal manager George Graham that cost Graham his job – FiFa introduced a licensing system in a bid to regulate and control transfer dealings and, in particular, the actions of the agent. PFA representative Mick McGuire felt that this was necessary as 'all sorts of monies were going missing in international deals … [and] obviously agents had to become licensed in a way of quality control'. Potential agents were required to attend a formal interview with FiFa and, if successful, were required to guarantee a bond of 200,000 Swiss francs for the international licence. It is also possible to obtain a national licence through the Football Association which allows agents to deal with transfers only within England. There are strict guidelines on the role and actions of the agents, with particular reference outlining what is considered to be unethical dealing, with licence revoking as the punishment. A significant network of agents is able to work within English football, though some British agents have teamed up with foreign agents to deal with United Kingdom representation. By 2001 there were over 100 licensed agents, mostly with international licences, operating from England.

There are at least four types of agent operating in the football world: the *Solo Agent* (who deals mainly with transfers and contracts – the most popular type: has a licence); the *Sports Agency* (which provides a wider support service beyond contracts: has a licence); the *Solicitor/Legal Advisor* (who provides legal service: may not have a licence); and the *Promotions Agency* (which provides career management and promotion opportunities: no licence). Agents are able to sign players on a two-year contract that guarantees them control and management of their client/player for that period in return for a service fee. From that point, the agent assumes control over the player as his financial representative, although Roy Evans did say that in his experience with transfers the commission fee demanded by the agent has been large enough to scupper the transfer. The role may be purely a negotiable one but could also involve financial management, promotions and publicity of the player. No player is able to have two agents, and some clubs have also become involved with using agents to represent them in negotiations such is their centrality to the business. Agents have grasped a strong position in the football business which has resulted in a gradual weakening of not only the power of the clubs but also of the football authorities themselves, and it is clear from this research that not all player representatives/agents are operating with a FIFA licence. The accepted involvement of unauthorised personnel points toward an unregulated and somewhat failing system, as well as raising questions about the commitment of the football authorities to legitimise transfer dealings.

There is a mass of licensed football agents seeking to establish themselves in the marketplace and, with a limited number of clients available, acquiring a client base is of fundamental importance. Without clients the agent has no player to represent or contract to negotiate for, no business to deal with and thus no income. Agent George Urquhart discussed the importance of 'building up and sustaining his player pool', while fellow agent Keith Park referred to 'the development of his player base' as being central to 'his business'. PFA representative Mick McGuire pointed out that 'there are a few top agents who have grabbed the market and then eighty per cent are fighting over the crumbs'. How agents become established in the market is questionable, though there are indicators that some agents have become illegally involved in representing players under the age of sixteen, thereby breaking licence regulations. The football authorities have been slow to act upon this and Mick McGuire of the PFA sees in this a worrying situation which the authorities are not dealing with stringently enough. Though he maintained he stayed within the regulations, agent Keith Park found that he needed to 'target young players to get established as they were not getting sufficient representation' and began to attract other players to his agency as a result of what he regards as 'his excellent service representation'. However there was a strong suspicion in the interviews with agents for this research that other agents were tapping already represented players, such is the strength of the competition and the lure of the extreme rewards on offer.

Roger Terrell, a lawyer who represents players, used his connections through his position as a Peterborough United director to attract players to his legal services, and as he became more established he left his post with Peterborough. Geoff Baker, who owns a sports promotion agency, decided to 'diversify into football and took on a former professional [player] with Manchester United to get me clients'. Whilst there were a varied degree of methods to acquire and develop a client base, one of the key struggles in this business involves competition between agents for players.

Mick McGuire, a representative and licensed agent with the players union, the PFA, was critical of the quality of representation of some fellow agents and highlighted one of the key power issues involved with agents:

> To become an agent there is very little quality control other than a ten minute interview at the FA. As long as you have not got a police record I think you have a great chance of becoming an agent ... Anybody can become an agent and, with the monies around, that has attracted every quality of individual. My real concern is that the quality of representation leaves something to be desired.

McGuire did recognise that there were 'some [agents] out there who were trying to do it the right way' but referred to a file on his shelf which was 'full of problems that players have had with agents, even licensed ones ... some are working in an immoral way'. George Urquhart, a fellow agent, admitted that 'there are a lot of people making money at it who are a bit 'dodgy', while Barry Nevill, another agent, succinctly summed up the delicacy around dealing with agents:

> Perhaps some of them are not really as interested in their client's welfare perhaps as they should be and they have ulterior motives to get their player to move to another club for another pay day for them ... Most agents, from what I gather, deal with contracts and transfers which is where the big money can be earned.

The delicacy of the situation involves the potential conflict of interests between the player's welfare/career and the agent's business needs to earn money through contract negotiations.

In most cases, agents earn most, if not all of their money, during contract negotiations but, if their client is not in a position to need a new contract, the agent effectively does not earn. Contracted and settled players are of little use to the agents and there is potential for a conflict of interests here because agents need players to move between clubs so that they can earn their service fee from the transfer but, by the same token, it may be advantageous to the player to remain at a club and establish stability. Longer-term contracts for some of the top players may reduce the involvement of the agent, though it has been proven time and again that football players are willing to move with time remaining on their contract. When this happens, suspicion is raised as to the motives behind the player's decision to seek a move, often a sudden change of attitude on the part of the player, and whether the agent has brokered a transfer through background covert work. The biggest criticism of agents in this research was about those who seek to unsettle their players when under contract to transfer them, guaranteeing another commission fee from the contract negotiations, without necessarily putting the player's welfare first. However, the weak stance of the football authorities in tackling this issue has allowed agents the freedom to get away with working outside the supposedly stringent regulations, and this again raises questions of the legitimacy of the licence as well as indicating the power assumed by agents in the business. Now that longer-term contracts are becoming standard for the top players, there is a trend developing in which players through their agent are able to get these renegotiated when some are only part way completed. The agent is able to utilise a situation whereby the club is informed that the player has become unsettled but will remain on a new contract if terms are improved. If the club refuses then a club-versus-player situation exists and the club is compromised somewhat in having a disgruntled player on its books. In most cases, the club either renegotiates the contract or is forced to sell the player, almost against their plans, such is the strength of modern-day player power.

It is on this issue that the role of the agents in football is most controversial, and Roy Evans, a former manager with Liverpool and Fulham, argued that:

agents are supposed to be for the benefit of the player but if you start moving them around every two years for the sake of money then there is a danger ... it's a hidden agenda with some agents ... when you get that many of them you don't get the quality.

Evans also said that 'some agents earn substantial amounts ... that's where the money goes out of football', whilst Joe Royle added further details into dealing with agents:

Some work purely to move their players. People ring me sometimes to tell me they have players at other clubs but they can be got out. And I'm afraid with the hypocrisy of this business we all use that if it suits us on the premise that if we don't someone will. I would be heavily hypo-critical if it happens to us and I'd fall out with that agent and not deal with them again.

Steve McMahon, manager of Blackpool, highlights the difficulties of working with agents: 'If you want a player you can't tell him "I'm not dealing with that agent" because the fact is he is going to use that agent'. Therefore, and despite doubts over their motives and their actions, it has become impossible for managers not to deal with certain agents as failure to do so would result in the manager not securing the services of a particular player. The power of the agents forces managers into dealing with them if they wish to have the services of particular players. Joe Royle held strong views on this issue:

There are some I won't deal with. Some I won't even speak to as I have had dealings with them in the past ... There are others I have dealt with who have been ethical and you have to listen to those people ... Like anything, you can't brand them all the same. Some are good to deal with, some I wouldn't trust as far as I could throw them and they are the unethical side.

Barry Fry, manager of Peterborough United, was unequivocal in his dismissal of agents when he said that 'I won't deal with them, won't do busi-ness with them and that's final'. Further research at Fry's club, however, pointed to an association that Fry had with a particular agent through whom he directed his transfer dealings.

The unethical side of agents' operations, and the power that agents have assumed, were graphically indicated during the very first interview for this research. This was with Andrei Kanchelskis at Everton, managed by Royle at the time. The player related how his agent had secured a transfer for him from Manchester United to Everton, despite there being three years left on his contract. The reason for this, according to Kanchelskis, was because 'I had a problem with the manager and I want to go', raising questions about agent advice and behind-the-scenes manoeuvres. The matter-of-fact way this account was related was startling and certainly raised questions regarding the transfer, its inception and the motives of those involved. In this instance, the agent, through behind-the-scenes moves, was able to obtain a transfer for his player whilst he was still under contract to another club, thereby financially benefiting both the player and the agent in the process. It is not illegal for agents to act like this, but it is unethical and contravenes the licensing regulations; however, it appears such a common practice that it is either ignored by the football authorities or informally accepted.

An interesting twist in this account was to occur in that Kanchelskis, not long after the interview, developed a similar 'problem' with Royle and, with covert work by his agent, now achieved a transfer to the Italian club Fiorentina. Again, another pay day came the way of the player and his agent. At the time Royle was scathing of how quickly the player became disgruntled and unsettled and of how his agent operated behind the scenes to move his player against Royle's wishes. However, Royle displayed a rather flexible and hypocritical position to dealing with agents and seemingly unsettled players, as he has benefited *and* lost from the behind-the-scenes manoeuvres of Kanchelskis and his agent. Even more interesting is that Royle re-signed Kanchelskis for his next club, Manchester City, and one can only assume that either Royle chose to suspend his rule of not dealing with problem agents or that Kanchelskis had acquired a new agent. The Kanchelskis account provides a clear illustration of the unregulated practices which exist in the football business, even among those who have acquired the necessary licence approval, indicating a failing system that allows agents to inhabit a space between player and club which permits agents to act unregulated. Kanchelsksis has been able to move freely without honouring the contract and to make vast amounts of money on the transfers, and this gives graphic detail of the type and scope of player power that those in club football are having difficulty in dealing with.

Clearly, the regulation of licensing agents seems to have fallen short of its intention, although without doubt there are some who are acting in the proper manner. Mick McGuire says that the global governing body is doing nothing about the licensing regulations and that immoral behaviour is being ignored as 'FiFa have realised it's an absolute minefield out there. It's an absolute free-for-all out there. It's disgraceful'. The market of players is very limited for the agents and so an obvious way to bolster the player bank has been to diversify and go abroad for clients. Joe Royle directly blamed agents for 'bringing about a massive influx of foreign players' and was dismissive of the amount of trade in foreign players. In most cases, agents only earn money from contract negotiating and thus are best suited if they can maintain the mobility level of their players between clubs. Becoming involved in transferring foreign players has been a sure way for agents to broaden their client base and guarantee themselves trade. With the levels of money flowing around English football, trading in football labour is a lucrative business, and so it is hardly surprising that the variety and quality of player representation is rather questionable.

Conclusion

As English football has become richer it has become more powerful on the European stage but, significantly, the football authorities have become weaker in terms of dealing with players and agents. This chapter has described the powerful profile of the English game, especially the Premiership, and has also indicated just how fragile and close to the precipice the business is. With the changes to the football market the ninety-two club professional league, already showing signs of great strain, will buckle. As Steve McMahon, the Blackpool manager, predicts, 'One thing is for sure, the rich are going to get richer and there'll be a big massive gap between top and bottom with some [clubs] dropping out of it at the bottom end'. Joe Royle blames the Bosman case for threatening the existence of lesser football clubs:

> It's [Bosman] changed the British game. I believe in ten years' time there'll be only two full-time professional leagues and maybe two part-time regional leagues because it [Bosman] has taken away the right of the smaller club to sell from strength and they'll hang themselves without transfer money.

Beyond the consequences of the Bosman case, notice of service is a further threat to the survival of clubs. Within this turbulent phase of transformation of the game, over the last decade or so players and agents have become unprecedentedly powerful in the football business. Roy Evans indicated that the commission fee of the agents has prevented the completion of some transfers he was involved with and it is clear that there are question marks hanging over the legitimacy, ethics and actions of some agents. Whilst there are some extremely reputable agents and sports agencies in operation who have cornered the football labour market, it is the actions of the lesser agents who invite criticism to be directed at agents. The pendulum of power now rests firmly with the totally emancipated player assisted by the agent. Such is the strength of player power that Steve McMahon, manager of Blackpool, was forced to admit that:

> The fear factor has gone. You can't tell players off anymore. You can't get players the sack, they get you [manager] the sack. The manager was always the one with all the aces ... and you shit yourself with the manager. He was always the one but now players get the manager the sack. A top player at a club can get the manager the sack. He can say to the Chairman 'I don't like that manager, I'm not signing for this club

unless that manager goes' and if he is the best player on £50,000 a week the Chairman will buckle. Players have such power now.

To assess McMahon's claims about the growth of player power, one must also look at the extent to which players are still exploited. As indicated, Sky Television has become a central organisation in the football business and has attained a powerful position that determines much of how and when football is delivered. Supporters also have a lot of untapped power and the nuances of the football supporter are founded upon extreme levels of club loyalty; a disgruntled player holding his club to ransom in a power conflict tends not to be looked upon favourably. Football would be a very weak product without supporters and, despite the actions of players and their agents, the intervention of television and the creation of the television supporter, albeit in the home or the public house, fortunately the clubs are still able to access a strong ally in the supporter. Also, even though the argument in this chapter is that the football authorities have weakened, the power of the governing bodies of the Football Association, UEFA, and FIFA cannot be discounted because no matter what changes are introduced to football these bodies are the ones who implement them. Ultimately the player is contracted to the governing body through his club contract, giving the authorities the ultimate power in the control of that player's career. It cannot be doubted that players are extremely well rewarded now and experience freedom unknown in previous phases of professional football, but claims of total player power need to be discounted. As the football labour market braces itself for more change that has the potential to threaten the existence of many clubs, the game has global power that will ensure its longevity. Within this power network of the new political economy of football, the player and agent have acquired more influence; but it is the commercial and media interests that provides the wherewithal on which that economy is based.

Appendix

Players interviewed:

Danny Allsopp (Manchester City and Australia)
Stig-Inge Bjornebyë (Liverpool and Norway)
Slaven Bilic (West Ham United and Croatia)
Isidro Diaz (Wigan Athletic and Spain)
Shaun Goater (Manchester City and Bermuda)
Bart Griemink (Peterborough United and Holland)
Marc Hottiger (Everton and Switzerland)
Sasa Ilic (Charlton Athletic and Yugoslavia)
Pontus Kaamark (Leicester City and Sweden)
Andrei Kanchelskis (Everton and Russia)

Anders Limpar (Everton and Sweden)
Roberto Martinez (Wigan Athletic and Spain)
Steve Mautone (West Ham United and Australia)
Toddy Orlygsson (Oldham Athletic and Iceland)
Andy Pettersen (Charlton Athletic and Australia)
Martin Pringle (Charlton Athletic and Sweden)
Franck Rolling (Leicester City and France)
Jürgen Sommer (Queens Park Rangers and United States of America)
Frank Talia (Swindon Town and Australia)
Mauricio Taricco (Ipswich Town and Argentina)
Claus Thomsen (Ipswich Town and Denmark)
Gerard Weikens (Manchester City and Holland)

Club representatives interviewed:

Don Howe (Arsenal, Director of Youth Coaching)
Barry Fry (Peterborough United, manager)
Kit Carson (Peterborough United, Academy Director)
Roy Evans (Liverpool, manager)
Colin Harvey (Everton, Academy Director)
Steve McMahon (Blackpool, manager)
Alan Hill (Leeds United, Academy Director)
George Smith (Leeds United, Academy Coach)
Joe Royle (Manchester City, manager)
Jim Cassell (Manchester City, Academy Director)
Terry Burton (Wimbledon, manager)
Dave Philpotts (Tranmere Rovers, coach)

Player representatives interviewed:

Keith Park (solicitor/sports agency – KP Sports Marketing)
George Urquhart (football agent – George Urquhart & Associates)
Roger Terrell (solicitor)
Barry Nevill (sports agency – IMG)
Geoff Baker (sports agency – MSB Marketing)
Mick McGuire (player representative – Professional Footballers' Association)

Notes

1   Based on initial research for doctoral work and subsequent follow-up research.
Initial interviews were conducted with sixteen foreign players during season
1997/98 as part of doctoral research. This was approximately 10 per cent of the
total number of foreign players contracted to English clubs at the time. As
numbers grew and post-doctorate research developed, further interviews were
conducted with players (total n=22 – approximately 5 per cent of the total
number of the foreign legion) as well as other key actors in the football network.

A full list of interviewees and their position at the time of interview can be seen in Appendix 1.

References

Boon, G. and Jones, D. (eds) (2001) *Deloitte & Touche Annual Review of Football Finance August 2001*, Manchester: Deloitte & Touche Sport.

Cashmore, E. (2000a) *Making Sense of Sports*, London: Routledge.

—— (2000b) *Sports Culture: An A–Z guide*, London: Routledge.

Collins, R. (1999) 'Is the bubble about to burst?', *Guardian Unlimited* 11 September 1999.

Dandelion, B.P. (1997) 'Insider dealing: researching your own private world', in A. Tomlinson and S. Fleming (eds) *Ethics, Sport and Leisure: Crises and Critiques*, Aachen: Meyer & Meyer.

Duke, V. (1994) 'The flood from the East? PERESTROIKA and the migration of sports talent from Eastern Europe', in J. Bale and J. Maguire (eds) *The Global Sports Arena*, London: Frank Cass.

Horne, J., Tomlinson, A. and Whannel, G. (1999) *Understanding Sport: An Introduction to the Sociological and Cultural Analysis of Sport*, London: Spon.

King, A. (1997) 'New directors, customers, and fans: the transformation of English football in the 1990s', *Sociology of Sport Journal* 14(3): 224–40.

Maguire, J. (1999) *Global Sport: Identities Societies Civilizations*, Cambridge: Polity Press.

Maguire, J. and Stead, D. (1997) 'Border crossings: soccer and labour migration and the European union', *International Review for the Sociology of Sport* 32(1): 59–73.

Middleton, G. (1997) *Football Industry Review 1997*, London: Football Trust.

Nelson, G. (1995) *Left Foot Forward*, London: Headline.

Professional Footballers' Association/*Independent* survey, April 2000.

Williams, J. (1994) 'The local and the global in English soccer and the rise of satellite television', *Sociology of Sport Journal* 11(4): 376–97.

bes on the beach, women in the surf

Researching gender, power and difference in the windsurfing culture

Belinda Wheaton

Introduction: insider accounts

> Studies of male subcultures are primarily explorations of masculinity.
> (Brake 1980, cited in Scraton 1987: 163)

Within the study of sport and leisure subcultures there has been a widespread recognition of the value of ethnographic research conducted by researchers who adopt 'insider' roles, whether by an originally 'native' association with the subculture studied, or a field role adopted during the research (see Redhead 1993; Giulianotti 1995; Donnelly 1985). Clearly there are some private worlds, including certain sport cultures, where only insiders have access to respondents. Nevertheless, in part this support for 'insider research' has stemmed from critiques of subcultural research such as Hebdige's (1979) seminal study of youth subcultures, in which his non-participatory role has been widely critiqued. It is argued that non-participant observers often misunderstand, or ignore, what the sport culture means to its participants – they do not explain the subjective experiences of everyday life. In the context of participatory sport cultures, such as surfing, some go so far as to argue that participation in the activity is a prerequisite to understanding the sports' meaning and aesthetic (see Doyle 1993).

However, it has become increasingly evident that in many of these sporting ethnographic texts the 'lived experience' that the researchers were detailing were specifically the realities, identities and experiences of white, Western, middle-class men. Despite reflection on the 'self' as cultural insider, researchers have often failed to investigate the 'self' as gendered or racialised subjects. Even fewer sporting ethnographies conducted by male researchers acknowledge – or make visible – their own maleness, or whiteness. Despite sport sociology's widespread acknowledgement of the *importance* of feminist theory, and increasingly postcolonial and black feminist critiques of the universalised and essentialised white male Western subject, it has not always led to an *engagement* with its implications in ethnographic practice.

In this chapter I raise a number of questions and tensions surrounding the methodological, epistemological and ontological issues in adopting a 'critical' ethnography that is sensitive to concerns around (the politics of) representing the 'Other'. The context for this discussion is ethnographic research that I conducted, focusing on a community of windsurfers in the south of England, a community in which I had an established participant role. I was an active and experienced windsurfer; I had been windsurfing at that beach for several years, and lived in the vicinity; I could be considered as an 'insider' to both the context (the windsurfing culture) and group (the specific South Coast community) (see Pink Dandelion 1997).

At the outset the research itself was neither consciously 'feminist', nor was it primarily concerned with women or their experiences. Yet this community, like many sport communities, was predominantly male. Contrary to the glamorised media representations of surf culture, I was one of just a handful of females who participated year round. My experiences as a 'woman in the surf' – an active woman windsurfer, not one of the spectating 'beach babes' – became central to the theoretical and methodological development of the research.

However, the realisation of the significance of Brake's statement – that my subcultural study was centrally an exploration of masculinity – took me almost two years to realise.[1] Of course, I had realised that 'masculinity' was significant to my research, but my prior understanding of 'masculinity' was as one of many emergent 'themes' I was grappling with. I had spent over eighteen months 'immersed' in the culture, and had analysed piles of data. Yet it was only when I tried to understand the complexities of competitiveness over status in the culture that I realised that almost every aspect of my research was in some way an investigation of the performance of sporting masculine identities. Each field incident and conversation I witnessed, each experience I noted, when examined under this new lens was in some way informing about masculinity or masculinity's relationship to 'other' categories – principally, in this research to feminities, class, age, and ethnicity, and centrally, masculinities relationship to my sense of 'self'.

In this chapter I reflect back on some fieldwork experiences to illustrate how my understanding of this social world, my theoretical interpretations of it as well as the methodological and practical problems encountered, were 'tied up' with the multiple and shifting roles and identities that I, as an embodied researcher, brought to and experienced during this ethnographic enterprise. I will focus on how being a *female* researcher, who was an *active windsurfer*, was central to the theoretical genesis of the study. Nevertheless, my positioning in this subculture was more complex and fluid than considerations solely of either 'insider status' or 'gender' indicate. My research provides some contextual examples to show how reflexively exploring the changing dimensions of my own subcultural identity, and how 'difference' was marked, gives important insight into the complexity and fluidity of the identities performed and power relations played out in this sport culture.

I begin the discussion by focusing on methodological debates around epistemology and ontology, particularly issues pertinent to researching issues of gendered identities. In the first section I outline and discuss the impact of debates around post-structuralism, postmodernism and feminisms, on the practices of critical ethnography generally, and the specificities of this ethnographic enterprise.

'Crisis of representation': the implications for a critical sports ethnography

The adoption of a research 'method' like ethnography is based on philosophical, ideological and epistemological assumptions about the social world, and the place of methodology within it. Over the past few decades, ongoing philosophical debates about the nature of knowledge and scientific enquiry in the social sciences, particularly in the context of post-structuralism and postmodernism's critique of the Enlightenment project, have contributed to a re-evaluation of many of the basic assumptions about (positivistic) scientific method, epistemology and, specifically, ethnography.

The implications of this epistemological 're-evaluation' are numerous, ranging from the rejection of grand narratives (a scepticism about discourses claiming to provide universal, rational, scientific explanations), to notions of a one-to-one relationship between reality and textually based accounts of it (Stanley and Wise 1993: 190). In this 'crisis' all certainties have been re-evaluated and all aspects of the research process have come under inspection. This critique, as I will illustrate, has wide-ranging implications for how we do ethnographic research, write about ethnographic research, for the role of the researcher and the claims we make about our research, and for ways of validating ethnography.

While these so-called crises of 'representation' (Marcus and Fisher 1986) and of 'legitimation' (Denzin and Lincoln 1994), which characterise what Denzin and Lincoln (1994) call the 'Fifth Moment' of qualitative enquiry, are often claimed to be a postmodern or post-structuralist development, many of the ideas and some of the resulting methodological initiatives have a longer history embedded in earlier critiques of method and epistemology,[2] most notably feminists' rejection of positivism and scientific objectivity (see Stanley and Wise 1993; Morgan 1992). Moreover, as the next section explores, feminist concerns continue to be central to this redefinition of the ethnographic project around these dual 'crises'. In the first part of this discussion I examine questions about the criterion we use for evaluating or legitimating ethnographic research, focusing around what constitutes 'truth' and 'value'. I go on to explore issues surrounding the text's claims to 'authority' and authenticity (Denzin 1994a), particularly focusing on issues of language, writing and representation in the ethnographic text. Of course these concerns are intimately linked. As Denzin and Lincoln put it: 'Clearly these two crises (of representation and legitimation) blur together, for any representation must now legitimate itself in terms of some set of criteria that allows the author (and the reader) to make connections between the text and the world written about' (Denzin and Lincoln 1994: 11).

Claims to truth and objectivity in ethnographic research

> Once upon a time, the lone ethnographer rode off into the sunset in search of his 'native'. After undergoing a series of trials, he encountered the object of his quest in a distant land. There he underwent his rite of passage but enduring the ultimate ordeal of 'fieldwork'. After collecting the 'data', the lone ethnographer returned home and wrote a true account of 'the culture'.
>
> (Rosaldo, *Culture and Truth* 1989, cited in Denzin (1994a: 500))

> Ethnographic truths are inherently partial, committed and incomplete.
>
> (James Clifford, introduction to the 'new ethnographies', Clifford and Marcus 1986: 7)

There is considerable debate and disagreement over what constitutes 'good interpretation' and rigour in ethnography (see Denzin and Lincoln 1994; Hammersley 1992). Extreme positions exist in this debate, from that of the positivists who believe that the same set of criteria should be used to assess all scientific research, to that of the postmodernists who conclude that the character of qualitative research is such that there can be no criteria for judging it – a position which 'doubts all criteria and privileges none' (Denzin and Lincoln 1994: 480). Critiques of this total or 'epistemological' (Harding 1991) relativist position championed by 'extreme' postmodernists have been well rehearsed (Ward 1997; Sokal 1999). My focus here, however, is with the ground between these extreme positions of positivism and post-modernism – that is, the many paradigms that have argued for, or have moved towards, 'alternative' research criteria that do not fit the positivistic criteria such as validity, objectivity, generalisability, repeatability. Such ethnographic practitioners hail from various feminisms, postcolonial theo-rists, cultural studies, critical and interpretative theories and varieties of postmodernism.

However, these are not just theoretical and methodological issues; under-lying these questions are issues of epistemology and ontology. Claims for objectivity and validity, the truth or value of research, are generally based on claims to knowledge referred to as epistemological stances (Abbott and Wallace 1997). Underlying these different paradigms, and the multiple positions within them, are *ontological differences* relating to views on the nature of social reality, and diverse *epistemological assumptions* about what is accepted as knowledge, and thus methods of 'objective' study:

An 'epistemology' is a framework or theory for specifying the constitution and generation of knowledge about the social world; that is, it concerns how to understand the nature of 'reality'. A given epistemological framework specifies not only what 'knowledge' is and how to recognise it, but who are the 'knowers'.

(Stanley and Wise 1993: 188)

These different theoretical perspectives I have demarcated do not share the same epistemological and ontological assumptions, but they are united in their critique of positivism and the assumptions underlying the enlightenment project. As Denzin and Lincoln (1994: 99) outline, the positivistic and post-positivistic paradigms 'provide the backdrop' against which these other paradigms and theoretical perspectives operate. My purpose here is to sketch out briefly the epistemological dimensions of my ethnography, specifically to highlight the (broadly) feminist constructionist and critical ethnography positions that underpin this research,[3] and how it is related to the claims to truth and objectivity made in ethnography.

A feminist constructionist perspective: beyond 'on/for/by women'

An array of different feminist epistemological stances has been adopted to provide the basis of feminist truth claims (Abbott and Wallace 1997).[4] Feminists such as Nancy Hartsock and Dorothy Smith contend that the feminist epistemological position is a privileged one – that is, the oppressed position is epistemologically privileged (see Hartsock 1987; Smith 1987). This position, commonly referred to as the feminist-standpoint, advocates that feminist research constitutes research done *by* women, *on* women and *for* women (see Stanley and Wise 1993: 30). It is argued that 'true knowledge' emerges from the *experiences* of oppressed people, thus women have better – or more direct access to – knowledge about the experience and (material) conditions of their subordination (Griffin 1996). Thus 'knowledge production and validation should be grounded in one's everyday life, and especially the everyday lives of the oppressed' (*ibid.*: 181). It is inferred that although men can challenge sexist assumptions, only the oppressed – women – can be 'feminists'.

The feminist constructionist position emerged, in part, from critiques of this feminist standpoint position. Three points are central: first, the feminist standpoint position assumes that gender issues are only *on* and *about* women (see discussion in Stacey 1988; Stanley and Wise 1993) rather than recognising and investigating the sex–gender binary systems that exist in society. As masculinity theorists (among others) argue, gender questions are not always women-centred questions – a viewpoint articulated in my windsurfing research. Researching masculinities helps to understand the part *men* play in women's oppression.

Second, the theoretical position inherent in the standpoint argument, assumes that *all* women are equally oppressed, rather then taking on board post-structuralist feminist and postcolonial debates around 'difference'. These have led to gender being understood in a more fluid way that deconstructs 'women' as a universal category and acknowledges the varied types of social oppression and power differentials *among* women.

Third, it is based on an assumption that there is a direct relationship between experience and 'true knowledge', which leads to a position of objectivity, the 'truth' (Abbott and Wallace 1997). It shares this *realist* view of the social world, with paradigms like positivism, believing that there is a universal underlying material reality (such as patriarchy) that structures it, and that reality is 'out there' independent of our understanding of it (*ibid.*: 292).

The feminist constructionist position challenges this foundationalism of positivistic and feminist standpoint positions, arguing that reality is socially constructed; there is no 'real' social world waiting to be discovered, only our individual subjective experiences of it (Abbott and Wallace 1997). Like critical ethnographers, constructionist feminists are sceptical of claims to any universal knowledge, including claims that feminist knowledge is epistemologically privileged (thus arguing for the existence of a variety of feminist epistemologies). Knowledge is contextual, thus different women have different experiences, and relationships to gendered, and other forms, of power inequalities. 'Women' as a universal category is deconstructed – although certainly not dissolved – to acknowledge the varied types of social oppression *among* women, and how accounts from these different standpoints help our understanding (see Hill Collins 1986).

A common critique of these positions, from those in the (positivistic and post-positivist) *realist* epistemological position, is that they are forms of cultural *relativism*. Relativism is the sociological assertion that 'what is thought to be a reasonable claim in one society or subculture is not thought to be so in another' (Harding 1991: 139). If, it is argued, there are no 'objective' standpoints from which to assess different claims to truth, all accounts or meta narratives become equally valid. However commentators attempt to lump together numerous relativists' perspectives under the banner of 'crude postmodernism';[5] Ward, for example, terms it the 'war between the realists and the relativists' (Ward 1997: 781), whereas a multitude of positions exists. The extreme relativist position that Harding terms 'epistemological relativism' (1991: 139), in which nothing exists outside of discourse, is clearly problematic. As Sugden and Tomlinson (1999: 386) outline, if there is no basis or criterion for adjudicating between competing truth claims then this 'plays into the hands of those who conceal a multiplicity of sins behind official histories of themselves'. It leaves no critical space to examine power relations, or (identity) politics at all.

However, to adopt a constructionist epistemology and ontology does not mean lapsing into this extreme relativist position (see also Harding 1991), but it highlights the localised sites and contingent perspectives where knowledge is created. Perspectives that see reality as socially constructed argue that such *realist* – and, feminists would argue, male-centred notions of objectivity and other traditional criterion such as validity or 'truth' – are inappropriate, even meaningless terms. They reject the idea of the dispassionate 'scientific' observer, suggesting that the experiences and feeling of the research need to be central to the production of cultural knowledge. Truth, like objectivity, is socially constructed: 'both are constructed out of experiences' (Stanley and Wise 1993: 171). Embracing such a worldview means that these traditional criteria become impossible aims from an epistemological and ontological standpoint (Bruce and Greendorfer 1994: 262). They 'simply reflect a concern for acceptance within a positivist concept of research vigour' (Kincheloe and McLaren 1994: 151), as the following discussion of objectivity illustrates.

Detached objectivity? Going, going, gone 'native'

Bell (1993: 29) outlines that in anthropology objectivity, considered to be the 'hallmark of science', is based on 'an absence of connection to one's subject matters'. This positivistic concern with 'detached objectivity' in ethnography is clearly illustrated in discussions of 'going native'. It is argued that the researcher must find a balance between personal involvement and detachment to maintain their 'critical' viewpoint. The term 'gone native' has been widely used (in the positivistic language) to describe researchers who have integrated so fully with the 'native' culture that they empathise with them, romanticising – even defending – the members' values. It is argued that they therefore lose 'detachment' (Woods 1986). However, the term itself (steeped in the discourses and practices of colonialism) and the concept of objectivity underlying 'going native' are problematical from a critical constructionist perspective. They assume that an external position exists where an apparent 'reality' can accurately be recorded. Yet, 'research' is a process which occurs through the medium of a person – 'the researcher is always and inevitably present in the research' (Stanley and Wise 1993: 175). Thus, the ethnographer is, in terms of experience, always the 'marginal native' (Atkinson 1990). As critical ethnographers have argued, 'going native' is the only way to engage with our 'subjects'.

Similarly, feminist critiques of objectivity in anthropology suggest that we should deconstruct the idea of objectivity and embrace the subjectivity central to a reflexive ethnography (Bell 1993: 29). Bell notes that once the line has been crossed into the subjective realm of declaring one's feelings and emotions, such work is seen to be 'biased, interested, partial'. It is no coincidence, she argues, that feminists in particular are accused of a lack of balance and detachment. In 'the gender-inflected dualism of post-enlightenment rational thought' such couplets as partial/impartial, personal/detached, emotional/rational are associated with 'woman' (*ibid.:*

29). As Harding argues, 'in a hierarchically organised society, objectivity cannot be defined as requiring (or even desiring) value-neutrality' (Harding 1991: 134).

It is for these reasons, that it is vital to emphasise the *procedures* that underlie the ways in which knowledge is produced, and the contextual specificity of feminist as of other knowledges (Stanley and Wise 1993) – particularly *who* the researcher is in terms of axes of their identity, such as class, 'race', gender, sexuality, and their status within the community they are studying.

Beyond the theory

The position that I advocated when writing up my doctoral research was, like many critical cultural studies theorists, somewhere in between these extremes of postmodern cultural relativism and positivistic realism. I rejected the assumption that a 'tangible, knowable, cause-and-effect reality exists and that research descriptions are able to portray that reality accurately' (Kincheloe and McLaren 1994: 151). I worked towards a reflexive approach to ethnography that denied a single interpretative truth, seeing validity as a process shaped by culture, ideology, gender and language (Lincoln and Denzin 1994: 481).

However it is also important to draw attention to the ways in which my position changed, both during the research and since completing it. I started this journey as a post-positivist. This is reflected in the Grounded Theory generic approach (Strauss and Corbin 1994, 1990) I adopted in my research, which reproduces a naturalistic approach to ethnography but one that is premised on the post-positivist approach. As Strauss and Corbin (1990: 250) put it, 'the usual canons of good science should be retained, but require redefinition in order to fit the realities of qualitative research'. For example, I used analytic induction, negative case testing and other means to 'validate' my emergent themes, and to ensure my account was rigorous and had theoretical and inductive generalisability.

My feeling at the time was that a 'good story was not enough'; it needed the 'appropriate' methodological legitimation of (post-) positivistic language to make it 'good ethnography'. My experiences are by no means novel. Andrew Sparkes, for example, writes at length about how assumptions about 'proper academic work' influenced how he wrote and presented his narrative of self called the 'Fatal flaw' (see Sparkes 2000). Sparkes's account is informing on many levels, but particularly in revealing the contradictions and tensions that exist between and within different reviewers of the journal who had to 'judge' this piece of 'experimental' qualitative writing. In his assessment he argues:

> It makes little sense to impose criteria used to pass judgement on one upon another. Attempts to do so are at best misguided and at worst,

arrogant and nonsensical, a form of intellectual imperialism that builds failure in from the start so that the legitimacy of other research forms is systematically denied.

(Sparkes 2000: 29)

That is, debates over truth and objectivity in ethnographic research need to acknowledge that different approaches and paradigms see the world differently – they have different realities and thus will have different methods and criteria to assess the research. However, the differences between different forms of inquiry – different paradigms – need to be acknowledged so that each are measured using criteria that are 'consistent with their own meaning structures' (Sparkes 2000: 29). Textual (re)constructions, such as a written ethnography, are always time- and culture-bound accounts of reality (see Atkinson 1990). Rather than claiming the existence of a reality that exists 'out there' independent of the researcher, as Thornton (1997) contends, as ethnographers we are attempting to 'map' a social world but, in the process of translating that world into the language of academia, we are inevitably involved in a process of constructing a particular reality. Thus, critical subcultural ethnography can best be described as the researcher's written representation of that culture. One of the challenges is to recognise and, as the next section illustrates, represent the 'polyphony of voices' (Hughson 1998: 53) within the communities we study.

Reporting ethnography

Another central aspect of this debate around the 'linguist and rhetorical' turn' is the concern with *reporting* ethnography, both in terms of the *style* in which ethnography is presented and the *procedures* used. As Bruce and Greendorfer (1994: 261) outline, the ground has shifted from concerns with 'how the study was produced' to 'what is produced' – that is, how to write 'credible texts'. These issues are part of the broader problematisation of cultural representation under which traditional writing genres have been put under intense scrutiny (for example, see Denzin 1994a, b; Atkinson 1990; Richardson 1994). I will discuss some of these concerns in this research context in relation to the initiatives termed the 'impressionist tale' (Van Maanen 1988) and the 'audit trail' or 'confessional'.

During the 1960s onwards, a new 'genre' of ethnography surfaced that has been referred to as the 'confessional' (Van Maanen 1988) or autobiographical account (Bryman and Burgess 1994). The role and authority of the ethnographer is problematised (Fontana 1994), as is the notion that the researcher is outside the research process, an invisible observer, with no influence on it:

[Postmodern] ethnographers seek to deconstruct the dominant position of the ethnographer. This is not done by making the ethnographer 'disappear', but by making him or her 'public'.

(Fontana 1994: 212)

The 'confessional' documents how the fieldwork was carried out and the many problems encountered in the field. Rather than omitting or glossing over the problematics of fieldwork in an attempt to present a more 'objective' study, they in themselves became topics of research (Fontana 1994). The researcher thus writes a 'research diary' or 'audit trail' that documents his or her experiences of the research process and focuses on the procedures of data collection and analysis (Burgess *et al.* 1994). By including observations about the researcher's interactions with the social actors and exploring the researcher's subjective experiences of the research setting, context and process, the 'audit trail' adds a dimension of reflexivity to ethnography (Fontana 1994). It thus illustrates, and makes explicit, the relations between the author, the object of analysis and the final constructed text.

Another important dimension of this discussion revolves around the *style of reporting* ethnography. Researchers have looked towards various literary and narrative models of writing, as well as ways of legitimating their research (Bruce and Greendorfer 1994). Increasingly, researchers have played with different forms and styles of reporting ethnography, deconstructing positivistic conventions, and challenging the ethnographer's authoritative influence (Marcus and Fisher 1986). Scholars have interpreted such a challenge in different ways (see Richardson 2000). Postmodern ethnographers advocate extensive 'poetic experimentation' (Foley 1992; 45), suggesting new forms of writing such as writing drama, poetry and performed dialogue, which transgress scientific conventions (Bruce 1998). In the sporting context, examples of the possibilities of the experimental texts can be seen in the work of Bruce (1998), Rinehart (1998a) and Kohn and Sydor (1998). Others have explored the connections between autobiographical ethnographic texts and auto-ethnographies in experimental texts (see Sparkes 2000).

My attempt to negotiate this 'representational crisis' took me down the post-positivistic route, following those who suggest that there is value in the traditional 'realist' narrative, but adopting some of the initiates such as the 'confessional' and the 'impressionist tale' outlined here. Rather than adhering to positivistic rhetorical practices in the ethnographic narrative — such as third person reporting — that make a text authoritative and persuasive, my ethnographic account is reported in the first person. As Fontana suggests, the *language* of ethnography has tended to imitate the language of the natural sciences, as if 'to add legitimacy to a scientifically suspect enterprise' (1994: 209). First person narratives help to produce a reflexive account as they situate the fieldworker *in* the ethnographic account, recognising explicitly who the ethnographer is — as Bourdieu describes it, their habitus — and how they actually produced the account. The dialogue and differences between the researcher and the informants is emphasised, reducing the ethnographer's authoritative influence (Marcus and Fisher 1986).

The 'impressionist tale' was another 'narrative' device adopted in this research. Rather than presenting typifications, such as 'a day in the life of the windsurfer', real events and characters are discussed, although, for ethical reasons, the real names of places and participants are masked. This approach avoids simplifying experiences into one voice, one reality, and emphasises the multiplicity of voices in the windsurfing culture. However, as the next section explores, all too often ethnographers do not consider these 'polyphonic voices' in relation to issues of power and difference.

Gender, power and difference in the ethnographic process

> There is no ungendered reality or perspective, but rather the power to declare one universal and the other partial.
>
> (Bell 1993: 30)

A central challenge for critical ethnographers is to reject accounts that present the white male as generic and to deconstruct and challenge those practices and assumptions that enable the 'male stream' to be presented as 'truth'. As Bell (1993) contends, while debates about difference, post-colonial theory and postmodern discourses have forced white Western male anthropologists to reflect on their 'otherness' and decentre their authority, 'gender blind' accounts still dominate ethnographic work. Feminists have drawn on Foucaultian concepts of knowledge production to understand the connection between power and knowledge, that all knowledge-making involves the exercise of power (Foucault 1979 in Ward 1997: 778), and thus that knowledge claims are intrinsically tied to the politics of identity, power and exclusion (Abbott and Wallace 1997). As Cain outlines, Foucault's concern with 'repressed knowledges' – that is, 'with the existence and voices of those who are silenced or subordinated by, or excluded from, dominant discourse' (1993: 74) – has been particularly important in this context. It raises questions about how and under what conditions knowledge is produced and whom it benefits. As Cole argues, 'What counts as critical, what counts as theory, and what counts as knowledge is contested territory' (Cole 1991: 45). Critical feminist ethnography thus aspires to 'create a space for minor voices and visions', particularly those voices that have been historically silenced or marginalised (*ibid.*: 34). (For a discussion of these issues in relation to the marginalisation of black women's voices and knowledge, see Hill Collins 1986 and hooks 1982).

However, as noted in the introduction, despite a general acceptance of the *importance* of feminist theory, this has not always led to an *engagement* with its implications in ethnographic practice. Les Back (Back 1993) explores this argument in relation to anthropology's attempts to manage the 'postmodern turn', particularly in relation to the crisis in intellectual authority (see Clifford and Marcus 1986). He argues that while there has been a greater critical awareness of 'feminist' issues, such as around truth, authority and reflexivity (what he calls a 'fetish' for 'self disclosure'), this does not necessarily lead to an analysis which examines *how* gendered power relations may be at work in the research process, nor an examination of the *production* of gendered subjects and selves. Male anthropologists have had a lot to say about their ethnographic experience, but have written comparatively little:

> Male autobiographies are confined to the bar-room confessional, or as anecdotes for the amusement of students or colleagues. ... [We] need a more sensitive appreciation of the politics of research. In short we need to respond positively to feminist anthropologists' critique of methodological practice.
>
> (Back 1993: 215)

Ultimately, he maintains (drawing on Said 1989 and Marcus and Cushman 1982) the response is an 'aesthetic not political one' (Back 1993: 216). Anthropologists have developed new ways of writing which are qualitatively different from the male as generic; they acknowledge feminist theory, but ultimately marginalise it.

Likewise, sport sociologists and anthropologists tend not to deconstruct — or make visible — their *maleness*, their *masculinity*. The exception is a small body of male researchers — men who write from a (broadly) critical constructionist position, who have vividly explored their gendered selves in their experimental texts about sport (for examples see Sparkes 1996, 1998; Rinehart 1998b; Thornton 1998; Spracklen 1996; and contributions to Messner and Sabo 1990). An apposite example of this is the way male ethnographers and investigative journalists write about 'risk taking' in fieldwork. For male ethnographers risk is often about penetrating public places and institutions, 'getting under the skin' of social life, as Sugden and Tomlinson (1999) term it. John Sugden (1997), for example, writes an extremely lively and reflective ethnographic account that documents the scrapes and scares he encountered in his various ethnographic adventures. David Morgan's comments are apposite:

> [Qualitative research] has its own brand of machismo with its image of the male sociologist bringing back news from the fringes of society, the lower depths, the mean streets.
>
> (Morgan 1992: 87)[6]

For women, the kinds of risk tend to be more 'personal' and private, personal security being a central issue for women attempting to do research in public places or institutions (see Flintoff 1997); such divisions again

te the gender-inflected cultural associations of the dualism of
rivate, male–female.

would not describe this research project as specifically a *feminist* ethnography. One fundamental tenet in almost all debates about feminist research and epistemological standpoints is that it should be 'for women' – that the emancipation of women, rather than the pursuit of knowledge is the, or a, central objective (Stanley and Wise 1993). While one of the intentions of this project was to make gender visible, particularly to contribute to debates about how gendered power differences are maintained and reproduced in the cultural space of the windsurfing subculture, I did not embark on this project believing that it would empower or even assist my (predominantly 'privileged' middle-class white) female respondents. Perhaps my research is best described as feminist-inspired research. However, whether the focus of research is on men or women, or both, researchers need to be aware of debates about how gender should be researched, which methodologies best serve a feminist agenda, and the broader issues around power, knowledge and disclosure of 'self' in the research process. In relation to critical ethnography, the central issue is to elevate the importance of the political and personal dimensions of ethnography such as: reflexivity, responsivity, a rejection of the hierarchical exploitative relationship between researcher and researched (in method and representation), and to foster an experiential, eclectic approach – one that is sensitive to, and engages with, gender and other (multiple) forms of oppression and difference in the research process (see Hammersley 1992b; Morgan 1992; Stanley and Wise 1993; Finch 1993; Roseneil 1993).

The remainder of the paper focuses on my attempts to produce such an ethnographic account. My starting point is a consideration of 'self' as a cultural insider.

Reflections on 'insider accounts'

As outlined, in adopting an 'insider' role I was following an established 'tradition' both within cultural studies and the sociology of sport. Observations centred not just on the windsurfing beaches, but other sites where the windsurfers gathered socially, such as pubs they frequented after windsurfing, shops, trade shows and festival events, windsurfing car boot sales, beach parties and informal gatherings at windsurfers' houses. My role was 'covert' in that I did not always declare my true intentions to the community (see Wheaton 1997b), although the distinction between covert and overt can be misleading as in practical terms, particularly in a public setting like the beach, the boundaries are rarely so distinct.

Insider research raises a number of theoretical *and* methodological debates, but particularly about the *nature* and *validity* of the insider. Theoretical analyses of the role of the participant observer, such as Hammersley and Atkinson's (1995) continuum from the 'complete participant' to the 'complete observer', often over-simplify the role that fieldworkers actually negotiate. I will argue that the distinction between 'insider' and 'outsider' is a misleading binary opposition rooted in an essentialist and fixed understanding of identities, one that fails to recognise the multiple ways in which difference or 'otherness' is marked and measured, so masking the fluidity and contingent nature of the researcher's role and identity. As Song and Parker (1995) argue, 'dichotomised rubrics', such as insider–outsider, 'put too much emphasis on difference, rather than on partial and simultaneous commonality and difference between the researcher and interviewees' (*ibid*.: 249). In the following discussion I will demonstrate that I was more of an 'insider' in some settings, while concurrently experiencing being an 'outsider' in others. Moreover, other positionality issues such as being a proficient windsurfer, a journalist,[7] middle class, a 'girlfriend', and, centrally, being female, heterosexual and white, also influenced my 'insider' role in different ways in different situations, times and contexts. In ethnographic research – as in other cultural settings – identities are continually made and remade. The incidents I discuss revolve around reoccurring problematics that I have discussed in the first section of the chapter – that is, ethnographic roles and detached 'objectivity' claims to truth and 'authenticity' and debates about subjectivity, gender and status. However, the central thread underlying these incidents is the reoccurring problematic of the self – other binary – that is, the ways in which I, as a researcher, simultaneously became the researched.

Degrees of 'otherness'

I found it hard initially to change my perspective from being a 'windsurfer' to a 'researcher', to make the subculture 'anthropologically strange' (Woods 1986: 34). Like many novice ethnographers, it seemed as if there 'wasn't anything to report', consequently the field notes in the early phase lacked substance and especially contextual detail. Over time my field notes became more detailed and seemingly more critical. Nevertheless, over-identification, at least with parts of the culture such as the advanced participants, was clearly a potential problem. A particular conversation with two 'occasional' windsurfers alerted me to the complexity of insider–outsider relations *within* the subculture, and importantly how *my* identity fitted into this characterisation and the methodological ramifications of my positioning.

Theoretically, I had explored the existence of different levels of subcultural membership, adapting – among others – Donnelly's (1981) model of the horizontal stratification of an achieved subculture from the 'core member' to the 'outsider'. Lived experience is infinitely more complex and fluid than any rigid appplication of a model of identity positions would suggest. Nevertheless, in the windsurfing setting, high levels of skill, a 'go-for-it' attitude and commitment in time and resources were key values, and forms of subcultural capital, that differentiated the 'core' windsurfer (see Wheaton 2000a). The existence of this cultural hierarchy, and particularly the recognition that windsurfers were competitive over subcultural status, had methodological implications for my 'insider' role. What kind of insider was I? How and where did I fit in? How were the boundaries marked, negotiated and contested? And how did my subcultural identity change during the process?

An apposite example of the fluid and contingent nature of subcultural identity lies in the conversation I noted above with the marginal wind-surfers. It helped me to realise that I was still too involved in the core of the subculture to understand the experiences of less involved windsurfers. As a consequence I focused my 'formal' interviews on more marginal participants. However during the progression of the research, my role and identity within the culture continued to change. As a consequence of the research, I became one of the beach regulars – my status in the community shifted from being a committed windsurfer to a 'core' member of the subculture. I became known as the person who was always hanging around the beach, always (over-) eager to talk about windsurfing and enthusiastic enough to take on things no one else wanted to do. I ended up on several windsurfing organisation commit-tees and wrote regular articles for a British windsurfing magazine. Then, later in the process, particularly once I began formal interviewing, I spent increasingly less time at the beach, and less time socialising with wind-surfers – I was withdrawing from the community. I was conscious of the way my identity was changing; I no longer felt a part of the group. As the central analytic themes began to emerge, the feelings of distance changed to antipathy, even resentment towards some individuals in the group – and to myself as my own (and my partner's, who was also a participant) involve-ment in it, was placed under the analytical microscope.

On reflection, I think at this time that my total identification with the Silver Sands community was at least partially suspended. My outlook or viewpoint had gradually transposed from windsurfer–researcher to researcher–windsurfer. The 'unease' that I felt in the windsurfing commu-nity continued, and I suspect that it was a necessary part of the progressive detachment process – it marked my critical distancing of self from both the 'native', and my own initial experiences. This tension between achieving 'critical distance' and 'involvement' (in an intellectual rather than physical way) continued throughout my study, even during the writing-up phase. The gradual and emotionally overwhelming process of withdrawal was one of the hardest intellectual and emotional challenges of this research.

Being a 'woman in the surf': reflections on researching a culture of commitment

> You can't write about surfing if you aren't a surfer. A lot of writers have tried over the years, and I think they've done the sport a lot of damage by making it appear silly, frivolous, and self-indulgent.
>
> (Doyle 1993: 37)

Early in the research process it became apparent that my role as a proficient and active windsurfer was vital in gaining access to this subculture. As discussed, sporting prowess and commitment were two central values of this culture and were necessary to participate in the activities of the group. To retain my legitimacy in the subculture as a participant, I had to go out windsurfing, at least for a short time. The few times I tried to avoid sailing, windsurfers at the beach made comments like: 'Are you an actor or a wind-surfer' or 'Stop being such a girlie and get out there'. As one of my interviewees suggested, reflecting on her own initiation into the wind-surfing scene, by 'hanging out at the beach' she learnt 'insider knowledge' about the sport – in particular, the argot and value system. However, without giving windsurfing 'a go', displaying commitment, she felt excluded by the windsurfing community:

> Actually just watching it helps – just being around and watching it and seeing people sail and things. So you can talk to them about their sailing and stuff. And just actually being willing to go down to the beach and hang around. But I think it's quite hard to get really accepted if you don't do it.
>
> (Debby)

As a female participant attempting to negotiate access into a male-domi-nated world, this ability to participate in the activity was especially important. My research revealed that within the subculture a range of competing femininities existed among these predominantly middle-class, white, heterosexual, 'privileged' women. These identities ranged from the 'windsurfing widows' – those women who participated in the lifestyle but didn't or rarely actually windsurfed – to the 'real women', a member-identi-fied term, used by windsurfers to distinguish the competent committed 'core' women (see Wheaton and Tomlinson 1998). The identities of 'real women', or 'core' women, were embedded in 'being a windsurfer' foremost. These women saw themselves as different from the windsurfing widows and, in some cases, actively differentiated themselves from them, particularly the 'girlies', whose identity they saw as based around 'emphasised femininity' (Connell 1995). The windsurfing widows had a lower status in the subcul-ture based on their low commitment to the windsurfing activity, and thus were a subordinated femininity. Widows I interviewed were aware of their subordinate statuses and discussed how they felt as relative 'outsiders':

> It makes me feel a bit unimportant because I can't windsurf very well, so they won't be interested in me, so I felt a bit of an outsider.
>
> (Fiona)

The role I adopted was that of the 'core woman'. Based on my windsurfing proficiency and perceived commitment to the sport, I was able to participate in most sporting and social activities. I even had access to interactions between men in the 'locker room' – women and men shared the changing room, although women were designated to a small curtained area in the corner. My access to the elite windsurfers – the men at the core of the culture – was based on my 'one-of-the-lads' status – that I could windsurf as well as them. As Stephanie, a committed female interviewee, explained, elite men treated her as one of them. 'As a token lad, I think. I mean I think I get quite a lot of respect for having a go, and getting out there and doing it.'

While this 'token lad' status was defined and negotiated in male terms, it was a role associated with masculinity. Like my female interviewees, I did not experience a sense of exclusion from being female and a windsurfer. The committed 'core' women in this study argued that their leisure experiences and identities shared many aspects with the windsurfing men. Due to this status, I had almost full access to the men's activities and conversations, including the times when their own female partners weren't 'welcome' in the group. In contrast, while observing the surfing groups at the same locations, I did not have the same access to the group. I do not think this is solely because the surfers were more sexist and excluding of female surfers (see Stedman 1997, Pearson 1982, who discuss the sexist, misogynist nature of the surfing culture). Rather, it was due to being both female and a *novice*. These dual axes of otherness clearly marked my positioning as 'non-surfer'. Moreover, although I did go out 'surfing', the craft I used was a 'boogie-board', which many surfers consider as inferior to the surfboard (forms of abuse include calling boogie boards, and people who use them, sponges, shark biscuits, etc.). This, in conjunction with my incompetence at the sport, denied me the same access I had to the windsurfing subculture.

Yet, my role as an active participant also caused unexpected problems. I wanted to understand the experiences of the 'windsurfing widows', who seemed to me to be an important part of the culture, with their own separate 'scene'. In particular, their experiences were important in understanding the exclusion process and barriers to participation. Because of my windsurfing role, I was denied access to their private activities and often their conversations. Being a woman did not in any way give me a 'way in' – my identity as a windsurfer, as one of the 'lads', made me as much the 'other' as their own male partners. I used informants – widows with whom I socialised, often the girlfriends of my windsurfing buddies – to establish links with at least some sections of this group. I also drew on my own experiences of being a beginner windsurfer, which time I spent 'just watching' my very skilful (male) partner. Like the women I observed in the same situation, I had probably been perceived to be a 'widow'. Nevertheless, I never really permeated this group of women.

'I ain't no beach babe': (re)making boundaries

One of the hardest tasks, personally and analytically, was understanding and explaining the ambiguities of gender relations in the windsurfing culture, specifically the experiences and exclusion of 'core' women windsurfers. My initial unwillingness to concede that the women in the subculture were being excluded, and wanting to privilege, give authenticity to the 'voices' of the 'active women' was because of my own personal subjectivity as a wind-surfer, and as a woman, as 'one of them'. In this, more than any other part of the project, I was a subject of my own research, and the research became my biography. I had my own experiences of being both a windsurfing 'widow' (albeit very briefly), and my existing role as a 'real woman'; I was my own 'native' informant. Like the women I researched, I found windsurfing an exhilarating experience that gave me a huge sense of self-achievement and confidence in myself and, as their narratives illustrated, for 'us' it was a physically and emotionally empowering experience.

I had documented the barriers that women faced, and understood the pervasiveness of the cultural and structural causes of female exclusion. Yet, like other female participants, I found it hard to understand why and how anyone could watch the activity without becoming involved. As Debby recounted: 'It just seemed such a waste of anybody's life to sit in the car'. I did not feel unity or a bond of 'womanhood' with the non-active wind-surfing widows. The differences between women in this context – specifically between their subcultural roles – were more significant than their 'shared femininity'. Despite the similarities in class, 'race', nationality and often age between the women I researched and myself, there was still a 'difference' based on subcultural commitment and status.

Most of the time I was windsurfing I thought of myself as a 'windsurfer', not specifically as a woman. My gender was not at the 'forefront' of [my] awareness' – it was as Riley (1988) suggests, a passive identity:

> It's having an identity as a person who is empowered to do their own thing, really or – you know, a professional identity is important, I think too. I don't like the idea of being just someone's wife, or mother, or whatever. ... It's given me a sense of identity, that is detached from other people.
>
> (Stephanie)

Nevertheless, the multiple and sometimes conflicting identities that individual women experienced were mirrored in my own fieldwork experiences. As the following two excerpts from my field diary illustrate, such dissonance in my subcultural femininity was most explicit when focusing on the experiences of the younger male elite whom I termed 'the lads'. It was during the times I was with the really 'laddish' men that I felt 'different' – specifically excluded as a woman:

it was a very weird feeling. In one sense it was hard to be 'female' and a windsurfer. All the guys started talking and bantering about the women. Suddenly being a windsurfer no longer matters. In fact when that happens it seems that my role of 'windsurfer and one of the lads' changed instantly to an outsider. It is not as if they expect me to join in the banter, in fact I become invisible – they seem to forget that I am there. But, at these times, I feel a role conflict between being a woman, and a windsurfer. … No one actually said anything to make me feel that way, it is just a sense of being a woman, the object of their banter, that is strange and uncomfortable.

It is hard to be involved with 'the lads' … James was in one breath saying how well I got on wakeboarding, how I really 'went for it' – judging my performance as one of them – a lad. Then in the next breath starting to discuss whether the women who windsurf are attractive, grading the women like objects. So it seems that by their standards, we have to be both 'really go for it on the water' and in other sports, but also look attractive. I certainly feel more comfortable with the former role.

I found this laddish behaviour shocking in that I was suddenly and unexpectedly no longer one of the group. I felt an acute sense of difference, based on my identity as a woman but, significantly, as a *heterosexual* women – the object of their banter. I was being 'judged', not on my windsurfing ability – my 'athleticism', but as a sexualised object. Yet I, like the women I interviewed, did not identify with this image of feminity. For 'us' being 'attractive' was not seen as an important factor underlying why we windsurfed or became involved with windsurfing. And, as my interviewees had claimed, being overly concerned about appearance, or displaying 'emphasised femininity' by looking the 'beach babe', was deemed the sphere of the 'girlies' and the non-serious women windsurfers, who were 'only really involved with windsurfing for social reasons or to attract the attention of men'. Thus it was an identity serious women windsurfers resisted. Nevertheless, 'core' women's narratives, and my own experiences, suggested that we acknowledged that we were judged – at least by the lads – on how we looked, as well as on our windsurfing ability and commitment.[8]

On reflection, I came to realise that these experiences were revealing in demonstrating the ways in which my feminity was framed specifically as *heterosexual*. Flintoff (1997) demonstrates how her assumed heterosexuality impacted her field role in her research in school PE culture (also exposing her potential vulnerability as a female researcher). The windsurfing culture was undeniably heterosexist and, as I have explored in relation to masculinities, heterosexual prowess was a central way that difference between men was marked (see Wheaton 2000b). However, my own heterosexuality was an assumed, but never explicitly addressed, identity. I did not appreciate the 'compulsory' character of my heterosexuality, perhaps because, as Kitzinger and Wilkinson (1996) note, when heterosexuality is experienced as pleasurable it feels 'natural and innate' (Bartky 1993). This is symptomatic of a wider neglect and lack of understanding of heterosexuality. As Kitzinger and Wilkinson (1996) outline, despite a plethora of research examining the ways in which individuals construct gay and lesbian identities, and the discursive practices and political contexts under which these identities are produced and reproduced, there is still remarkably little research examining the social construction of heterosexuality.

In the next section, I explore how my whiteness, like my heterosexuality, was a 'taken-for-granted', naturalised and, thus, hidden axis of my 'insider status'.

Tanned skin, white beach

> One effect of colonial discourse is the production of an unmarked, apparently autonomous white/Western self, in contrast with the marked, Other racial and cultural category with which the racially and culturally dominant category is coconstructed.
>
> (Frankenberg 1993: 17)

The windsurfing culture in Great Britain was almost exclusively a white space. Yet I did not take into account how whiteness was an identity that was an integral part of the process of 'self'-presentation and construction of the windsurfer. As Frankenberg (1993: 17) outlines, 'the white Western self as a racial being has for the most part remained unexamined and unnamed'. In the sporting context, this failure to 'unmask' and 'name' whiteness, and to challenge the structures and practices that maintain its privileged position – particularly gendered whiteness – is especially pronounced (Scraton 2001).

Yet, despite this burgeoning literature examining whiteness as a racial category, methodological issues have received less attention. As Carrington (forthcoming) observes, considerable literature has focused on the dilemmas for white social scientists researching non-white cultures, yet for researchers from the same ethnic background it is assumed to be unproblematic. 'Race is only perceived to be an issue when white researchers begin to investigate the racial Other' (*ibid.*). These accounts, he argues, 'tend to portray racial identities as fixed and unchanging, negating the very contested nature of their construction' (*ibid.*).

My experiences support these claims. The only times I started to unpack issues of whiteness as a lived identity was when confronted with the racial 'Other' – in this specific case, the Polynesian males in Hawaii. 'The dominance of white culture and identity makes it invisible, other than as "difference" to the status of non-white groups' (Griffin 1996: 137). In Hawaii, the racial conflict between Polynesians and 'haolies' (the white 'colonialists') is well documented in the surfing media and popular literature (see Doyle 1993; Booth 1995), and plays a central part in understanding tensions between surfers and windsurfers (predominantly 'haolies'), as well as so-called 'localism' – or turf wars – in the surf culture. This competitiveness among and between male surfers and windsurfers from different geographical locations was based in part on competing masculine identities and cultural styles (differing attitudes to the meaning of surfing and surfing styles). However, as Doyle (1993) proposes in the context of surfing in Hawaii, differences in class, nationality and, particularly, ethnicity is central to this often aggressive exclusion process in the surfing and windsurfing culture.

In Hawaii I was a cultural-outsider, a 'haole' (white person), but not 'Euro' (Europeans who tended to be characterised as blonde), and critically I wasn't male. As one blond male windsurfer told me: 'Maui is the only place I know where you are a hell of a lot safer walking the streets as a woman, than as a blond-haired male' (field notes, Maui). As a woman, despite my 'whiteness', I was more able than some men to avoid confrontation and potential exclusion from parts of the surf culture. Similarly, in the Dominican Republic, surfing with a group of Hispanic male surfers, my male partner – who was blond – was told by our 'gatekeeper', a local Hispanic surfer, to 'keep his head down, not to drop in on any locals'. Again, while we were both outsiders to the group, context and culture, my positioning as 'outsider' was different as a 'dark-haired female surfer' to my partner as a 'blond-haired male surfer'. In both locales the discourses of localism perpetuated racially coded representations of the indigenous populations (of surfers) as 'hostile' and 'violent'.

I recount these incidents to illustrate that, in the main part, I *failed* to acknowledge and reflexively unpack the ways in which my white ethnicity was constructed, or how whiteness, like other racial identities, is subject to change and contestation.

Closing comments

This chapter has tried to raise and exemplify a number of the methodological issues and tensions that emerged during my ethnographic research on windsurfing, which are indicative of current debates around adopting critical ethnography. Its scope has been somewhat ambitious and so, rather than attempting to come to any overarching conclusions, I summarise the key issues I have addressed.

I have described some of the methodological issues and problems associated with a female researcher doing research in a male-dominated setting, illustrating that my positioning as a 'core', white, middle-class, heterosexual female was pivotal. While the researcher's self-identity and experiences may not inflexibly *determine* particular perspectives, 'they do give researchers variable standpoints in relation to the subjects of the research' (Holland and

Ramazanoglu 1994: 13, cited in Flintoff 1997: 169). However, these stand-points are also multiple and change temporally, spatially and contextually. My positioning in the subculture was more complex than consideration of gender or any epistemological standpoint alone. Similarly, I have argued that, in the light of this research, the methodological distinction between insider and outsider seems a misleading binary that does not fit with my experiences as a fieldworker. As Atkinson suggests: 'No ethnographer can ever claim to have been one or the other in an absolute sense. The very fact of negotiating one's status in the community precludes any such possibility' (Hertzfeld 1983: 151, cited in Atkinson 1990: 157). Such a categorisation fails to recognise the different ways in which *difference* is constructed and contested, and the multiple and shifting identities and boundaries negoti-ated and experienced during the research process.

These issues lead me into reiterating the implications of this ethno-graphic project for understanding gender, identity and power. John Sugden and Alan Tomlinson have argued for the retrieval of the 'investigative ethno-graphic tradition' for the sociology of sport as a way to 'stimulate democratic reform' (1999: 386). My interpretation of this challenge is to underline that questions of power are central to the ethnographic process, and that knowl-edge production is an inherently political process. This chapter illustrates that ethnographic research is particularly well suited for examining the rela-tionship between 'experience, identity, politics and power' (Griffin 1996: 181) – for example, to examine the cultural construction and contestation of masculinities, and other identities, through sport. Ethnographic research is well suited to teasing out and exposing both the conditions in which men can and do mobilise patriarchal forms of power and how men's structural position affects men differently – that is, how men experience power in different ways, particularly in relation to their positioning in terms of 'race', class, age and sexuality, and subcultural status (see Griffin 1996). Moreover, as this research illustrates, there are also occasions when particular types of women benefit from their power relations through their heterosexuality, class and ethnicity, and subcultural positioning. By critically reflecting on my own shifting identity position, I have shown how the 'participant observer's gender identity become entwined with the process of knowing' (Back 1993: 218). Such a process has helped to gain a fuller understanding of identity (re)construction – both masculinities and feminities – and of the meanings made by participants in and of this sporting culture.

Methodologically, I have argued for a reflexive approach to critical ethnography, one that denies a single interpretative truth or reality, chal-lenging the positivistic foundationalist understanding of 'scientific' validity and objectivity. In a process in which the role and authority of the ethnogra-pher is problematised (Fontana 1994), the dialogue between the researcher and the informants is emphasised (Marcus and Fisher 1986), and the researcher, as a member of the culture, becomes their own 'native informant' (Grossberg 1994: 58).

Perhaps the hardest analytical task for an ethnographer is to negotiate a path that understands and acknowledges the participants' worldview, their subjectivities, yet also gains that critical distance that is needed to situate those views and actions into wider social structures. This is not just about demystifying the familiar, but involves analysing the respondents' views and then engaging with those views from a 'different perspective'. However this difference can be marked in multiple ways, and unequal power relations are always part of this location process. Moreover, this research alerts us to the ways in which as researchers we often fail to 'see' the parts of our 'selves' that are most personal and most obvious. The autobiographical voice can be used to question 'the relation of the self to experience, researchers to researched and the production of knowledge itself' (Probyn 1993: 105). Whether the researcher's original positioning is insider or outsider, the critical distance is achieved through the processes of constructing or writing the ethnography, and centrally experiencing and grappling with the constant and multiple tensions between 'self' and 'other' (Atkinson 1990). This recognition of, and attention to, the reflexive situating of the researcher to their subjects, perhaps inevitably, ends up as a biography of self.

Notes

1   That my study was centrally a study of whiteness took me even longer to comprehend, and I largely failed to develop an integrated race and gender reflexivity in my analysis.
2   These authors also point to the work of 1930s philosophers, such as Wittgenstein, as well as earlier strands of late nineteenth-century sociology influenced by German philosophy (Stanley and Wise 1993: 190). Initiatives to reduce the researcher's authority were considered, if not adopted, by the Chicago School ethnographers.
3   I say broadly, as I am aware that by labelling my position, I am perhaps masking the complexity inherent in both constructionism and critical theory approaches, and the 'multiple discourses that now circulate' around such qualitative research paradigms (Denzin and Lincoln 1994; 100).
4   These feminist epistemological stances range from the realist–empiricist to postmodern feminist positions, which have been outlined in great depth elsewhere (see Abbott and Wallace 1997; Stanley and Wise 1993). Moreover, as Stanley and Wise (1993: 190) outline, it is important to recognise that feminist epistemologies are a model – a simplified rather than literal account of epistemological possibilities that exist – and that in practice feminists combine elements of a number of epistemologies, which, as Abbott and Wallace (1997) suggest, is indicative of the contradictory nature of social reality.
5   This debate highlights the ways in which a false dualism is often constructed between 'standpoint epistemology' and 'scientific realism' (cf. Sokal 1999; Ward 1997). In this dualism, all 'standpoint positions' are unproblematically assumed to be equivalent.
6   It is for this reason that Stanley and Wise (1993) reject the direct identification of 'feminist research' with certain methods, particularly the assumption that qualitative methods are inherently preferable because of being less sexist.
7   I was working as a freelancer for a British windsurfing magazine. For a discussion of how I negotiated the ethnical issues that emerged in this role,

particularly the power inequalities in the journalist–interviewee relationship, see Wheaton (1997a, b).

8   It is interesting to note the ways in which, both in my field notes and this narrative, I move from the pronoun *them* (or *windsurfers*) to *we* and *us*, again indicating the fluidity of my insider and outsider relations.

References

Abbott, P. and Wallace, C. (1997) 'The production of feminist knowledges', in P. Abbott and C. Wallace (eds) *An Introduction to Sociology: Feminist Perspectives*, London: Routledge.

Atkinson, P. (1990) *The Ethnographic Imagination: Textual Constructions of Reality*, London: Routledge.

Back, L. (1993) 'Gendered participation: masculinity and fieldwork in a south London adolescent community', in D. Bell, P. Caplan and W. Jahan Karim (eds) *Gendered Fields: Women, Men and Ethnography*, London: Routledge.

Bartky, S. (1993) 'Hypatia unbound: a confession', in C. Kitzinger and S. Wilkinson (eds) *Heterosexuality: A Feminism and Psychology Reader*, London: Sage.

Bell, D. (1993) 'Yes Virgina, there is a feminist ethnography. Reflections from three Australian fields', in D. Bell, P. Caplan and W. Jahan Karim (eds) *Gendered Fields: Women, Men and Ethnography*, London: Routledge.

Booth, D. (1995) 'Ambiguities in pleasure and discipline: the development of competitive surfing', *Journal of Sport History* 22: 189–206.

Brake, M. (1980) *The Sociology of Youth Culture and Youth Subcultures*, London: Routledge & Kegan Paul.

Bruce, T. (1998) 'Postmodernism and the possibilities for writing "vital" sports texts', in G. Rail (ed.) *Sport and Postmodern Times*, Albany: SUNY.

Bruce, T. and Greendorfer, S. (1994) 'Postmodern challenges: recognising multiple standards for social science research', *Journal of Sport and Social Issues* 18(4): 258–68.

Bryman, A. and Burgess, R. (1994) *Analysing Qualitative Data*, London and New York: Routledge.

Burgess, R., Pole, C., Evans, K. and Priestley, C. (1994) 'Four studies from one or one study from four? Multi-site case study research', in A. Bryman. and R. Burgess (eds) *Analysing Qualitative Data*, London and New York: Routledge.

Cain, M. (1993) 'Foucault, feminism and feeling. What Foucault can and cannot contribute to feminist epistemology', in C. Ramazonoglu (ed.) *Up Against Foucault: Explorations of Some Tensions Between Foucault and Feminism*, London: Routledge.

Carrington, B. (forthcoming) 'Black skin, white flannels: a study of the role of sport in the construction of black identity', unpublished PhD thesis, University of Leeds.

Clifford, J. and Marcus, G. (1986) *Writing Culture: The Poetics and Politics of Ethnography*, Berkley: University of California Press.

Cole, C. (1991) 'The politics of cultural representation: visions of fields/fields of vision', *International Review for Sociology of Sport* 26(1): 37–49.

Connell, R. (1995) *Masculinities*, Cambridge: Polity Press.

Denzin, N. (1994a) 'The art and politics of interpretation', in N. Denzin. and Y. Lincoln (eds) *Handbook of Qualitative Research*, Thousand Oaks, CA: Sage.

—— (1994b) 'The Fifth Moment', in Denzin, N. and Lincoln, Y. (eds) *Handbook of Qualitative Research*, Thousand Oaks, CA: Sage: 575–86.

Denzin, N. and Lincoln, Y. (1994) *Handbook of Qualitative Research*, Thousand Oaks, CA: Sage.

Donnelly, P. (1981) 'Toward a definition of sport subcultures', in M. Hart and S. Birrell (eds) *Sport in the Sociocultural Process*, 3rd edn, Dubuque, Iowa: Wm. C. Brown.

—— (1985) 'Sport subcultures', *Exercise and Sport Sciences Review* 13: 539–78.

Doyle, M. (1993) *Morning Glass: The Adventures of a Legendary Waterman*, Three Rivers, CA: Manzantia Press.

Finch, J. (1993) ' "Its great to have someone to talk to": the ethics and politics of interviewing women', in M. Hammersley (ed.) *Social Research: Philosophy, Politics and Practice*, London: Sage.

Flintoff, A. (1997) 'Gender relations in physical education initial teacher education', in G. Clarke and B. Humberstone (eds) *Researching Women and Sport*, Basingstoke: Macmillan.

Foley, D. (1992) 'Making the familiar strange: writing critical sport narratives', *Sociology of Sport Journal* 9(1): 36–47.

Fontana, A. (1994) 'Ethnographic trends in the postmodern era', in D. Dickens and A. Fontana (eds) *Postmodernism and Social Enquiry*, London: UCL Press.

Frankenberg, R. (1993) *White Women, Race Matters: The Social Construction of Whiteness*, London: Routledge.

Giulianotti, R. (1995) 'Participant observation and research into football hooliganism: reflections on the problems of entree and everyday risks', *Sociology of Sport Journal*, 12(1): 1–20.

Griffin, C. (1996) 'Experiencing power: dimensions of gender, "race" and class', in N. Charles and F. Hughes-Freeland (eds) *Practising Feminism: Identity, Difference, Power*, London: Routledge.

Grossberg, L. (1994) 'The formations of cultural studies: an American in Birmingham', in V. Blundell, J. Shepherd and I. Taylor (eds) *Relocating Cultural Studies: Developments in Theory and Research*, London and New York: Routledge.

Hammersley, M. (1992a) *What's Wrong With Ethnography: Methodological Explorations*, London: Routledge.

—— (1992b) 'On feminist methodology', *Sociology* 26(2): 187–206.

Hammersley, M. and Atkinson, P. (1995) *Ethnography: Principles in Practice*, London and New York: Routledge.

Harding, S. (1991) *Whose Science? Whose Knowledge? Thinking From Women's Lives*, Milton Keynes: Open University Press.

Hartsock, S. (1987) 'The feminist standpoint', in S. Harding (ed.) *Feminism and Methodology*, Bloomington: Indiana University Press.

Hebdige, D. (1979) *Subculture, the Meaning of Style*, London and New York: Routledge.

Hill Collins, P. (1986) 'Learning from the outsider within: the sociological significance of Black feminist thought', *Social Problems* 33: 14–32.

hooks, B. (1982) *Ain't I a Woman? Black Women and Feminism*, Boston, MA: South Park Press.

Hughson, J. (1998) 'Among the thugs: the "new ethnographies" of football supporting subcultures', *International Review for Sociology of Sport* 33(1): 42–57.

Kincheloe, J. and McLaren, P. (1994) 'Rethinking critical theory and qualitative research', in N. Denzin and Y. Lincoln (eds) *Handbook of Qualitative Research*, Thousand Oaks, CA: Sage.

Kitzinger, C. and Wilkinson, S. (1996) 'Deconstructing heterosexuality: a feminist social-constructionlist analysis', in N. Charles and F. Hughes-Freeland (eds) *Practising Feminism: Identity, Difference, Power*, London: Routledge.

Kohn, N. and Sydor, S. (1998) '"How do you warm up for a stretch class?" Sub/In/Di/verting hegemonic shoves towards sport', in G. Rail (ed.) *Sport and Postmodern Times*, Albany: SUNY.

Lincoln, Y. and Denzin, N. (1994) 'The art of interpretation, evaluation, and presentation', in N. Denzin and Y. Lincoln (eds) *Handbook of Qualitative Research*, Thousand Oaks, CA: Sage.

Marcus, G. and Cushman, M. (1982) 'Ethnographies as text', *Annual Review of Anthropology* 11: 25–69.

Marcus, G.E. and Fisher, M.J. (1986) *Anthropology As Cultural Critique: An Experimental Moment in the Human Sciences*, Chicago: University of Chicago Press.

Messner, M. and Sabo, D. (1990) *Sport, Men and the Gender Order: Critical Feminist Perspectives*, Champaign, Illinois: Human Kinetic Books.

Morgan, D. (1992) *Discovering Men*, London and New York: Routledge.

Pearson, K. (1982) 'Conflict, stereotypes and masculinity in Australian and New Zealand surfing', *Australian and New Zealand Journal of Sociology* 18: 117–35.

Pink Dandelion, B. (1997), 'Insider dealing: researching your own private world', in A. Tomlinson and S. Fleming (eds) *Ethics, Sport and Leisure: Crises and Critiques*, Aachen: Meyer & Meyer.

Probyn, E. (1993) 'True voices and real people: the problem of the autobiographical in cultural studies', in V. Blundell, J. Shepherd and I. Taylor (eds) *Relocating Cultural Studies*, London: Routledge.

Redhead, S. (1993) *Rave Off: Politics and Deviance in Contemporary Youth Culture*, Aldershot: Avebury.

Richardson, L. (1994) 'Writing: a method of inquiry', in N. Denzin and Y. Lincoln (eds) *Handbook of Qualitative Research*, Thousand Oaks, CA: Sage.

—— (2000) 'New writing practices in qualitative research', *Sociology of Sport Journal* 17(1): 5–20.

Riley, D. (1988) *Am I That Name?* London: Routledge.

Rinehart, R. (1998a) 'Born-again sport: ethics in biographical research', in G. Rail (ed.) *Sport and Postmodern Times*, Albany: SUNY.

—— (1998b) *Players All: Performances in Contemporary Sport*, Bloomington and Indianapolis: Indiana University Press.

Roseneil, S. (1993) 'Greenham revisited: researching myself and my sisters', in D. Hobbs and T. May (eds) *Interpreting the Field: Accounts of Ethnography*, Oxford: Clarendon Press.

Said, E. (1989) 'Representing the colonized: anthropology's interlocutors', *Critical Inquiry*, 15: 205–25.

Scraton, S. (1987) '"Boy's muscle in where angels fear to tread": girls' sub-cultures and physical activities', in J. Horne, D. Jary and A. Tomlinson (eds) *Sport, Leisure and Social Relations*, London: Routledge & Kegan Paul.

—— (2001) 'Reconceptualizing race, gender and sport: the contribution of black feminism', in B. Carrington and I. McDonald (eds) *'Race', Sport and British Society*, London: Routledge.

Smith, D. (1987) *The Everyday World As Problematic: A Feminist Sociology*, Boston: Northeastern University Press.

Sokal, A.D. (1999) *Intellectual Impostures: Postmodern Philosophers' Abuse of Science*, London: Profile.

Song, M. and Parker, D. (1995) 'Commonality, difference and the dynamics of disclosure in in-depth interviewing', *Sociology* 29(2): 241–56.

Sparkes, A. (1996) 'The fatal flaw: a narrative of the fragile body-self', *Qualitative Inquiry* 2: 463–94.

—— (1998) 'Athletic identity: an Achilles' heel to the survival of self', *Qualitative Health Research* 8: 644–64.

—— (2000) 'Autoethnography and narratives of self: reflections on criteria in action', *Sociology of Sport Journal* 17(1): 21–43.

Spracklen, K. (1996) 'Playing the ball: constructing community and masculine identity in sport', unpublished PhD thesis, Leeds.

Stacey, J. (1988) 'Can there be a feminist ethnography?', *Women's Studies International Forum*, 11: 21–7.

Stanley, L. and Wise, S. (1993) *Breaking Out Again*, Routledge.

Stedman, L. (1997) 'From gidget to gonad man: surfers, feminists and postmodernisation', *Australian and New Zealand Journal of Sociology* 33: 75–90.

Strauss, A. and Corbin, J. (1990) *Basics of Qualitative Research*, Sage.

Strauss, A. and Corbin, J. (1994) 'Grounded theory methodology: an overview', in M. Miles and M. Huberman (eds) *Qualitative Data Analysis*, Thousand Oaks, California: Sage.

Sugden, J. (1997) 'Fieldworkers rush in (where theorists fear to tread): the perils of ethnography', in A. Tomlinson and S. Fleming (eds) *Ethics, Sport and Leisure: Crises and Critiques*, Aachen: Meyer & Meyer.

Sugden, J. and Tomlinson, A. (1999) 'Digging the dirt and staying clean: retrieving the investigative tradition for a critical sociology of sport', *International Review for Sociology of Sport* 34(4): 385 – 97.

Thornton, A. (1998) 'Ultimate masculinities: an ethnography of power and social difference in sport', unpublished PhD thesis, Ontario Institute for Studies in Education of the University of Ontario.

Thornton, S. (1997) 'General introduction', in K. Gelder and S. Thornton (eds) *The Subcultures Reader*, London and New York: Routledge.

Van Maanen, J. (1988) *Tales of the Field: On Writing Ethnography*, Chicago: University of Chicago Press.

Ward, S. (1997) 'Being objective about objectivity: the ironies of standpoint epistemological critiques of science', *Sociology* 31(4): 773–91.

Wheaton, B. (1997a) 'Consumption, lifestyle and gendered identities in postmodern sports: the case of windsurfing', unpublished PhD thesis, University of Brighton.

—— (1997b) 'Covert ethnography and the ethics of research: studying sport subcultures', in A.Tomlinson and S. Fleming (eds) *Ethics, Sport and Leisure: Crises and Critiques*, Aachen: Meyer & Meyer.

—— (2000a) 'Just do it: consumption, commitment and identity in the windsurfing subculture', *Sociology of Sport Journal* 17(3): 254–74.

—— (2000b) ' "New Lads?" Masculinities and the new sport participant', *Men and Masculinities* 2: 436–58.

Wheaton, B. and Tomlinson, A. (1998) 'The changing gender order in sport? The case of windsurfing', *Journal of Sport and Social Issues* 22(3): 252–74.

Woods, P. (1986), 'Observation', in *Inside Schools*, London: Routledge.

14 Sport, masculinity and black cultural resistance

Ben Carrington

On sport's level playing field, it is possible to challenge and overturn the dominant hierarchies of nation, race and class. The reversal may be limited and transient, but it is nonetheless real. It is, therefore, wrong to see black sporting achievement merely as an index of oppression; it is equally an index of creativity and resistance, collective and individual.

(Mike Marqusee 1995: 5)

Introduction

This chapter traces the meanings associated with sport in relation to black masculinity by examining the role of sport as a form of cultural resistance to the ideologies and practices of white racism.[1] First, an argument for the use of ethnographic case study methods within cultural studies is made. The chapter then shows the absences within contemporary sociology of sport theorising around 'race' that has led to incomplete understandings of the complex ways in which gender is articulated with and through discourses of 'race'. It is argued that it is necessary to produce more critical theorisations of the intersections of 'race' with gender, nation and class if we are to fully appreciate how social identities are constructed. A theoretical account follows of the historical and contemporary significance of sport within racialised societies (the 'racial signification of sport'). These arguments are then explored in more detail by an empirical analysis. Drawing on participant observation and in-depth semi-structured interviews, an account is given of how a black cricket club in the north of England is used by black men as both a form of resistance to white racism and as a symbolic marker of the local black community. Three themes are traced in this regard: namely, (i) the construction of black sports institutions as 'black spaces'; (ii) the use of black sports clubs as symbolic markers of community identity; and (iii) the role of cricket as an arena of both symbolic and material, racial and masculine contestation. The chapter attempts, therefore, to advance the state of knowledge concerning the meanings, importance and social significance of sport within black communities which, as a number of commentators have acknowledged (Hargreaves 1986; Williams 1994), is currently inadequate.[2]

Cultural studies and the ethnographic case study

> Popular culture is a site where the construction of everyday life may be examined. The point of doing this is not only academic – that is, as an attempt to understand a process or practice – it is also political, to examine the power relations that constitute this form of everyday life and thus to reveal the configuration of interests its construction serves.
>
> (Turner 1996: 6)

From Richard Hoggart's (1958) *Uses of Literacy* through to Paul Willis's (1977) *Learning to Labour* and beyond, ethnographic research methodologies have been central to the development of cultural studies as a critical field of study.[3] The development of qualitative methodologies has been vital in allowing cultural studies to develop 'grounded analyses' of the complex and subtle ways in which people come to understand culture and identity as unfinished social processes, connecting both wider structures of power to the lived experience of individual and collective actors. This point is taken up by Alasuutari (1995) when he argues that qualitative analysis is more suited to deal with the question of 'culture' and with explaining meaningful action. Thus 'cultural studies means that one takes culture seriously, without reducing it to a mere effect or reflection of, for instance, economy. On the other hand, cultural studies treats culture and systems of meaning in connection with questions of power and politics' (*ibid.*: 2).

Culture should be seen, in part, as the result of the processes of social interaction, therefore attention needs to be paid to the *symbolic* dimensions of these multi-faceted forms in constructing notions of self and Other through cultural practices. Thus how people themselves create collective meanings through their everyday activities, as well as the conditions within which this is possible, are central issues for cultural studies analysis. Cultural studies is fundamentally concerned therefore with questions of power, identity and meaning. In seeking to locate and trace the ways in which cultural practices enable agents to give meaning to their lives, it politicises the act of cultural participation/consumption and extends political economic readings of the effects of cultural activities beyond the predetermined 'moment of production'. In effect, cultural studies grapples with the twin polars of subordination–resistance within the realm of the everyday. As Grossberg summarises:

> Cultural studies does assume that people live their subordination actively; that means, in one sense, that they are often complicit in their own subordination, that they accede to it, although power often works through strategies and apparatuses of which people are totally unaware. Be that as it may, cultural studies does believe that if one is to challenge the existing structures of power, one has to understand how that complicity, that participation in power, is constructed and lived, and

that means looking not only at what people gain from such practices, but also at the possibilities for rearticulating such practices to escape, resist, or even oppose particular structures of power.

(Grossberg 1997: 8)

However, in recent years there have been some worrying developments that have failed to follow through the earlier thrust of cultural studies, exemplified in the work of Raymond Williams and Stuart Hall, amongst others, which have sought to keep questions of social inequality, power and cultural politics as central concerns. One has been the drift towards 'cultural populism' where analyses of the connections between the 'consumption' and meanings of popular cultural forms and the economic basis of its production – that is, a theorisation of a *critical* political economy of culture – have been lost, leading to what some have labelled an uncritical celebration of popular culture and a tacit endorsement of the logic of consumer capitalism (McGuigan 1992; Murdock 1997).

A separate, but related, concern emerging from the influence of literary theory and certain deconstructionist perspectives can be seen in the growth within cultural studies of reading and interpreting cultural texts isolated from any social context – that is, textual analysis divorced from material relations of power, or what McRobbie has referred to as the 'textual trap' (1994: 39). This has led to the valorisation of often incomprehensibly obscure theoretical debates – a form of elitist theoreticism which produces 'a particularly self-regarding kind of writing, couched in an exclusive and intimidating jargon that is deployed as proof of the academic seriousness of the field of study and its objects' (Turner 1996: 5).[4] Against some of these trends, the current work via the theoretical and historical analysis and the ethnographic material presented seeks to develop a more integrative mode of analysis that blends the historical, structural and ethnographic (Hall and Jefferson 1976) in tracing the political possibilities of people's involvement with a particular cultural practice.

Black masculinity and the limits to sports sociology theorising

In analysing the historical development and social significance of sports during the nineteenth and early twentieth century, it is now commonplace within the sociology of sport to assert that sport functioned as a key male homosocial institution whereby 'manly virtues and competencies' could be both learned and displayed as a way of avoiding wider social, political and economic processes of 'feminisation' – sport, in effect, symbolising and reinforcing a patriarchal structure of domination over women. However, such accounts have consistently failed to acknowledge that this view can only be sustained if the inherently *racialised* nature of social relationships and the position of black peoples within Western societies generally, and within sport in particular, is ignored. Historically, the entry of black males into the social institutions of sport was conditional with formal segregation, particularly in America, often imposed. When black males did compete directly and publicly with whites, such competition was organised on the premise that the 'white man' would eventually win, thereby maintaining the racial order, and where this could not be guaranteed the prohibition of blacks was quickly instated. Thus, the claim that is repeatedly made concerning sport's early development as the preservation of male authority needs to be extended as it more accurately relates to the preservation of certain heterosexual notions of *white* male identity and authority. To acknowledge this challenges many of the Eurocentric accounts which have inadvertently been guilty of reproducing, in their analyses, racist discourses that have denied both the importance, and the very presence, of black peoples throughout the modern history of the West.[5]

A notable exception to such accounts can be found in the work of Messner (1992, 1997), who has argued that men's historical and contemporary experiences in sport clearly demonstrate that it is overly simplistic to view sport as a patriarchal institution that reinforces men's domination and power over women. Rather, 'the rise of sport as a social institution in the late nineteenth and early twentieth centuries had at least as much to do with men's class and *racial relationships* with other men as it did with men's relations with women' (Messner 1992: 17, emphasis added). Messner continues:

> we can see that the turn-of-the-century 'crisis of masculinity' was, in actuality, a crisis of legitimation for *hegemonic* masculinity. In other words, upper- and middle-class, white, urban heterosexual men were the most threatened by modernization, by changes in the social organization of work, by the New Woman's movement into public life, by feminism, and by the working-class, ethnic minority, immigrant, and gay men.
>
> (*ibid.*: 18)

Such a radical reconceptualisation of the meaning of sport's historical development would help us to understand better the heightened significance of sport within colonial and contemporary societies and, specifically in relation to this chapter, the critical public role that sport continues to play in narrating relations between black men and white men. Clearly, the historical position of black males does not fit those models of analysis developed within the sociology of sport that have constructed a universal and 'non-raced' male subject who obtains and reproduces his dominance over 'women' in a society conceptualised as lacking racial inequalities. Mercer (1994) has drawn attention to these questions in criticising the Eurocentrism of many of the theoretical approaches to masculinity that have stubbornly refused 'to recognize that not all men in the world are white or even that white masculinities are informed by the ethnicity of whiteness' (*ibid.*: 153).[6] The historically constructed social position of black males, which raises important questions for contemporary sports sociology theorising, is accurately described by Mercer when he writes:

> Whereas prevailing definitions of masculinity imply power, control and authority, these attributes have been historically denied to black men since slavery. The centrally dominant role of the white male slave master in eighteenth- and nineteenth-century plantation societies debarred black males from patriarchal privileges ascribed to the masculine role ... In racial terms, black men and women alike were subordinated to the power of the white master in hierarchical social relations of slavery, and for black men, as *objects* of oppression, this also cancelled out their access to positions of power and prestige which in gender terms are regarded as the essence of masculinity in patriarchy. Shaped by this history, black masculinity is a highly contradictory formation of identity, as it is a *subordinated* masculinity.
>
> (Mercer 1994: 142–3)

It is clear then that we need to move towards more sophisticated and non-reductionist models of analysis that do not treat the significance of 'race' and racism as being epiphenomenal to the development of modern sports and modernity itself, and that take seriously the 'intersectionality' (Brah 1996) of 'race', gender, nation, class, and the other multiple relational identities individuals have, as constitutive elements of the social field.

The racial signification of sport

> When you talk about race in basketball, the whole thing is simple: **a black player knows he can** go out on the court and **kick a white player's ass.** He can beat him, and he knows it. It's that simple, and it shouldn't surprise anyone. The black player feels it every time. He knows it from the inside.
>
> (Rodman 1996: 129)

Given that sport is one of the few arenas where public displays of competition, domination and control are openly played out (Birrell 1989), it is not surprising, as hooks suggests, that, historically, 'competition between black and white males has been highlighted in the sports arena' (1994: 31). Messner (1992), drawing on a Gramscian analysis of the hegemonic nature of sport, highlights the way in which sport provides opportunities for subordinated groups to challenge the established order. Messner argues that subaltern groups are able to 'use sport as a means to resist (at least symbolically) the domination imposed upon them. Sport must thus be viewed as an institution through which domination is not only imposed, but also contested; an institution within which power is constantly at play' (1992:

13). Therefore within racially inscribed societies we can see how the socio-cultural, psychological and political meanings of public displays of sporting contestation come to take on specifically racial significance. As Mercer notes:

> As a major public arena, sport is a key site of white male ambivalence, fear and fantasy. The spectacle of black bodies triumphant in rituals of masculine competition reinforces the fixed idea that black men are 'all brawn and no brains,' and yet, because the white man is beaten at his own game – football, boxing, cricket, athletics – the Other is idolized to the point of envy ... *The ambivalence cuts deep into the recess of the white male imaginary.*
>
> (Mercer 1994: 178–9, emphasis added)

Mercer's perceptive analysis highlights the implicit role of sport as central to the racial, and national, imaginary and the wider social and (unacknowledged) psychological meanings invested in the physical and competitive struggles played out in the sports arena between black and white men. What Mercer is describing is a reading of the meanings inscribed in the public representation of sporting spectacles. A further, pertinent, question would be to ask what happens when sporting contests between black men and white men actually take place? That is, to move from cultural representations to cultural practices. What is the significance for those involved, both black and white, and how do wider racialised discourses affect the game itself?

Messner's arguments pertaining to the role of sport in allowing for the realisation of a masculine identity for subaltern groups is relevant here. Messner suggests that '[s]ubordinated groups of men often used sport to resist racist, colonial, and class domination, and their resistance most often took the form of a claim to "manhood"' (1992: 19). It is precisely this attempt to reconstruct black masculinity, which colonialism had configured 'as feminised and emasculated' (Vergès 1996: 61), that is central to Frantz Fanon's (1986) analysis of colonial racism, and further shows why it is impossible to separate, in any simple way, questions of masculinity from 'race'. For Fanon the claim to manhood is realised via a claim to *black* manhood because it is on the basis of the black male's racialised identity – that is, because he is black – that his masculine identity is denied: 'All I wanted was to be a man among men' (Fanon 1986: 112). Confronted with this denial, or lack of recognition, Fanon responds, 'I resolved, since it was impossible for me to get away from an *inborn complex*, to assert myself as a BLACK MAN. Since the other hesitated to recognize me, there remained only one solution: to make myself known' (*ibid*.: 115).

It is not surprising, then, that it is the traditionally highly masculinised arena of sports through which black men often attempt to (re)assert their black identity; that is, gender acts as the modality through which a racialised identity is realised (Gilroy 1993: 85). As the epigraphic quote from the enigmatic basketball player Dennis Rodman suggests, sports can be seen at one level as a transgressive liminal space where black men can attempt, quite legitimately, to (re)impose their subordinated masculine identity through the symbolic, and sometimes literal, 'beating' of the Other – that is, white men. Interestingly Rodman's comments were echoed by a black professional rugby league player when interviewed as part of a survey looking at racism within rugby league in the north of England (Long *et al.* 1995). He said, 'I think a lot of black players play rugby league, in my opinion … as they see it as a way to get their own back, or to take their aggression out on people, *white* people … You couldn't do it on the street, but you can do it on the pitch' (quoted in Long *et al.* 1996: 13; see also Long *et al.* 1997a). It is also within this context that we can understand the comments made by the West Indian cricketer Brian Lara after his side's inexplicable loss to Kenya in the cricket World Cup in 1996. In private remarks to the Kenyan side after the game, which were eventually reported by the media and for which he later apologised, he said, 'It wasn't that bad losing to you guys. You are black. Know what I mean. Now a team like South Africa is a different matter altogether. You know, this white thing comes into the picture. We can't stand losing to them' (quoted in Marqusee 1996: 136).[7] Therefore, what we might term the 'racial signification of sport' means that sports contests are more than just significant events, in and of themselves important, but rather that they act as a key signifier for wider questions about power and identity within racially demarcated societies in which racial narratives about the self and society are read both *into* and *from* sporting contests which are imbued with racial meanings.

Cricket, colonialism and cultural resistance

> The whole issue [of racism] is quite central for me, coming as I do from the West Indies at the very end of colonialism. I believe very strongly in the black man asserting himself in this world and over the years I have leaned towards many movements that follow this basic cause.
>
> (Viv Richards 1991: 188)

It is within this context that we can begin to understand more fully the centrality of sports as a form of black cultural resistance. As Hartmann points out, sport has 'long constituted an important, if under-appreciated, set of activities and institutions in the black community providing many of its leaders and one of its most established spaces for collective action (second only perhaps to the Church itself)' (1996: 560).[8] In the Caribbean, complex class, gendered and racial antagonisms across the Caribbean itself, and of course between the West Indians and the British, were most often played out in the arena of cricket. C.L.R. James's (1994 [1963]) *Beyond A Boundary* is testament to what he saw as the inherent relationship between culture and, in particular, cricket, politics and black resistance in the anti-colonial struggles of the time. James argued that cricket was central in helping to shape a *political* sense of West Indian identity during the period of colonial rule by the British. In a way, cricket could be seen as being more than a metaphor for Caribbean politics; in many ways *it was* Caribbean politics.[9]

Cricket, in particular, due to its position both as perhaps *the* cultural embodiment of the values and mores of Englishness, and its 'missionary' role within British imperialism and colonialism, occupied a central site in many of the anti-colonial struggles within the Caribbean and elsewhere within the Empire. Thus the game itself assumed political importance in narrating the unequal power relations between the British and West Indians: 'beating them at their own game' taking on deeper and more profound meanings. In discussing this, Farred has argued that it 'is precisely because the colonised were immersed in and observant of the codes of the native British game that they were able to transform the sport into a vehicle for Caribbean resistance' (1996: 170–1).

Viv Richards, captain of one the most successful West Indian teams in cricket history, extends this connection between sport and black resistance to the black diaspora, when he reflects: 'In my own way, I would like to think that I carried my bat for the liberation of African and other oppressed people everywhere' (1995: vii).[10] Cricket, especially for certain generations of West Indian men, came to occupy a central position in their social identities, whether they were living in the Caribbean or elsewhere within the black diaspora. As Stuart notes, for many black men cricket itself occupied a symbolic position in articulating an empowered sense of self within white supremacist societies: 'cricket represented social status, social mobility, it meant modernisation and it meant West Indian success' (1996: 125). It is to ground these theoretical issues, relating to the importance of cricket and notions of cultural resistance in the lived experiences of black men, that I now turn.

The setting: the racialisation of Chapeltown

This study focuses on the Caribbean Cricket Club (CCC) which is situated near an area of Leeds, a large city in the north of England, where the majority of the city's Asian and black residents live.[11] The 1991 census data for Leeds showed that those classified as 'Black-Caribbean' numbered just under 7,000, of whom nearly 60 per cent lived within the two electoral districts known as 'Chapeltown' (Policy Research Institute (PRI) 1996). Because of the relatively large concentration of black people, Chapeltown has come to be known in the city as a 'black area' and, as such, has been subject to a racialised discourse, fuelled by local and national media (mis)representations (Farrar 1997), that have labelled the area (and by default the black residents of Chapeltown) as deviant, dangerous and sexually promiscuous.

In keeping with many of Britain's multi-racial, inner-city areas,

Chapeltown is a largely working-class area with few public amenities and considerable economic problems, such as higher than average levels of unemployment and poor housing conditions (PRI 1996; Farrar 1997). Partly as result of these socio-economic conditions, the area has twice seen major disturbances, which have attracted both regional and national attention in 1975 (see Farrar 1981; Sivanandan 1982; Gilroy 1987) and during the summer of 1981, when many areas of Britain were gripped with black and working-class violent political revolts (see Farrar 1981). More recently, during the summer of 2001, these underlying tensions have manifested themselves in violent clashes between Asian youths and the police. Despite, and probably because of, these economic conditions and the difficulties faced by the city's Asian and black populations, the large number of political and cultural organisations in the area, of which the cricket club is a central part, have maintained, and even increased, their importance to the social life of Chapeltown.

The club: Caribbean Cricket Club

Caribbean Cricket Club (CCC) is one of the oldest black sports clubs in Britain. It was originally formed in the late 1940s as a social and sporting club by a group of West Indian soldiers who had fought in the Second World War and had settled in the city (Wheatley 1992; Zulfiqar 1993). Over the years the club became more successful, culminating in the late 1970s when it won the league three years running, and won the treble on a number of occasions. In the late 1980s, CCC moved on to play in one of the strongest leagues in the Yorkshire county, the Leeds League. It has three senior men's teams and three junior boy's teams. Nearly all of the senior players are black except for three Asian players and three white players.

The club's current ground, called 'The Oval', was a relatively new acquisition. With money from the local council, wasteland just outside of Chapeltown was transformed, over many years, into a cricket pitch, and a few years later the club's current pavilion was built – the plaque inside proudly confirming the opening as 'The Realisation of a Dream'. The surrounding area is largely overgrown grassland, overlooked by a working-class council estate and tower blocks on one side, with a panoramic view of the city's skyline on the other. The clubhouse has been the subject of constant vandalism and break-ins over the years – another break-in occurred during the research, in which the television, phone, drinks and money from the till and pool table were stolen. The most serious set-back to the club has been an arson attack which unfortunately destroyed nearly all of the club's memorabilia. This has left the clubhouse looking somewhat empty without all the team photos that usually adorn cricket clubhouses. There is often talk within the club that such attacks are racially motivated, with the prime suspects being the youths from the nearby, predominantly white, council estate, although on each occasion the police have been unable to prosecute anyone. Earl, the third team wicket-keeper, suggested:

> I think it's down to, 'Oh, it's a black club, we don't want them to get far'. I think it's a racial thing again because I've seen words daubed up, 'Niggers Out', and things like that ... Because once you've been done over once, and it happens again, you know there is a pattern to it.

The spacious wasteland of the surrounding area tends to attract youngsters riding motor bikes, and sometimes cars. Presumably due to this activity, a police car or two, and sometimes even a police helicopter, will circle the ground (as occurred on my very first visit to a game at the club). The well-documented history of police and state regulation, surveillance and harassment of black community spaces within Britain (Sivanandan 1982; Gilroy 1987; Keith 1993; Hesse 1997), a key factor in the disturbances in Chapeltown in 1975 and 1981, gives this constant police activity (that symbolically infringes on the bounded space of the club) heightened significance. This inevitably leads to the feeling amongst many that the police are keeping an eye on the club as much as looking out for the 'joy riders'. The location of the club and its somewhat troubled history seem to give the club and its members an 'embattled' feel, and adds to the widely held notion of the club's 'struggle' both on and off the pitch.

Black space as cultural resistance

I wish now to explore how members of the club use CCC as a discursively constructed black social space. The concept of 'space' invoked here is not used simply as reference to a geographically bounded area, although clearly this is a dimension of any use of the term, but rather refers to the social production of space, that is, the ways in which socio-economic, cultural and political discourses construct spatial relations *and* the ways in which individuals themselves negotiate, and reconstruct, these discourses. As Lefebvre argues, space should be seen as having been 'shaped and moulded from historical and natural elements ... this has been a political process. Space is political and ideological. It is a product literally filled with ideologies' (1976: 31, quoted in Farrar 1996: 295). In relation to the 'racialisation of space', Farrar remarks:

> In everyday speech, many residents of an urban area of black settlement would readily comprehend a phrase such as 'black space' ... in terms of their effort to forge discourses and practical activities in a particular part of town which are, to some extent, 'free' from the discourses and practices which they associate with a coercive white power structure. Establishing nearly autonomous territory is the conscious aim of all sorts

of actors in the black inner city – in churches, mosques, temples, community centres, clubs, pubs, and in certain 'open' spaces.

(1997: 108)

Such movements to create 'nearly autonomous' spaces are an attempt to resist what might be described as the 'terrorising white gaze' (hooks 1992) within public spaces. Here, black people, and black bodies, become subject to a panoptic form of 'white governmentality' (Hesse 1997) that seeks to oversee, control and regulate the behaviour of black people and is underpinned by the constant threat of racial harassment and violence. In this sense, we can see how the club's significance goes beyond merely being a cricket club and assumes a heightened *social* role as a *black* institution within a wider white environment, providing many of the black men with a sense of ontological security. This can operate on a number of related levels, from being a space removed, albeit not entirely, from the overt practices of white racism, as a social and cultural resource for black people, and as an arena that allows for black expressive behaviour. These elements can be traced in the various ways in which the importance of CCC was discussed by its members. The club was often labelled by the players and members in the interviews and discussions as a *black space*, by which was often meant a place where black people could 'be themselves' (for example, in being able to tell certain jokes and speak in Caribbean patois), free from the strictures imposed by the white gaze. Thus the club's importance transcended its sporting function.

The current chair and manager of CCC, Ron, came to Leeds in the late 1950s and joined CCC in the 1970s, when in his early twenties. For Ron, it was important to acknowledge the historical social role of the club within the area. When asked whether he saw the club as being more than just a sporting club, he replied:

> Oh yeah, because when it started in '47 it wasn't just a sports club, it was a focal point for those people who were black and in a vast minority, because in 1947 I don't think there were the amount of black people in Leeds that there are now. It was a focal point, it was a survival point for the people that were here. So it was more than a club then and it's still more than a club now, so it will always be that.

The use of the language of 'survival' is interesting. It highlights the historical social significance of the club in providing a safe space within a wider (hostile) environment for the earlier Caribbean migrants, which is then mapped onto the present, showing the continuities of the club and its role in the light of the persistence of racism: 'it was more than a club then and it's still more than a club now, so it will always be that'.

Nicholas, a 17 year old who played for both the senior and junior sides, referred to CCC as being an important social space for black people. As he also played for another junior cricket team in another part of Yorkshire, he was able to contrast his experiences of playing for 'white' and 'black' teams. Nicholas had experienced racial abuse from an opposing player whilst playing junior cricket for his other team, Scholes, which had increased his feelings of isolation at his predominantly white club:

NICHOLAS: Some teams, if you're batting against them, and you start hitting them all over the place they always have to come out with their racist remarks to try and put you off … It even happened to me this season when we played a team from Garforth, and I was hitting the opening bowler who has played for Yorkshire [Juniors]. I was hitting him for quite a lot of fours, and then he started to go on and call me names on the pitch … and then he got me out, and then, he was all 'mouthy mouthy'.

BC: But how did that make you feel?

NICHOLAS: Well, it's the first time it's happened, it made me feel kind of funny. I didn't know whether to answer him back or to walk away from him.

BC: If you were playing for Caribbean do you think he would have said it?

NICHOLAS: If I were playing for Caribbean he wouldn't have dared say it because if he was saying it to one person he's really saying it to the whole team … but at Scholes there is only two of us there, and all the rest are white, so it was more easier for him to say it there.

Such incidents compounded his feeling of isolation and 'otherness' in a white setting and he thus felt more relaxed and secure when at CCC. In this sense, the CCC can be seen as providing Nicholas with an environment where his blackness takes on a lesser significance – 'As long as the black man is among his own, he will have no occasion, except in minor internal conflicts, to experience his being through others' (Fanon 1986: 109) – and offers, in both a symbolic and very real sense, protection from the more overt practices of white racism.

The achievement of creating and sustaining a cricketing 'black space' within a white environment was often reflected on, somewhat nostalgically, by the club's members, particularly the older ones. There was a sense of pride amongst many of the players and members that despite all the problems the club had faced, including increasing financial pressures, the CCC was still going and now had its own ground and pavilion. Pete, one of the older players who had come to England from Barbados in the late 1960s, echoed these views, whilst being interviewed in his car at 'The Oval'. He said:

I tend to think there are people out there who don't want us to have this … But I hope we can carry on. I mean look at this [he gazes at the panoramic view across the ground over-looking the city], this is great as far as I'm concerned!

Community, resistance and cricket

It is important to remember the wider context of the CCC's developments. Its ground and clubhouse materialised in the 1980s and can be seen as emerging from a wider black political struggle that was taking place during this period. Following the violent disturbances of the early 1980s, there was a shift in government spending towards 'social expenses' as a means of trying to placate inner-city tensions. The provision of leisure facilities was a key part of this process, even whilst government expenditure generally was being squeezed as the welfare state was restructured (Henry 1993). Although state funding of such leisure provisions has been criticised as being merely a form of 'soft policing' (Hargreaves 1986) that increased state control of black and working-class communities and simultaneously diverted attention away from the underlying (economic) causes of the social deprivation these areas were facing, the outcomes of such policies were more ambiguous. Although it was clear that the primary motive behind such funding was designed to (re)impose 'social integration', many black organisations were willing to take the money available and to use it to their own advantage. Thus the negotiations with the local state, in order to achieve the aims of CCC, were contradictory. To a degree, this allowed the state to use sport, as Hargreaves (1986) suggests, to further its own ends, whilst, simultaneously, the black community also fought for space to negotiate a different set of cultural possibilities (cf. Hall 1996).

Ron, who worked for the local council and was instrumental in securing local government funding for the development of the ground, and the subsequent building of the clubhouse, was well aware of the underlying political motives of such provision:

> It was after 1981, the uprisings, or the disturbances, whatever you want to call them. The authorities decided that they had to keep the 'natives' happy, and they looked at something that the natives liked, and obviously cricket was what the natives liked.

Ron's deliberately ironic self-description of the 'natives' is instructive. It highlights how the colonial discourse of British imperialism still resonates as a point of reference within the popular contemporary white imaginary in relation to black people living in Leeds. Indeed, as late as the 1970s, Chapeltown was actually referred to in the local press as 'the colony within' (Farrar 1996), reinforcing popular local misconceptions of Chapeltown and its residents as an alien and potentially violent place, to be overseen and policed as a colonial settlement.

The 'natives', then, had, after almost 40 years, secured their own ground and clubhouse – a physical marker of the club's (and in some ways Chapeltown's black communities') presence and progress in the area. However, it is argued here that although CCC now has a physical presence – a clubhouse and a pitch – the sense in which the club comes to represent 'the community' for some of its members is largely as a symbol, that is to say, it is imagined. As Cohen (1985: 19) notes, 'symbols are mental constructs: they provide people with the means to make meaning. In so doing, they also provide them with the means to express the particular meanings which the community has for them'.

The polyvocal nature of signs can be seen in the way in which the CCC is itself used interchangeably with 'the black community' in discussions at the club, standing as a symbolic marker of the community (which depending on the context can take on both local, i.e. Chapeltown, or wider, i.e. diasporic, dimensions), and assumes a specifically racial, that is black, association. We can see then that the language of 'community', especially for blacks living in Britain, connotes both political (as a form of resistance) and moral (as a place of transcendence) associations. What we might term 'black community discourse' (Back 1996) is used strategically as a way of articulating wider black struggles within a specific locality by labelling it as a 'black area'. The black community discourse can be understood as a narrative that locates a particular area 'as the site of black struggles and institutions, a place where black people have fought to make something their own. This construct is also invested with a notion of political agency and locates black resistance to racism and self-affirmation in this particular area' (*ibid.*: 113). Such attempts at establishing (partially) autonomous institutions and spaces, such as CCC, as part of wider community projects are mechanisms in the development of 'communities of resistance' (Sivanandan 1990) which are inherently political manoeuvres. As Gilroy (1987) notes, the invocation of 'community' refers to more than just the concentration of black people within a particular bounded area:

> It has a moral dimension and its use evokes a rich complex of symbols surrounded by a wider cluster of meanings. The historical memory of progress from slave to citizen actively cultivated in the present from resources provided by the past endows it with an aura of tradition. Community, therefore, signifies not just a distinctive political ideology but a particular set of values and norms in everyday life: mutuality, co-operation, identification and symbiosis. For black Britain, all these are centrally defined by the need to escape and transform the forms of subordination which bring 'races' into being.
>
> (1987: 234)

Thus, given the symbolic significance attached to the club and its central position within the local black community discourse, the success of the club on the field came to be seen as reflecting on the standing of the black community of Chapeltown too. For example, during team meetings the management and other senior players would often stress the need for the players to be aware that they were not just playing for themselves, or even the team, but also for 'the community' as a whole: 'for everyone down at

Chapeltown' as Ron once put it. Despite CCC's achievements over the years, the club had not won the Leeds League since its acceptance, after a number of unsuccessful applications, in 1988 and this was a constant source of frustration for many at the club. Both Ron and Earl felt the need for the club to win the league:

Ron: Because we need to be champions one day.
Earl: For the community as well as the club.
Ron: And it would lift the community like Earl says.

Errol, too, acknowledged the importance of the CCC for the black community of Chapeltown, especially for some of the older members. When asked what importance the club had for the residents of Chapeltown, Errol replied:

> To me it [CCC] is still important, it's still important, that's my view, I think it's important for the community. Because everybody, especially for the older generation as well, the people who have actually played, it's part of their history, no matter what, you can't take that away from them, because there are times when they go to games and they watch and they say, 'Well, I used to play for these', so it's important for them.

Another player, Tim, also believed that the club served a wider purpose than merely being a cricket club, in the sense that it could have an important social role and even a moral purpose, especially in relation to offering something positive to Chapeltown's disadvantaged youth. When asked if he felt CCC was important in any way for Chapeltown he said:

Tim: Oh yeah, very important, very important for Chapeltown, very important from a community point of view.
BC: In what ways?
Tim: From the club's history, it's nearly 50 years old, I think we should continue ... Chapeltown has got this reputation and the Caribbean Cricket Club should be a shining light. We need role models at the club. We should be role models for those kids, we should set examples, we should set standards. I look at Caribbean Cricket Club as a focal point. We've got access to all these kids in the area and we should bring them along and show them what is right.

For Pete, CCC was important to Chapeltown because 'it's the only sporting club, cricket club, that black people have got in the area, and when I say black I mean West Indian'. Pete was aware that CCC was perceived by white people as a 'black club' and symbolically represented Chapeltown and black people in general to them, therefore it was vitally important that the club was not only successful but run well: 'I've had my hands down the loo! "Wash this, wash that". Because I'm buggered if I want anyone to come up here and believe, "Ah, is this the way black people live?".' He therefore spoke disparagingly, and with a sense of bewilderment and incomprehension, about those members who did not realise the wider social significance of the club; 'Most members come up here and all they want to do is play cricket!'.

Cricket and racial contestation

C.L.R. James (1994 [1963]: 66) noted long ago the wider social significance of cricket contests: 'the cricket field was a stage on which selected individuals played representative roles which were charged with social significance'. Given that CCC has a predominantly black membership (and its name and location signify the club as 'black') and given too that it plays its cricket in a league in the 'heart of Yorkshire' (a regional identity historically constructed through a notion of 'whiteness'), the racial meanings invested in the actual matches are heightened even further. Due to a number of high profile incidents of racist abuse from supporters at Yorkshire cricket grounds, and statements, widely seen as racist, by prominent members of Yorkshire County Cricket Club over the years, the county has a reputation as 'unwelcoming territory for black cricketers' (Searle 1990: 43; see also Searle 2001). As Marqusee notes

> the roots of racism in Yorkshire cricket are set deep in the county's peculiar regional chauvinism, a chauvinism warped by years of cricket failure ... The powers that be at Yorkshire have for many decades preferred the spurious roots of racial and cultural identity to the living roots of the game as it is actually played in the locality. It stands proudly not for the mixed culture of contemporary Yorkshire – industrial and urban, black and white, immigrant and native – but for a reified, hollow culture of boastfulness and bigotry. It is, at its core, profoundly exclusive.
>
> (Marqusee 1994: 143–4)

Despite over a century of Asian and black involvement in cricket throughout England, at both county and national level, Yorkshire disgracefully remains the only county cricket club never to have fielded a British-born Asian or black cricketer in its first team. Although Yorkshire County Cricket Club now officially promotes an open policy in its selection, evidence suggests that racial discrimination is still prevalent in Yorkshire cricket despite the work of a number of committed individuals at the club to change this situation (see Long *et al.* 1997b). The county's emblem, a white rose, has therefore become a powerful signifier for racist sentiments in the county in wanting to keep the 'white rose white'. Many of the players at CCC were sure that the opposing teams were well aware of the wider racial significance of the contests, and that the cricket matches were more than 'just a game'; the metaphor of war was often used to describe the contests.

Overlaid on this, of course, as outlined earlier, is the specificity of cricket itself as a cultural practice and its central, almost metaphoric, position as a site of hegemonic struggle between the British and West Indians. The competition between black and white men within this context becomes a symbolic and real contestation of masculine and racial pride, and specifically for the black participants, a way of attempting to reassert a unified sense of self and of rejecting, even if temporarily, the notion that their black identity is a subordinated, and inferior, identity. As Westwood (1990: 68) notes, in her brief analysis of a black men's football team, the victories of black teams over white teams 'is, in effect, an injury to white masculine pride and a source of power and celebration to black masculine pride when white teams are beaten'.

These themes emerged constantly during the discussions at the club and the interviews conducted. For instance, referring to opposing white sides, Nigel said, 'I think they see us purely as colour first, end of story, and then the cricket club comes [second]'. Nigel was therefore dismissive of the notion that the cricket arena was somehow free of racial contestation and significance and that it could 'bring people together'. When I suggested this to him he replied:

> Oh come on, come on! We are talking about cricket here aren't we Ben? We're talking about the one county that we're based in being the one that always said (*puts on a strong mock Yorkshire accent*), 'You can't play for Yorkshire unless you're born in bloody Yorkshire lad!'. That's still got to come through and that's been so strong within Yorkshire, the country on its own inside of another country, that's almost how strong they feel, and particularly around cricket.

This passage is important as it pulls together a number of key issues. It shows how a regional identity can become conflated with notions of nation and indeed 'race'. The view that Yorkshire is a 'country on its own inside of another country' is a powerful one which gives the county a particularly strong regional identity. That sport, and in particular cricket, is central to this, and that until recently only those born in Yorkshire could play for Yorkshire, thereby excluding Asian and black immigrants from being 'true Yorkshiremen' and thus giving the identity a racial connotation, means that the players come to assume representative roles which are charged with social significance; the games themselves becoming, in effect, black (West Indian)–white (Yorkshire) contests.

For example, Pete was clear, as he saw it, of the wider significance of the CCC and the matches within a context of a racist society. The relationship of the players to the actual national West Indian Test team went beyond rhetorical support and extended to a deeper identification and the view that they actually were in some sense part of the West Indies side:

Pete: As far as I'm concerned we're just an extension of the West Indies national team.

BC: Is it more than just a cricket game to you?

Pete: Yes it is. You see I've heard the opposing teams talk you see. I've been at a game when we've lost and I've heard the words coming out of the dressing room, 'We've beaten the fucking black bastards dem, again!' (*thumps steering wheel*). So then it takes the game away from being a game, it's war then.

Such views were reflected in a number of the interviews undertaken in this study. Errol, who was in his thirties and had played for the club for a number of years and had also played with a predominantly Asian cricket team, similarly noted the racial, and hence national, significance that was attached to the games: 'They [white teams] don't want a West Indian team to beat them or they don't want an Asian team to beat them. For them it's like, England versus the West Indies, or England versus India'. Errol continued, suggesting that white teams would consciously raise their game to ensure they were not beaten by a black side:

ERROL: At the end of the day we are living in England. Nobody want us to do better. It's like if there were an English [i.e. white] team in the West Indies, there's no way that the West Indies players or teams are gonna want them to win.

BC: How do you think other teams see Caribbean?

ERROL: It's like, to me, they don't want a *black* team to beat them. We've played against teams who never win a game but yet when they're playing Caribbeans you'd think that they were unbeatable! ... It's because they don't want a black man to beat them.

We can begin to see here how the wider discourses of the racial signification of sport become constituted in the actual contests themselves. The view that other teams played differently against the CCC because they were seen as a black club was widely held amongst the players and supporters. Brett, the first team captain, was again typical when he said:

If you are wise, it's like any sport, football's the same, if it's a team of black guys playing against a team of white guys they are desperate to beat you ... You get guys, who for the rest of the season they'll never take three wickets but against us they've taken five, because they've worked that bit harder, they go out there and fight a bit harder, because they're playing Caribbean, it's the black team in the league.

Given the racial signification of the contests, the immense emotional and personal investment made in the games for the black men was significant. At both a symbolic and everyday level, winning became a way of challenging the logic and efficacy of the racism they faced in their day-to-day lives, even if the victories were always, ultimately, transitory. As Bob, an older player in his forties, acknowledged, racial and masculine pride was at stake in contests between CCC and other white sides, thus it became paramount for CCC, and the players themselves, not to lose:

> At the end of the day you don't want to be beaten. You think 'Let's show these lads who's the boss here'. You try your best because you don't want to be beaten because it's like they go away all cocky and that, 'We showed them, they can't play cricket, English game's the best!', all that business. You want to go out there and hopefully shut them up.

Conclusion

Westwood (1990: 61) has argued that as 'a counter to racism black masculinity is called up as part of the cultures of resistance developed by black men in Britain'. This chapter has shown how for a number of black men, sport, and in particular cricket, can provide a modality through which black cultural resistance to racism can be achieved. Sports provide an arena whereby black men can lay claim to a masculine identity as a means of restoring a unified sense of racial identity, freed, if only momentarily, from the emasculating discourses imposed by the ideologies and practices of white racism.

However, we should be cautious not to overstate unproblematically the benefits of such 'sites of resistance'. For one, black women often occupy marginal positions within sports clubs such as CCC (especially those that do not have women's teams), which are perhaps more accurately described, as I have made clear throughout, as black *men's* cricket clubs. Without acknowledging such limitations, the complex positioning of black women, in particular, within 'white supremacist capitalist patriarchal societies' (hooks 1994), gets overlooked. Thus any claims for such cultural practices as being in some way emancipatory must be qualified. Otherwise, as black feminists have consistently pointed out, the requirements for black resistance become equated with the need for black *male* emancipation. The overcoming of the so-called crisis of black masculinity is frequently misrecognised as the panacea for the black community as a whole, thereby silencing the voices and needs of black women; the politics manifest within certain (conservative) black nationalisms being the most obvious example of this (see Carbado 1999).

There is also, of course, the further problematic with the 'zero-sum' notion of resistance and power, most evidenced in the competitive sports arena, which inevitably leads to a conceptualisation of resistance which can only be understood via notions of domination and physical conflict. Burton (1991, 1997), for instance, has provided an interesting analysis in arguing for cricket to be situated within carnivalesque aspects of Caribbean street culture. Burton suggests that the carnival's symbolic subversion is central to how cricket is watched and played, as a more diffuse and stylised site of popular cultural resistance in challenging dominant social hierarchies.[12] This should alert us to the fact that such modes of resistance, that have been analysed here, should not be thought of as the only positionings possible, which ultimately need to be embedded within wider struggles. Indeed, for those of us interested in the politics of culture, the extent to which popular culture offers *transformative* possibilities for social change is something which requires much greater analytical attention.

It is necessary, therefore, to understand and explore both the benefits that such forms can have for a number of black men, and the limitations of sport as a modality of resistance to racism. Only when we have more ethnographically informed analyses, in a greater variety of different communities across differing locations, and a deeper theoretical understanding of the cultural sphere as a site of contestation, will we be able to more fully appreciate the complexities of black cultural resistance through sport and its emancipatory potential.

Notes

1   This chapter is a slightly amended version of the article 'Sport, masculinity, and Black cultural resistance' which first appeared in the *Journal of Sport and Social Issues* 22(3) August 1998.

2   Throughout the 1970s and 1980s a sophisticated sociological approach to understanding the dynamics of class relations within the sociology of sport was developed. During the 1980s and early 1990s sport's role as a site for gender construction became more fully understood, with a concomitant interest in issues of sexuality. It could be argued, however, that with the exception of Harry Edwards's political interventions, no such critical approaches to understanding sport's role in the reproduction of racial ideologies, and its place as a site of racial contestation has been developed. It is only since the late 1990s that sufficiently theorised accounts of the relationship between racialisation and sport has emerged, although mainly from those at the margins of, or outside, the terrain of 'sport studies'. I am thinking, in particular, of the work of David Andrews, Grant Farred, Brett St Louis and David Hartmann, amongst others.

3   Strictly speaking Hoggart's work was not ethnographic in the sense that it did not explicitly use a clearly delineated case study methodology. However, the broadly qualitative and partly autobiographical nature of the analysis, as well as the careful descriptions of the lived experiences of the subjects studied, enables us to situate the book within the broad methodologies embraced by cultural studies, in opposition to the positivistic tendencies of certain sociological approaches. As Hoggart himself noted, in the preface to the original Pelican paperback edition, 'this book is based to a large extent on personal experience, and does not purport to have the scientifically-tested character of a sociological survey' (1958: ix).

4   Stuart Hall makes a similar point in warning of the dangers of the institutionalisation of cultural studies, particularly in America, as a merely esoteric academic pursuit removed from everyday practices, and his uneasiness about the loss of the *political* impulse of early cultural studies' concerns – for instance, see 'Cultural studies and its theoretical legacies' in Morley and Chen (1996) and also Hall (1997). For a discussion of the extent to which cultural studies has

neglected questions of political economy, see the exchange between Garnham (1998) and Grossberg (1998). For an overview of contemporary debates within cultural studies, see Miller (2001).

5   Eurocentrism is used conceptually to refer to those discourses and relations of power that privilege culturally hegemonic European notions of Western universality and that therefore elide, within their frame of reference, the voices of 'Others', both within and outside the West. In another sense, Eurocentrism can be understood as an attempt to recentre 'the West' in conditions when its universality can no longer be guaranteed due to the multi-faceted interrogations of the Occident by various post-colonial movements and critical multiculturalisms (see Hesse 2000; Sayyid 1997; Shohat and Stam 1994).

6   If the literature within the sociology of sport and leisure studies (and indeed elsewhere) on 'race', racism and sport is inadequate, then the acknowledgement within these fields of study of *white* ethnicity is even worse. There are too few studies that have seriously considered how sport is central to the construction of white racial identities, or even demonstrated an awareness of the fact that whiteness is a racial category. 'Race' is too often equated with the black (and/or Asian) experience (just as in an earlier period when gender equalled female experience) which, as a number of scholars have demonstrated, only serves to reinforce current racist discourses and obscures the normalising power of whiteness (see Dyer, 1988, 1997; hooks 1992; Ware and Back 2002; Feagin *et al.* 2001; Frankenburg 1993; Bonnett 2000).

7   St Pierre similarly suggests, in relation to cricket, that West Indian Test players 'will tell you, privately, that a victory against England carries with it a special savour' (1995: 77).

8   There is a complex history, which is yet to be fully theorised, or indeed written, concerning the connections, cross-overs and inter-play between the roles and lives of black athletes and black political radicals within the black diaspora. I have begun to map this out elsewhere via the concept of the 'sporting black Atlantic' (see Carrington *et al.* 2001). I am thinking here, for example, of the relationships between figures such as C.L.R. James and Learie Constantine (see note 10) and Muhammad Ali and Malcolm X (see Marqusee 1999), and in a somewhat different context, the quite literal connections made by Jean-Michel Basquiat in his painting *All Colored Cast (Part II)* 1982, between the boxer 'Jersey' Joe Walcott and Toussaint L'Ouverture.

9   The continuing relevance of, and insights from, James can still be seen in contemporary writings on cricket and the Caribbean which demonstrate the constitutive relationship between black political struggle and cricket; for example, see Beckles (ed.) (1994) *An Area of Conquest: Popular Democracy and West Indies Cricket Supremacy*; Beckles and Stoddard (eds) (1995) *Liberation Cricket: West Indies Cricket Culture*; Birbalsingh (1996) *The Rise of West Indian Cricket: From Colony to Nation*; see also the essays by St Pierre (1995) 'West Indian cricket as cultural resistance' and Yelvington's (1995) 'Cricket, colonialism, and the culture of Caribbean politics'.

10 Richards can be seen to be operating within a longer lineage of great West Indian cricketers who were aware of the wider significance of cricket, which can be traced back to Learie Constantine. The grandson of a slave, Constantine was a vocal advocate of West Indian independence and spoke out against racial injustice, both within cricket and, more generally, eventually serving in Dr Eric Williams's government in Trinidad and Tobago from 1957 to 1961 (Birbalsingh 1996). Indeed C.L.R. James credits Constantine as being a central figure in James's political development in relation to his racial awareness, anti-colonial sensibility and views on West Indian nationalism. As James remarks, 'Constantine had always been political, far more than I had ever been. My senti-

ments were in the right place, but I was still enclosed within the mould of nine-teenth-century intellectualism. Unbeknown to me, however, the shell had been cracked. Constantine's conversations were always pecking at it' (1994: 113).

11 The research is based on my doctoral study. In-depth semi-structured interviews conducted between 1995 and 1997, and participant observation during the summer cricket seasons of 1995, 1996 and 1997, have been used to collect the data. Pseudonyms for the players and club members are used throughout. I am using the nomenclatures 'black' and 'Asian' to refer to those groups who, due to the process of racialisation, are visibly marked as belonging to different 'races'. Within this context those referred to as 'black' are those people of sub-Saharan African descent, and those referred to as 'Asian' of south Asian descent.

12 In fact, following Michel de Certeau, Burton (1997) makes the distinction between *resistance* (i.e. those forms of contestation from *outside* a particular discursive regime) and *opposition* (i.e. those forms of contestation from *within* a system). Discerning readers will have noticed that I have used the term 'resistance' rather more generally and descriptively in this chapter when perhaps 'opposition' would have been more analytically precise. Such distinctions have not been central to my arguments here.

References

Alasuutari, P. (1995) *Researching Culture: Qualitative Method and Cultural Studies*, London: Sage.

Back, L. (1996) *New Ethnicities and Urban Culture: Racisms and Multiculture in Young Lives*, London: UCL Press.

Beckles, H. (ed.) (1994) *An Area of Conquest: Popular Democracy and West Indies Cricket Supremacy*, Jamaica: Ian Randle.

Beckles, H. and Stoddard, B. (eds) (1995) *Liberation Cricket: West Indies Cricket Culture*, Manchester: Manchester University Press.

Birbalsingh, F. (1996) *The Rise of West Indian Cricket: From Colony to Nation*, Antigua: Hansib.

Birrell, S. (1989) 'Racial relations theories and sport: suggestions for a more critical analysis', *Sociology of Sport Journal*, 6(3): 212–27.

Bonnett, A. (2000) *White Identities: Historical and International Perspectives*, Harlow: Prentice Hall.

Brah, A. (1996) *Cartographies of Diaspora: Contesting Identities*, London: Routledge.

Burton, R. (1991) 'Cricket, carnival and street culture in the Caribbean', in G. Jarvie (ed.) *Sport, Racism and Ethnicity*, London: Falmer.

——— (1997) *Afro-Creole: Power, Opposition and Play in the Caribbean*, London: Cornell University Press.

Carbado, D. (ed.) (1999) *Black Men on Race, Gender, and Sexuality*, London: New York University Press.

Carrington, B., Andrews, D., Jackson, S. and Mazur, Z. (2001) 'The Global Jordan-scape', in D. Andrews (ed.) *Michael Jordan, Inc.: Corporate Sport, Media Culture, and Late Modern America*, Albany: State University of New York Press.

Cohen, A. (1985) *The Symbolic Construction of Community*, London: Routledge.

Dyer, R. (1988) 'White', *Screen* 29(4): 44–64.

———(1997) *White*, London: Routledge.

Fanon, F. (1986 [1953]) *Black Skin, White Masks*, London: Pluto Press.

Farrar, M. (1981), 'Riot and revolution: the politics of an inner city', *Revolutionary Socialism* 2: 6–10.

—— (1996) 'Black communities and processes of exclusion', in G. Haughton and C. Williams (eds) *Corporate City? Partnership, Participation and Partition in Urban Development in Leeds*, Aldershot: Avebury.

—— (1997) 'Migrant spaces and settlers' time: forming and de-forming an inner city', in S. Westwood and J. Williams (eds) *Imaging Cities: Scripts, Signs, Memory*, London: Routledge.

Farred, G. (ed.) (1996) *Rethinking C.L.R. James*, London: Blackwell.

Feagin, J., Vera, H. and Batur, P. (2001) *White Racism: The Basics*, 2nd edn, London: Routledge.

Frankenburg, R. (1993) *White Women, Race Matters: The Social Construction of Whiteness*, London: Routledge.

Garnham, N. (1998) 'Political economy and cultural studies: reconciliation or divorce?', in J. Storey (ed.) *Cultural Theory and Popular Culture: A Reader*, 2nd edn, London: Prentice Hall.

Gilroy, P. (1987) *There Ain't No Black in the Union Jack: The Cultural Politics of Race and Nation*, London: Hutchinson.

Gilroy, P. (1993) *The Black Atlantic: Modernity and Double Consciousness*, London: Verso.

Grossberg, L. (1997) *Bringing It All Back Home: Essays On Cultural Studies*, London: Duke University Press.

—— (1998) 'Cultural studies vs. political economy: is anyone else bored with this debate?', in J. Storey (ed.) *Cultural Theory and Popular Culture: A Reader*, 2nd edn, London: Prentice Hall.

Hall, S. (1996) 'Politics of identity', in T. Ranger, Y. Samad, and O. Stuart (eds) *Culture, Identity and Politics: Ethnic Minorities in Britain*, Aldershot: Avebury.

—— (1997) 'Culture and power', *Radical Philosophy: A Journal of Socialist and Feminist Philosophy*, 86: 24–41.

Hall, S. and Jefferson, T. (eds) (1976) *Resistance Through Rituals: Youth Subcultures in Post-war Britain*, London: Hutchinson.

Hargreaves, J. (1986) *Sport, Power and Culture: A Social and Historical Analysis of Popular Sports in Britain*, Cambridge: Polity Press.

Hartmann, D. (1996) 'The politics of race and sport: resistance and domination in the 1968 African American Olympic protest movement', *Ethnic and Racial Studies* 19(3): 548–66.

Henry, I. (1993) *The Politics of Leisure Policy*, London: Macmillan.

Hesse, B. (1997) 'White governmentality: urbanism, nationalism, racism', in S. Westwood and J. Williams (eds) *Imaging Cities: Scripts, Signs, Memory*, London: Routledge.

—— (ed.) (2000) *Un/Settled Multiculturalisms: Diasporas, Entanglements, Transruptions*, Zed Press: London.

Hoggart, R. (1958) *The Uses of Literacy: Aspects of Working-Class Life With Special Reference to Publications and Entertainments*, Harmondsworth: Penguin.

hooks, b. (1992) 'Representing whiteness in the black imagination', in L. Grossberg, C. Nelson and P. Treichler (eds) *Cultural Studies*, London: Routledge.

—— (1994) *Outlaw Culture: Resisting Representations*, London: Routledge.

James, C.L.R. (1994 [1963]) *Beyond a Boundary*, London: Serpent's Tail.

Keith, M. (1993) *Race, Riots and Policing: Lore and Disorder in a Multi-Racist Society*, London: UCL.

Lefebvre, H. (1976) 'Reflections on the politics of space', *Antipode* 8(2), trans Michael Enders from French journal *Espaces et Sociétés* 1970 (1).

Long, J., Carrington, B. and Spracklen, K. (1996) 'The cultural production and reproduction of racial stereotypes in sport: a case study of rugby league', paper presented to British Sociology Association annual conference, Reading, April.

—— (1997a) ' "Asians cannot wear turbans in the scrum": Explorations of racist discourse within professional rugby league', *Leisure Studies* 16(4): 249–60.

Long, J., Nesti, M., Carrington, B. and Gilson, N. (1997b) *Crossing the Boundary: A Study of the Nature and Extent of Racism in Local League Cricket*, Leeds: Leeds Metropolitan University Working Papers.

Long, J., Tongue, N., Spracklen, K. and Carrington, B. (1995) *What's the Difference? A Study of the Nature and Extent of Racism in Rugby League*, Leeds: Rugby Football League/Leeds City Council/Commission for Racial Equality/Leeds Metropolitan University.

Marqusee, M. (1994) *Anyone But England: Cricket and the National Malaise.* London: Verso.

—— (1995) 'Sport and stereotype: from role model to Muhammad Ali', *Race and Class* 36(4): 1–29.

—— (1996) *War Minus the Shooting: A Journey Through South Asia During Cricket's World Cup*, London: Heinemann.

—— (1999) *Redemption Song: Muhammad Ali and the Spirit of the Sixties*, London: Verso.

McGuigan, J. (1992) *Cultural Populism*, London: Routledge.

McRobbie, A. (1994) *Postmodernism and Popular Culture*, London: Routledge.

Mercer, K. (1994) *Welcome to the Jungle: New Positions in Black Cultural Studies*, London: Routledge.

Messner, M. (1992) *Power at Play: Sports and the Problem of Masculinity*, Boston: Beacon Press.

—— (1997) *Politics of Masculinities: Men in Movements*, London: Sage.

Miller, T. (ed.) (2001) *A Companion to Cultural Studies*, Oxford: Blackwell.

Morley, D. and Chen, K-H. (eds) (1996) *Stuart Hall: Critical Dialogues in Cultural Studies*, London: Routledge.

Murdock, G. (1997) 'Cultural studies at the crossroads', in A. Gray and J. McGuigan (eds) *Studying Culture: An Introductory Reader*, 2nd edn, London: Arnold.

Policy Research Institute (PRI) (1996) *Community Profile of Chapeltown Leeds*, Leeds: Leeds Metropolitan University.

Richards, V. (1991) *Hitting Across the Line: An Autobiography*, London: Headline.

—— (1995) 'Foreword', in H. Beckles and B. Stoddard (eds) *Liberation Cricket: West Indies Cricket Culture*, Manchester: Manchester University Press.

Rodman, D. (1996) *Bad As I Wanna Be*, New York: Delacorte Press.

St Pierre, M. (1995) 'West Indian cricket as cultural resistance', in M. Malec (ed.) *The Social Roles of Sport in Caribbean Societies*, Luxembourg: Gordon & Breach.

Sayyid, B. (1997) *A fundamental Fear: Eurocentrism and the Emergence of Islamism*, London: Zed Books.

Searle, C. (1990) 'Race Before Wicket: Cricket, Empire and the White Rose', *Race and Class* 31(3): 31–48.

—— (2001) *Pitch of Life: Writings on Cricket*, Manchester: Parrs Wood Press.

Shohat E. and Stam, R. (1994) *Unthinking Eurocentrism: Multiculturalism and the Media*, London: Routledge.

Sivanandan, A. (1982) *A Different Hunger: Writings on Black Resistance,* London: Pluto Press.

—— (1990) *Communities of Resistance: Writings on Black Struggles for Socialism*, London: Verso.

Stuart, O. (1996) 'Back in the pavilion: cricket and the image of African Caribbeans in Oxford', in T. Ranger, Y. Samad and O. Stuart (eds) *Culture, Identity and Politics: Ethnic Minorities in Britain*, Aldershot: Avebury.

Turner, G. (1996) *British Cultural Studies: An Introduction*, 2nd edn, London: Routledge.

Vergès, F. (1996) 'Chains of madness, chains of colonialism: Fanon and freedom', in A. Read (ed.) *The Fact of Blackness: Frantz Fanon and Visual Representation*, London: ICA.

Ware, V. and Back, L. (2002) *Out of Whiteness: Color, Politics, and Culture*, Chicago: University of Chicago Press.

Westwood, S. (1990) 'Racism, black masculinity and the politics of space', in J. Hearn and D. Morgan (eds) *Men, Masculinities and Social Theory*, London: Unwin Hyman.

Wheatley, R. (1992) *100 Years of Leeds League Cricket*, Leeds: White Line Publishing.

Williams, J. (1994) ' "Rangers is a black club": "Race", identity and local football in England', in R. Giulianotti and J. Williams (eds) *Game Without Frontiers: Football, Modernity and Identity*, Aldershot: Arena.

Willis, P. (1977) *Learning To Labour: How Working Class Kids Get Working Class Jobs*, Farnborough: Saxon House.

Yelvington, K. (1995) 'Cricket, colonialism, and the culture of Caribbean politics', in M. Malec (ed.) *The Social Roles of sport in Caribbean Societies*, Luxembourg: Gordon & Breach.

Zulfiqar, M. (1993) *Land of Hope and Glory? The Presence of African, Asian and Caribbean Communities in Leeds*, Leeds: Roots Project.

Index